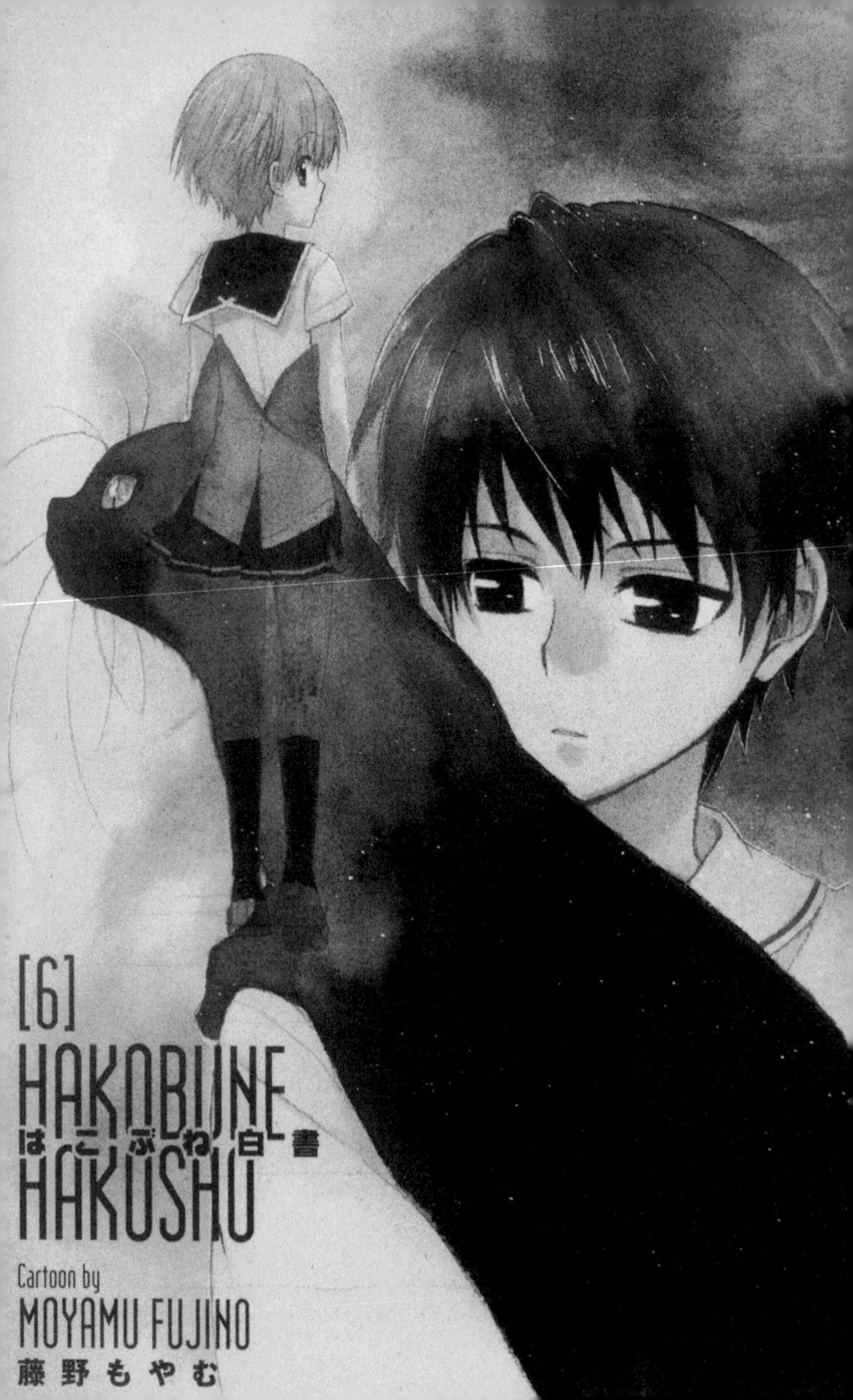
[6]
HAKOBUNE
はこぶね白書
HAKUSHO
Cartoon by
MOYAMU FUJINO
藤野もやむ

Animal Academy: Hakobune Hakusho Volume 6
Created by Moyamu Fujino

Translation - Katherine Schilling
English Adaptation - Ysabet Reinhardt MacFarlane
Retouch and Lettering - Star Print Brokers
Copy Edit - Joseph Heller
Production Artist - Michael Paolilli
Graphic Designer - Louis Csontos

Editor - Lillian Diaz-Przybyl
Print Production Manager - Lucas Rivera
Managing Editor - Vy Nguyen
Senior Designer - Louis Csontos
Art Director - Al-Insan Lashley
Director of Sales and Manufacturing - Allyson De Simone
Associate Publisher - Marco F. Pavia
President and C.O.O. - John Parker
C.E.O. and Chief Creative Officer - Stu Levy

A **TOKYOPOP** Manga

TOKYOPOP Inc.
5900 Wilshire Blvd. Suite 2000
Los Angeles, CA 90036

E-mail: info@TOKYOPOP.com
Come visit us online at www.TOKYOPOP.com

ISBN: 978-1-4278-1632-0

First TOKYOPOP printing: November 2010
10 9 8 7 6 5 4 3 2 1
Printed in the USA

Animal Academy

HAKOBUNE HAKUSHO

はこぶね白書

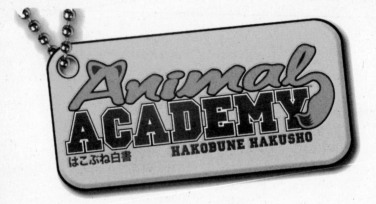

Volume 6
by
MOYAMU FUJINO

TOKYOPOP®

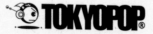

HAMBURG // LONDON // LOS ANGELES // TOKYO

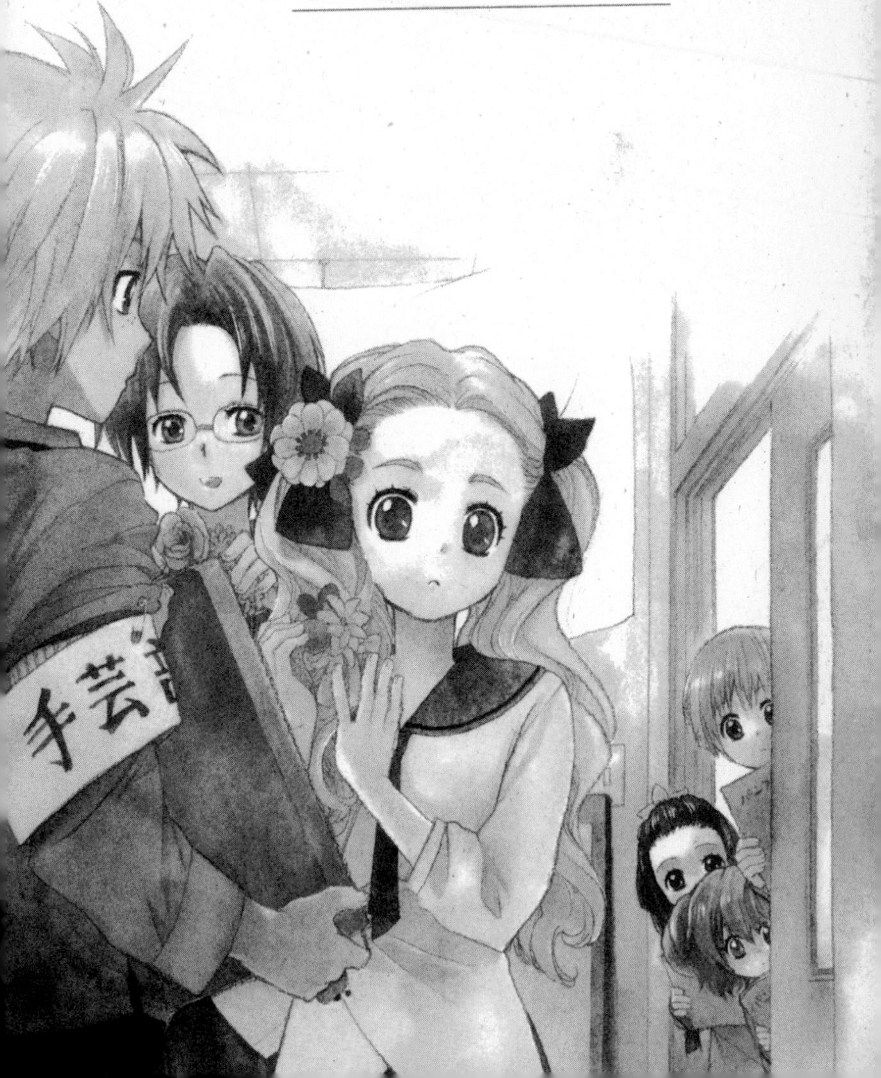
手芸

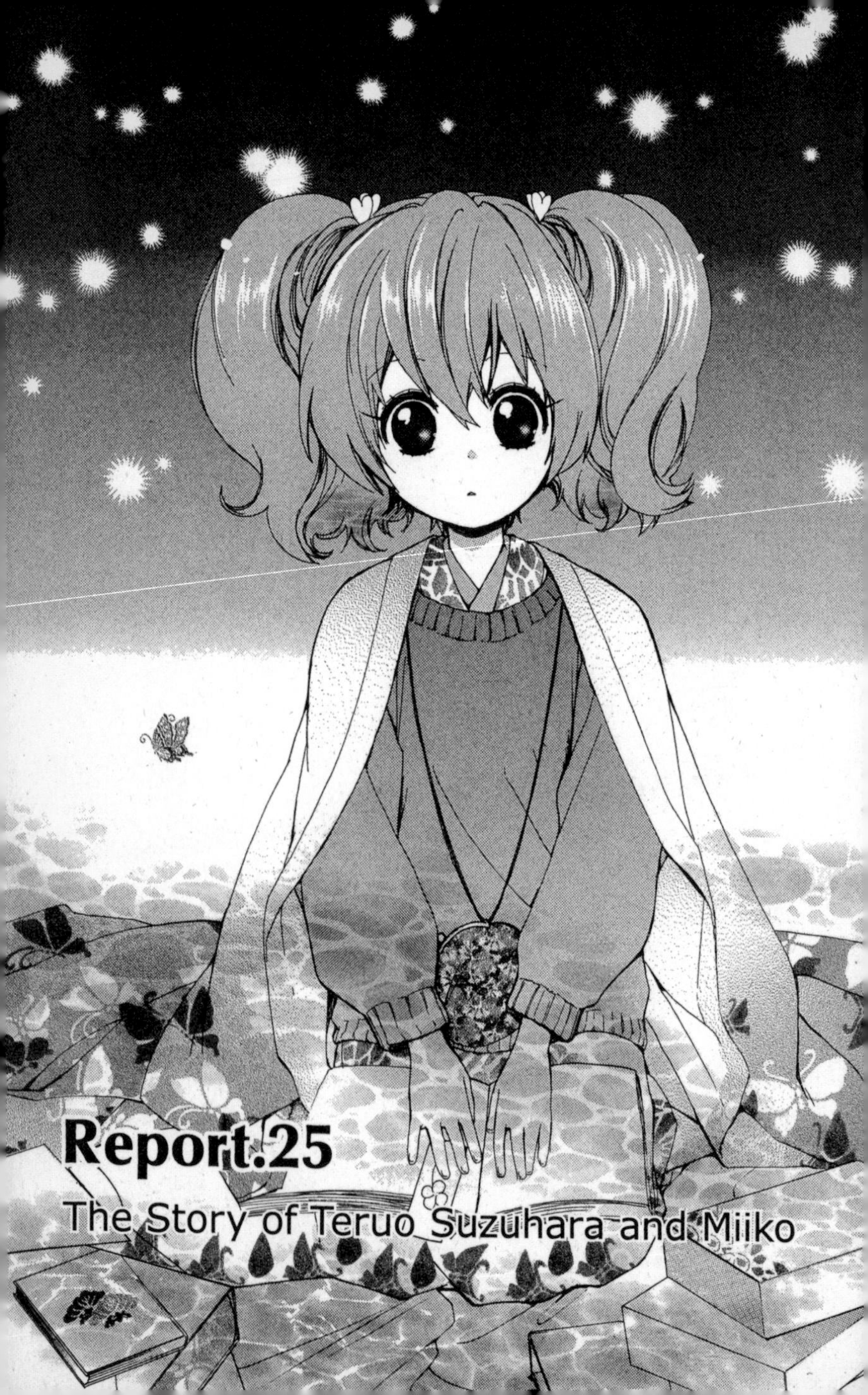
Report.25
The Story of Teruo Suzuhara and Miiko

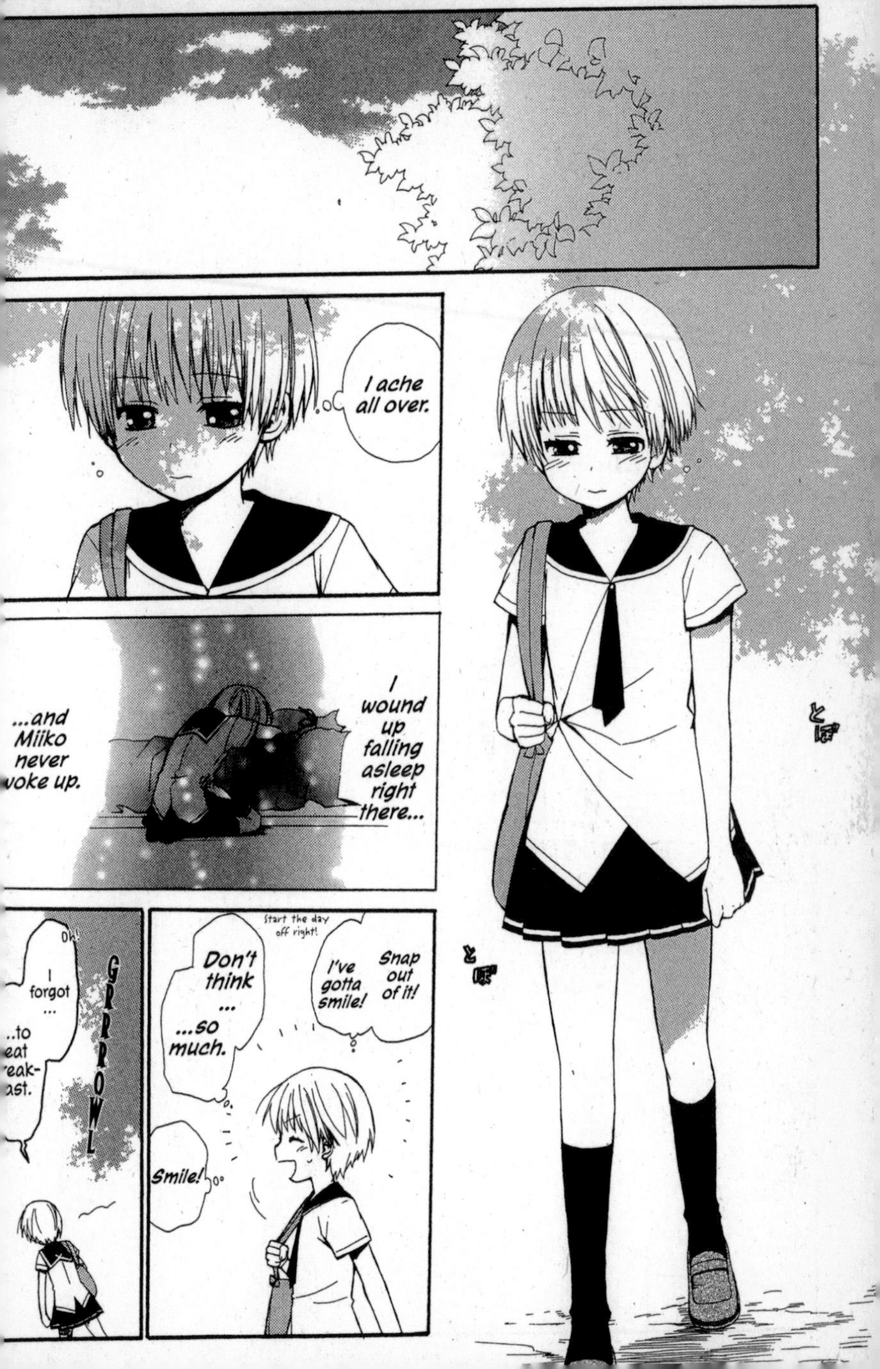
とぼ
とぼ
I ache all over.
I wound up falling asleep right there...
...and Miiko never voke up.
Snap out of it!
I've gotta smile!
Start the day off right!
Don't think ... ...so much.
Smile!
Oh!
I forgot ...
..to eat reak- ast.
GRRROWL

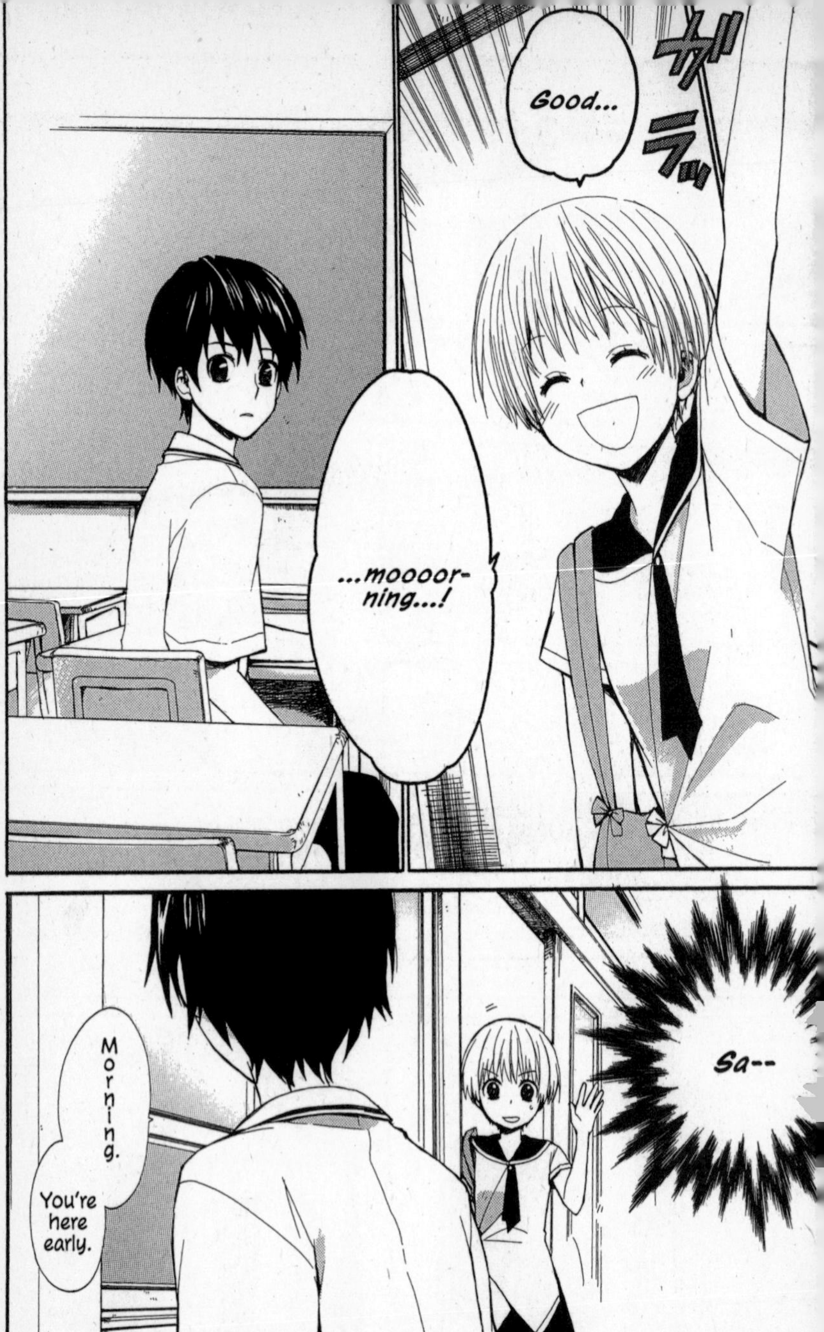
ガラッ
Good...
...moooor-ning...!
Sa--
Morning.
You're here early.

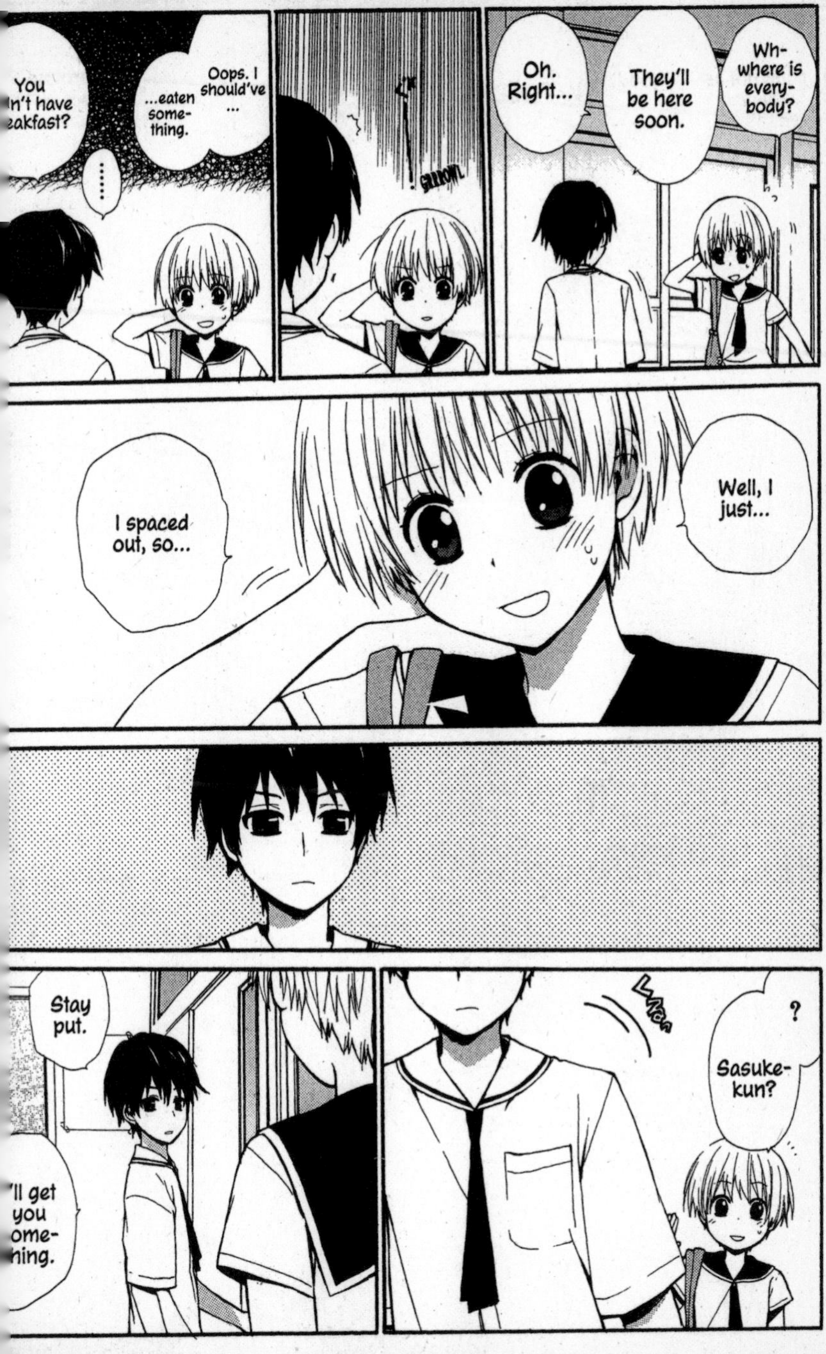

Wh- where is everybody?
They'll be here soon.
Oh. Right...
GRRROWL
Oops. I should've ...
...eaten something.
You n't have eakfast?
......
Well, I just...
I spaced out, so...
?
Sasuke-kun?
Stay put.
'll get you ome-hing.

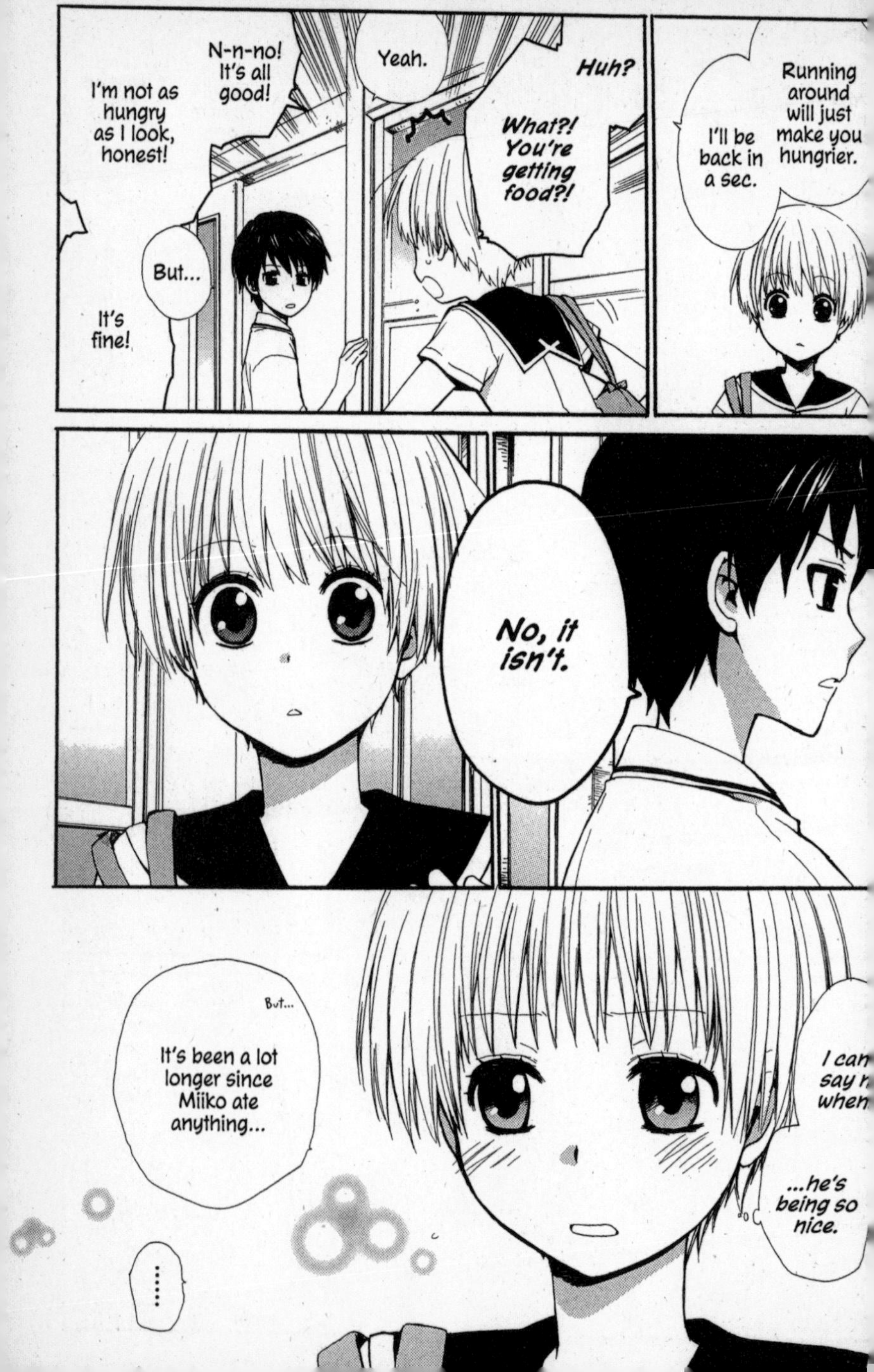
Running around will just make you hungrier.
I'll be back in a sec.
Huh?
What?! You're getting food?!
Yeah.
N-n-no! It's all good!
I'm not as hungry as I look, honest!
But...
It's fine!
No, it isn't.
I can say when
...he's being so nice.
But...
It's been a lot longer since Miiko ate anything...
......

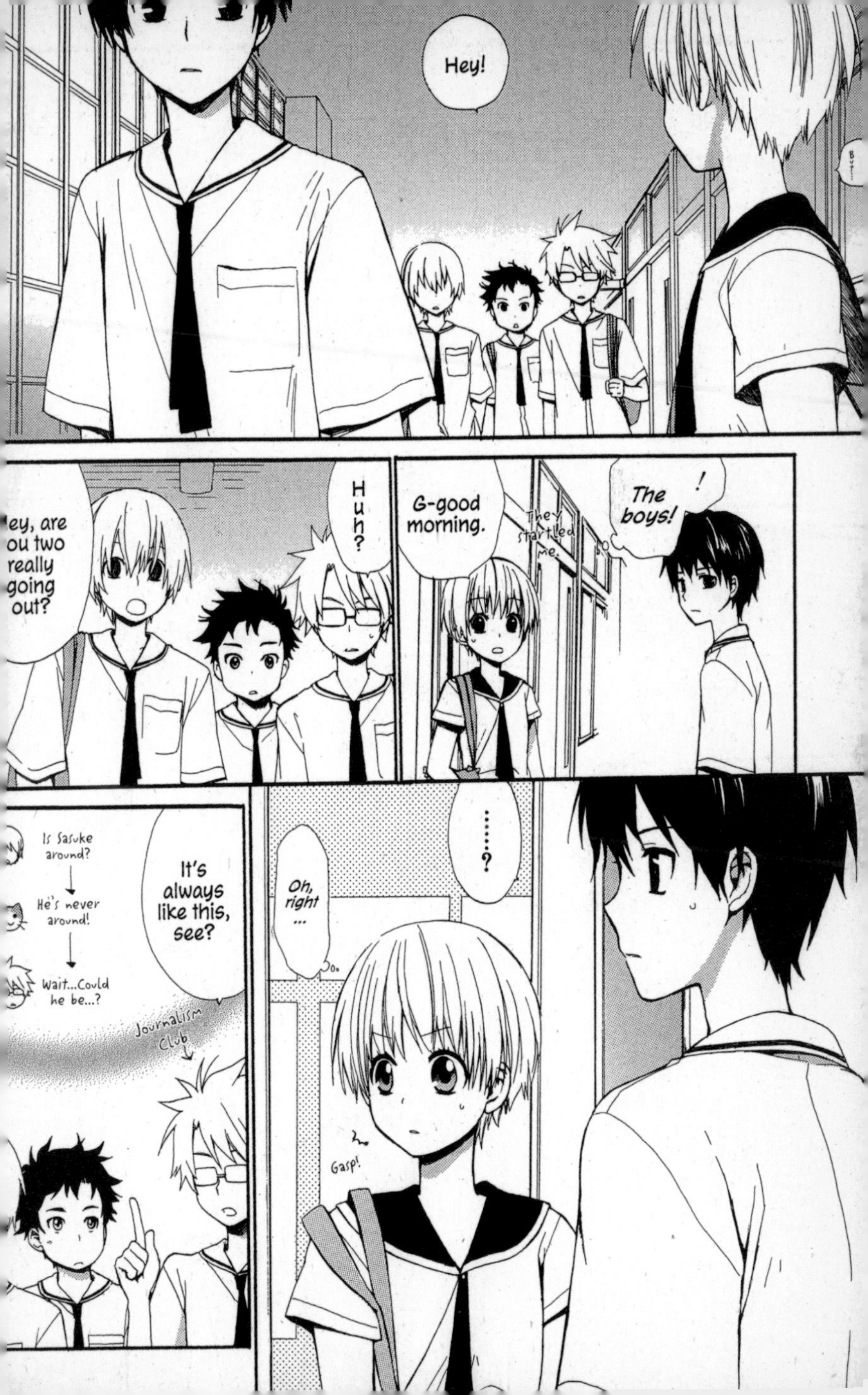
But...
Hey!
!
The boys!
They startled me.
G-good morning.
Huh?
ey, are ou two really going out?
......?
Oh, right...
Gasp!
It's always like this, see?
Is Sasuke around?
He's never around!
Wait...Could he be...?
Journalism Club

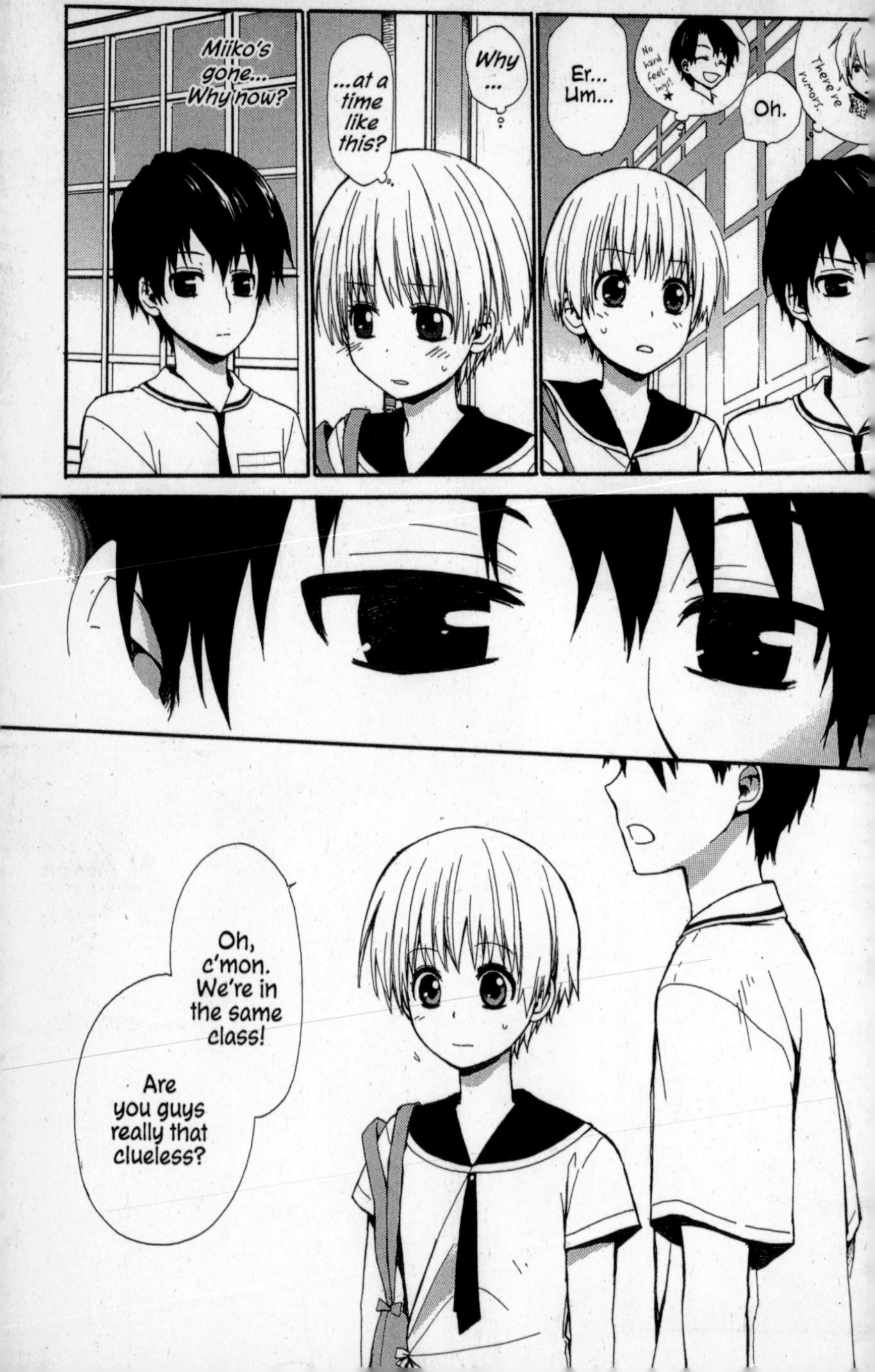
There're rumors.
Oh.
No hard feel-ings! ★
Er... Um...
Why ...
...at a time like this?
Miiko's gone... Why now?
Oh, c'mon. We're in the same class!
Are you guys really that clueless?

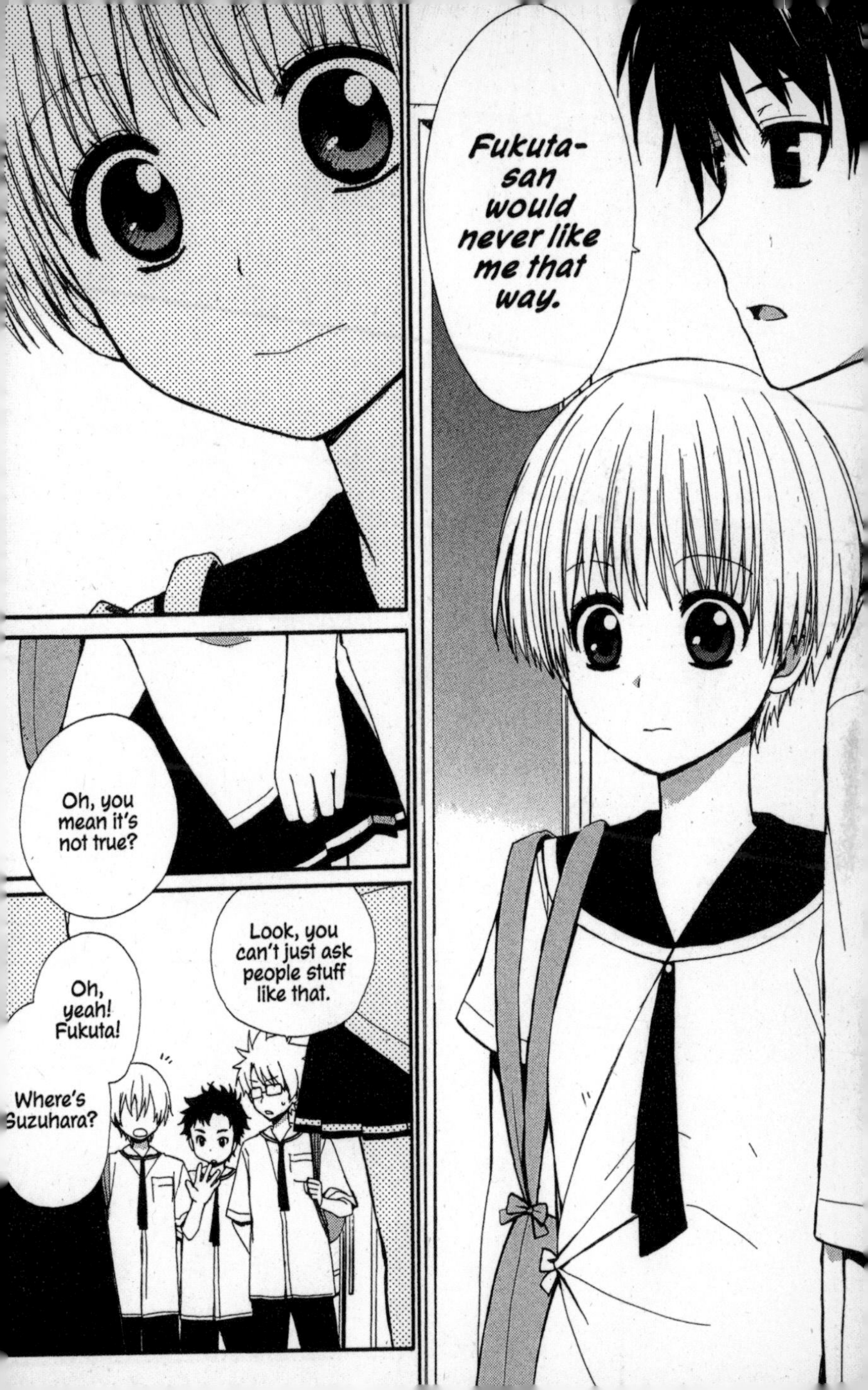
Fukuta-san would never like me that way.
Oh, you mean it's not true?
Look, you can't just ask people stuff like that.
Oh, yeah! Fukuta!
Where's Suzuhara?

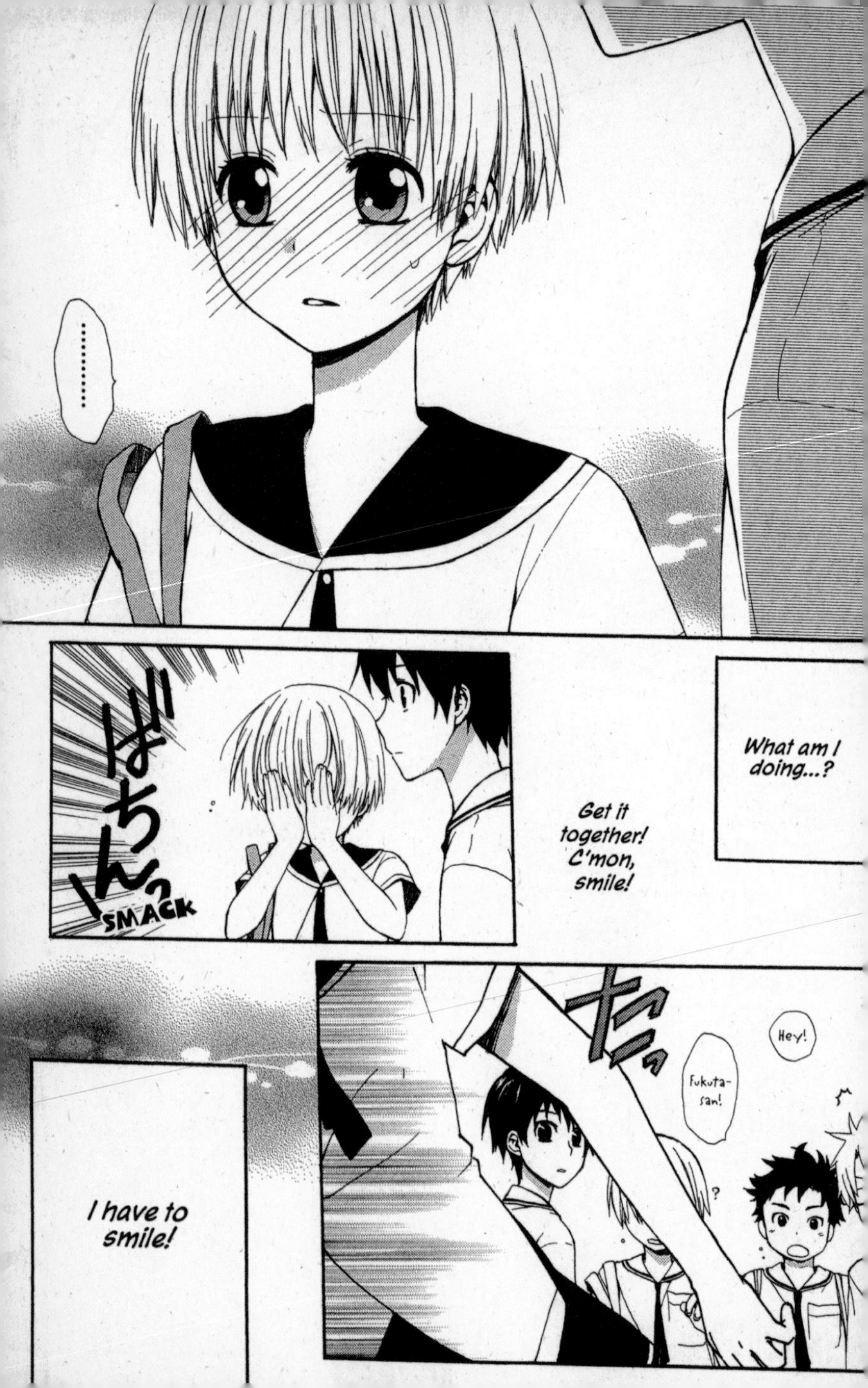
......
What am I doing...?
Get it together! C'mon, smile!
ぱちんっ
SMACK
Hey!
Fukuta-san!
I have to smile!

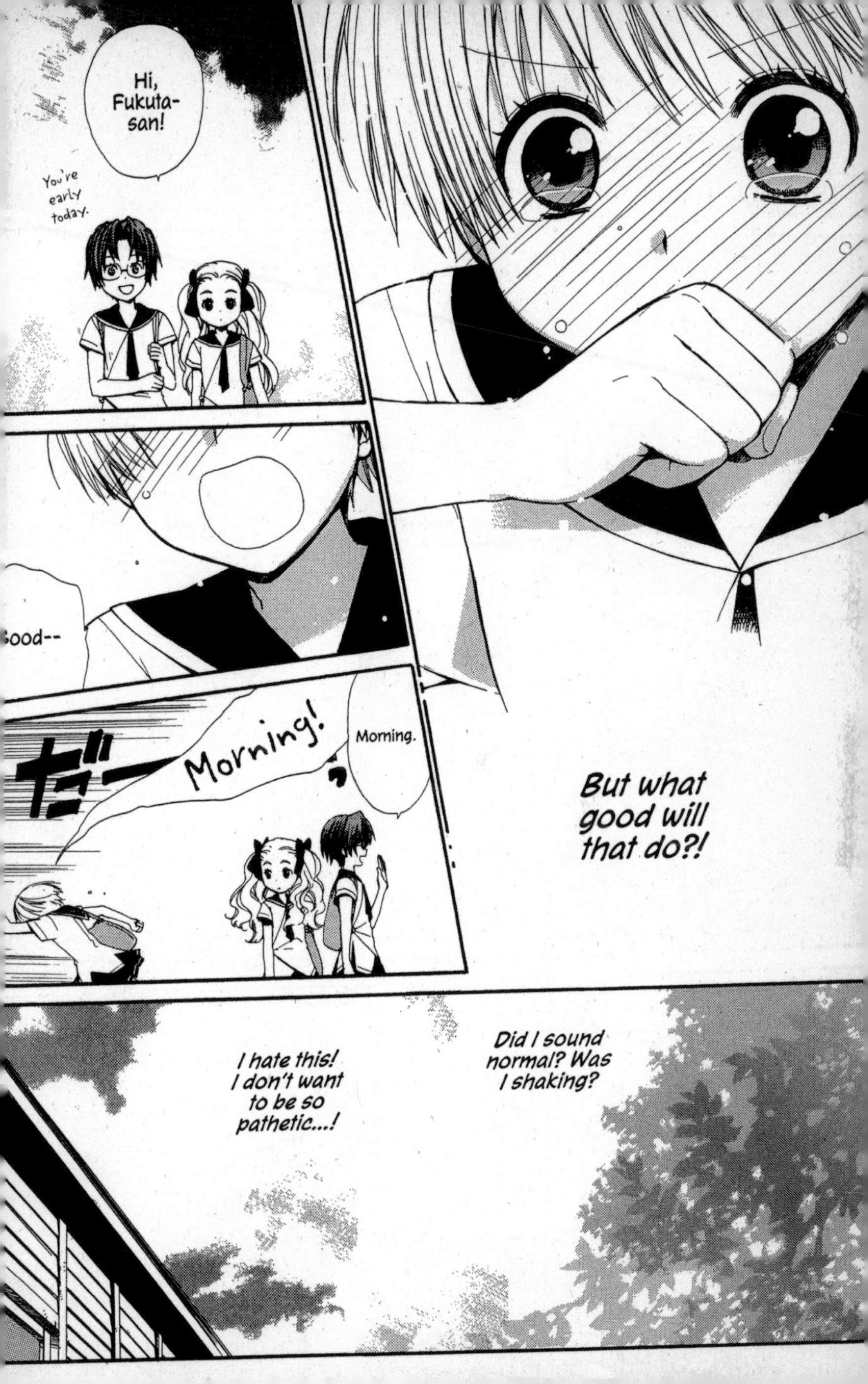
But what good will that do?!
Hi, Fukuta-san!
You're early today.
Good--
Morning.
Morning!
ダー
Did I sound normal? Was I shaking?
I hate this! I don't want to be so pathetic...!

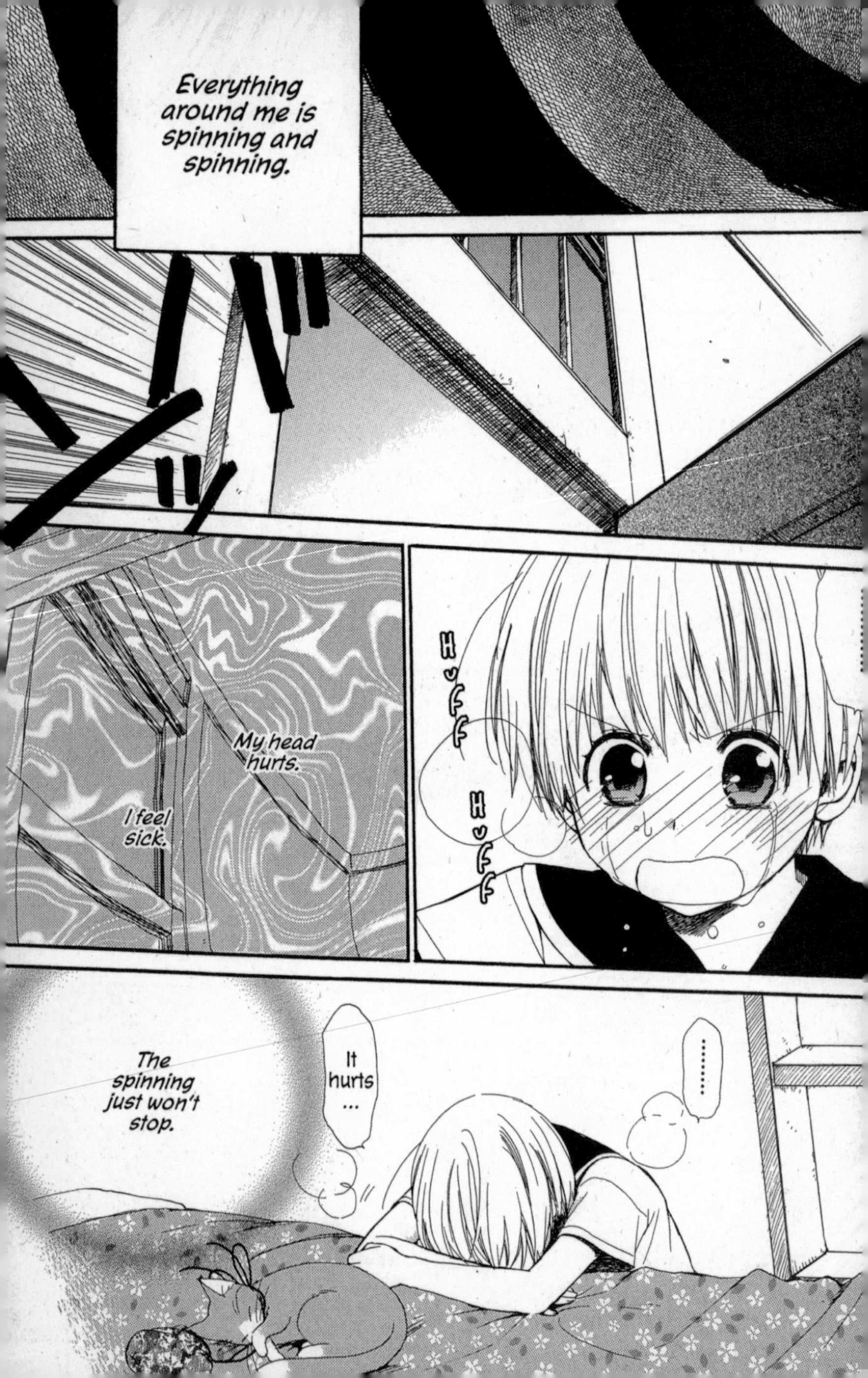
Everything around me is spinning and spinning.
HUFF HUFF
My head hurts.
I feel sick.
......
It hurts ...
The spinning just won't stop.

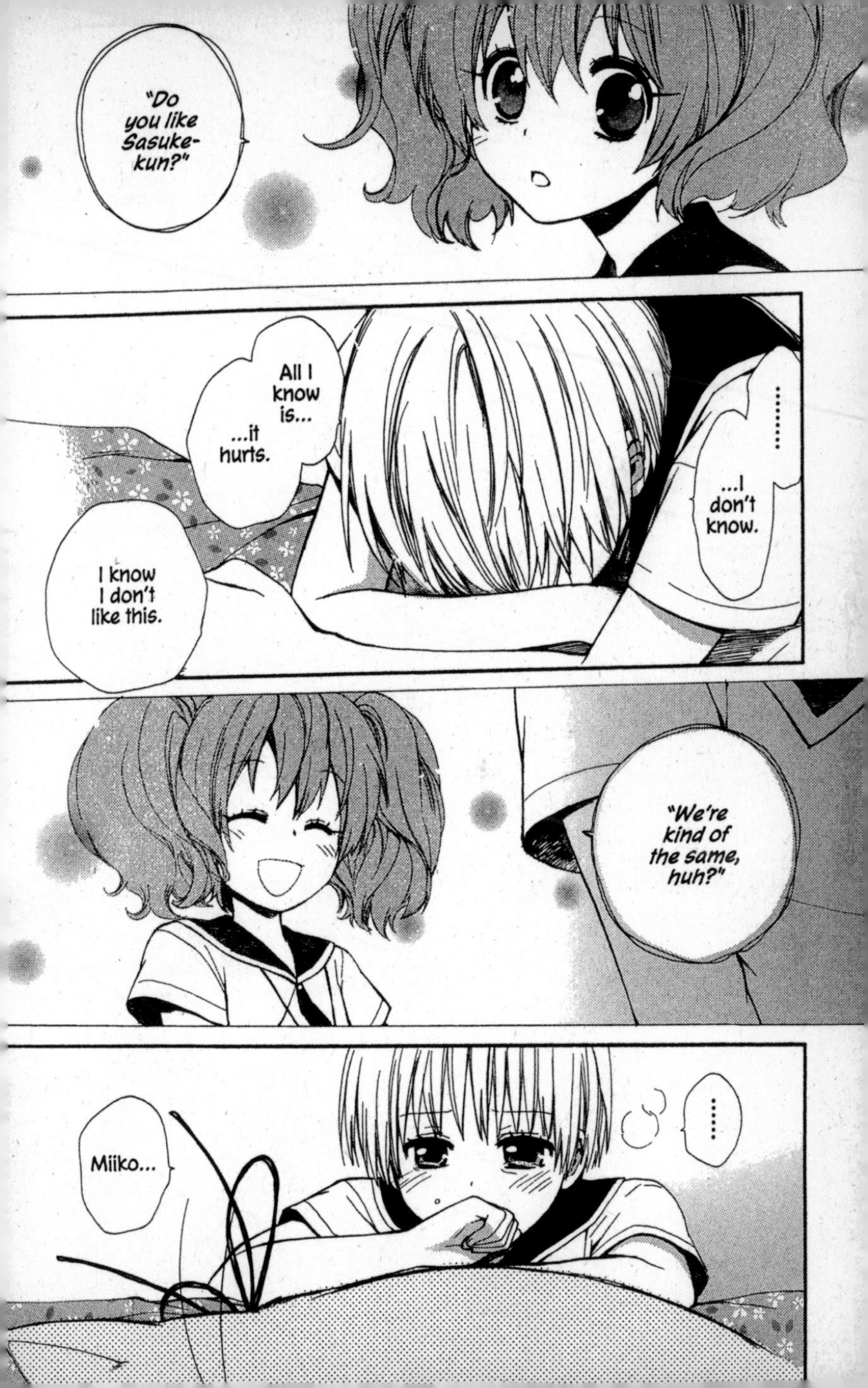
"Do you like Sasuke-kun?"
......
...I don't know.
All I know is...
...it hurts.
I know I don't like this.
"We're kind of the same, huh?"
......
Miiko...

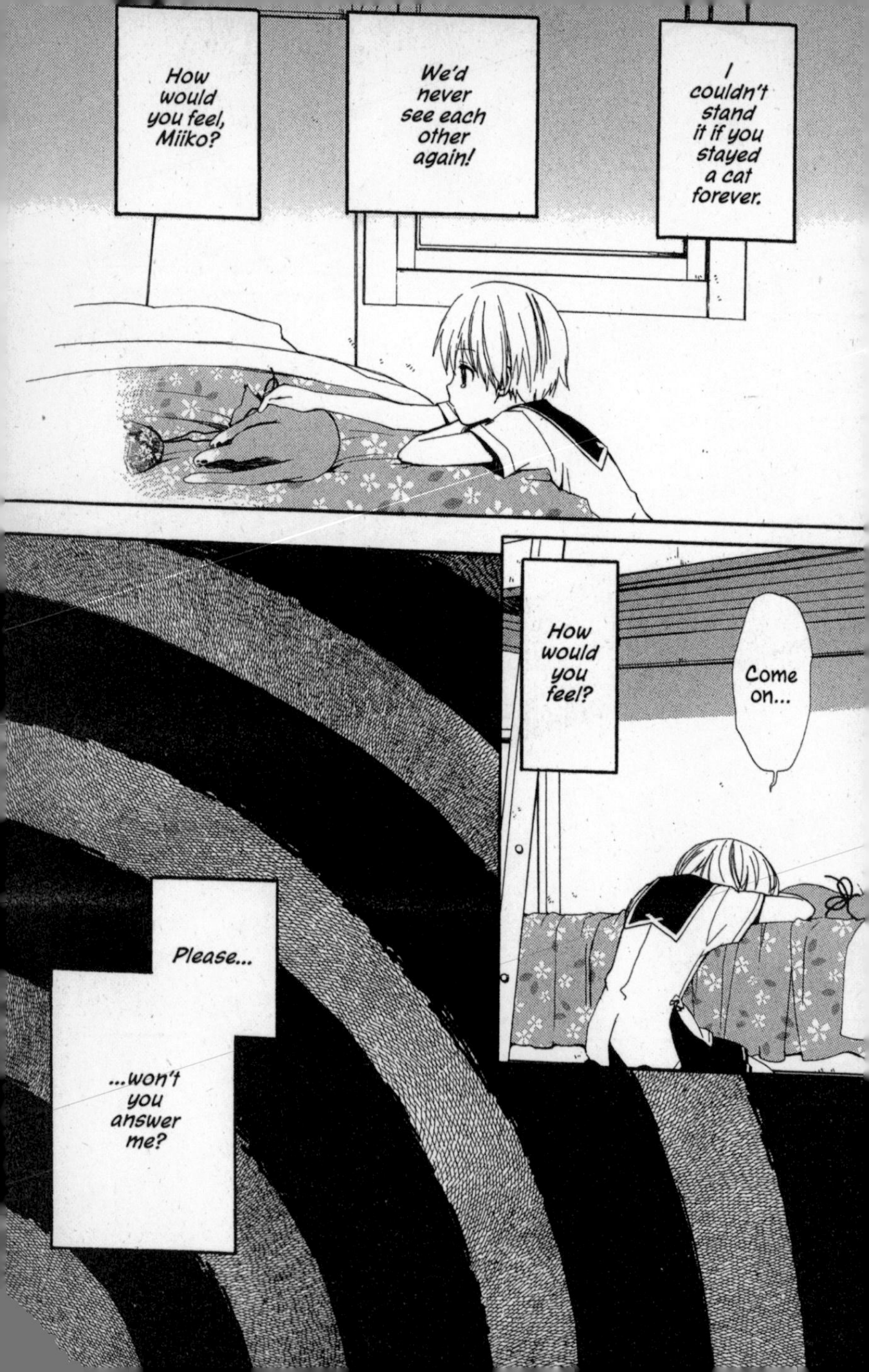
I couldn't stand it if you stayed a cat forever.
We'd never see each other again!
How would you feel, Miiko?
Come on...
How would you feel?
Please...
...won't you answer me?

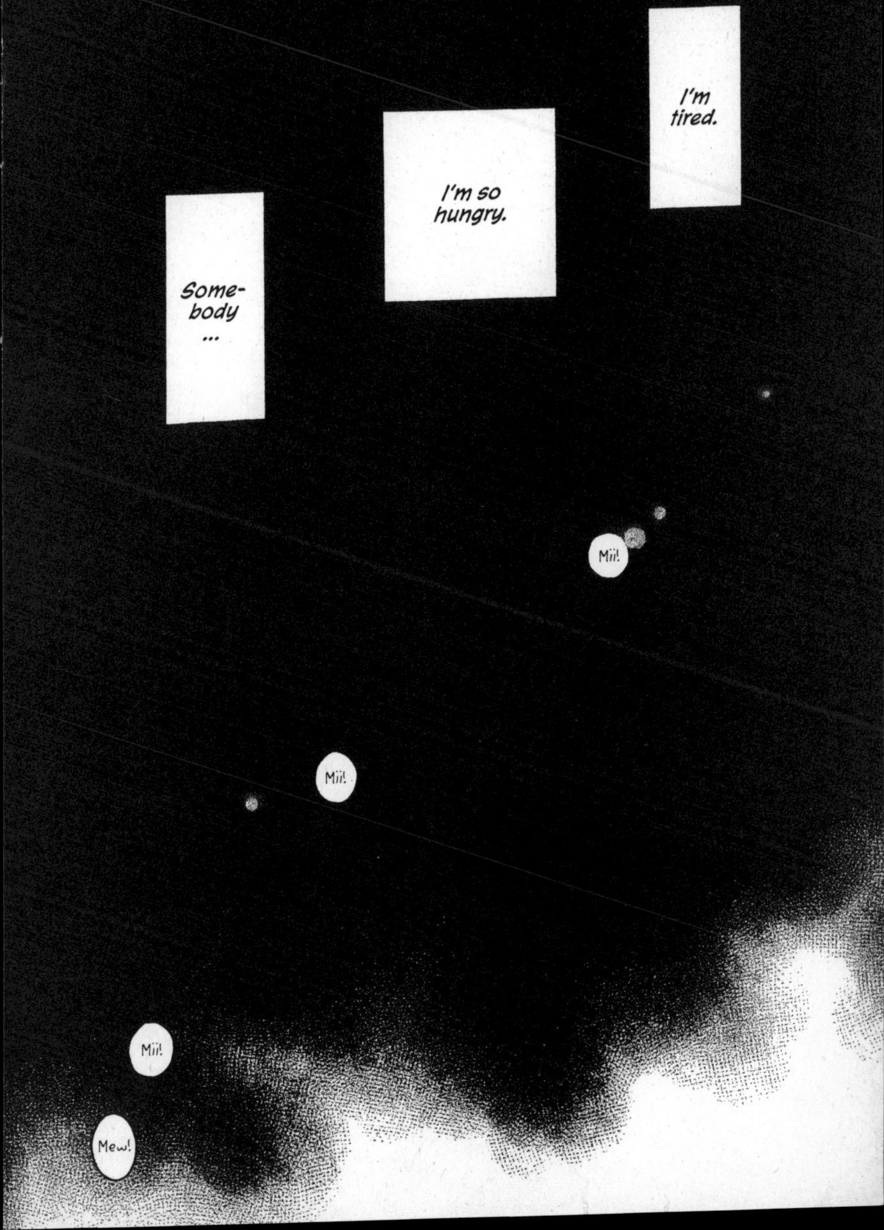
I'm tired.
I'm so hungry.
Some-body ...
Mii!
Mii!
Mii!
Mew!

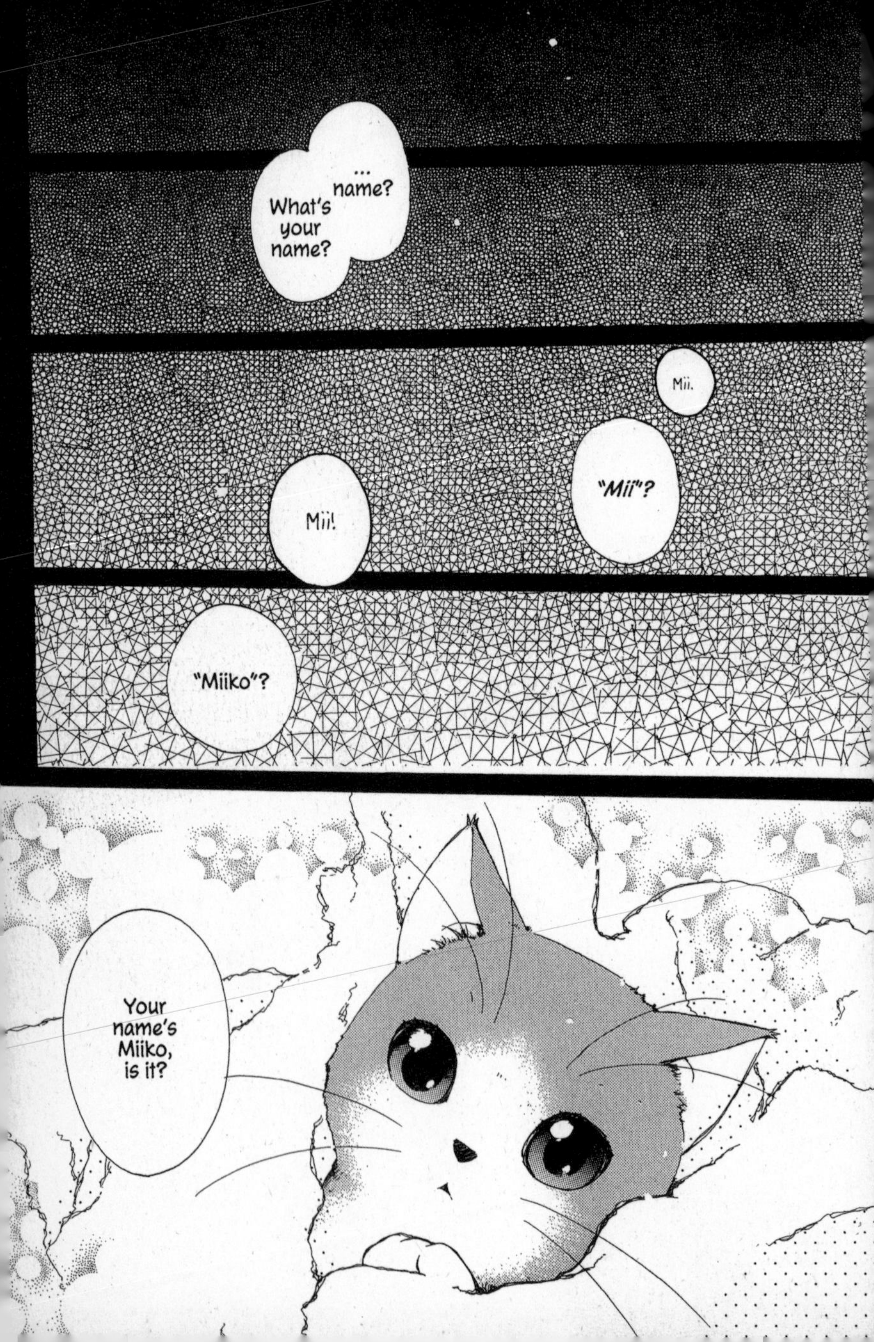
... name?
What's your name?
Mii.
"Mii"?
Mii!
"Miiko"?
Your name's Miiko, is it?

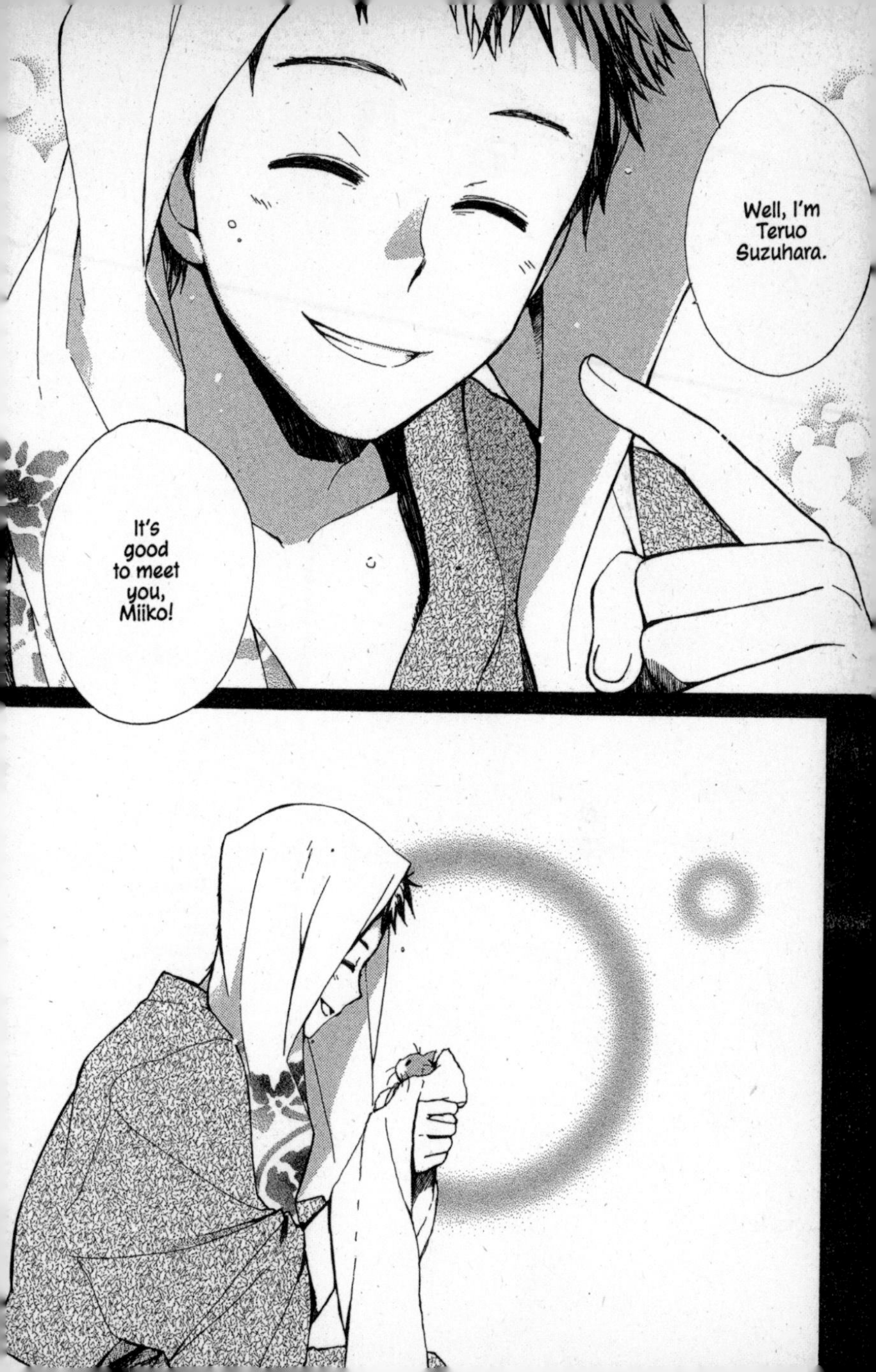
Well, I'm Teruo Suzuhara.
It's good to meet you, Miiko!

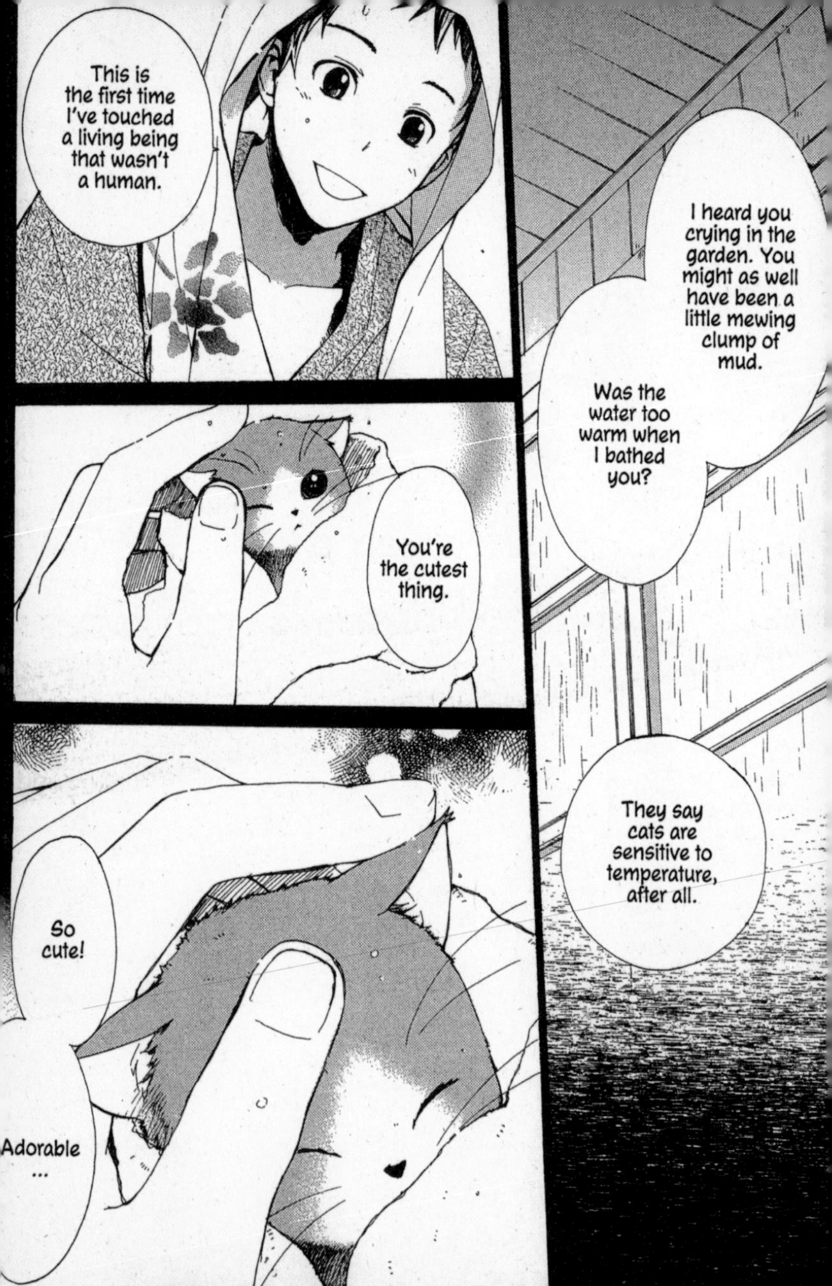
I heard you crying in the garden. You might as well have been a little mewing clump of mud.
Was the water too warm when I bathed you?
They say cats are sensitive to temperature, after all.
This is the first time I've touched a living being that wasn't a human.
You're the cutest thing.
So cute!
Adorable ...

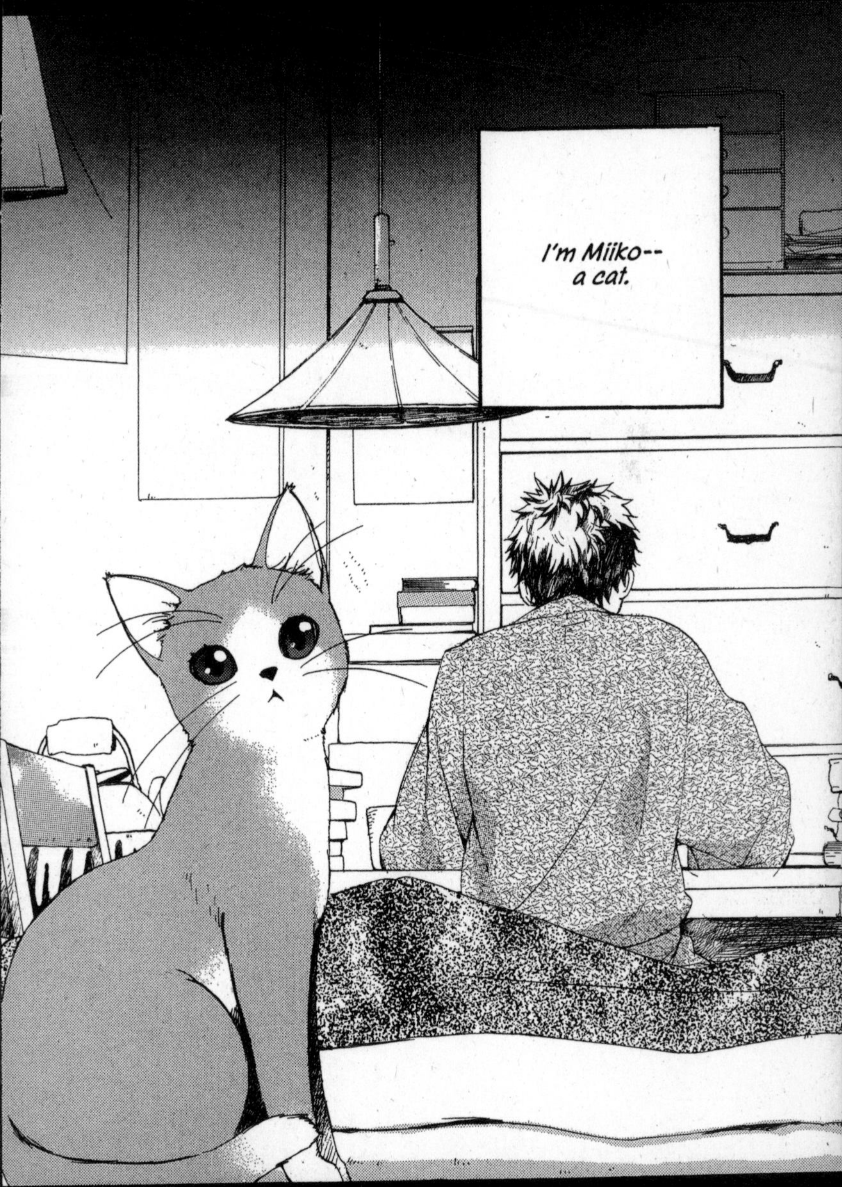
I'm Miiko--
a cat.

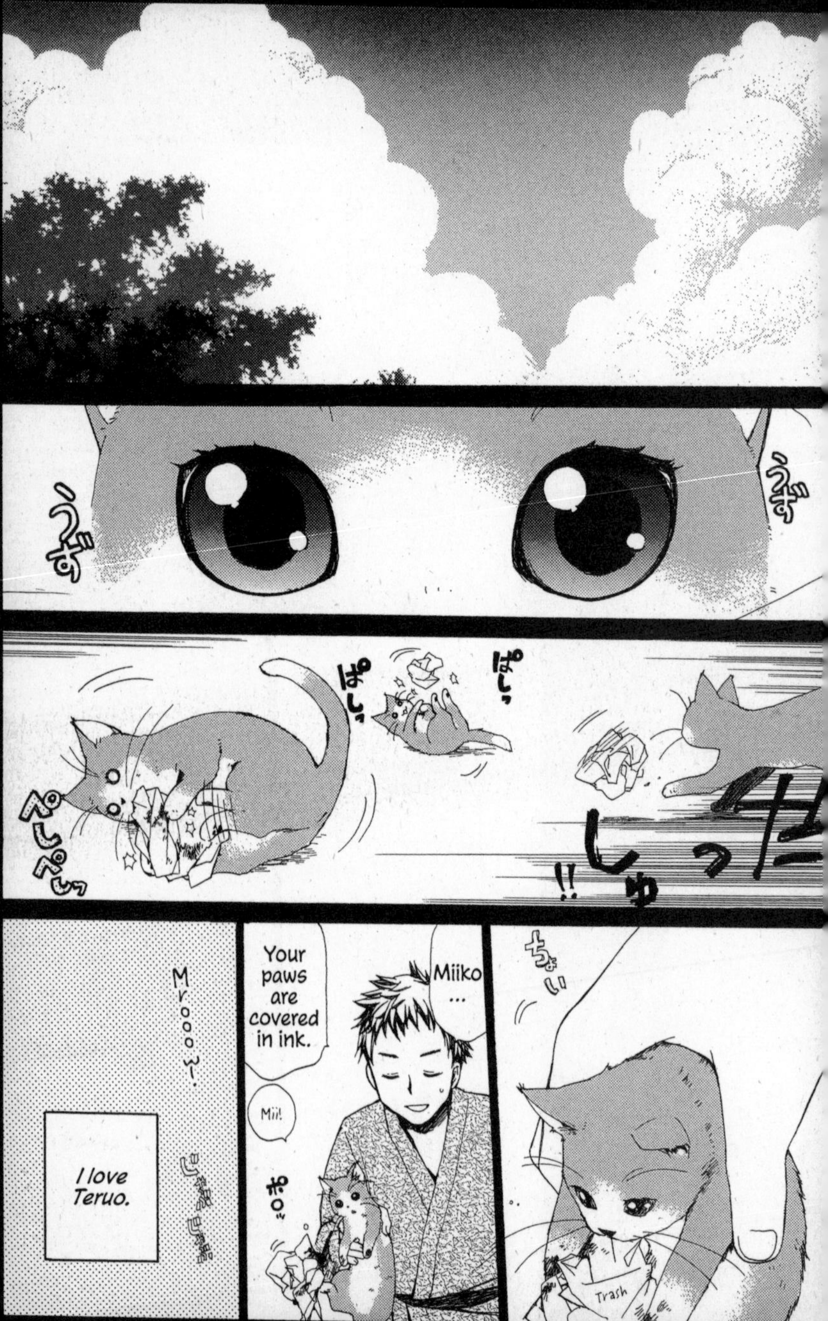

うず
うず
たっ
しゅっ!!
ぱし
ぱし
ぺしぺしっ
ちょい
Trash
Miiko...
Your paws are covered in ink.
Mii!
Mroooow.
I love Teruo.

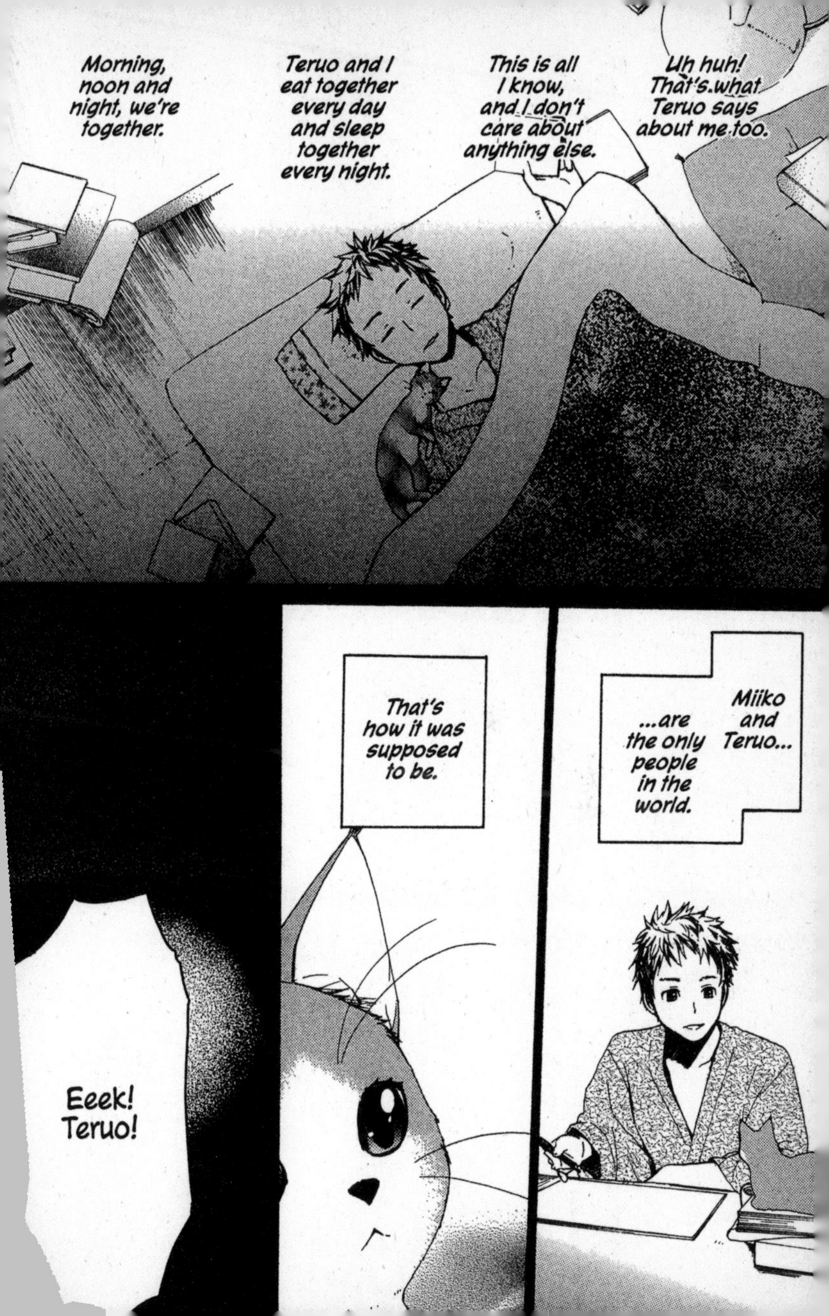
Morning, noon and night, we're together.
Teruo and I eat together every day and sleep together every night.
This is all I know, and I don't care about anything else.
Uh huh! That's what Teruo says about me too.
Miiko and Teruo...
...are the only people in the world.
That's how it was supposed to be.
Eeek! Teruo!

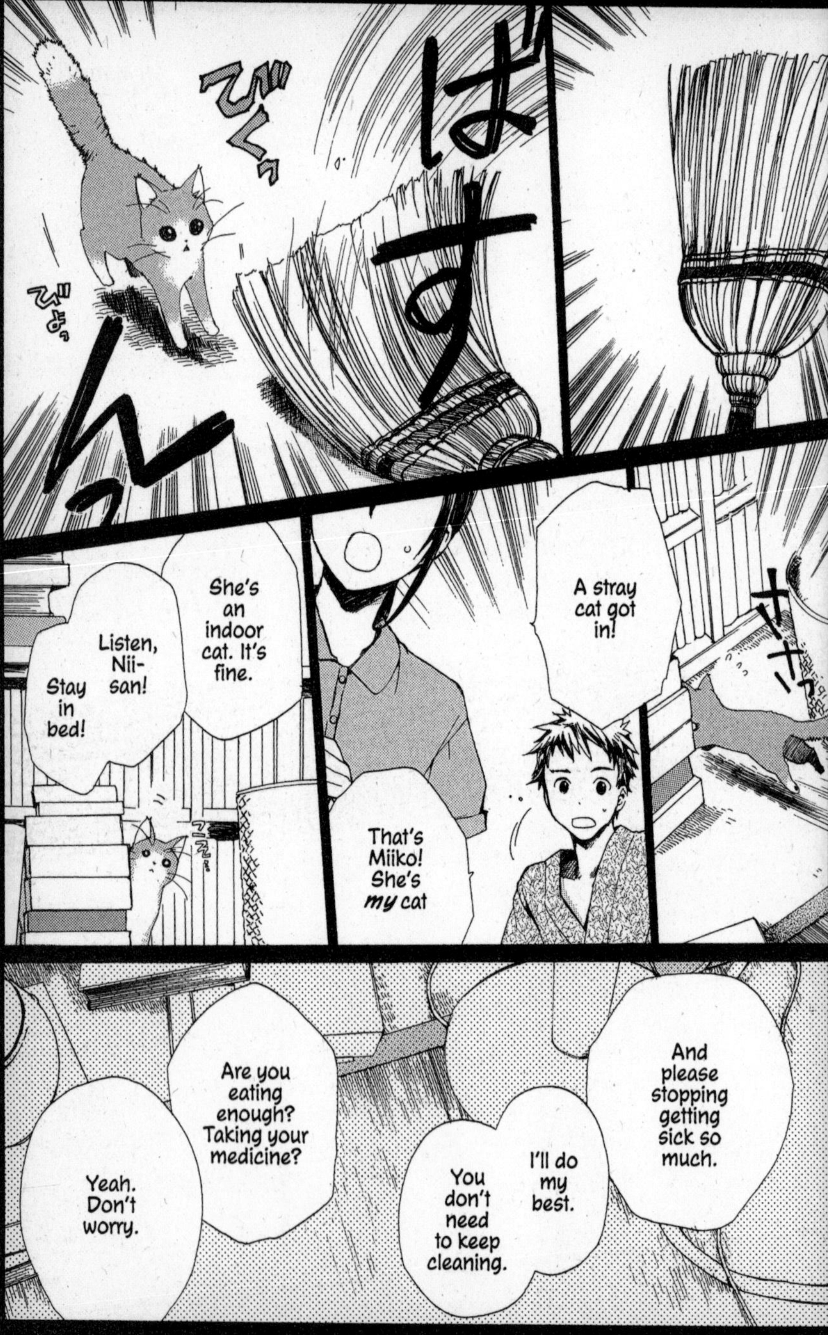
ばすんっ
びくっ
びょっ
さささっ
A stray cat got in!
That's Miiko! She's *my* cat
She's an indoor cat. It's fine.
Listen, Nii-san! Stay in bed!
And please stopping getting sick so much.
I'll do my best.
You don't need to keep cleaning.
Are you eating enough? Taking your medicine?
Yeah. Don't worry.

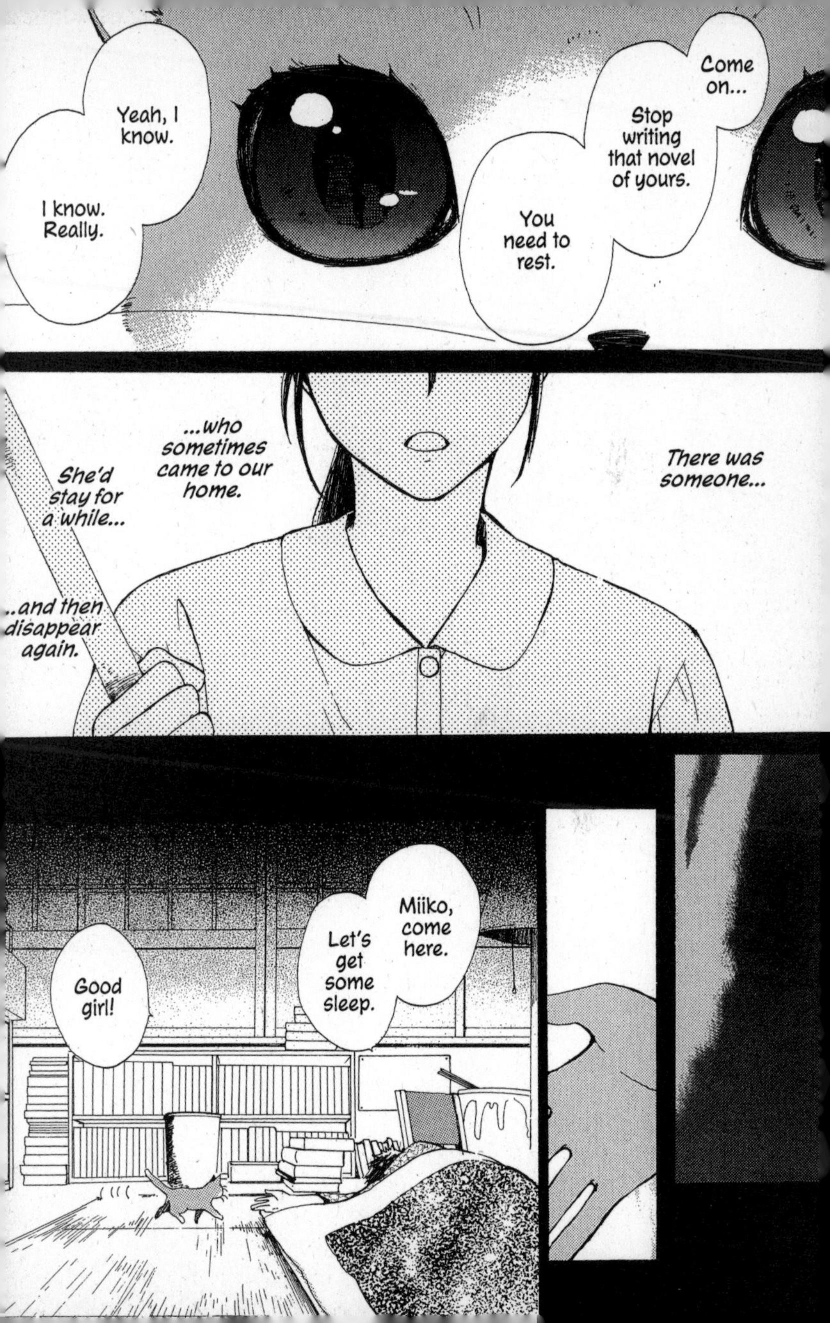
Come on...
Stop writing that novel of yours.
You need to rest.
Yeah, I know.
I know. Really.
There was someone...
...who sometimes came to our home.
She'd stay for a while...
...and then disappear again.
Miiko, come here.
Let's get some sleep.
Good girl!

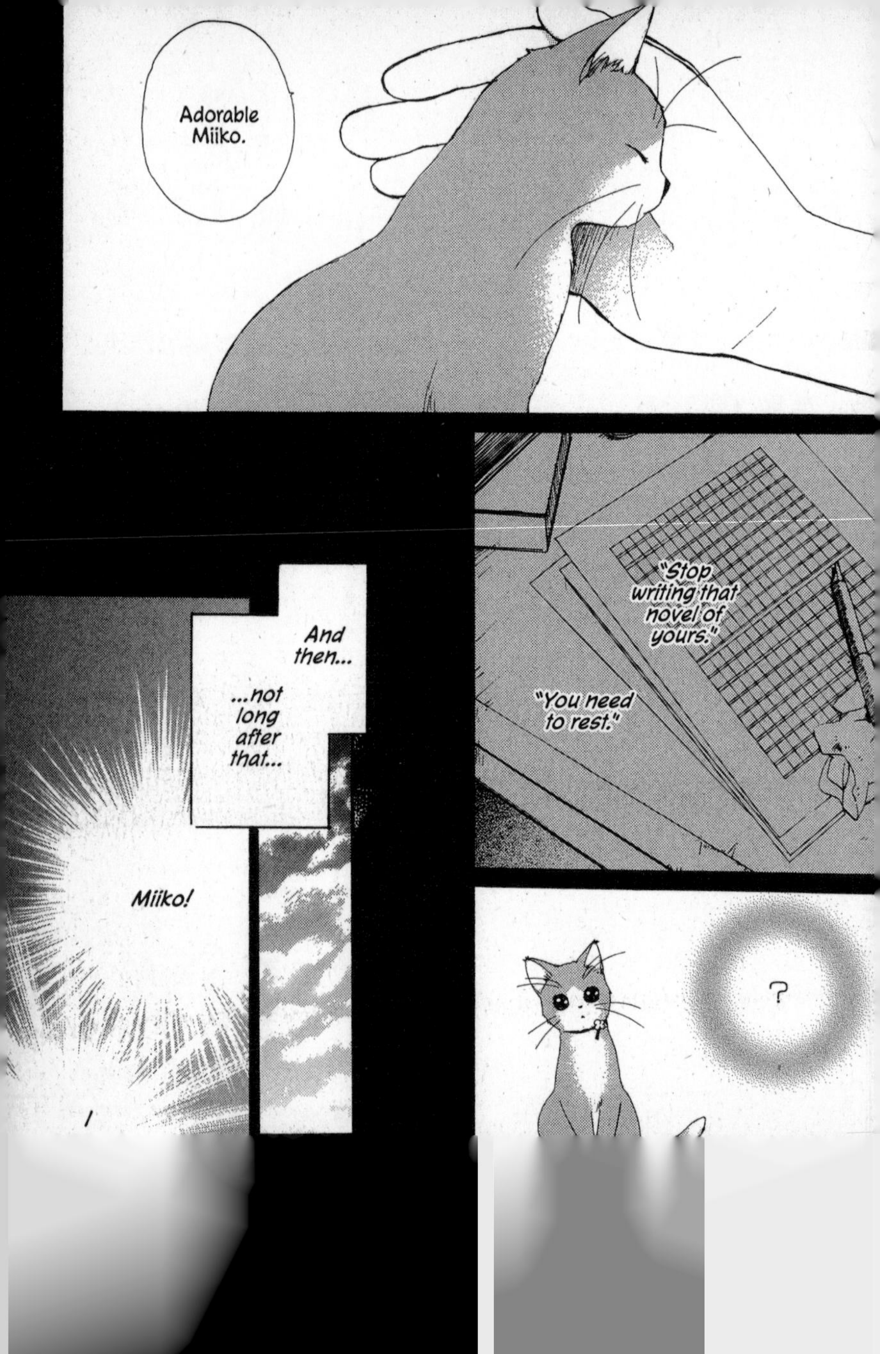
Adorable Miiko.
"Stop writing that novel of yours."
"You need to rest."
?
And then...
...not long after that...
Miiko!

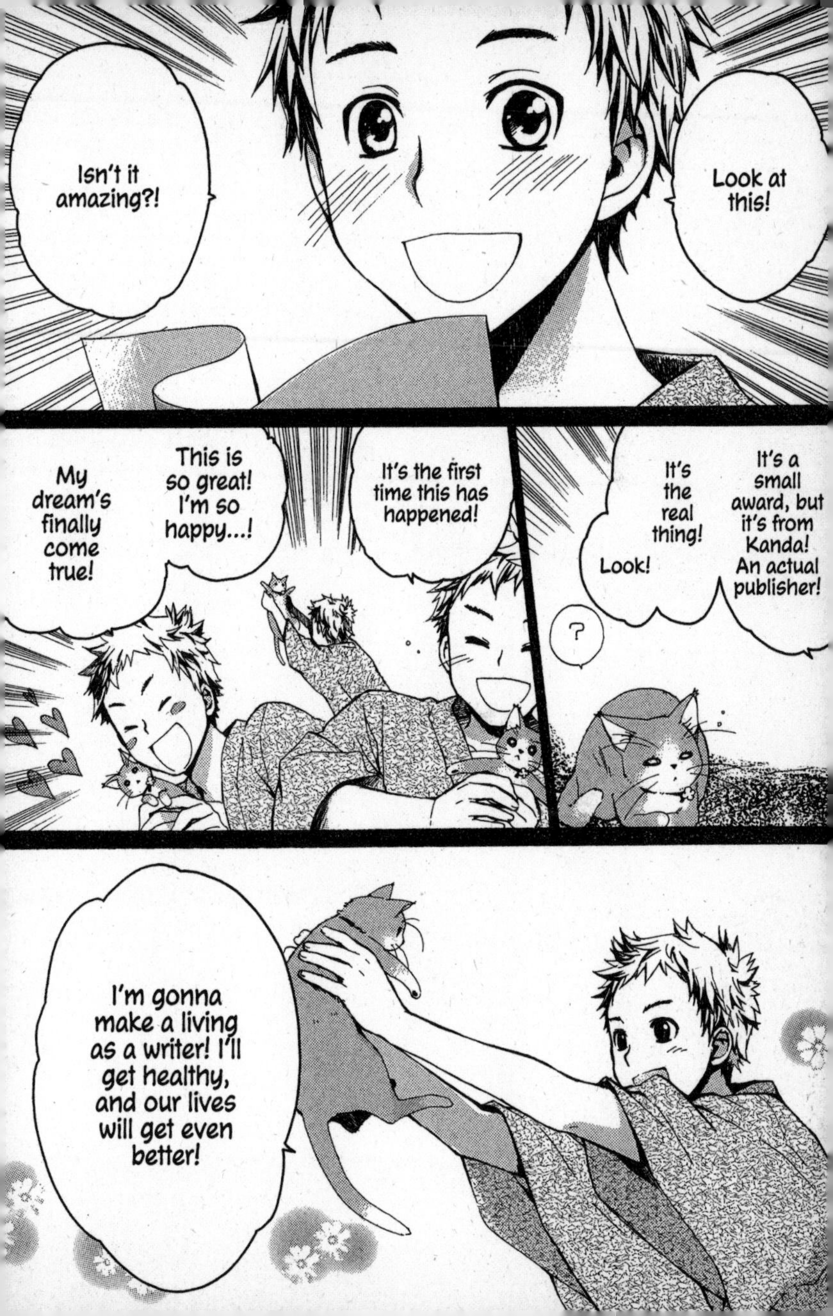
Look at this!
Isn't it amazing?!
It's a small award, but it's from Kanda! An actual publisher!
It's the real thing!
Look!
?
It's the first time this has happened!
This is so great! I'm so happy...!
My dream's finally come true!
I'm gonna make a living as a writer! I'll get healthy, and our lives will get even better!

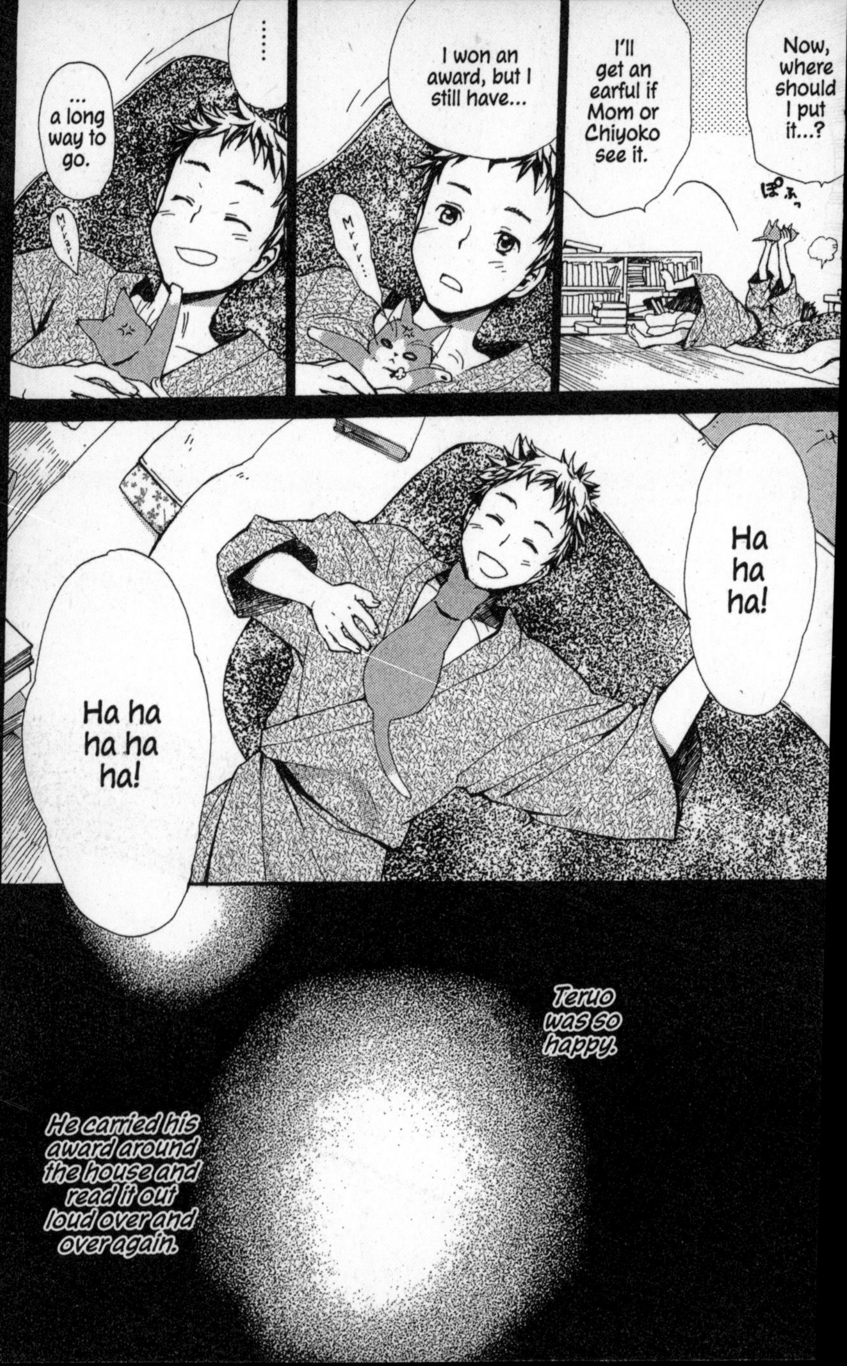

Now, where should I put it...?
ぽふっ
I'll get an earful if Mom or Chiyoko see it.
I won an award, but I still have...
Mrrr...
......
... a long way to go.
Mrrar!
Ha ha ha!
Ha ha ha ha ha!
Teruo was so happy.
He carried his award around the house and read it out loud over and over again.

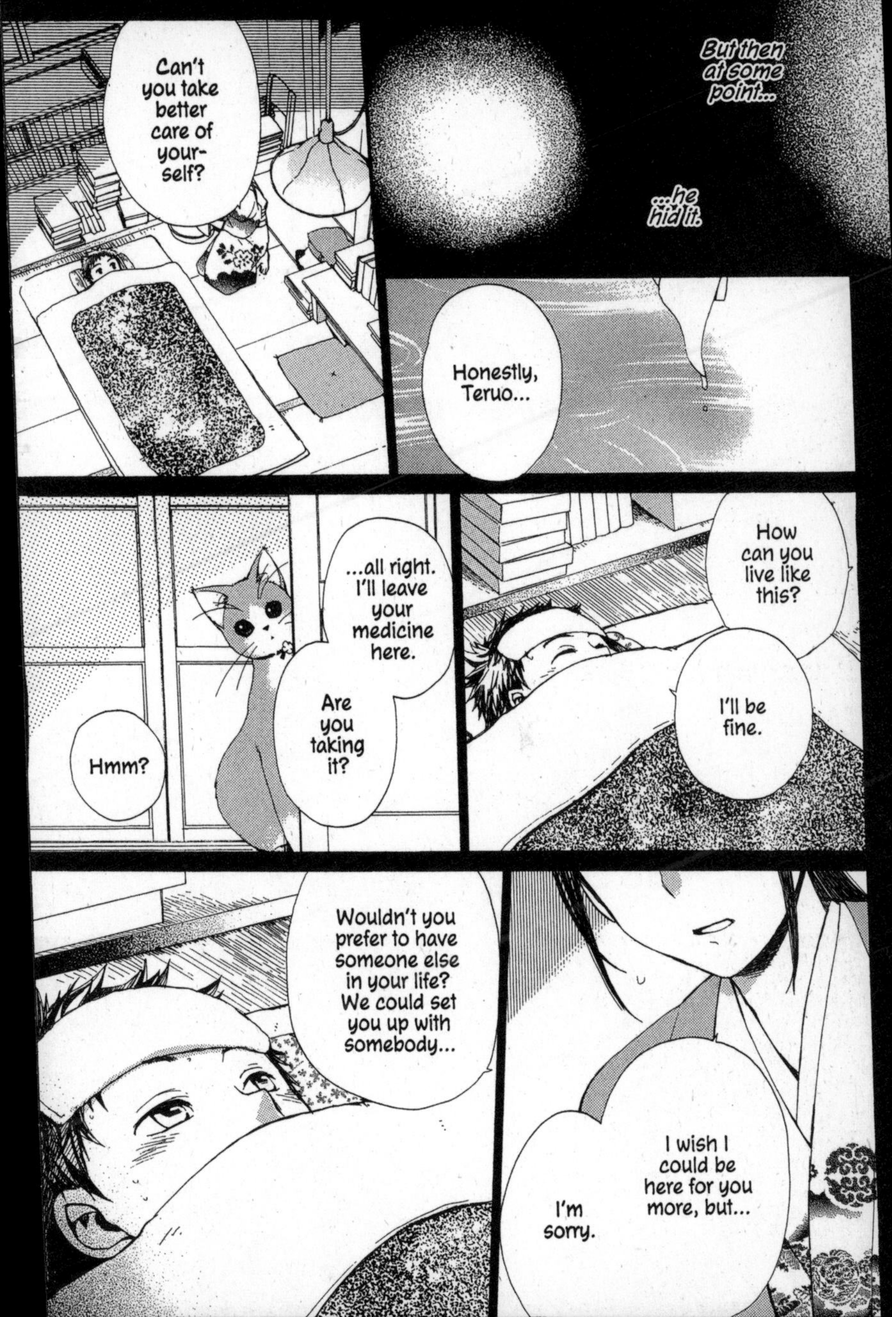
But then at some point...
...he hid it.
Honestly, Teruo...
Can't you take better care of your-self?
How can you live like this?
I'll be fine.
...all right. I'll leave your medicine here.
Are you taking it?
Hmm?
I wish I could be here for you more, but...
I'm sorry.
Wouldn't you prefer to have someone else in your life? We could set you up with somebody...

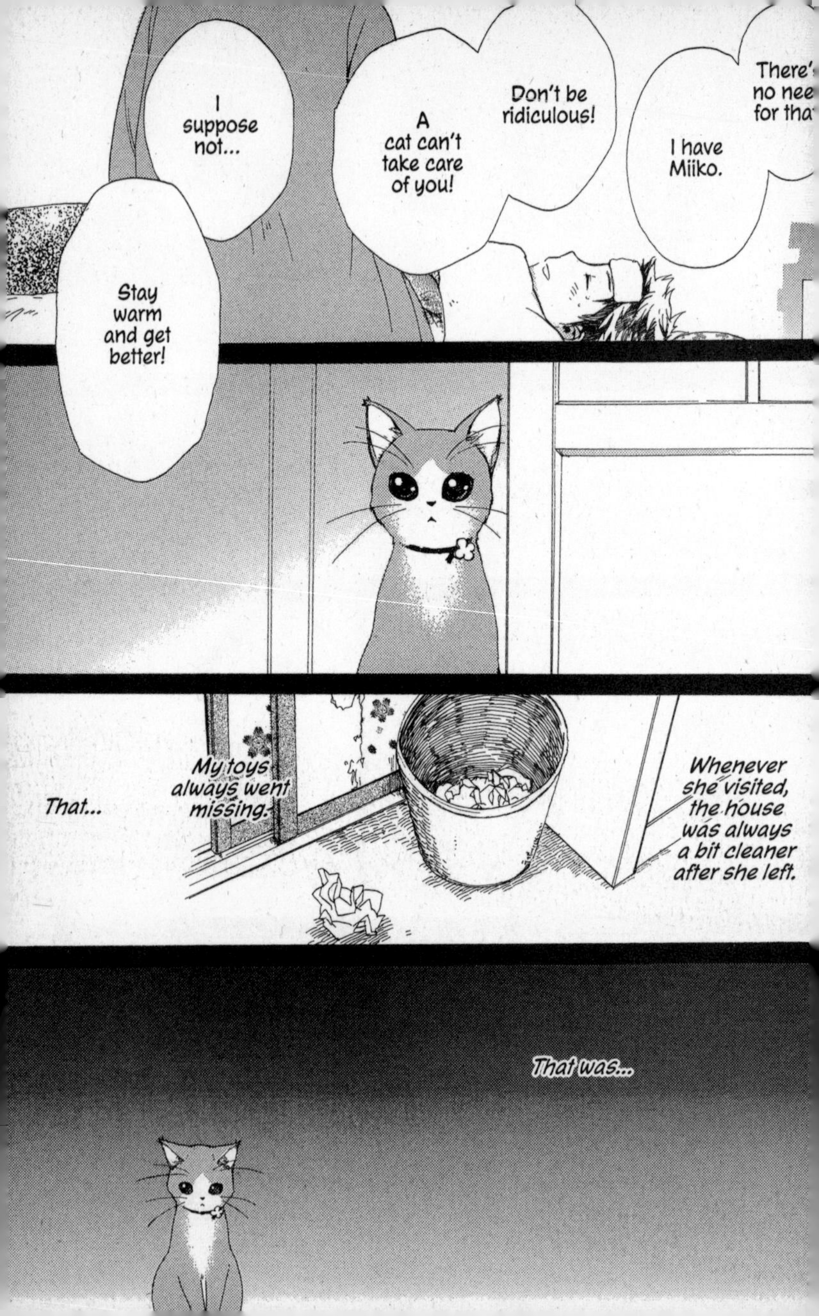
There' no nee for tha
I have Miiko.
Don't be ridiculous!
A cat can't take care of you!
I suppose not...
Stay warm and get better!
Whenever she visited, the house was always a bit cleaner after she left.
My toys always went missing.
That...
That was...

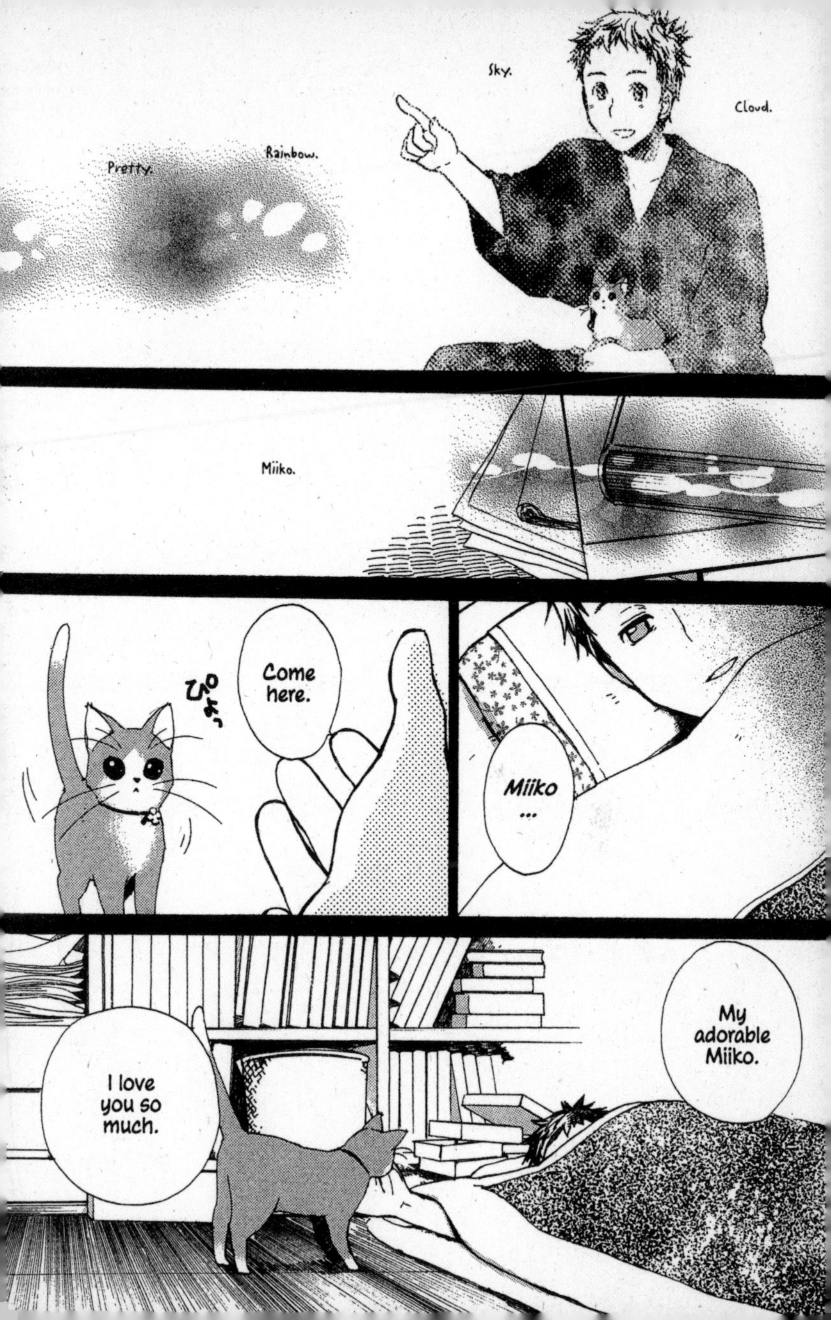
Cloud.
Sky.
Rainbow.
Pretty.
Miiko.
Miiko ...
Come here.
ぴょ
My adorable Miiko.
I love you so much.

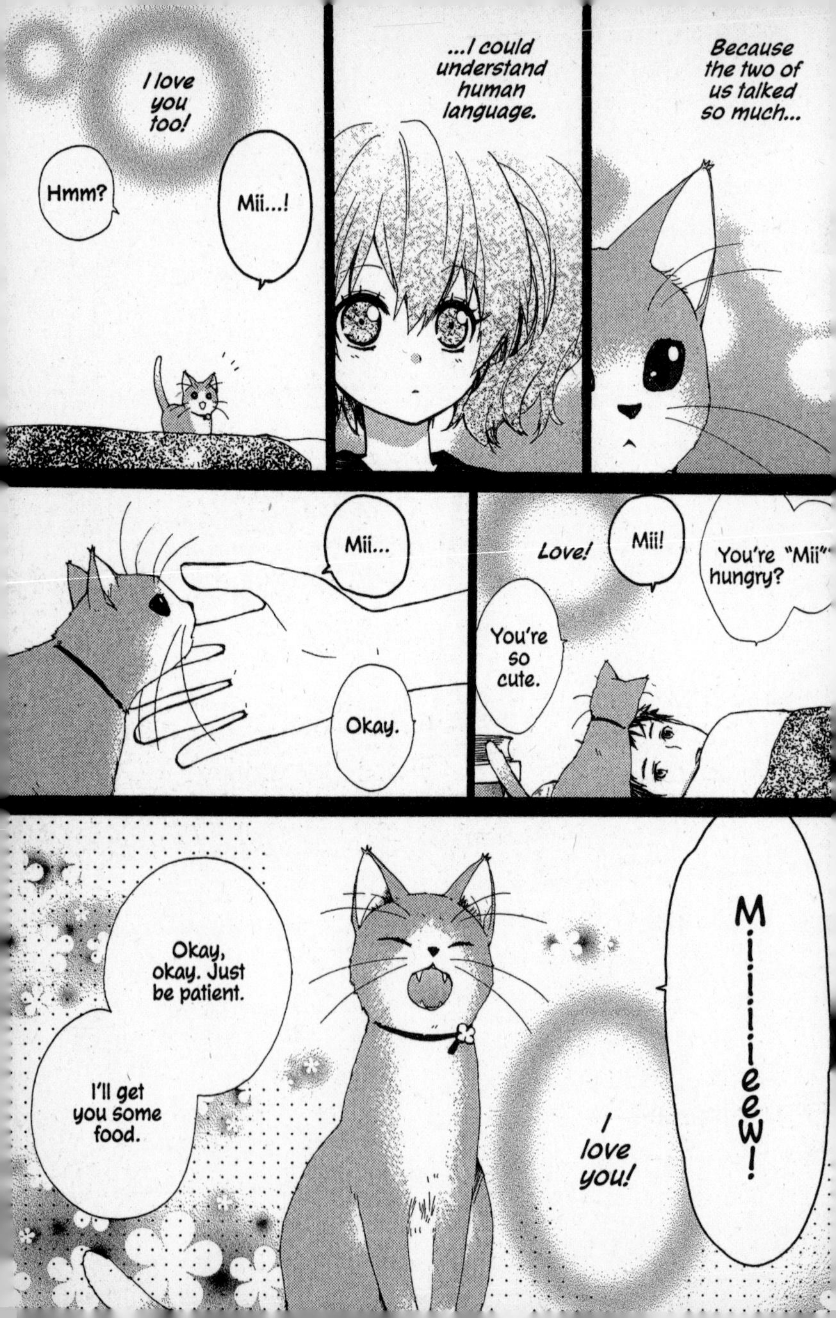

Because the two of us talked so much...
...I could understand human language.
I love you too!
Mii...!
Hmm?
You're "Mii" hungry?
Mii!
Love!
You're so cute.
Mii...
Okay.
Miiiieew!
I love you!
Okay, okay. Just be patient.
I'll get you some food.

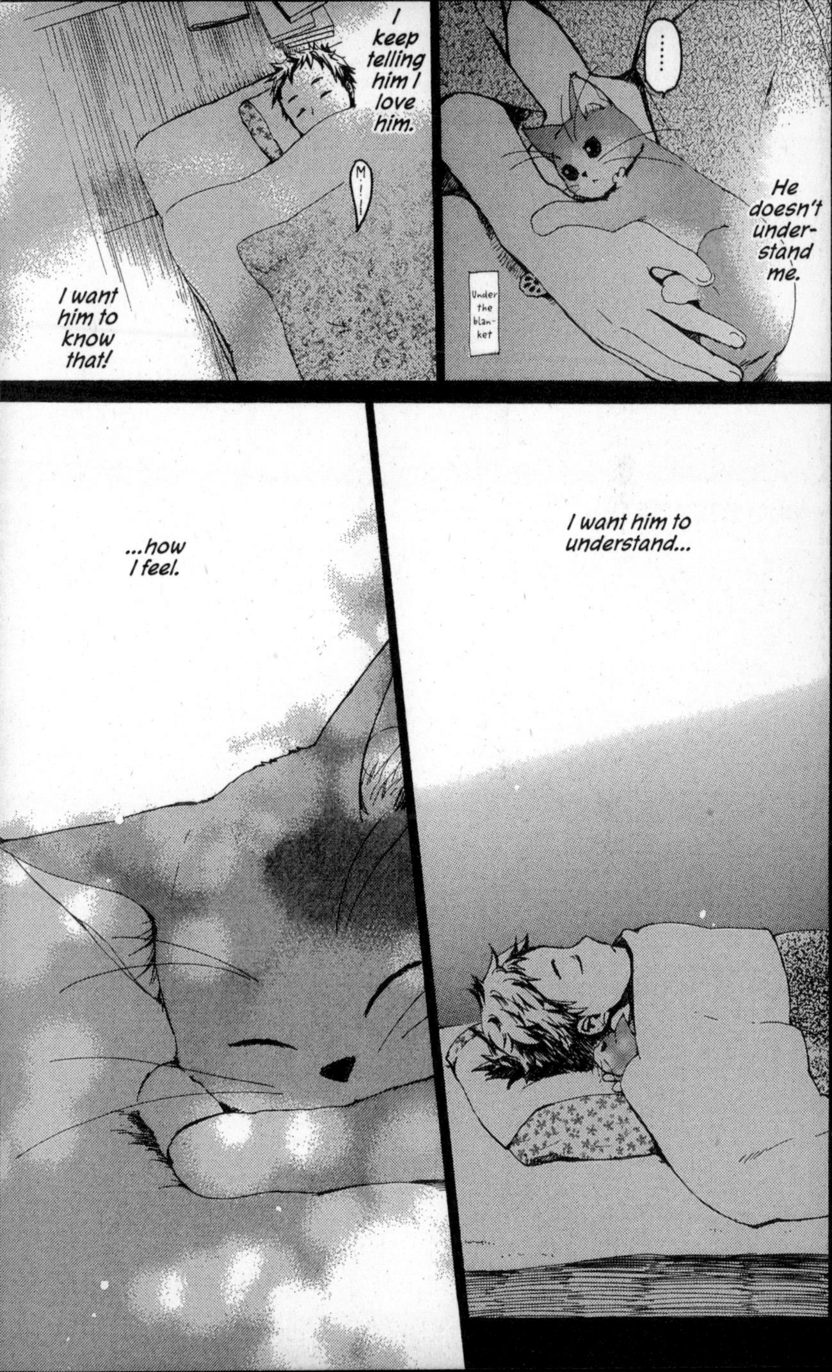
......
He doesn't under-stand me.
Under the blan-ket
I keep telling him I love him.
M!!!
I want him to know that!
I want him to understand...
...how I feel.

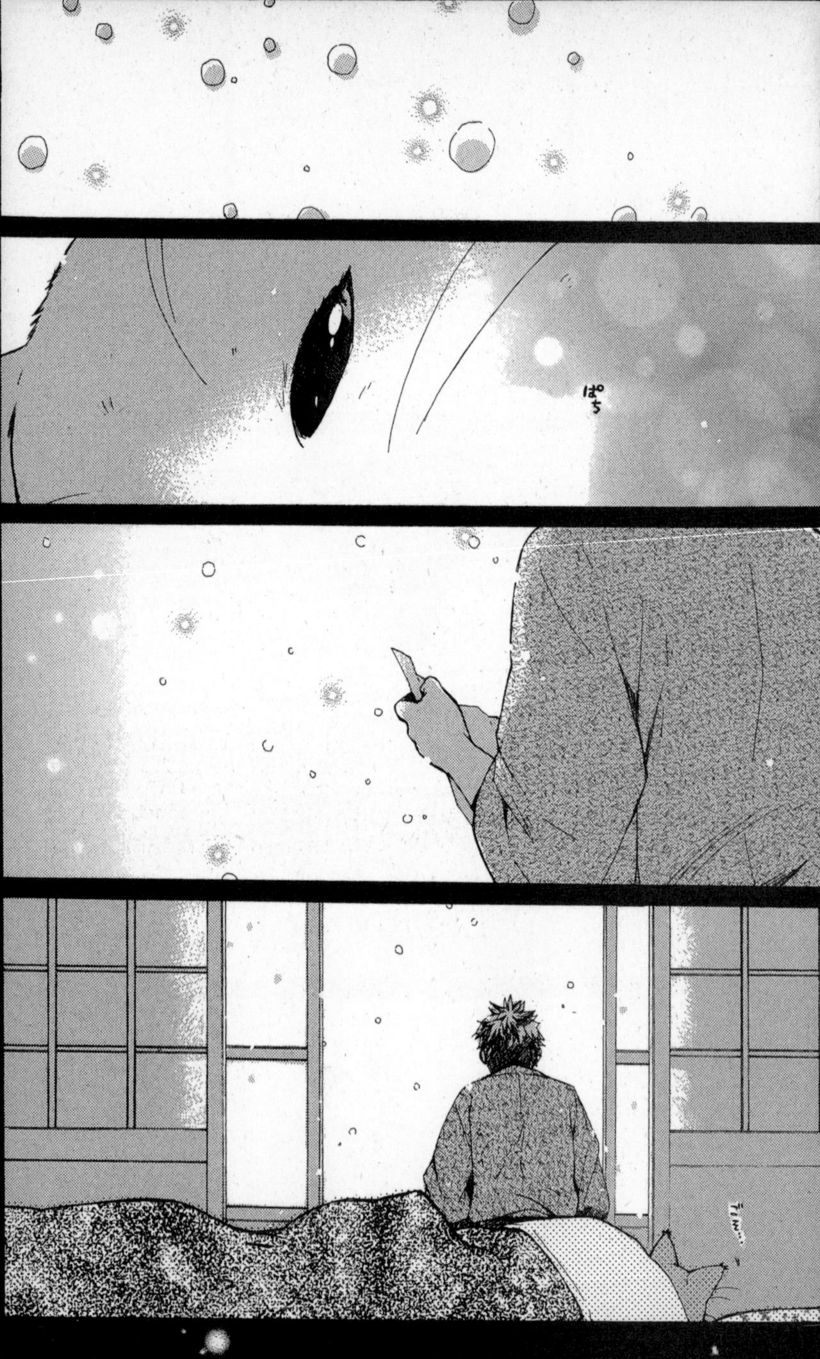
ぱち
ブゥ…

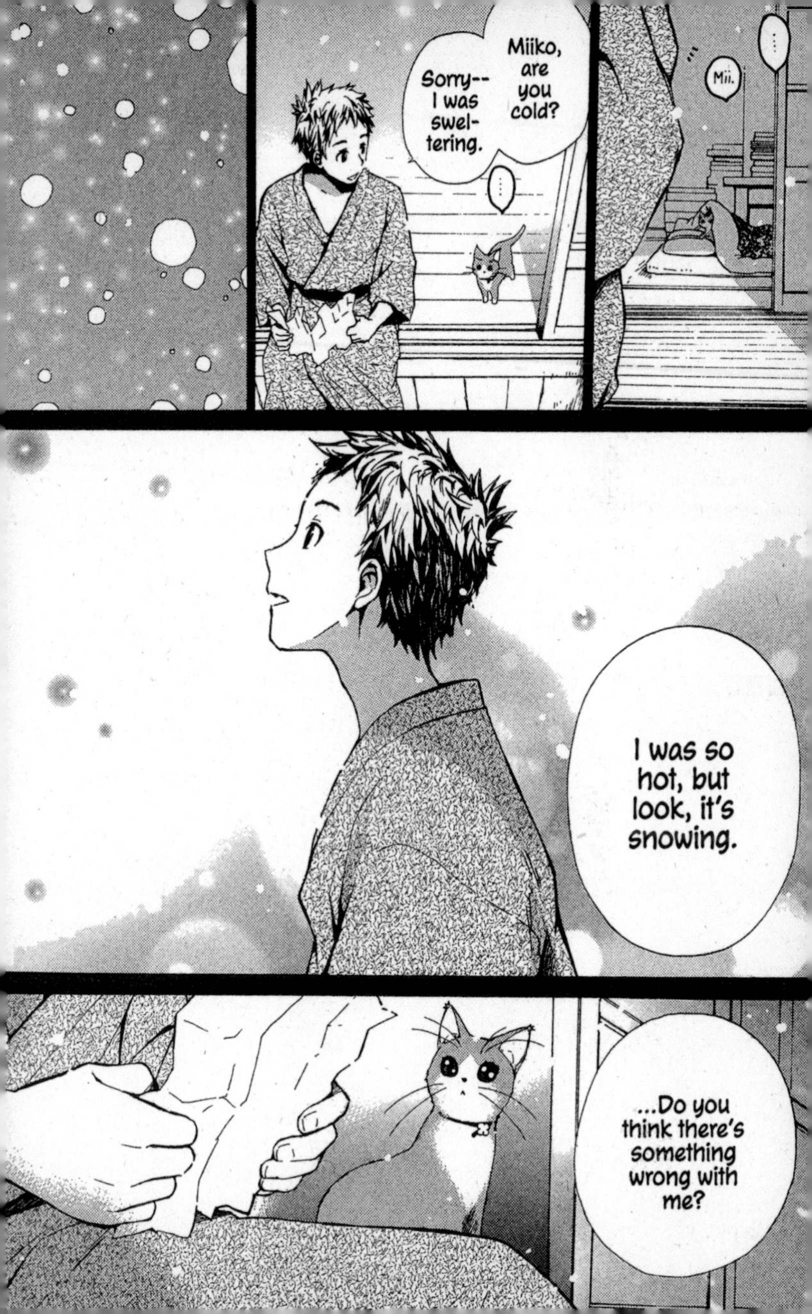
....
Mii.
Miiko, are you cold?
Sorry-- I was swel-tering.
...
I was so hot, but look, it's snowing.
...Do you think there's something wrong with me?

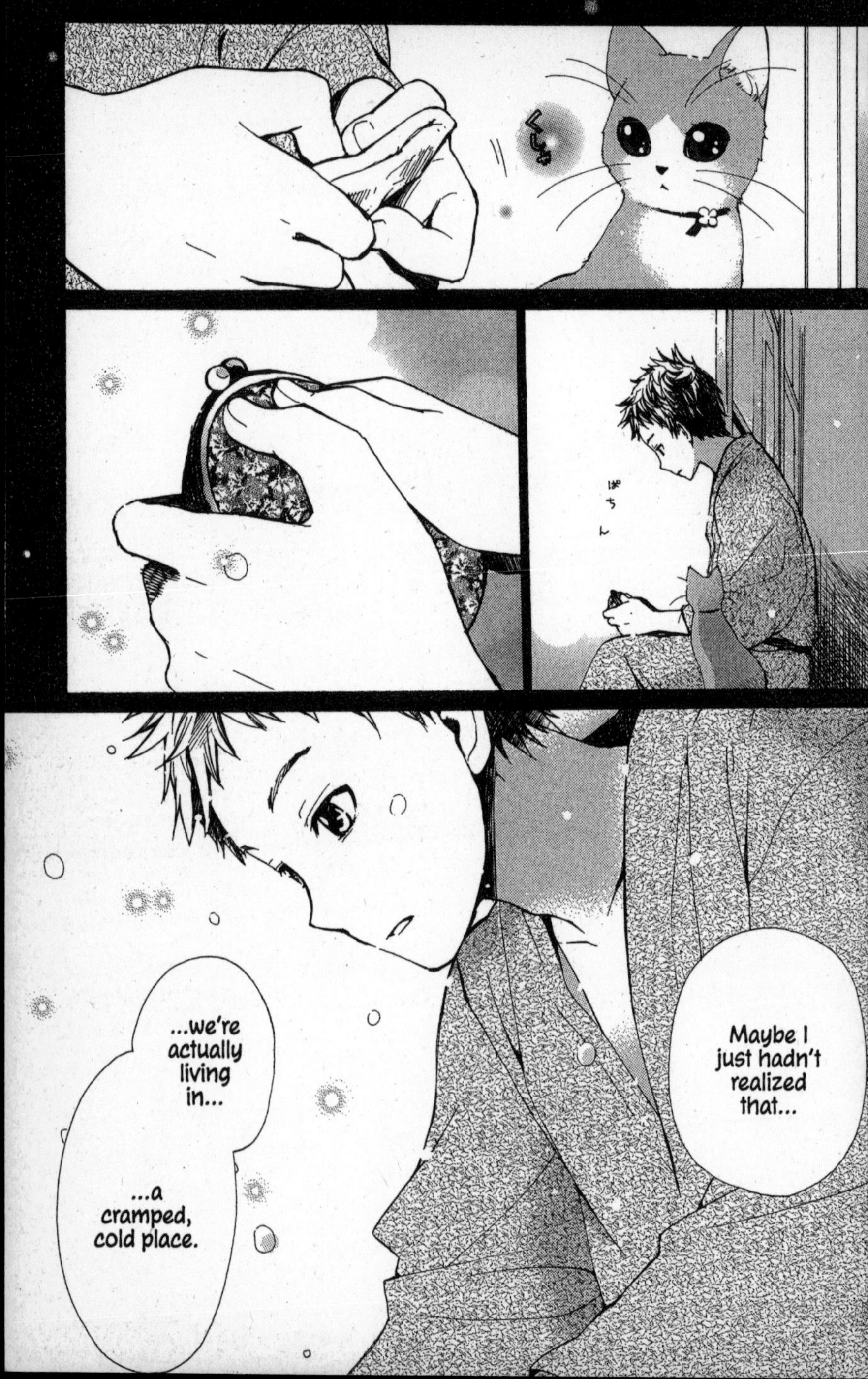
くしゅ
ぱちん
Maybe I just hadn't realized that...
...we're actually living in...
...a cramped, cold place.

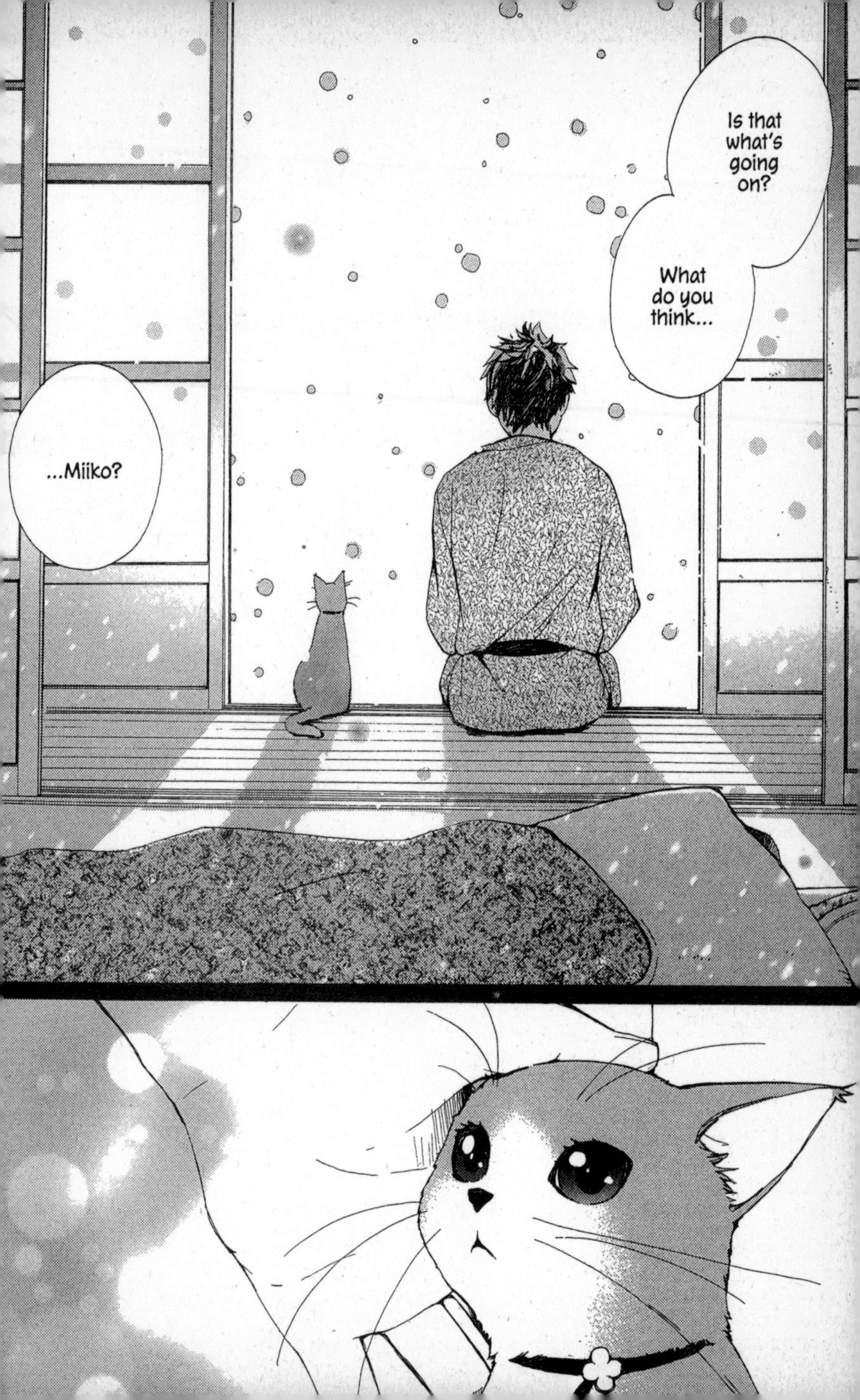
Is that what's going on?
What do you think...
...Miiko?

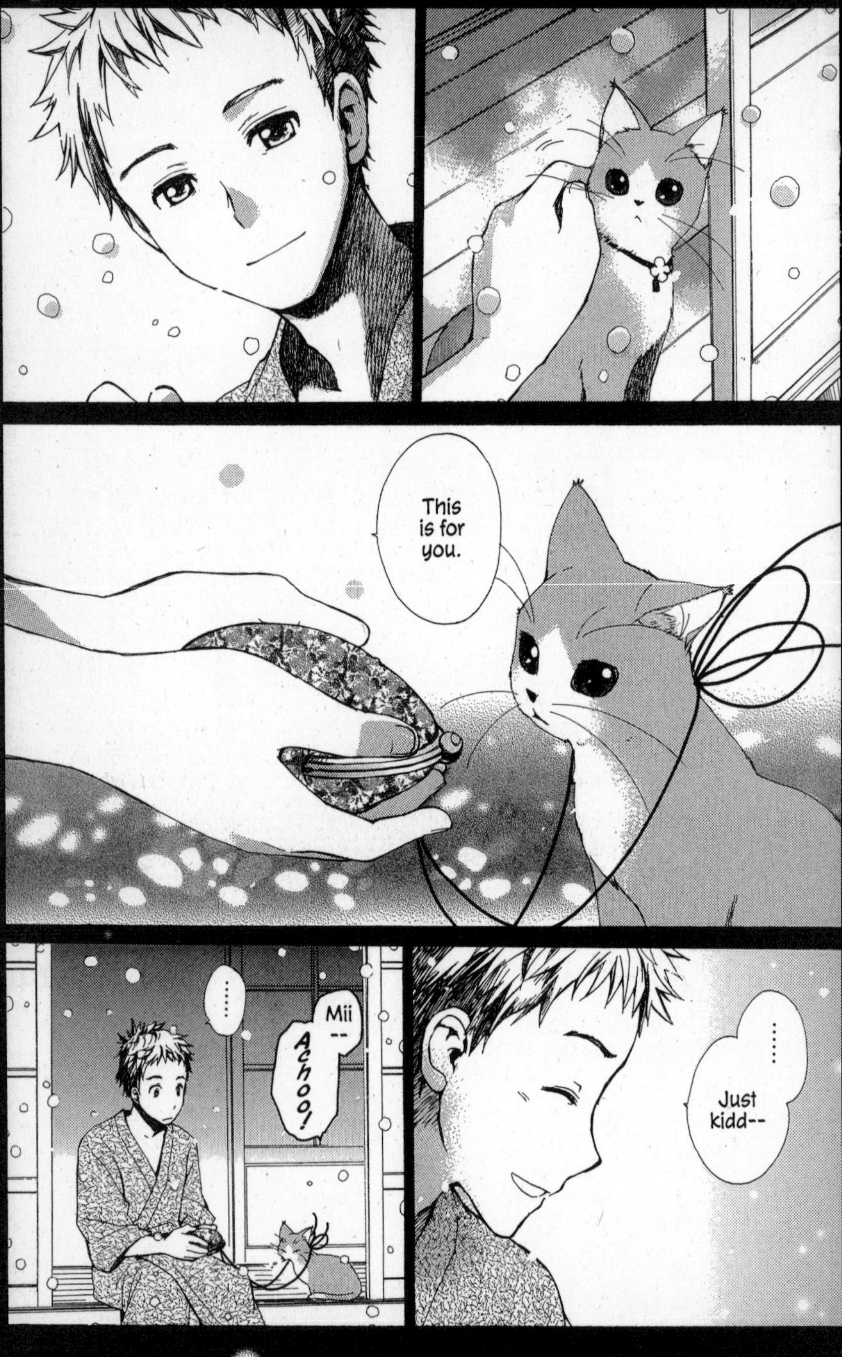
This is for you.
...... Just kidd--
......
Mii--
Achoo!

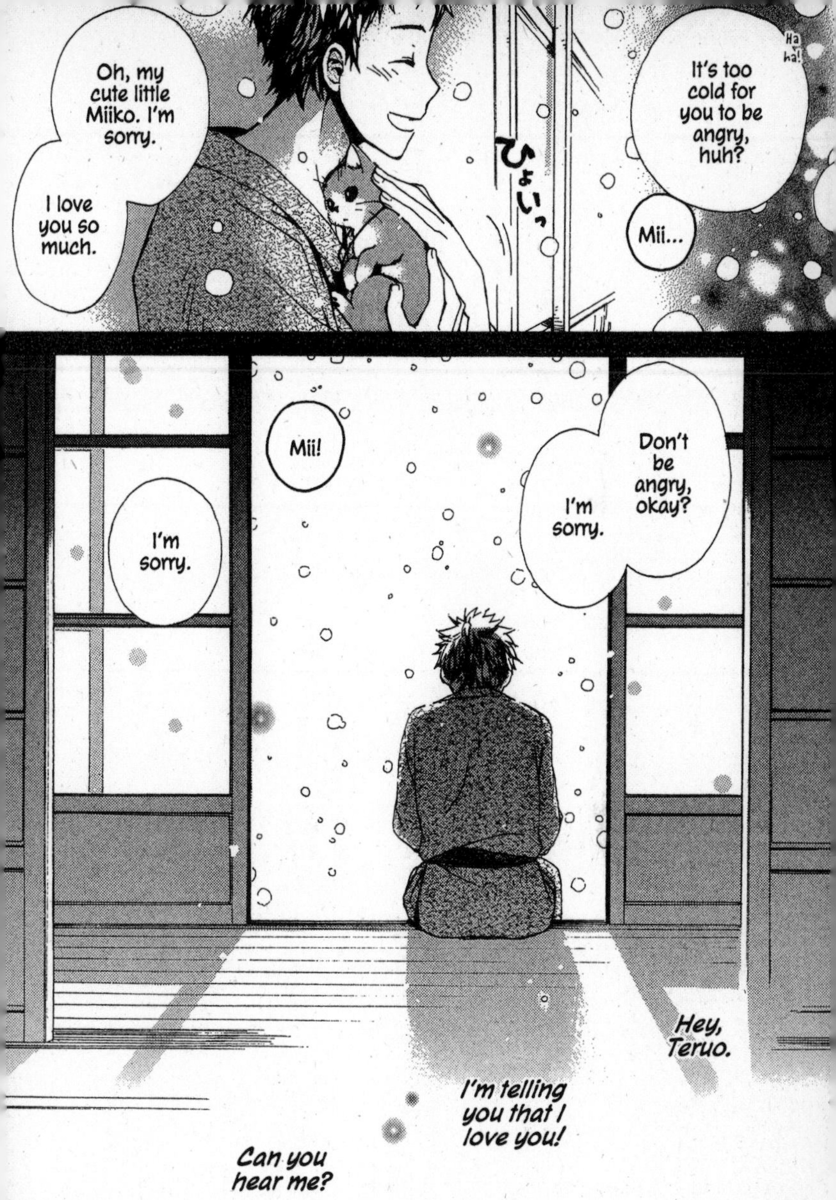
Ha ha!
It's too cold for you to be angry, huh?
Mii...
ひょいっ
Oh, my cute little Miiko. I'm sorry.
I love you so much.
Don't be angry, okay?
I'm sorry.
Mii!
I'm sorry.
Hey, Teruo.
I'm telling you that I love you!
Can you hear me?

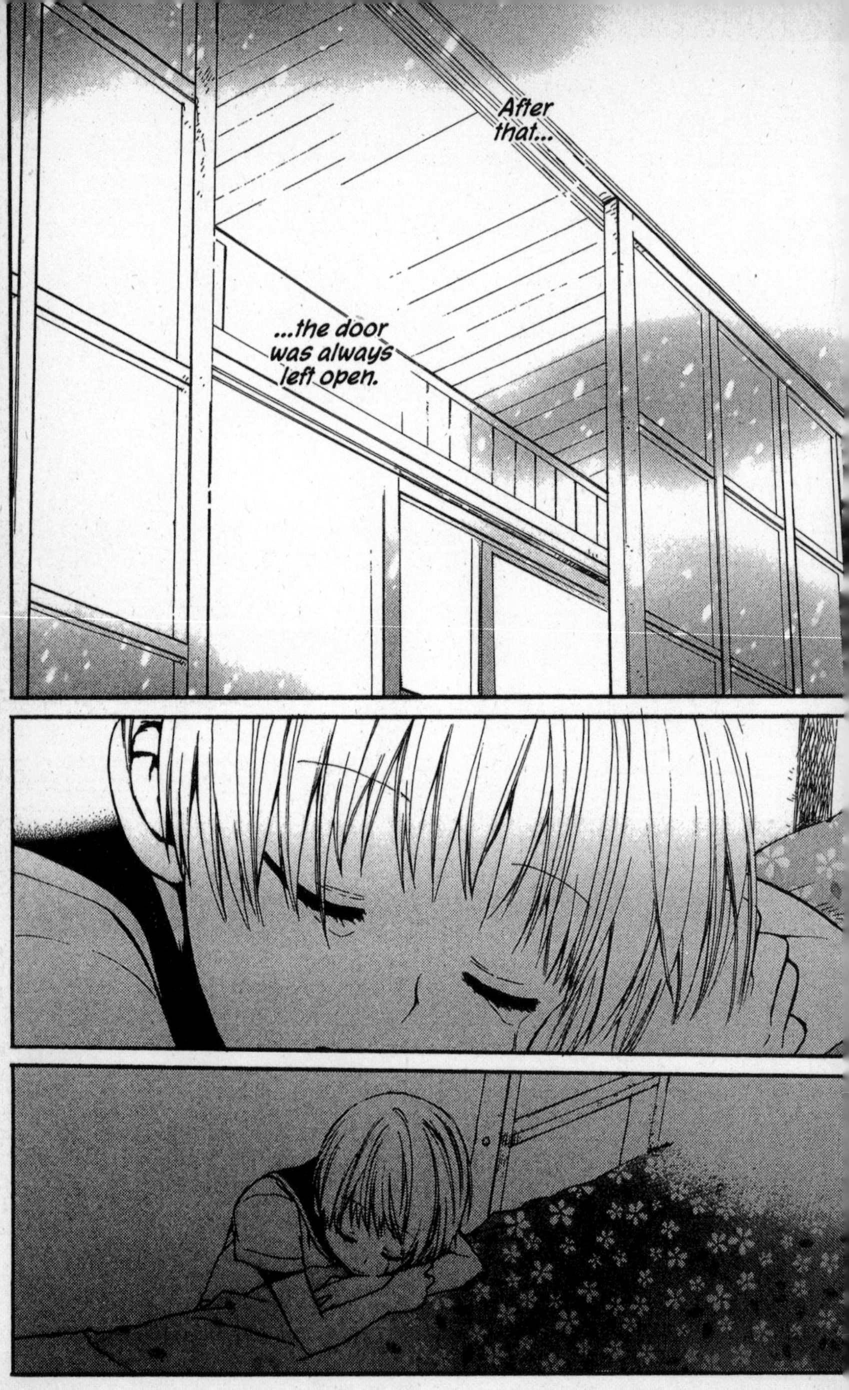
After that...
...the door was always left open.

Report.26 One Distant Morning

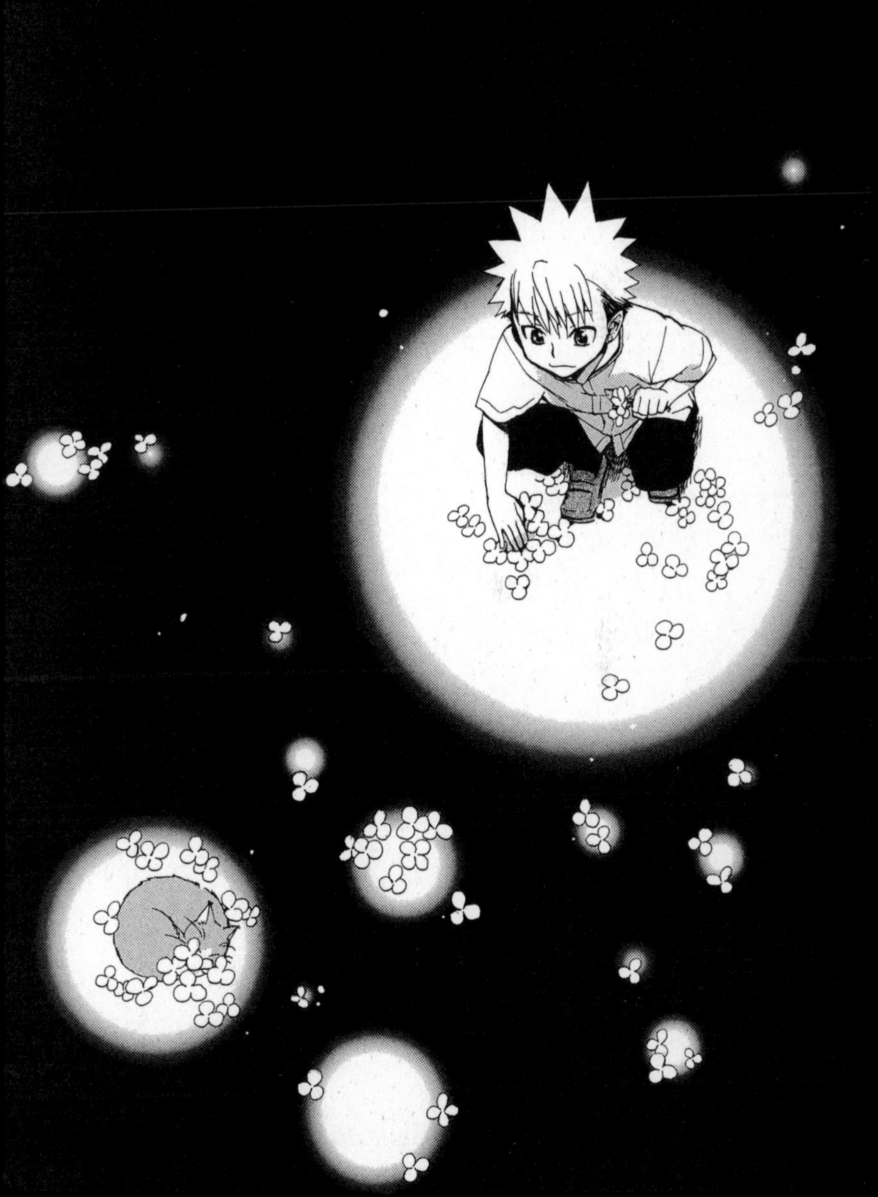

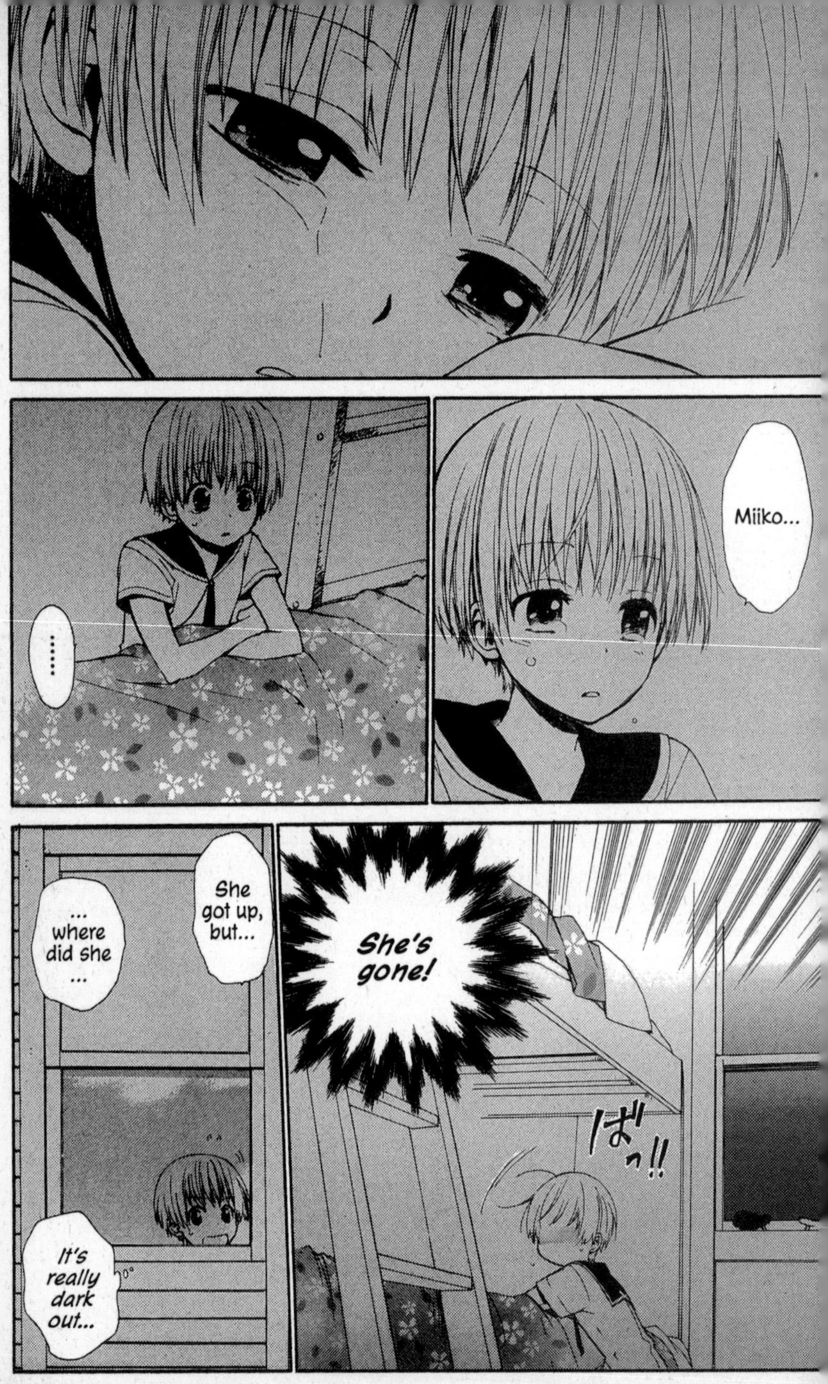
Miiko...
......
She's gone!
ぱっ!!
She got up, but...
... where did she ...
It's really dark out...

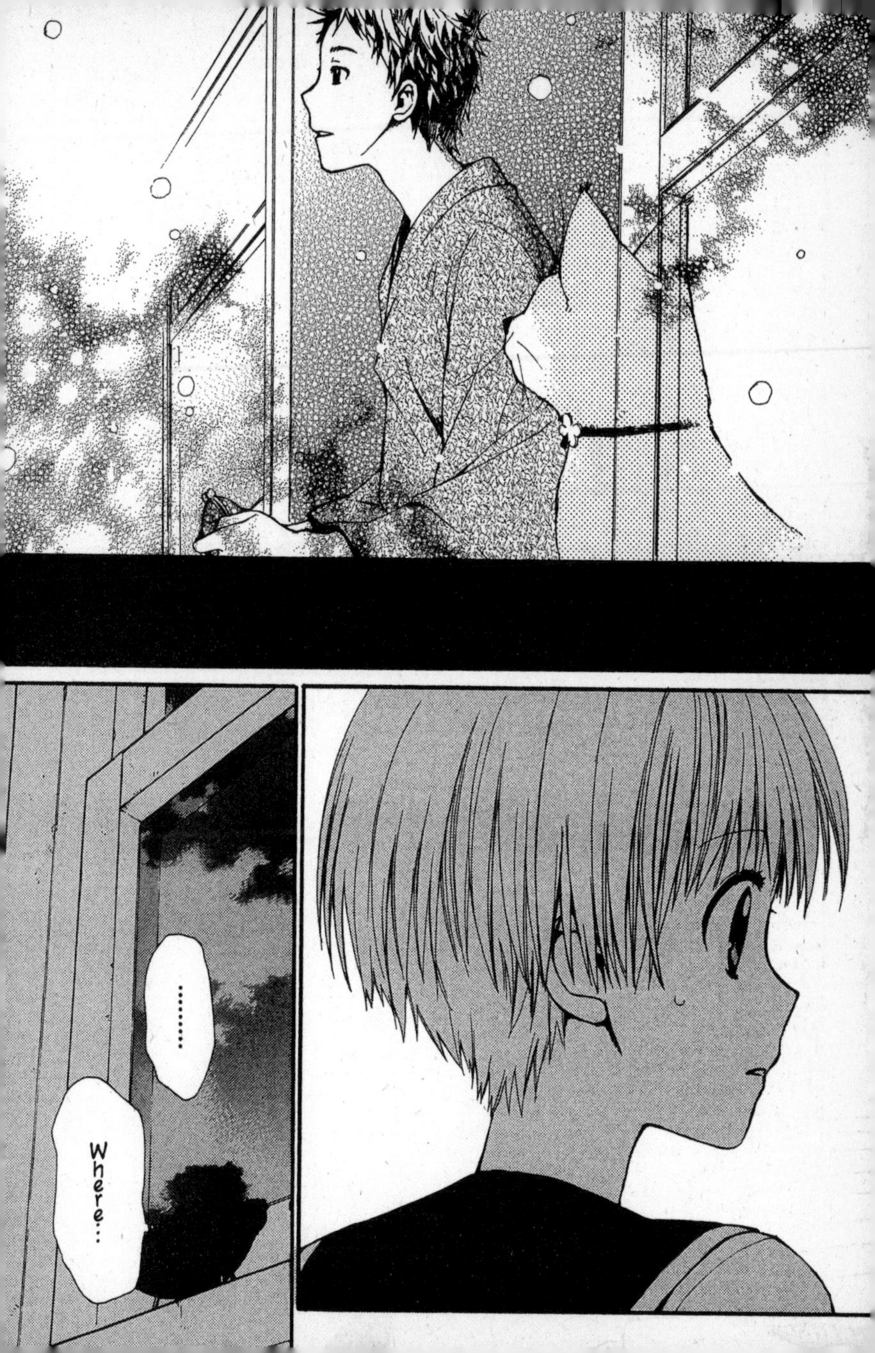
....
Where...

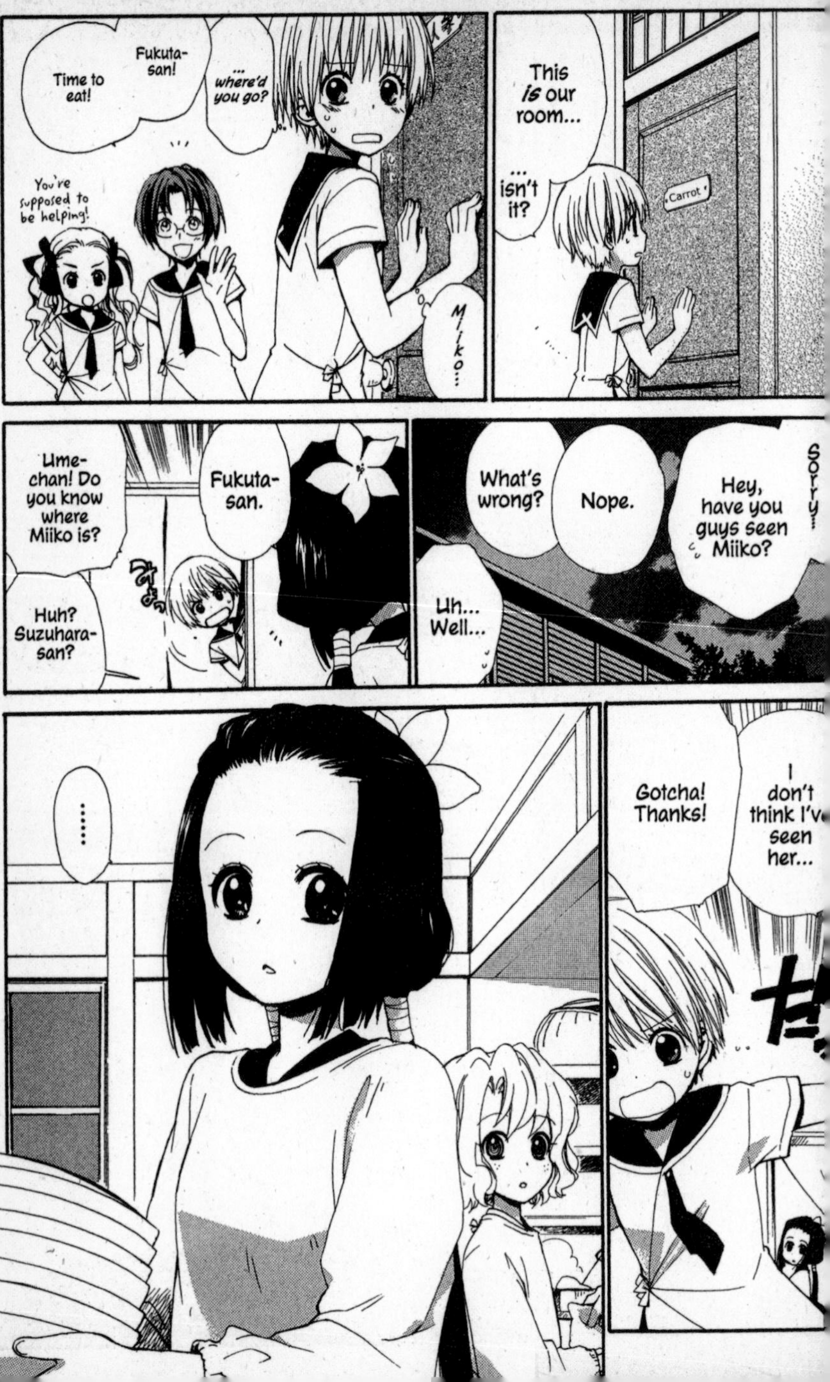
This is our room...
...isn't it?
Carrot
Miiko...
...where'd you go?
Fukuta-san!
Time to eat!
You're supposed to be helping!
Sorry...
Hey, have you guys seen Miiko?
Nope.
What's wrong?
Uh... Well...
Fukuta-san.
Ume-chan! Do you know where Miiko is?
Huh? Suzuhara-san?
I don't think I'v seen her...
Gotcha! Thanks!
......

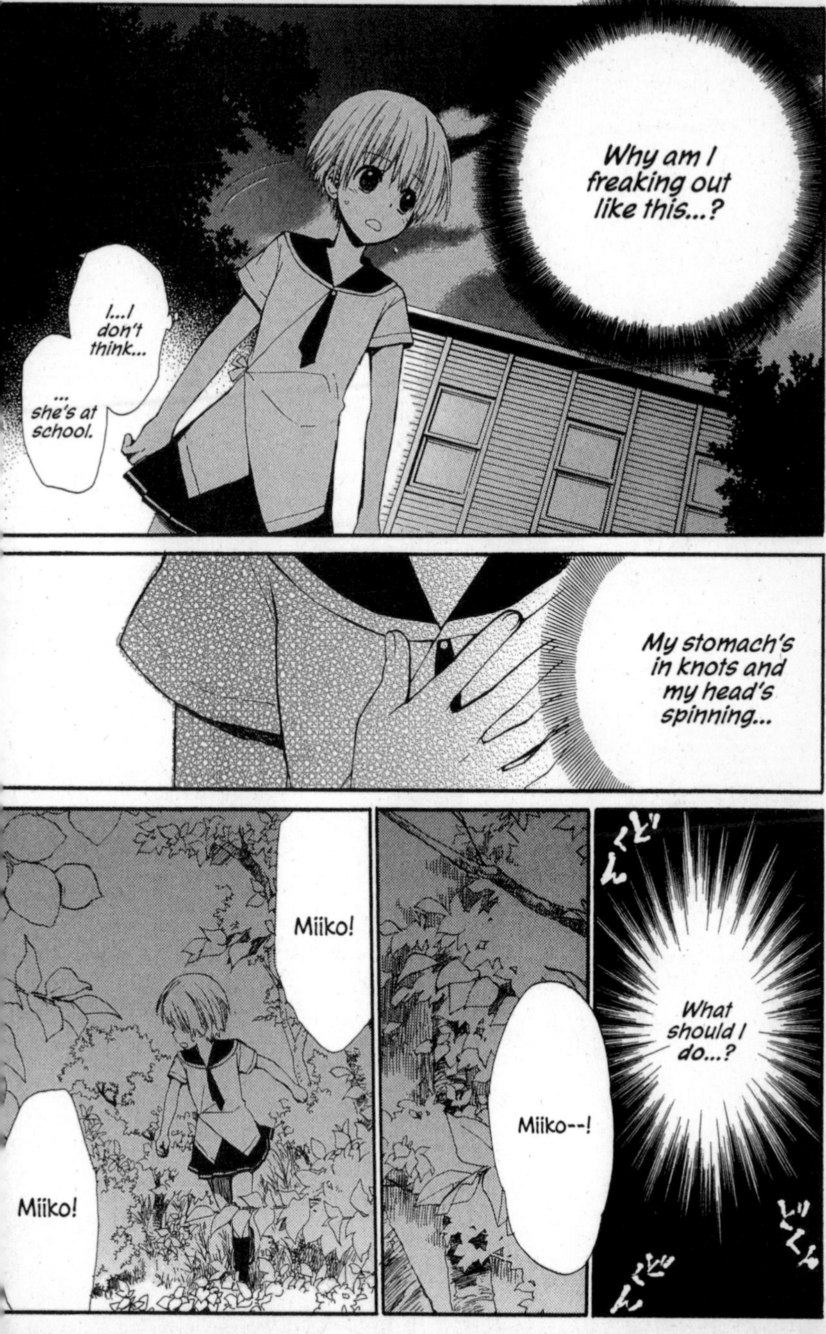
Why am I freaking out like this...?
I...I don't think...
...she's at school.
My stomach's in knots and my head's spinning...
どくん
What should I do...?
どくん
どくん
Miiko--!
Miiko!
Miiko!

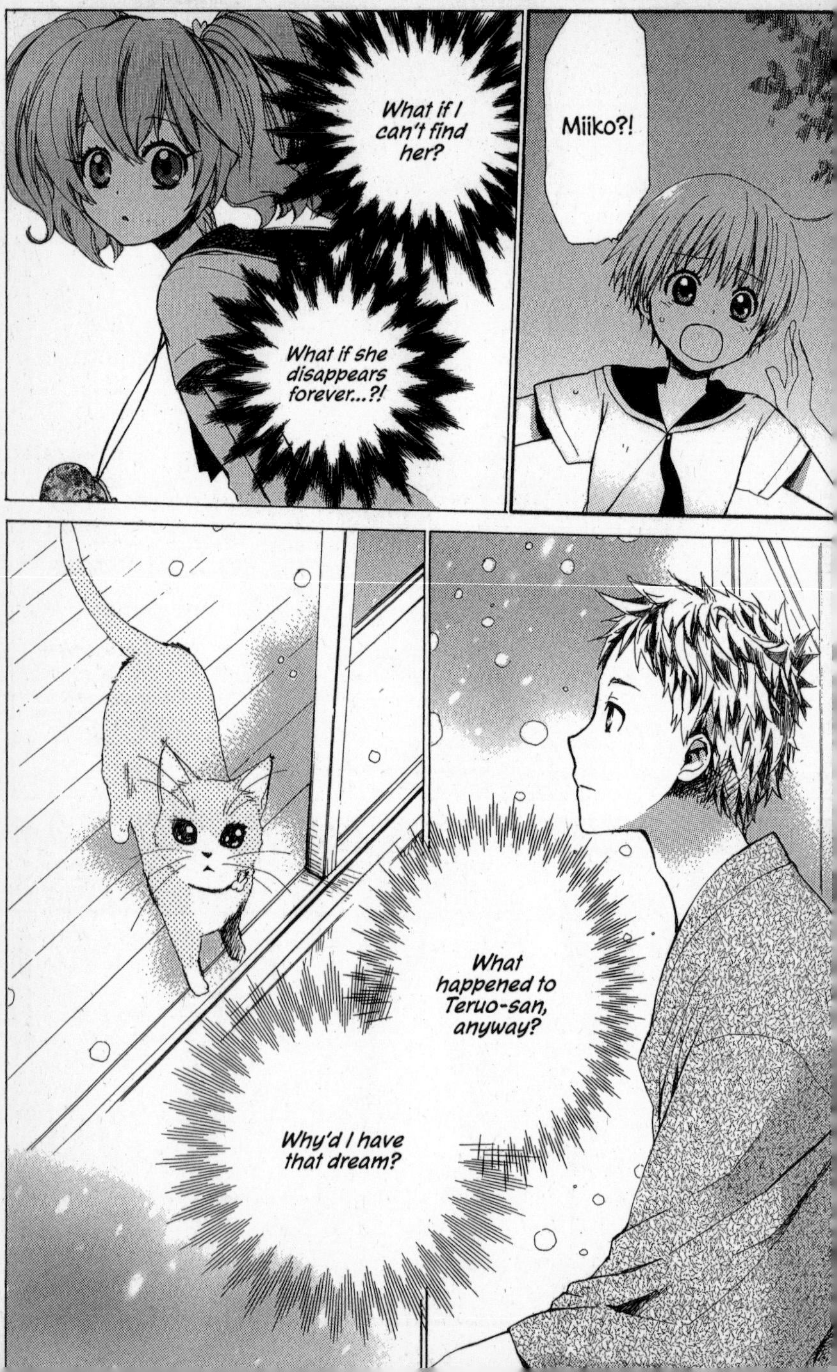
Miiko?!
What if I can't find her?
What if she disappears forever...?!
What happened to Teruo-san, anyway?
Why'd I have that dream?

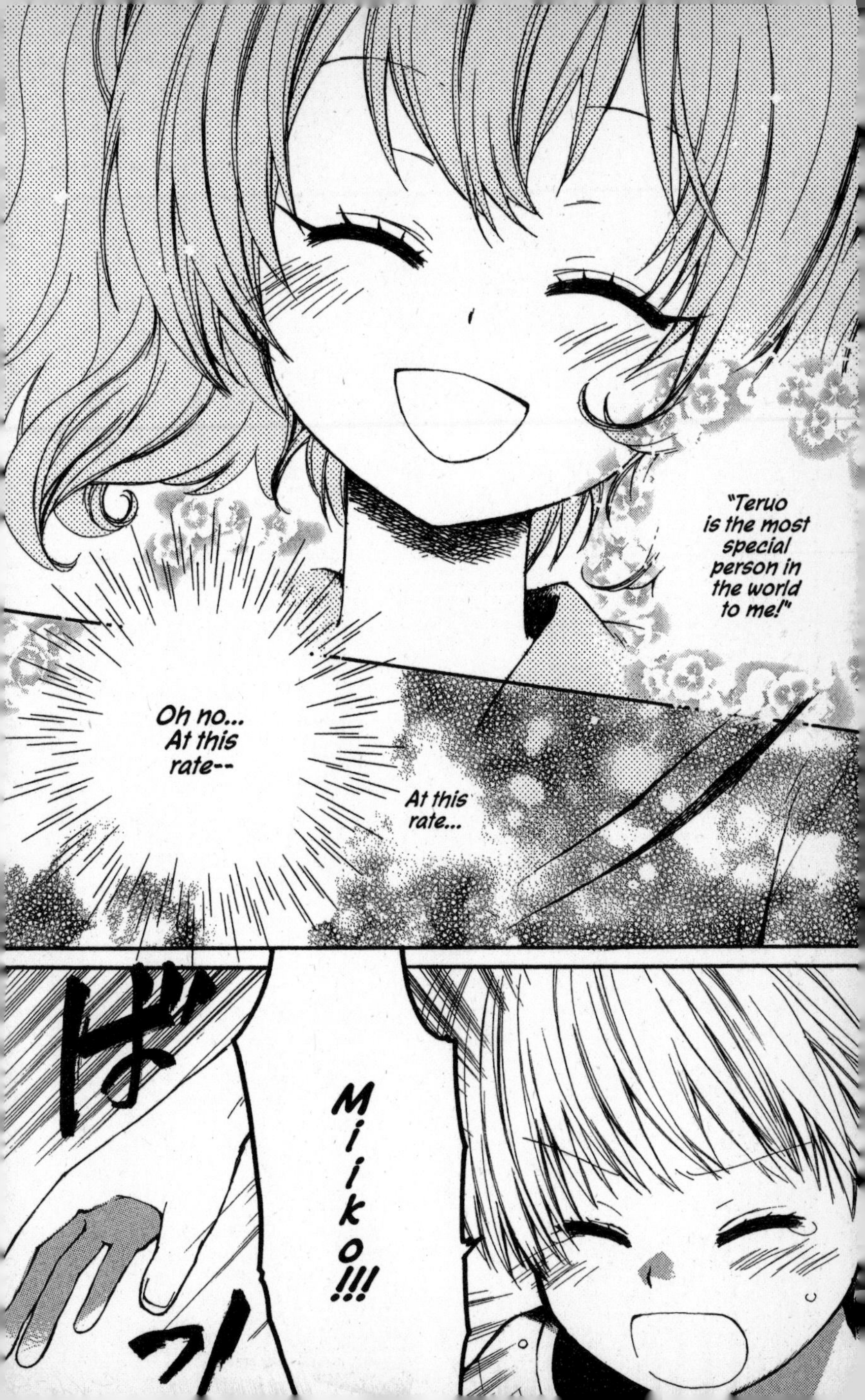
"Teruo is the most special person in the world to me!"
At this rate...
Oh no... At this rate--
Miiko!!!
ばっ

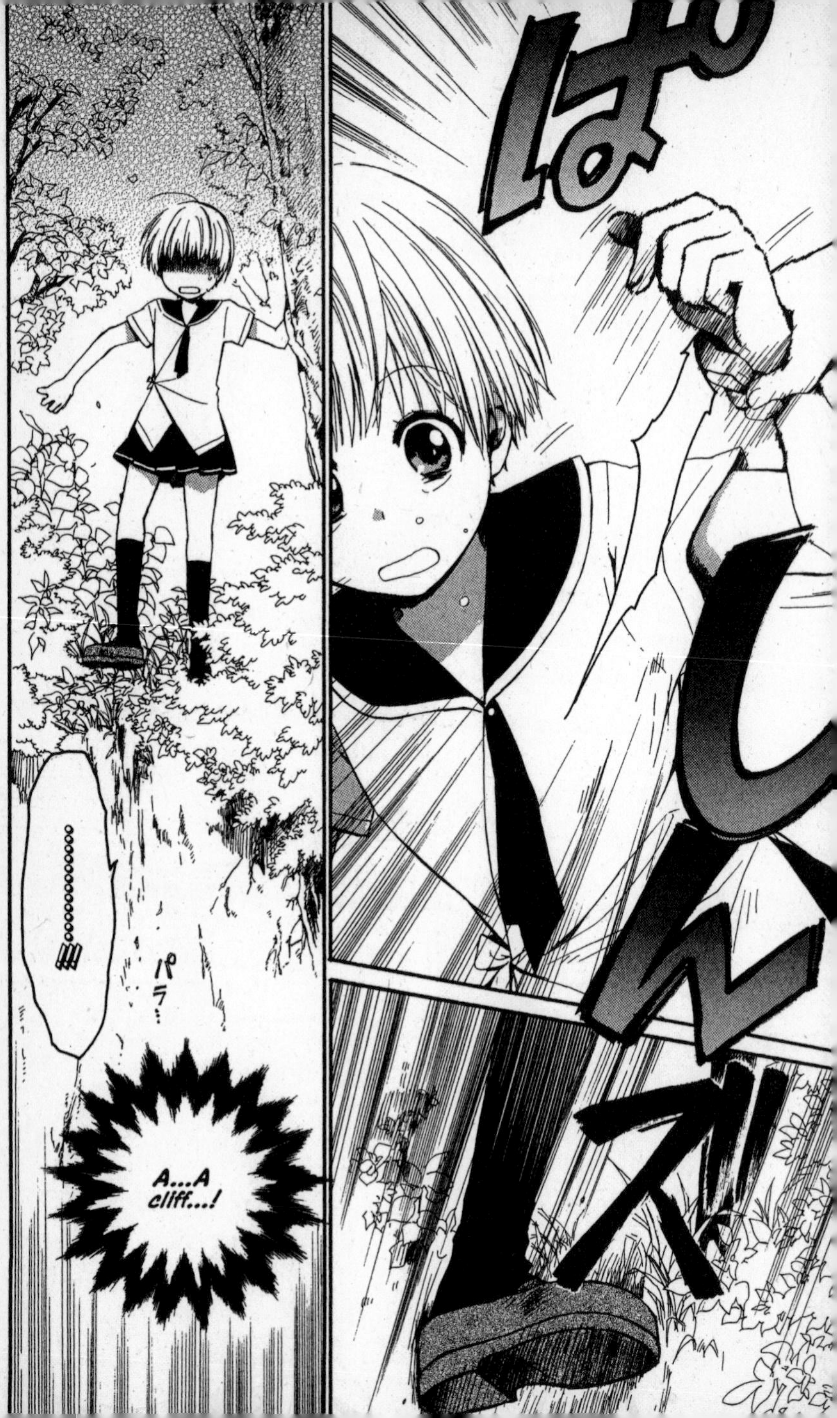
パラ…
A...A cliff...!

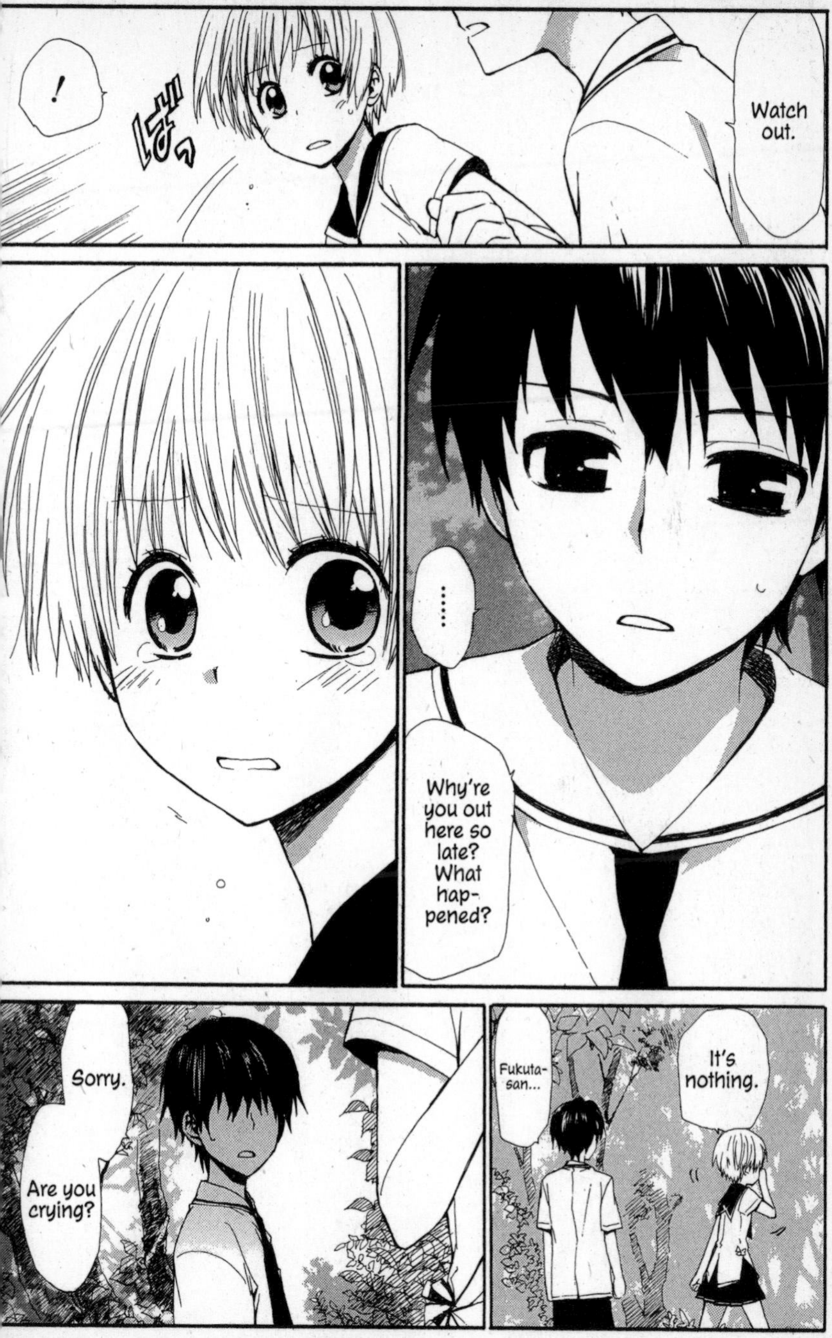
Watch out.
!
ばっ
......
Why're you out here so late? What hap-pened?
It's nothing.
Fukuta-san...
Sorry.
Are you crying?

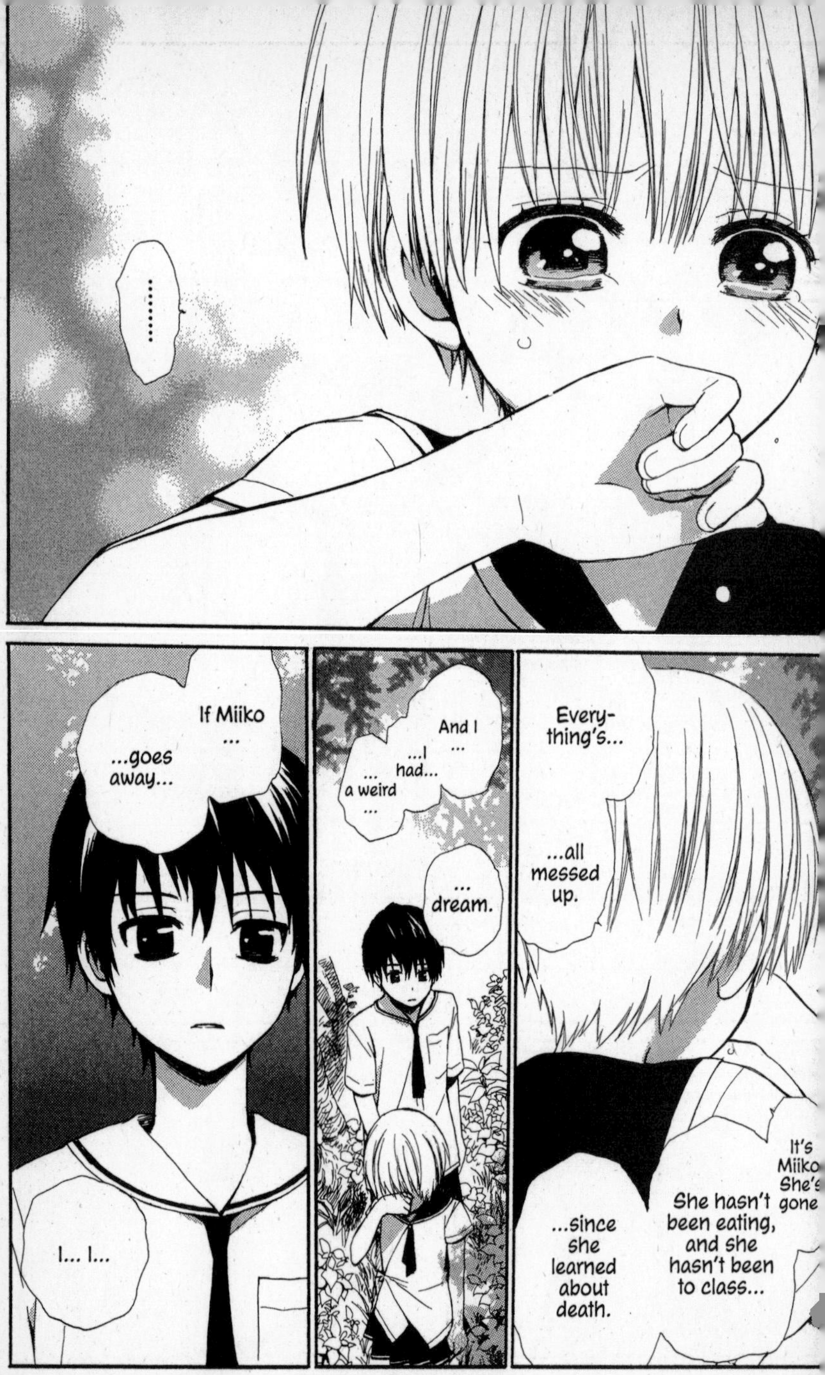
....
Every-thing's...
...all messed up.
It's Miiko She's gone
She hasn't been eating, and she hasn't been to class...
...since she learned about death.
And I ...
...I had...
... a weird ...
... dream.
If Miiko ...
...goes away...
I... I...

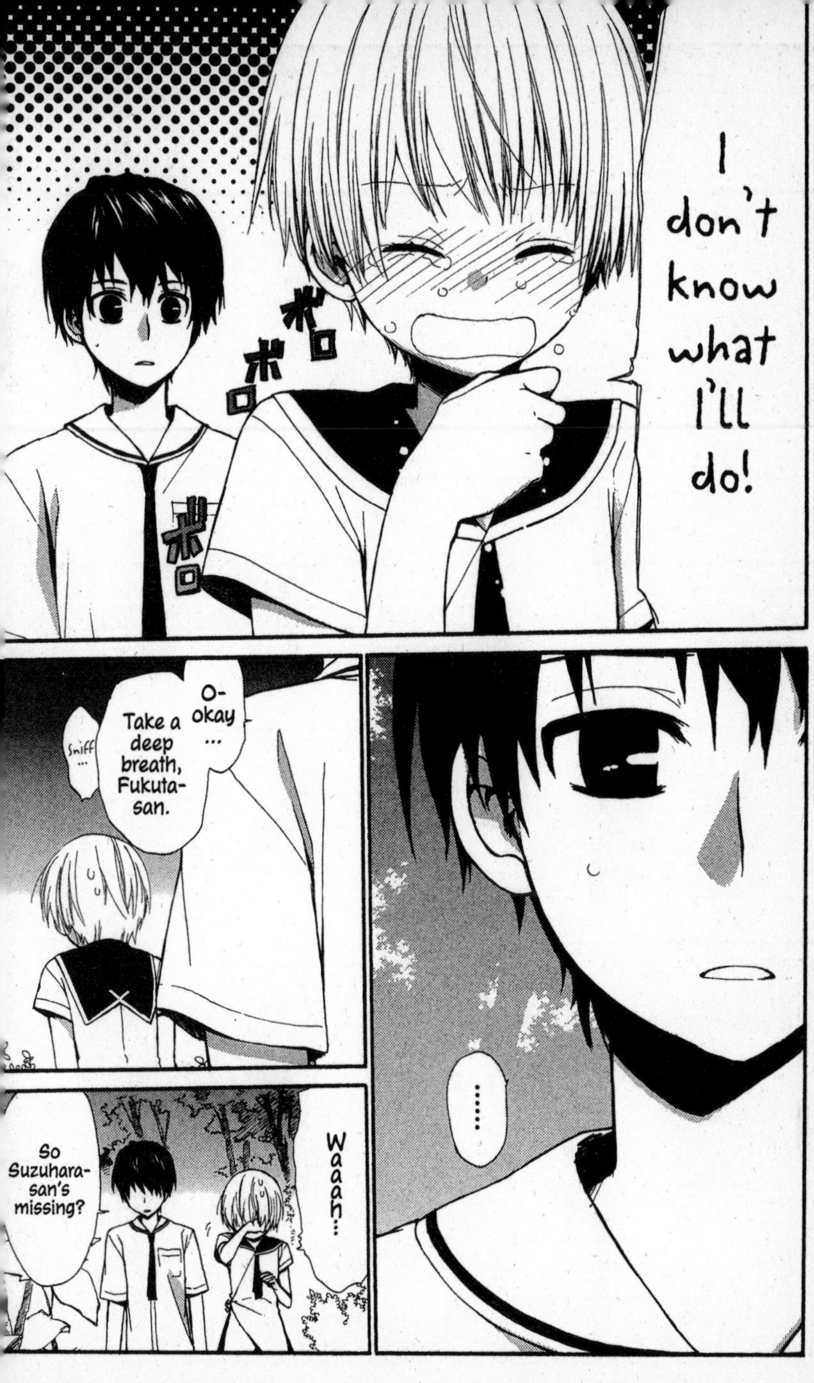
I don't know what I'll do!
ボロ
ボロ
ボロ
......
O-okay ...
Take a deep breath, Fukuta-san.
Sniff ...
Waaah...
So Suzuhara-san's missing?

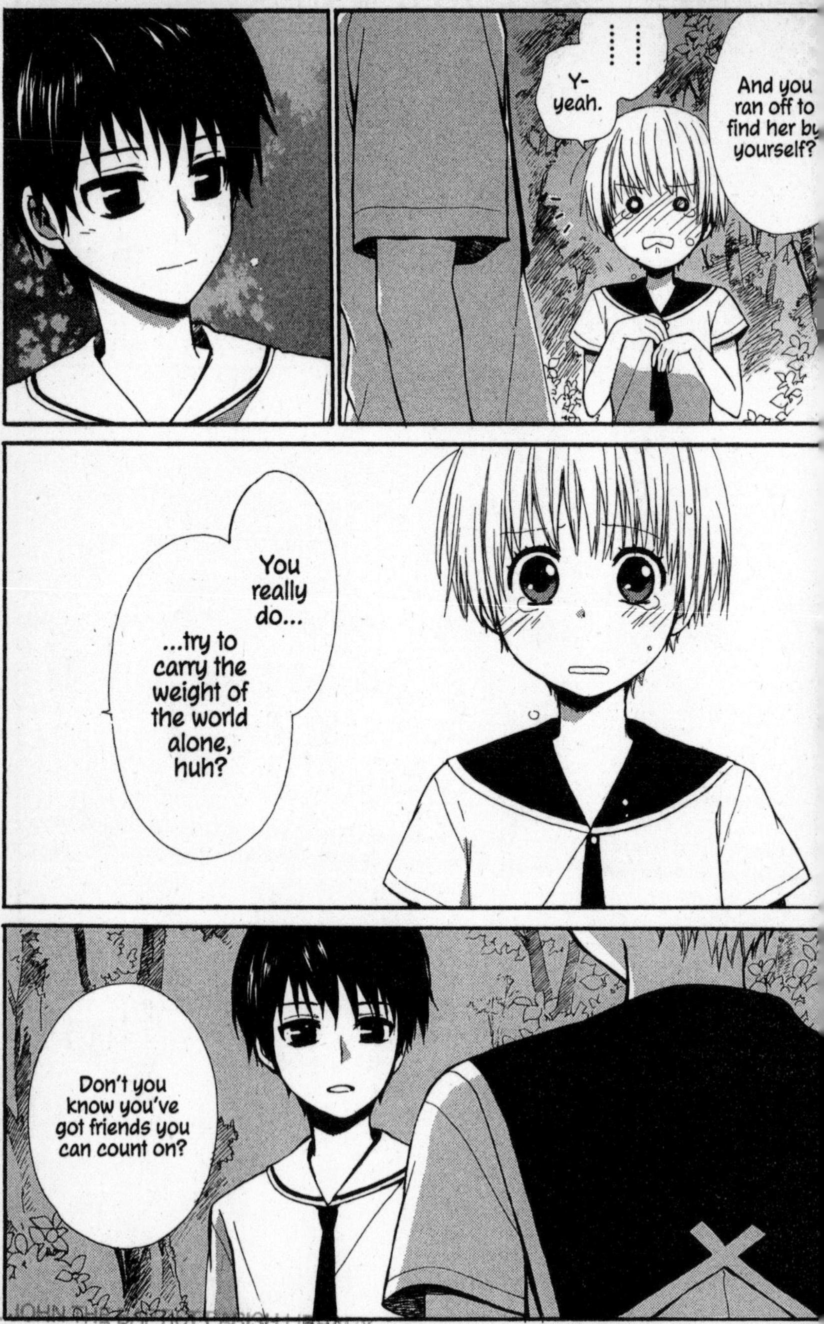

And you ran off to find her by yourself?
......
Y-yeah.
You really do...
...try to carry the weight of the world alone, huh?
Don't you know you've got friends you can count on?

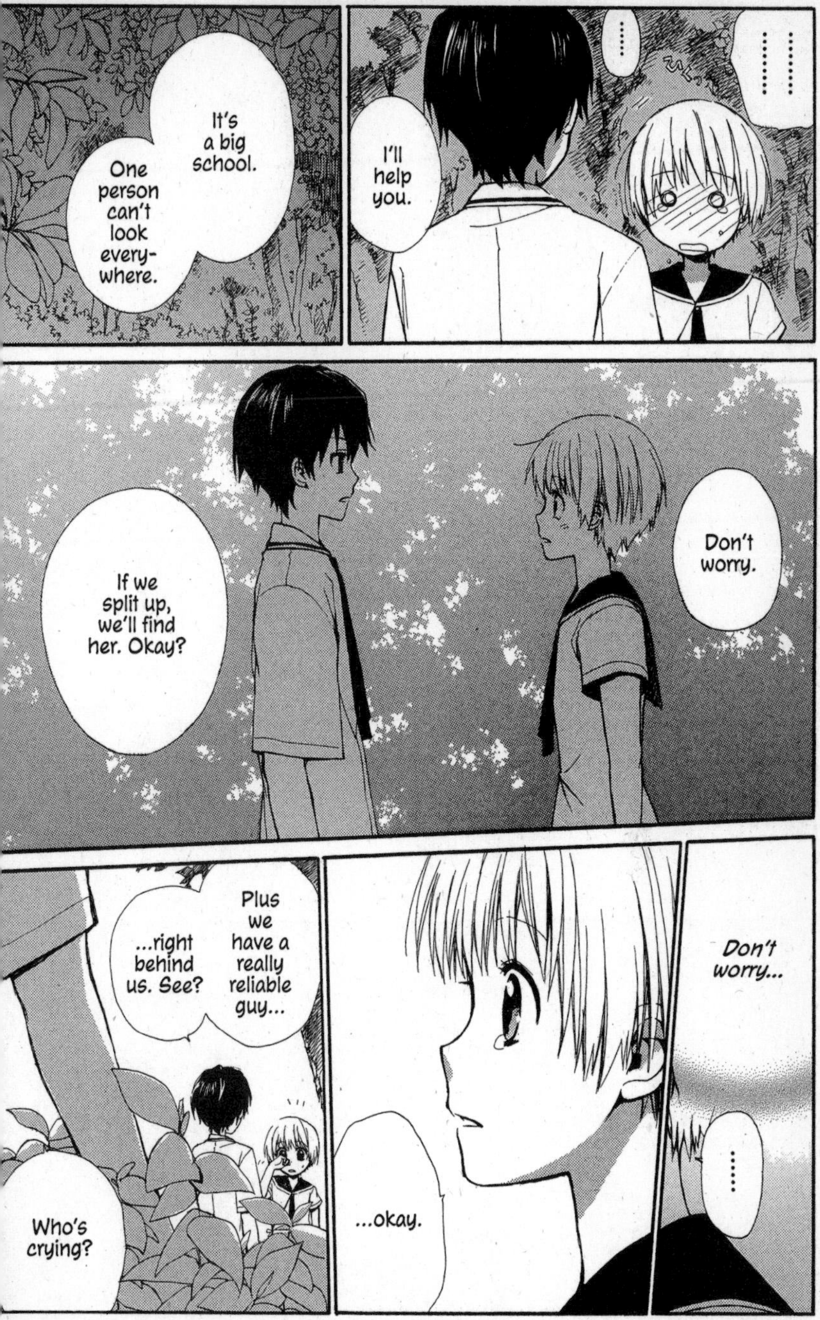
……
……
I'll help you.
It's a big school.
One person can't look every-where.
Don't worry.
If we split up, we'll find her. Okay?
Don't worry...
……
...okay.
Plus we have a really reliable guy...
...right behind us. See?
Who's crying?

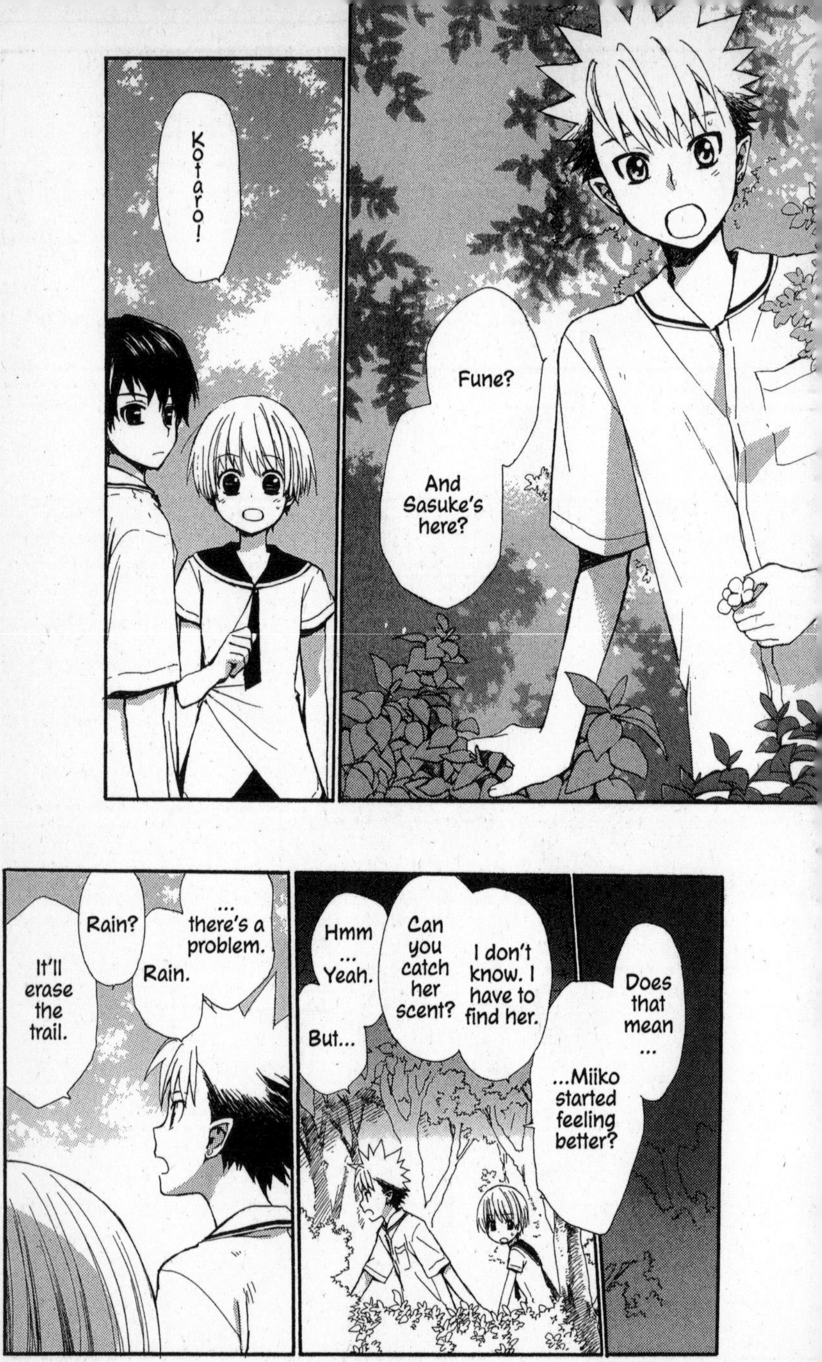
Fune?
And Sasuke's here?
Kotaro!
Does that mean...
...Miiko started feeling better?
I don't know. I have to find her.
Can you catch her scent?
Hmm... Yeah.
But...
...there's a problem.
Rain?
Rain.
It'll erase the trail.

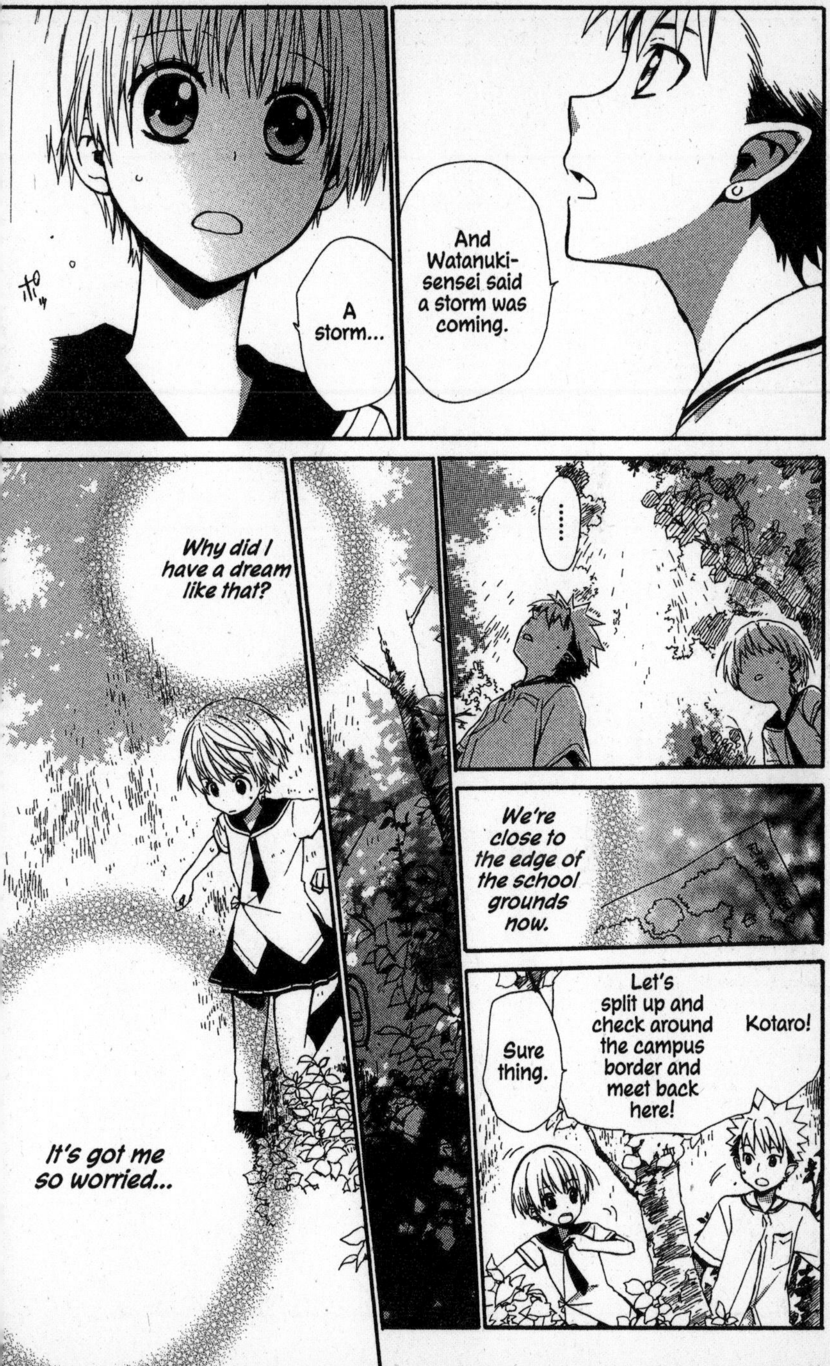
And Watanuki-sensei said a storm was coming.
A storm...
......
We're close to the edge of the school grounds now.
Kotaro!
Let's split up and check around the campus border and meet back here!
Sure thing.
Why did I have a dream like that?
It's got me so worried...

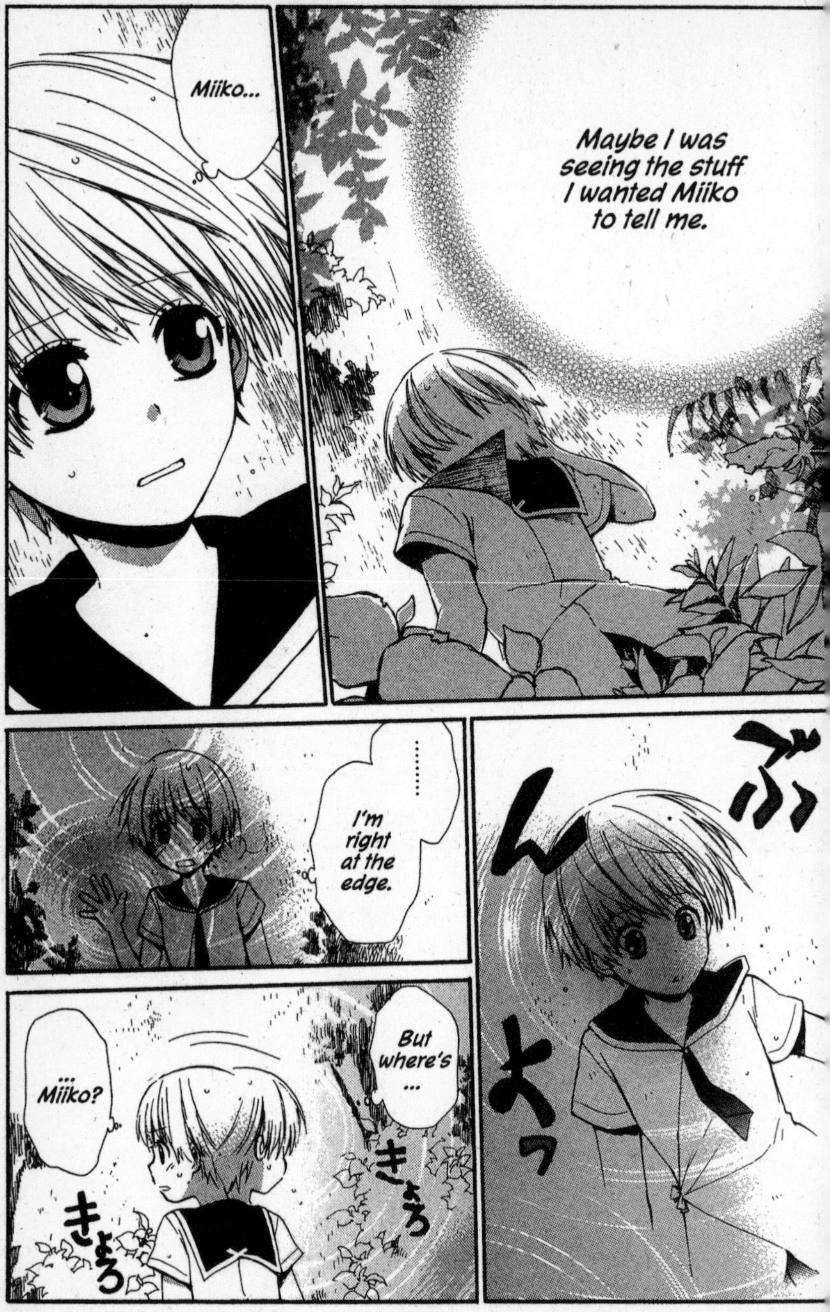
Maybe I was seeing the stuff I wanted Miiko to tell me.
Miiko...
ぶんよっ
......
I'm right at the edge.
But where's ...
... Miiko?
きょろ
きょろ

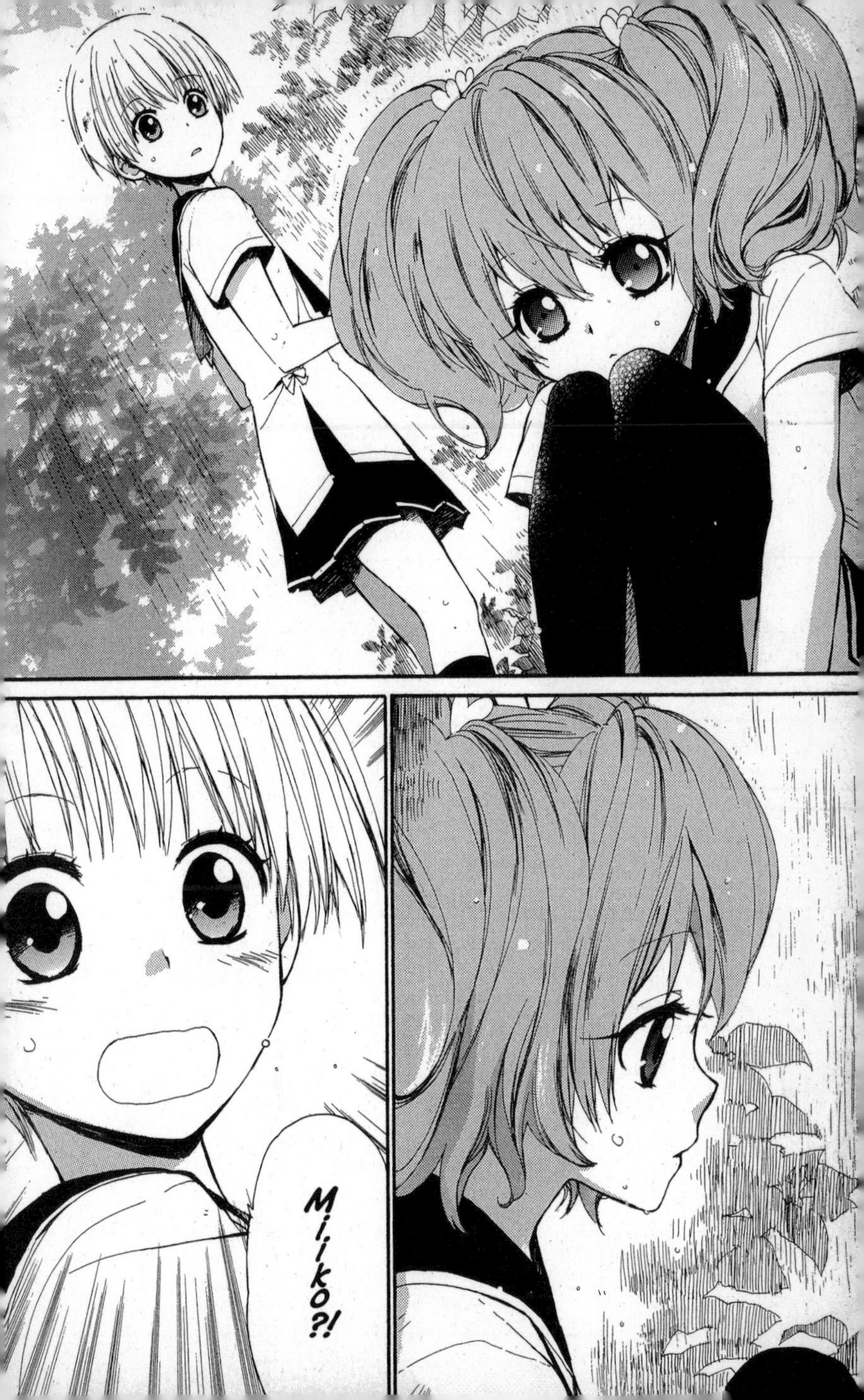
Miiko?!

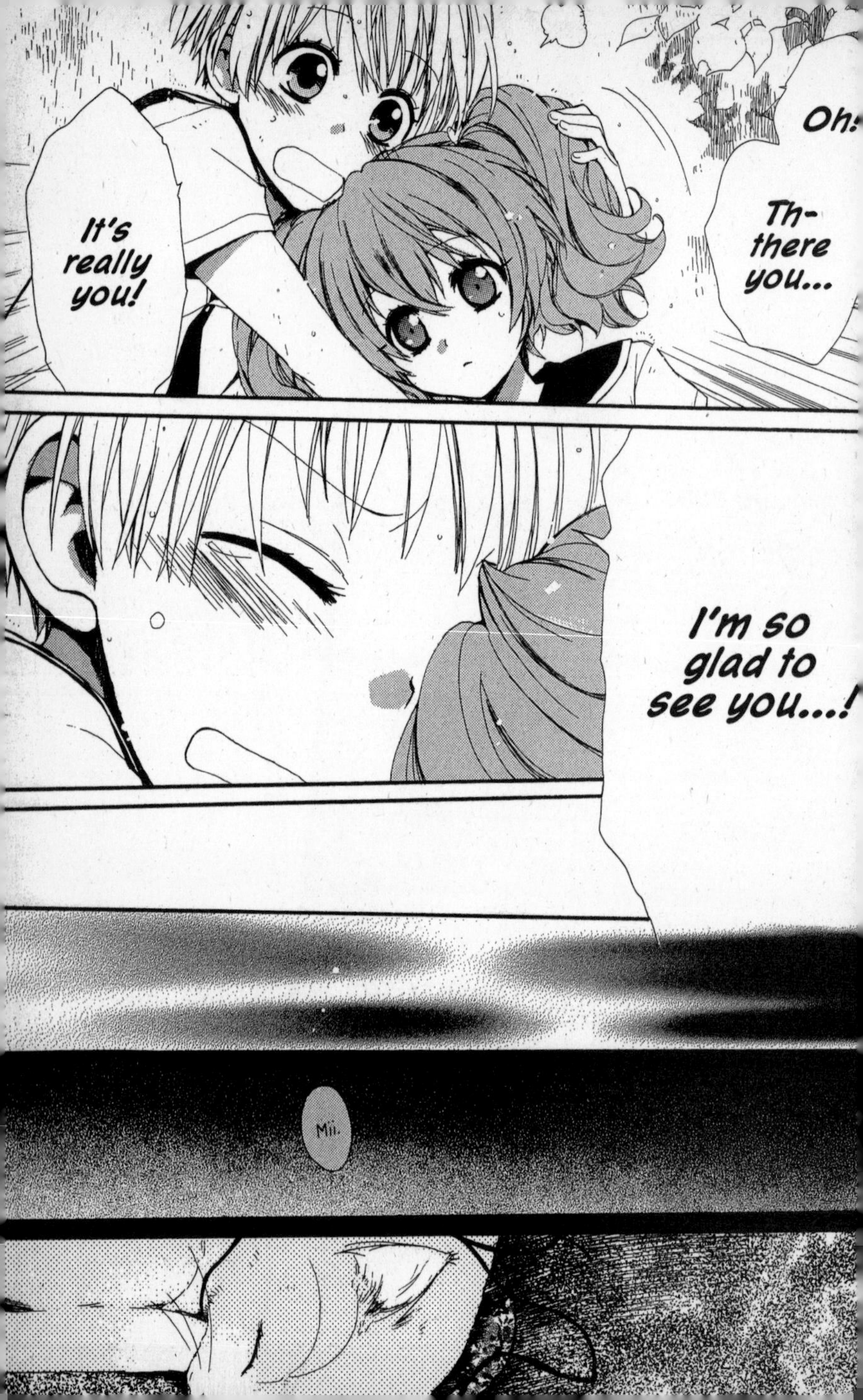
Oh!
Th- there you...
It's really you!
I'm so glad to see you...!
Mii.

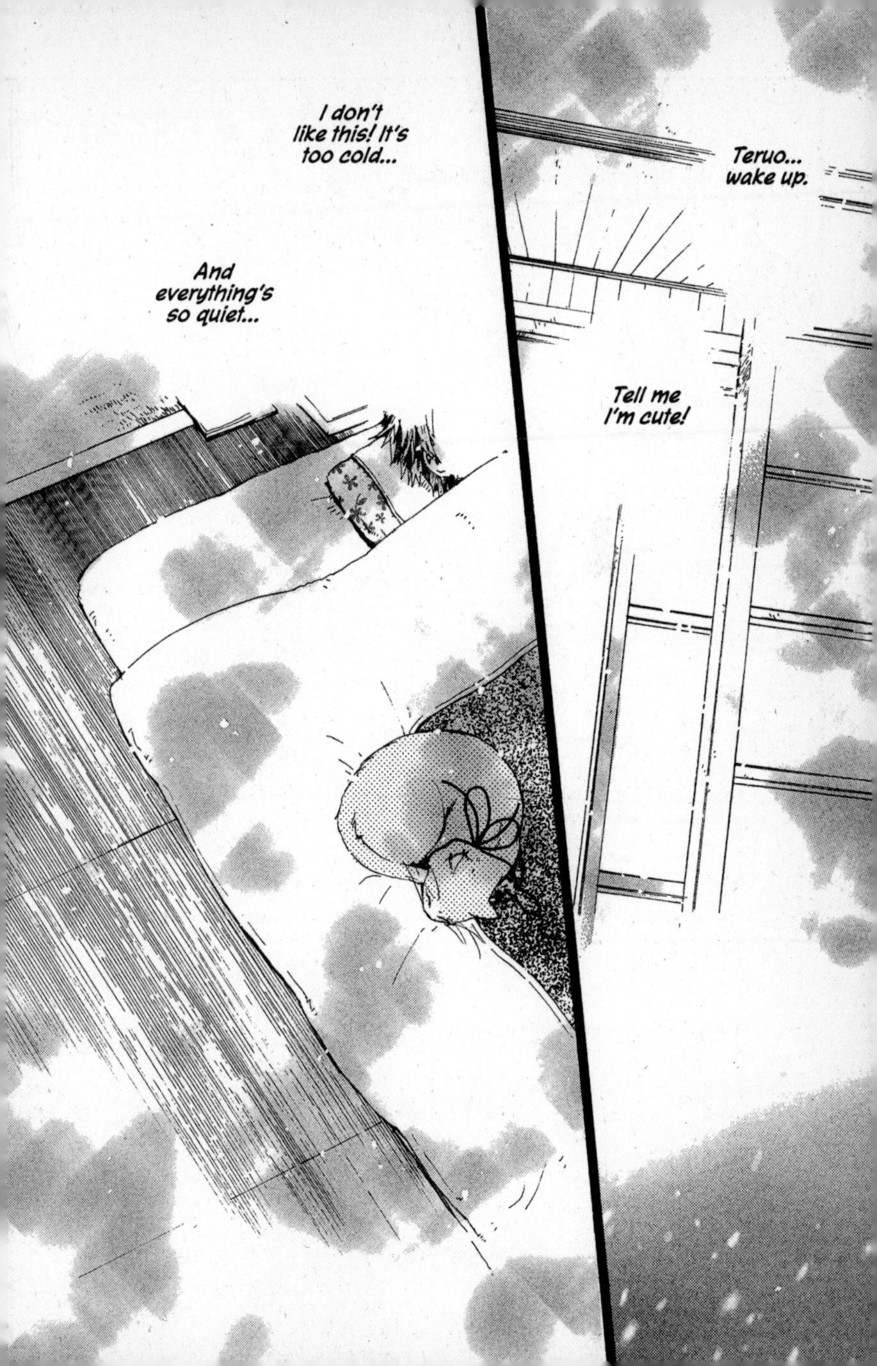
Teruo... wake up.
Tell me I'm cute!
I don't like this! It's too cold...
And everything's so quiet...

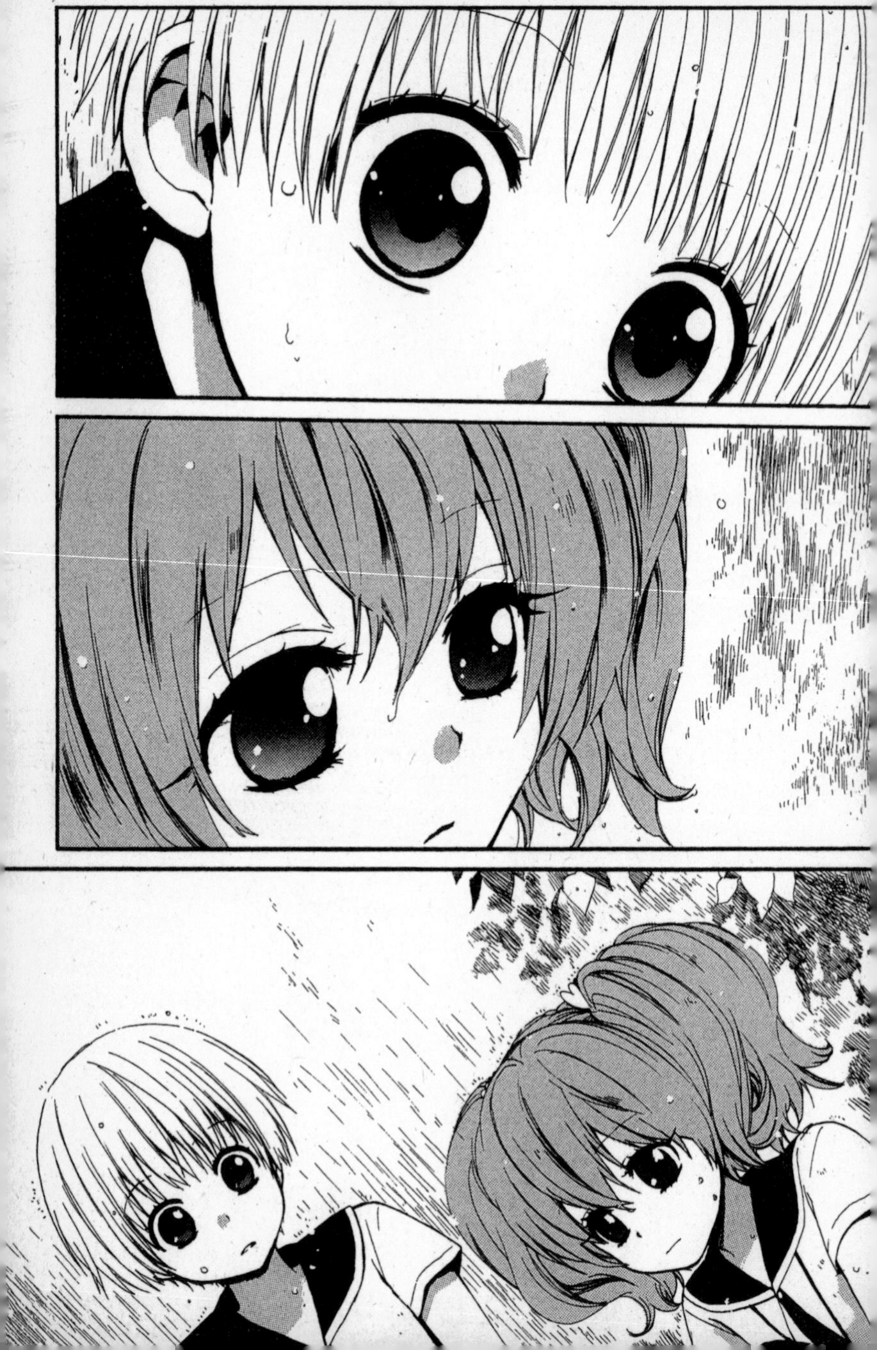

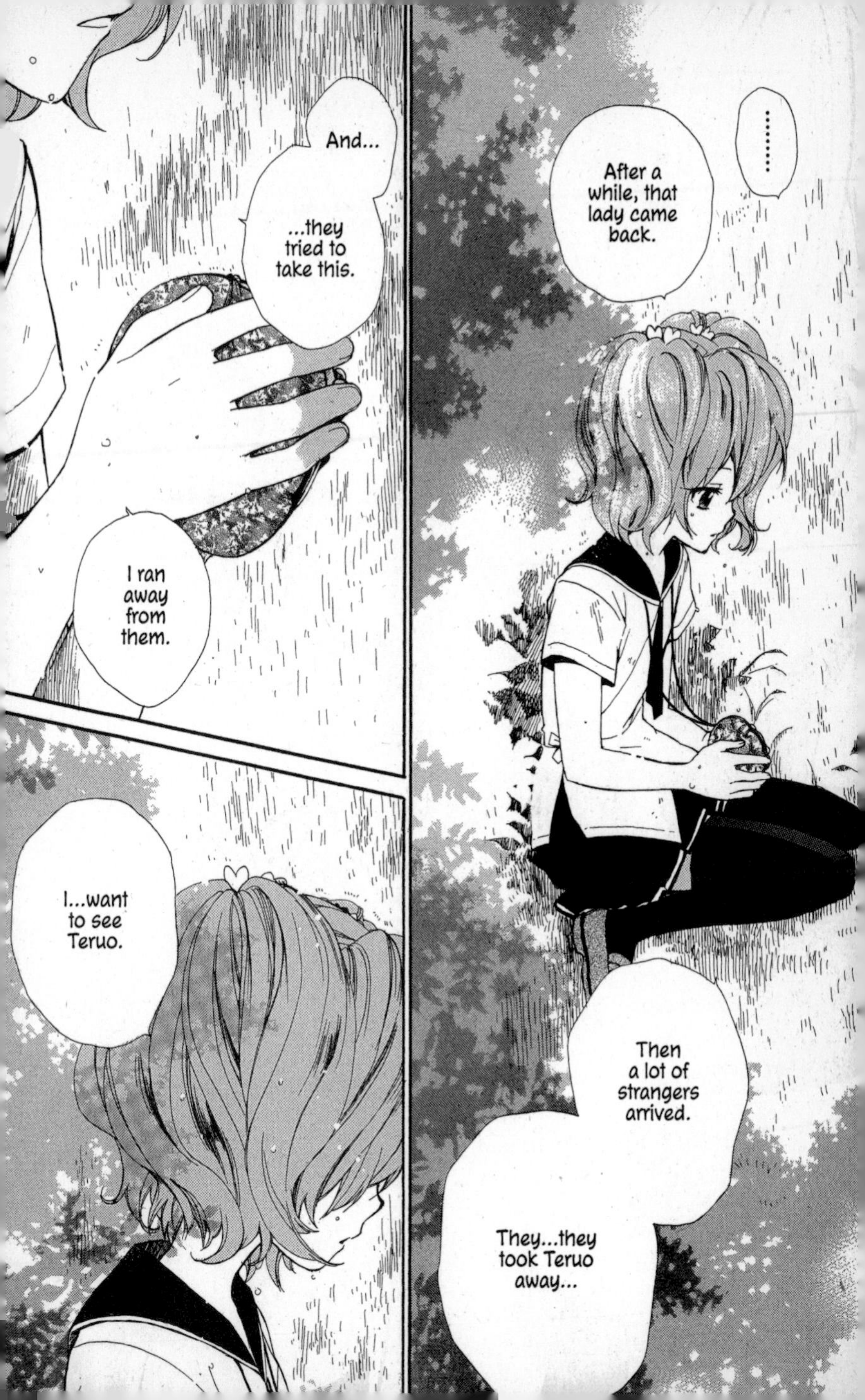
……
After a while, that lady came back.
Then a lot of strangers arrived.
They...they took Teruo away...
And...
...they tried to take this.
I ran away from them.
I...want to see Teruo.

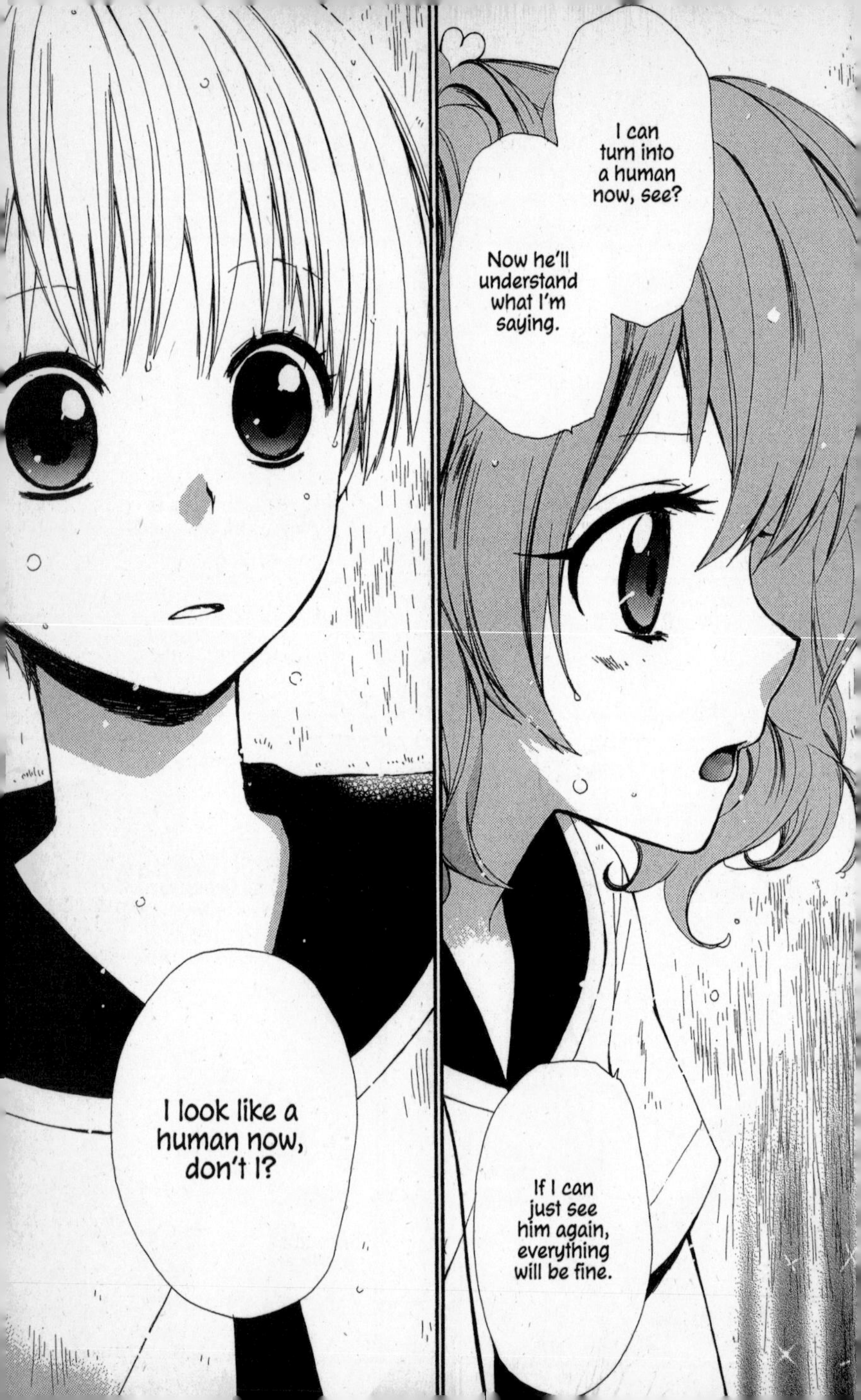
I can turn into a human now, see?
Now he'll understand what I'm saying.
If I can just see him again, everything will be fine.
I look like a human now, don't I?

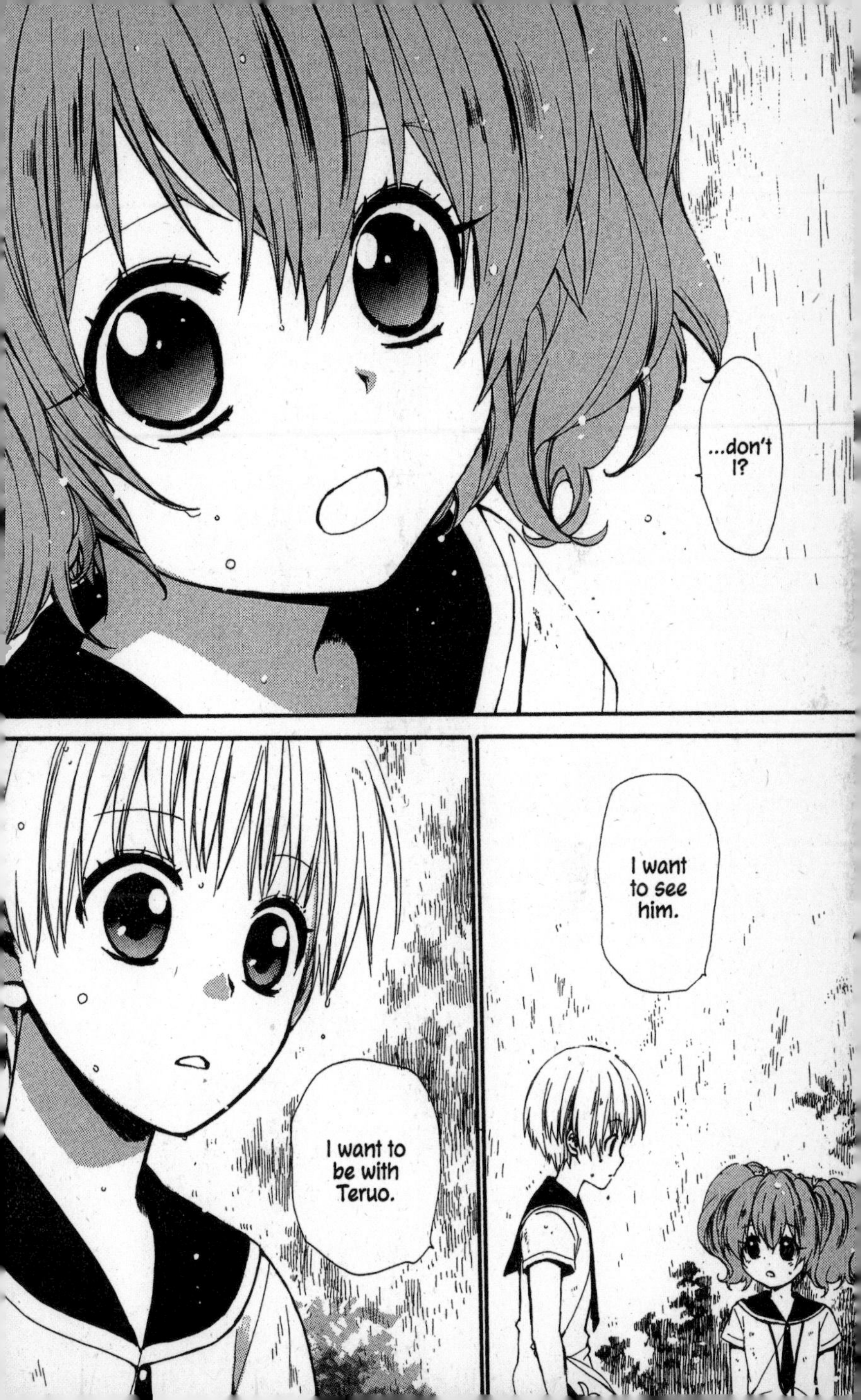
...don't I?
I want to see him.
I want to be with Teruo.

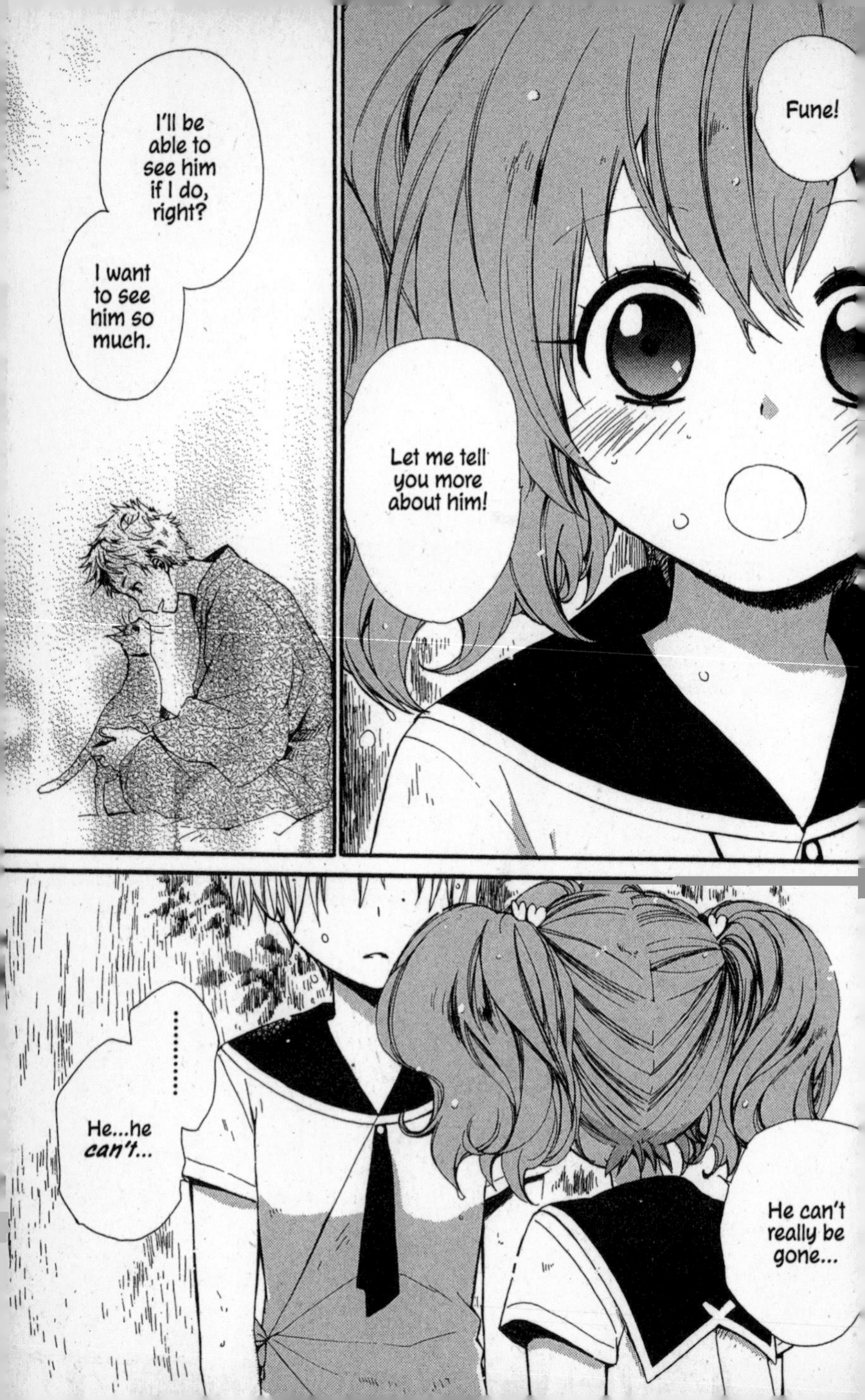

Fune!
Let me tell you more about him!
I'll be able to see him if I do, right?
I want to see him so much.
He can't really be gone...
....
He...he *can't*...

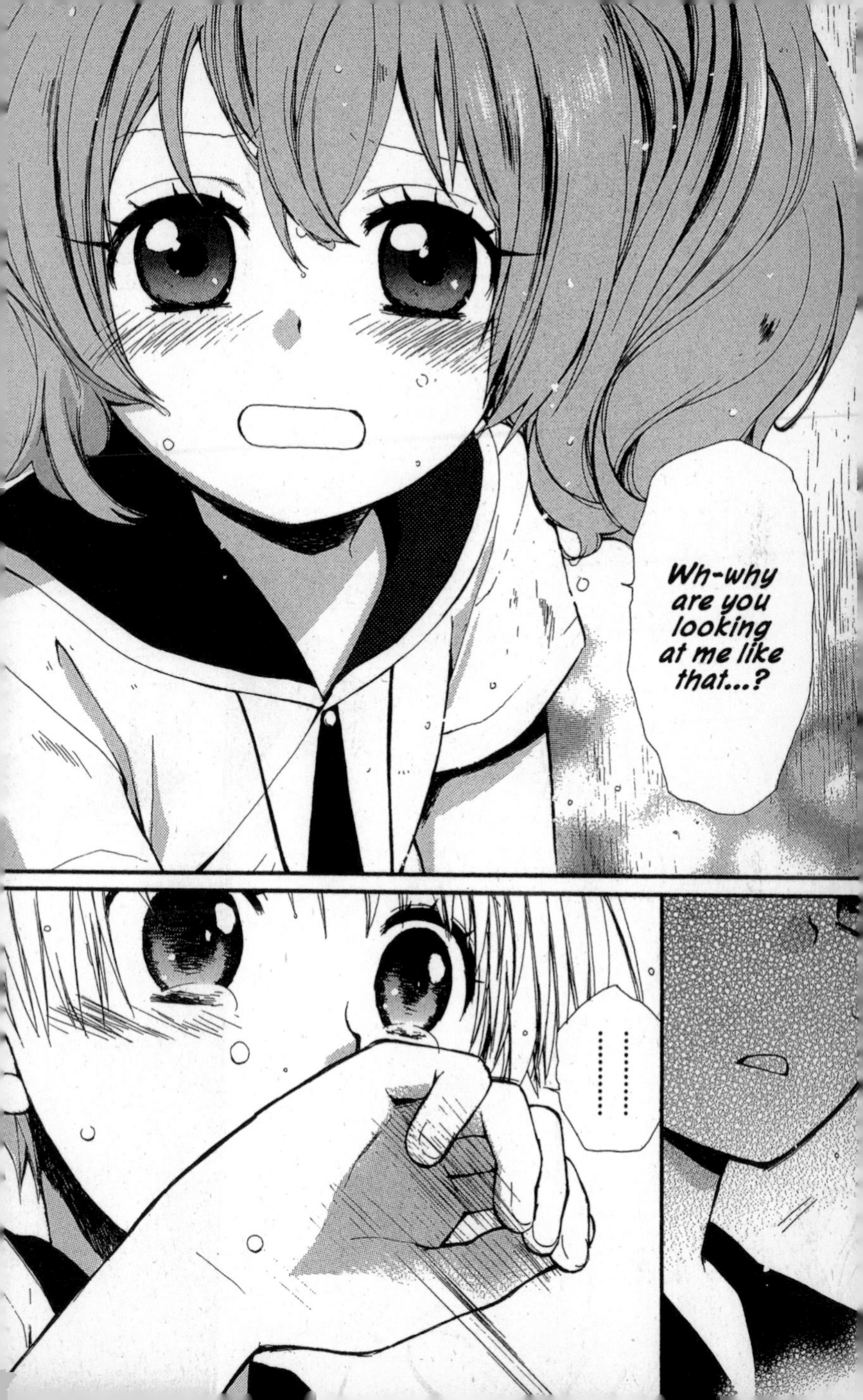
Wh-why are you looking at me like that...?
......

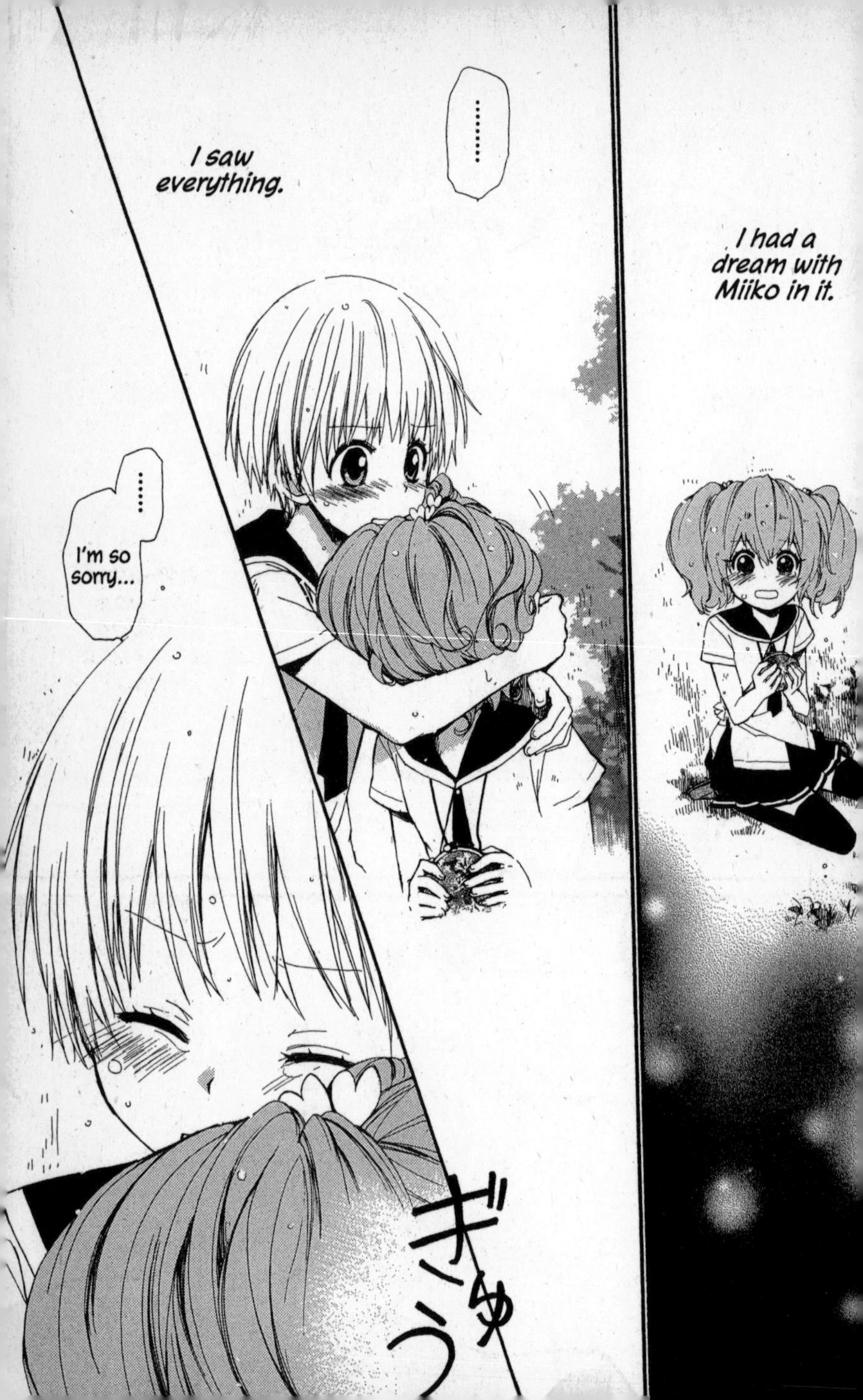
I had a dream with Miiko in it.
......
I saw everything.
...... I'm so sorry...
ぎゅう

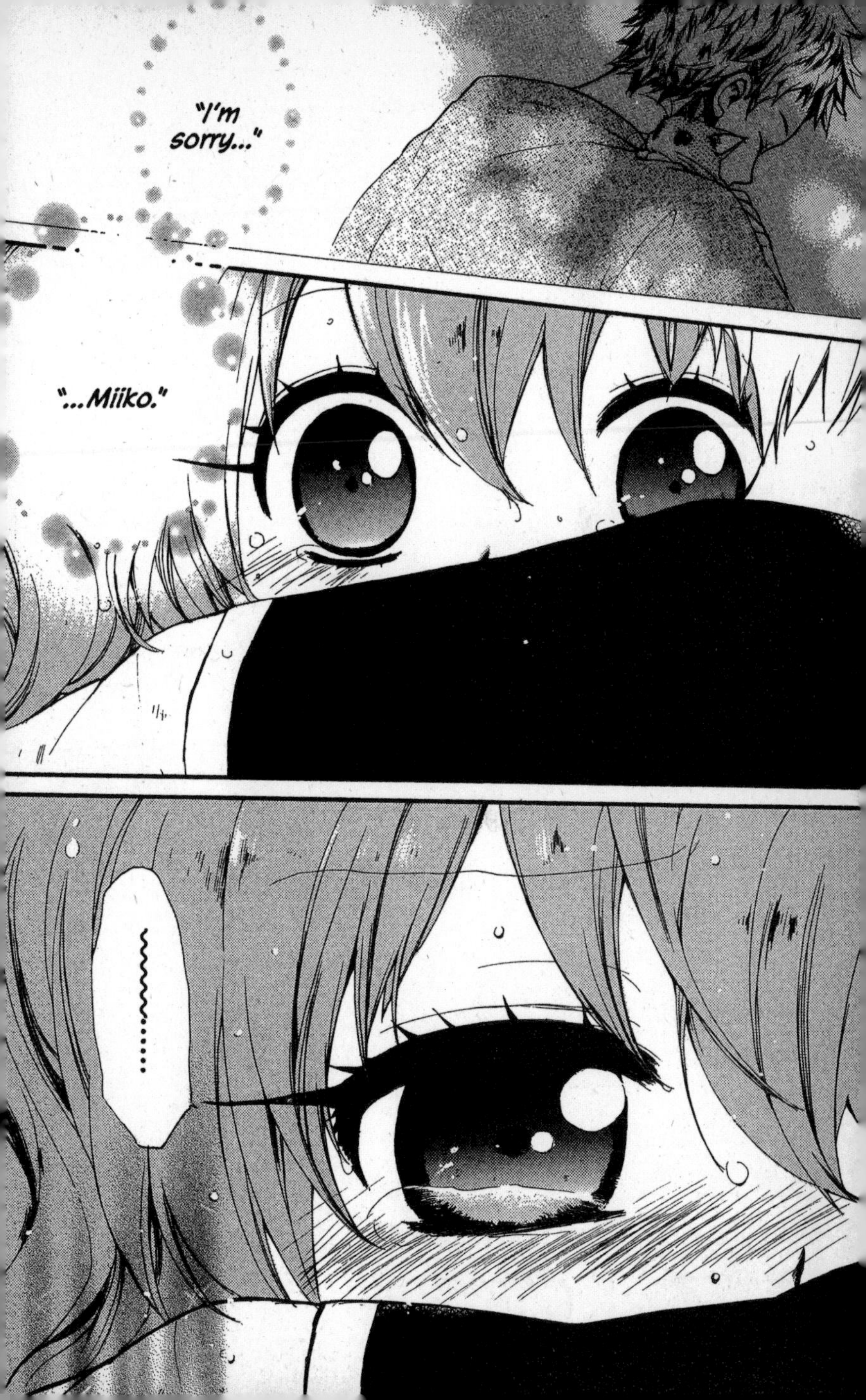
"I'm sorry..."
"...Miiko."
~~~~~~......
~~~~~~

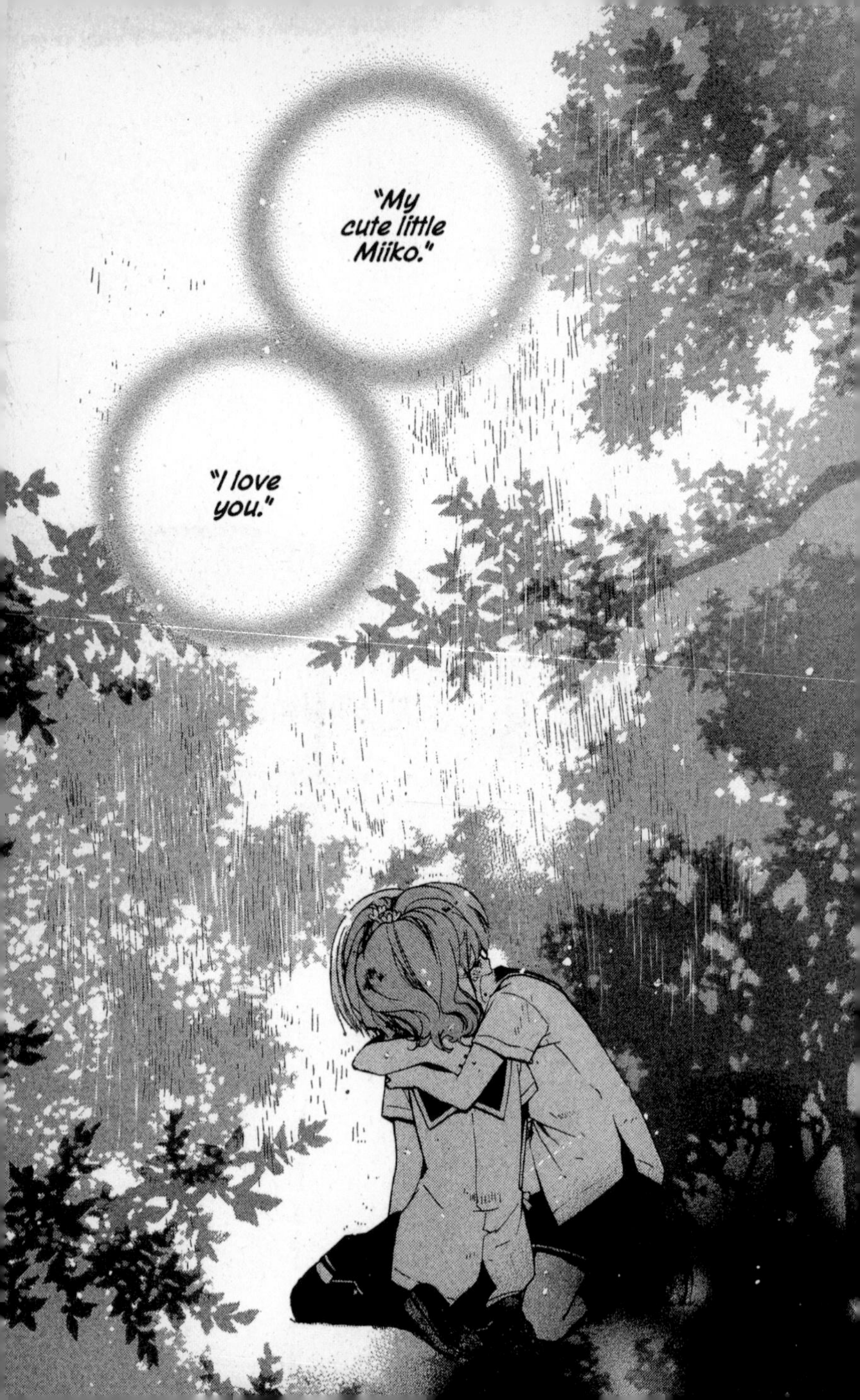
"My cute little Miiko."
"I love you."

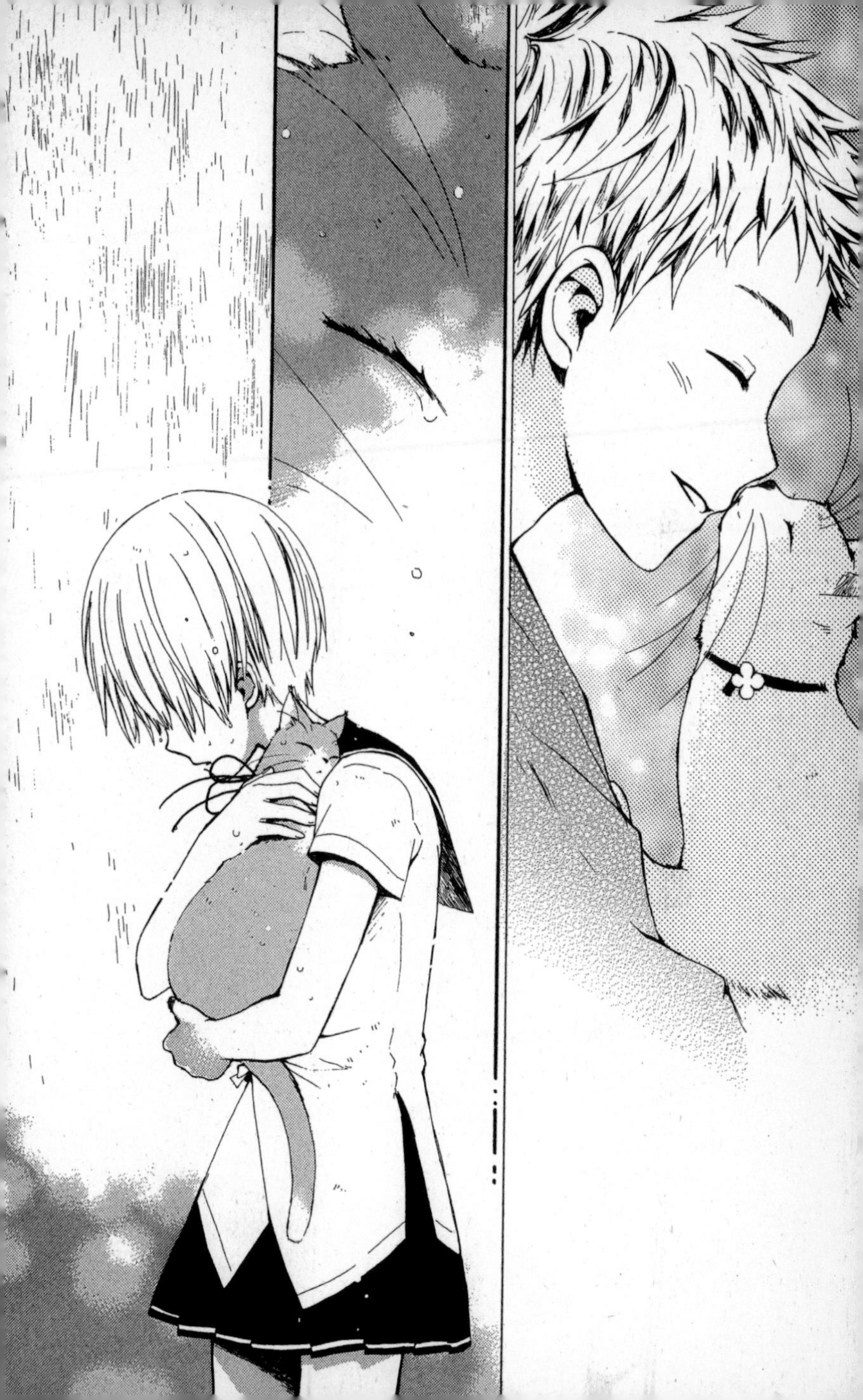

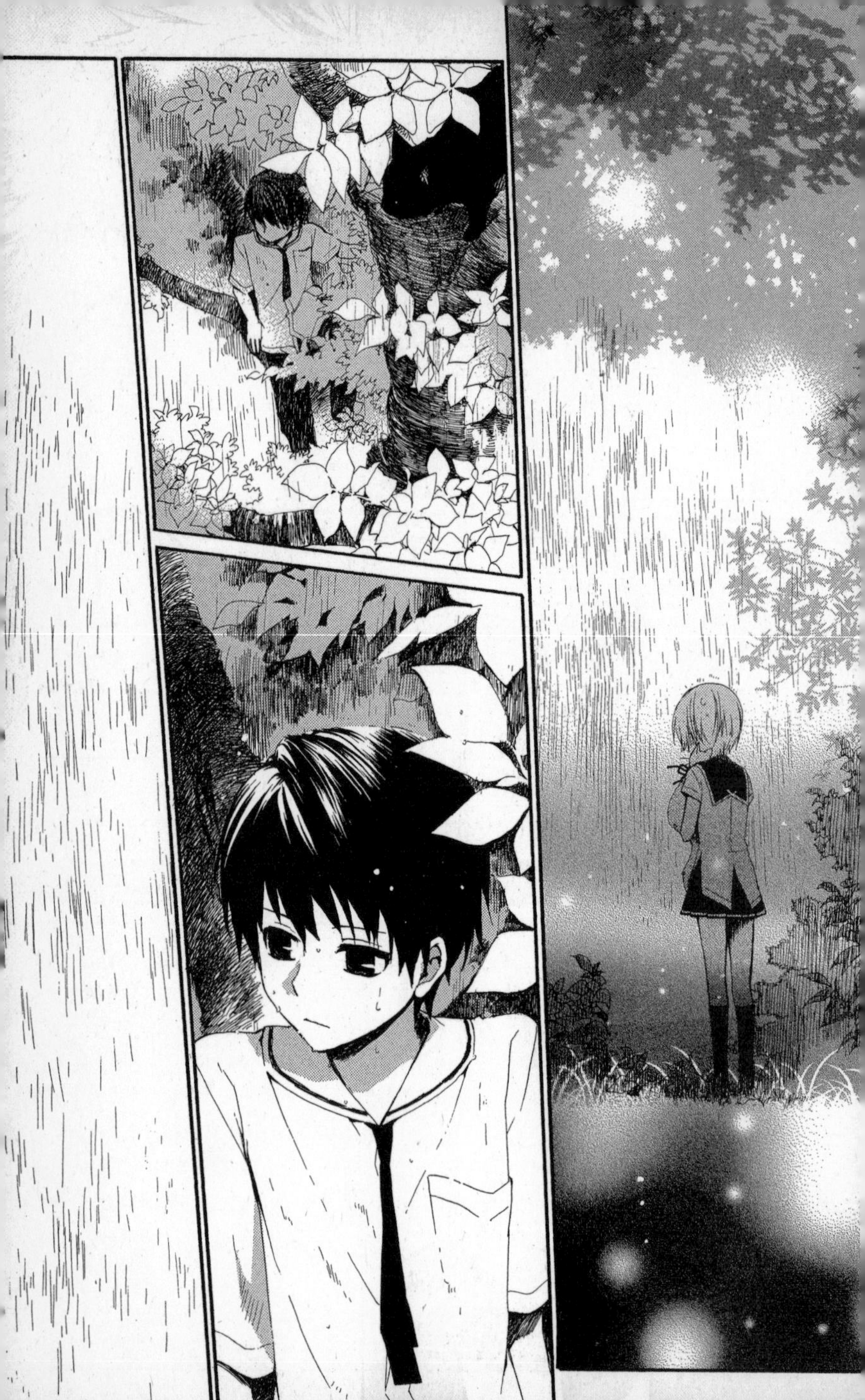

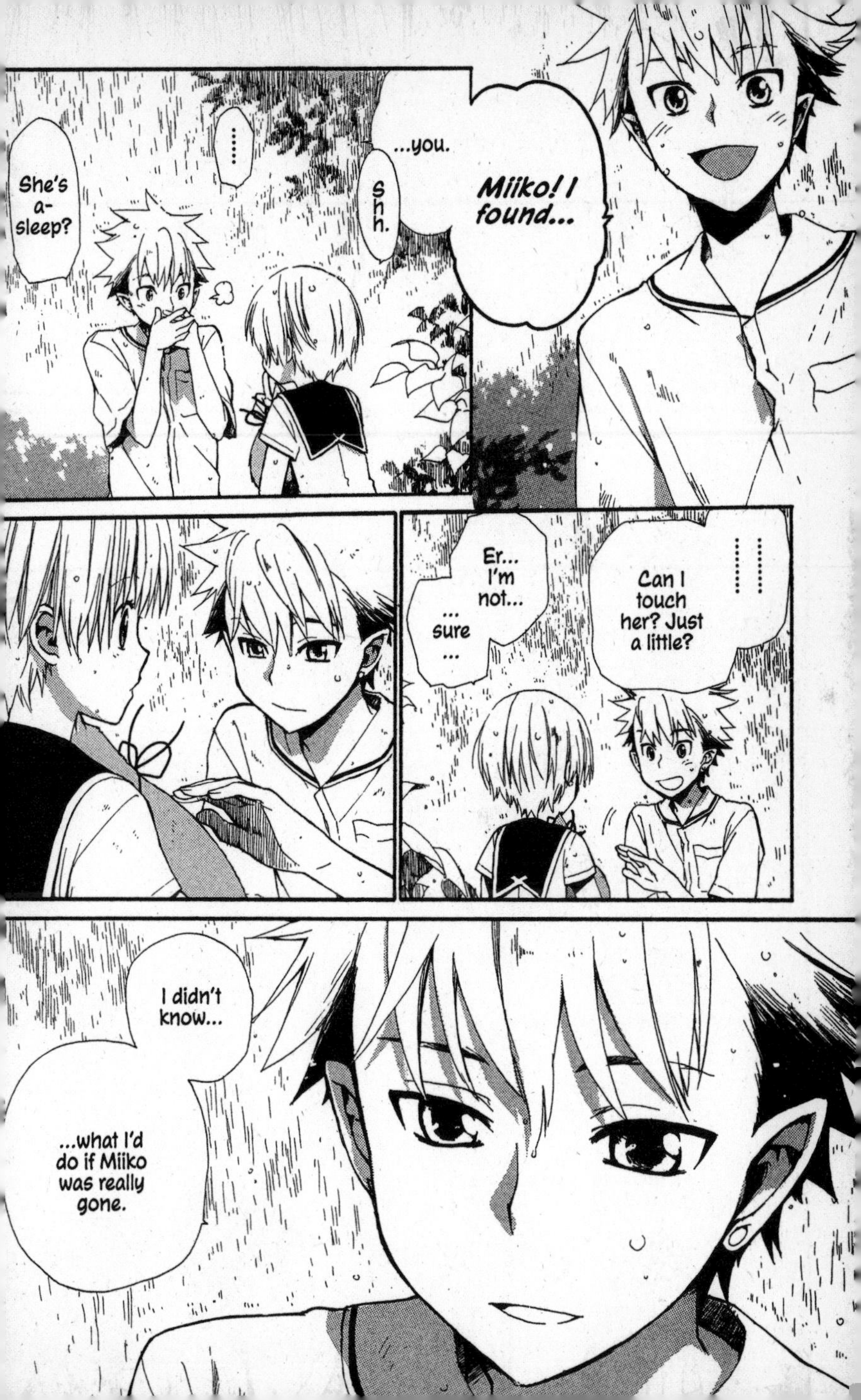
Miiko! I found...
...you.
Shh.
......
She's a-sleep?
......
Can I touch her? Just a little?
Er... I'm not...
...sure...
I didn't know...
...what I'd do if Miiko was really gone.

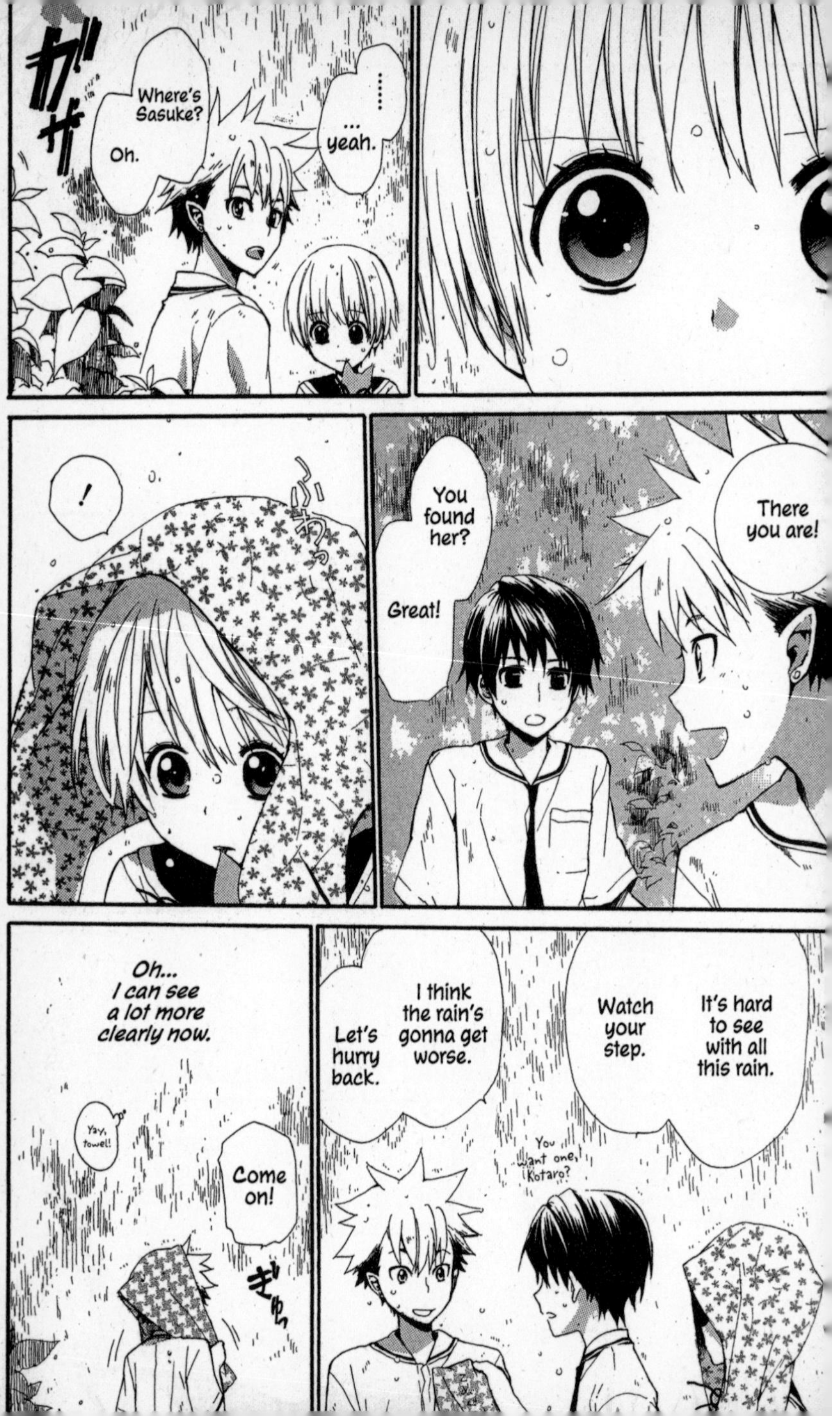
......
... yeah.
Where's Sasuke?
Oh.
ガザ
There you are!
You found her?
Great!
ふわっ
!
It's hard to see with all this rain.
Watch your step.
I think the rain's gonna get worse.
Let's hurry back.
You want one, Kotaro?
Oh... I can see a lot more clearly now.
Come on!
Yay, towel!
ぎゅっ

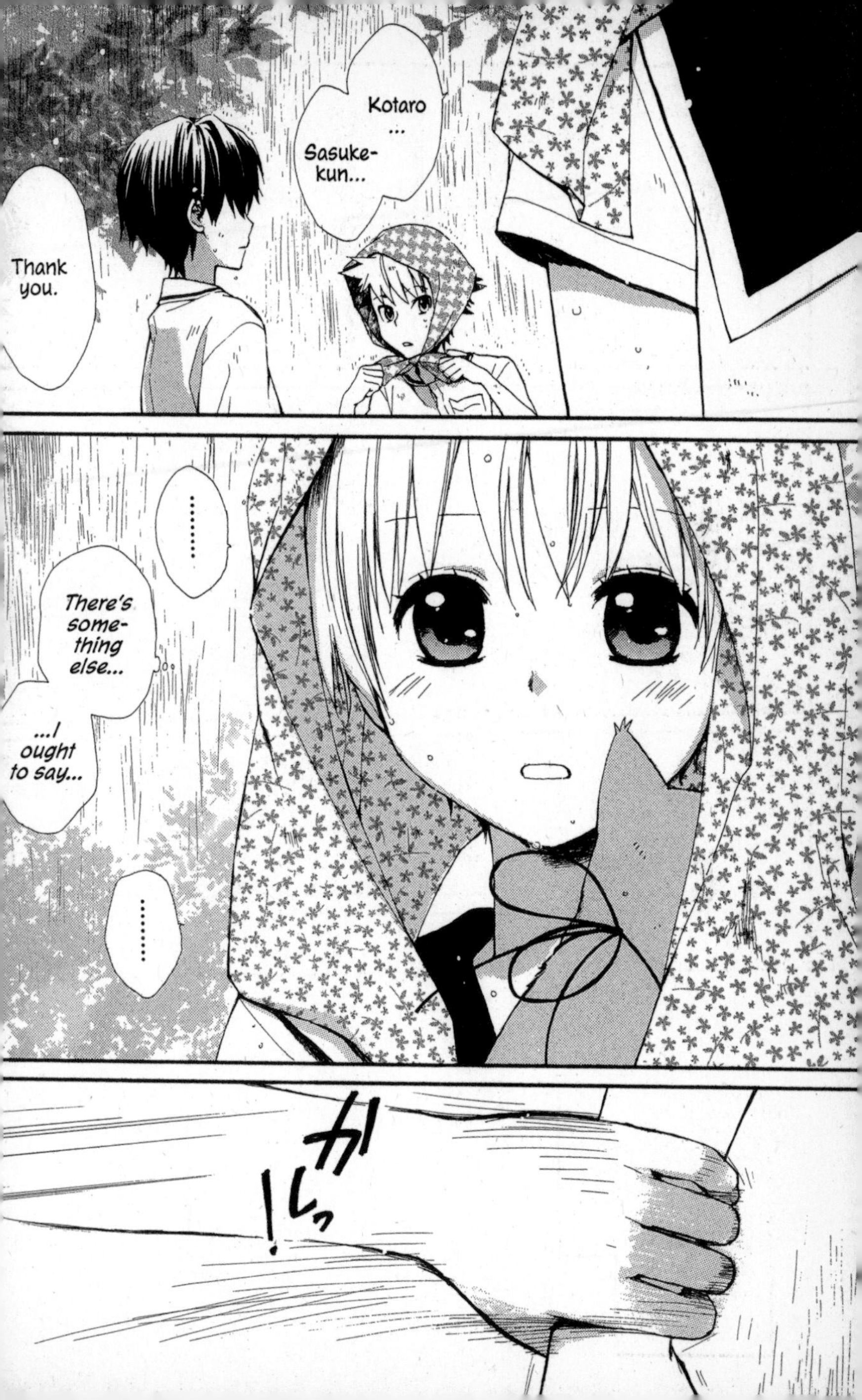

Kotaro ... Sasuke-kun...
Thank you.
....
There's something else...
...I ought to say...
....
ガしっ!

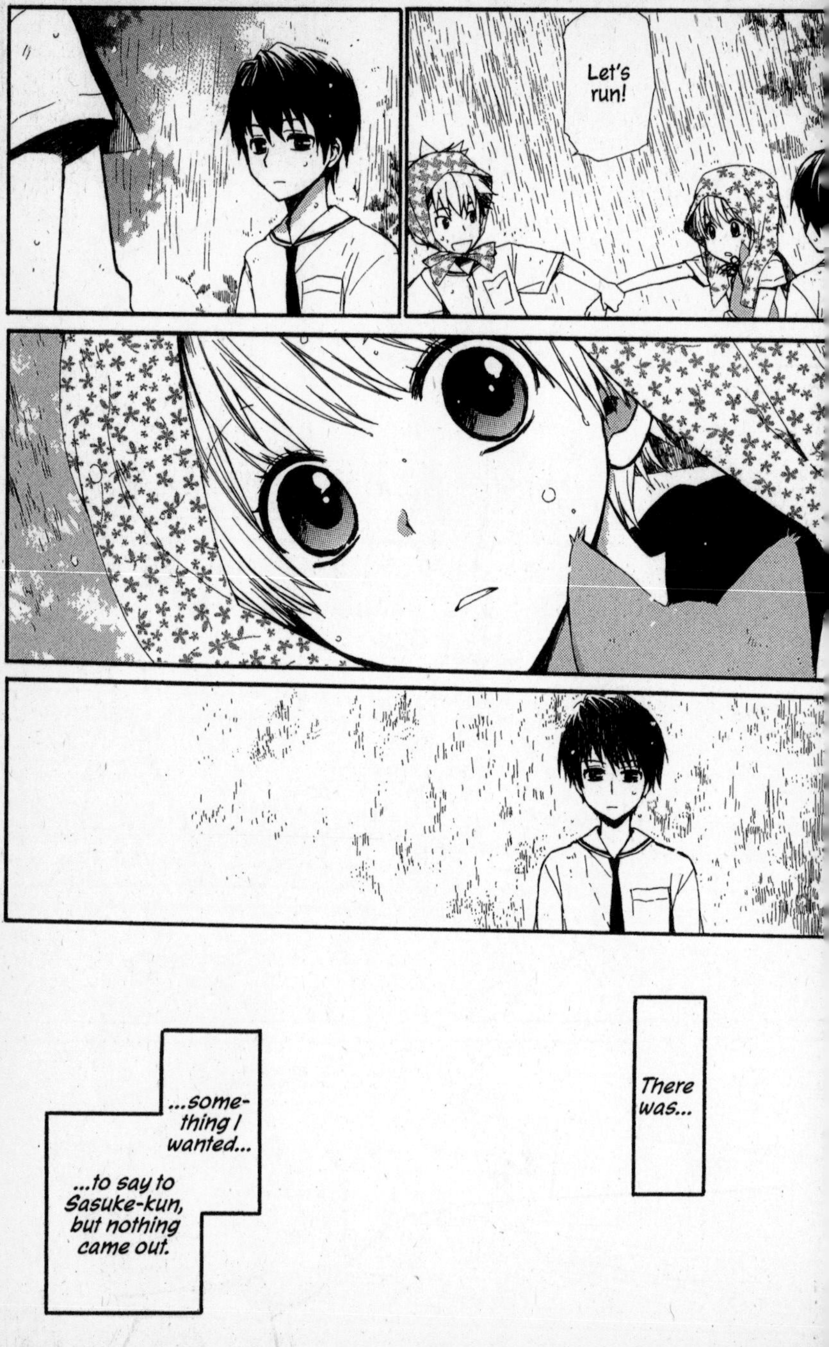
Let's run!
There was...
...something I wanted...
...to say to Sasuke-kun, but nothing came out.

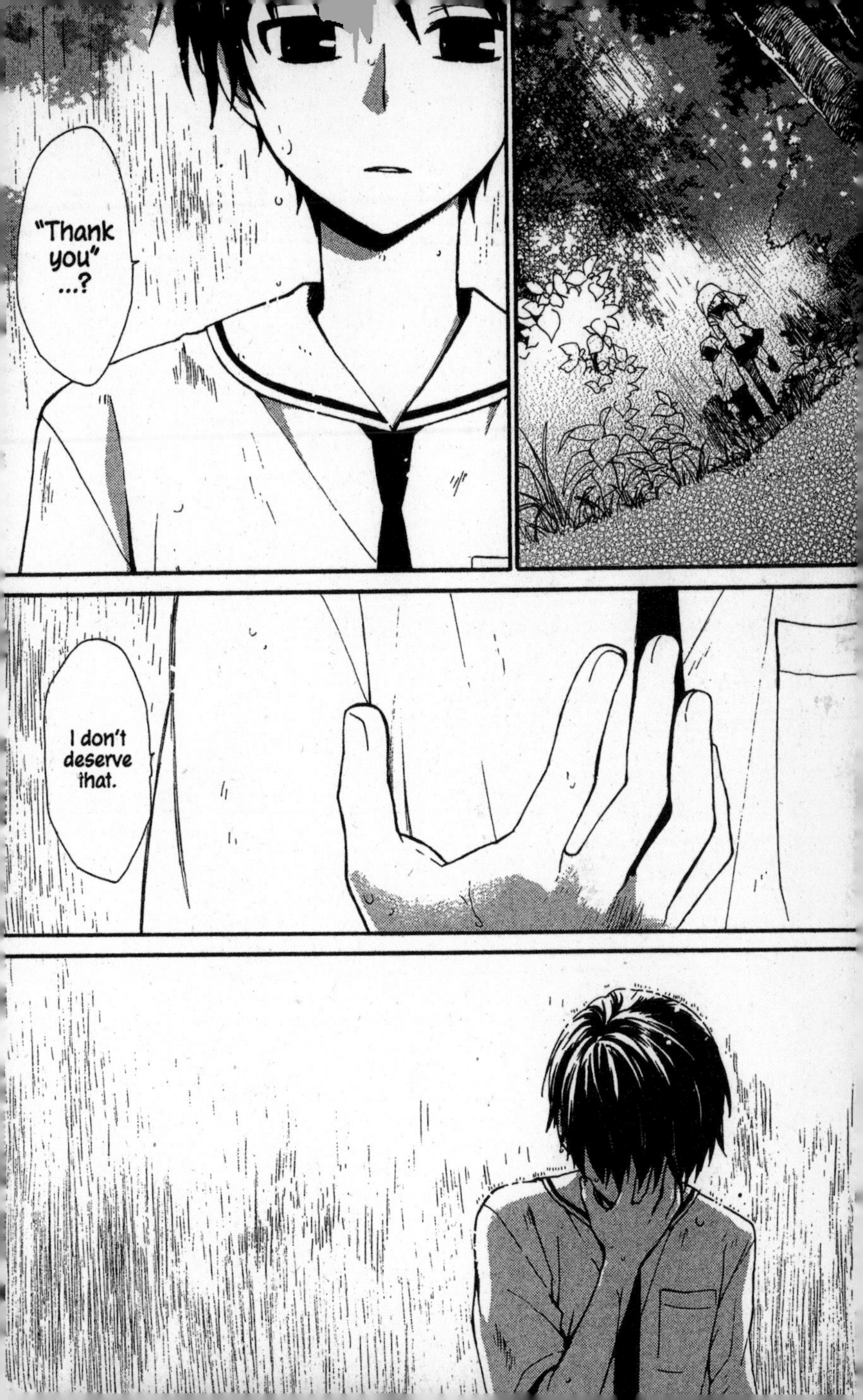
"Thank you" ...?
I don't deserve that.

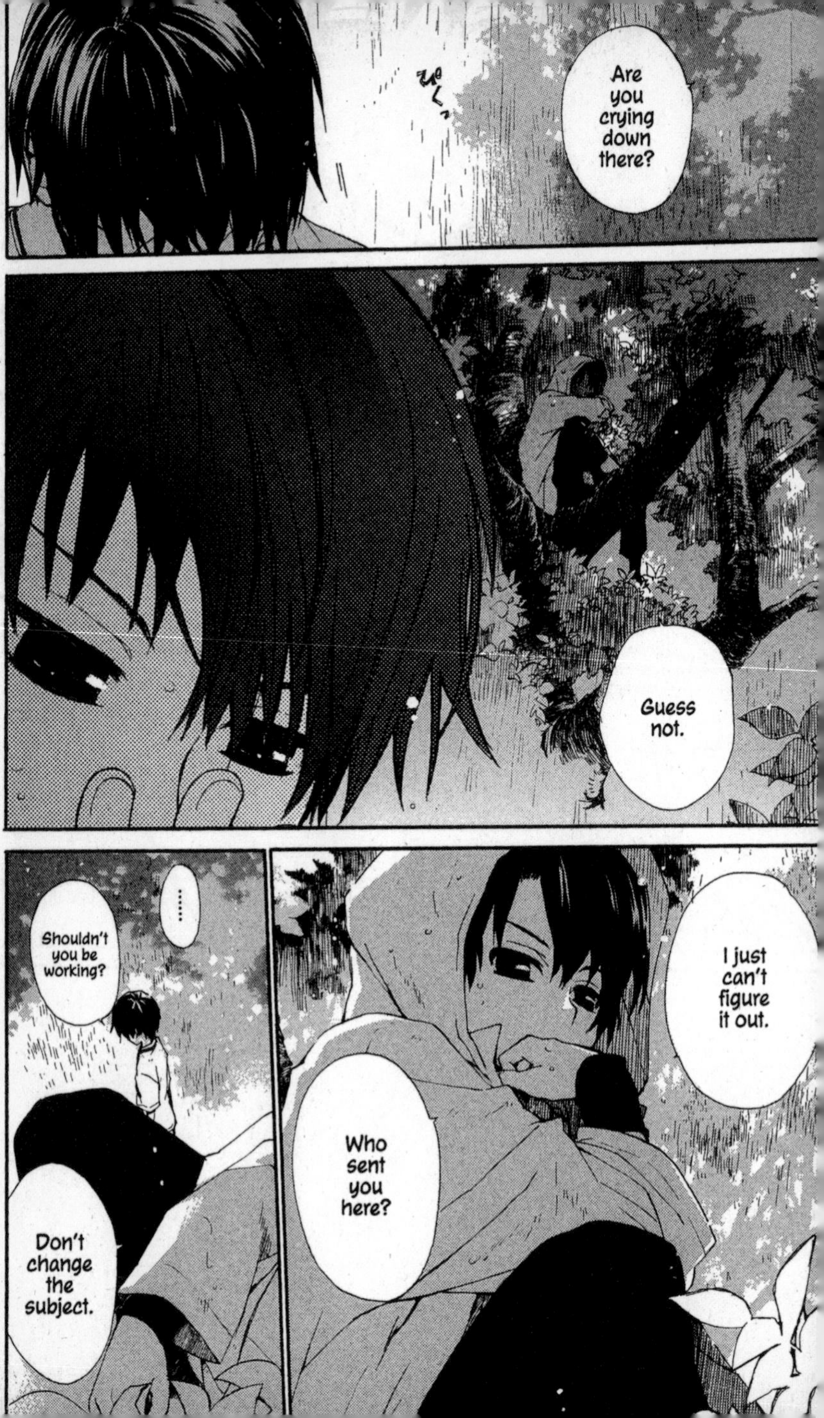
Are you crying down there?
Guess not.
I just can't figure it out.
Who sent you here?
......
Shouldn't you be working?
Don't change the subject.

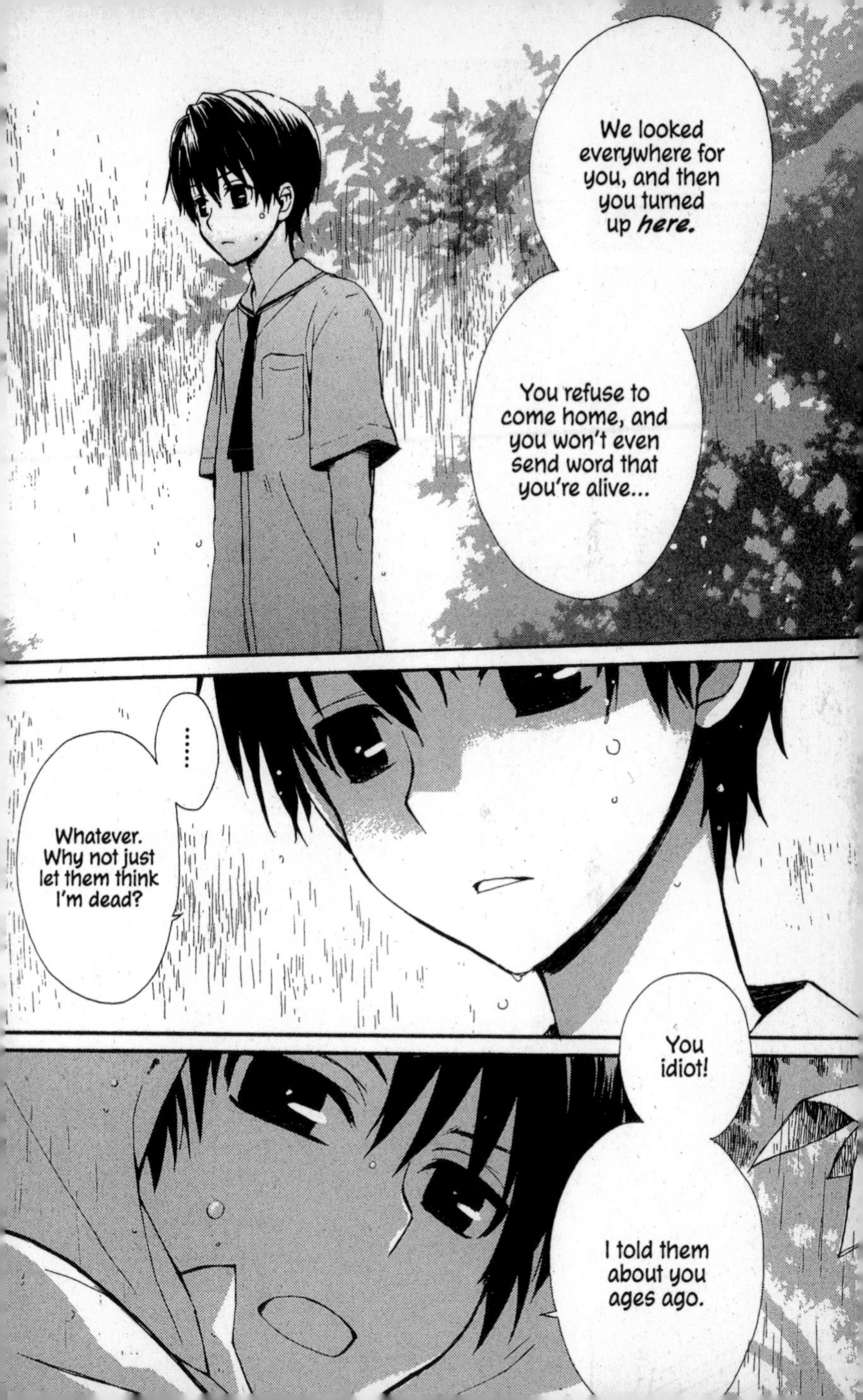
We looked everywhere for you, and then you turned up *here.*
You refuse to come home, and you won't even send word that you're alive...
......
Whatever. Why not just let them think I'm dead?
You idiot!
I told them about you ages ago.

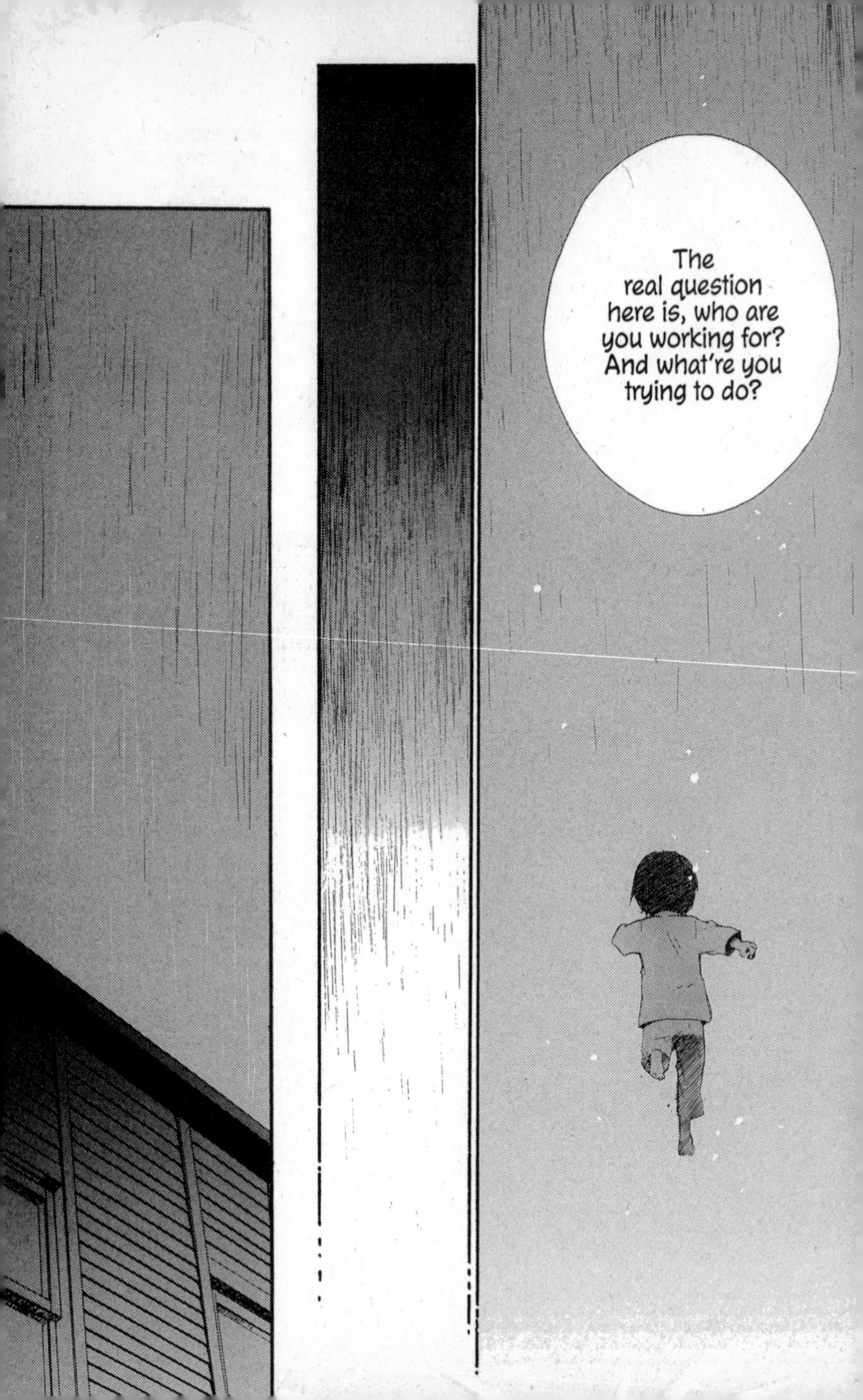
The real question here is, who are you working for? And what're you trying to do?

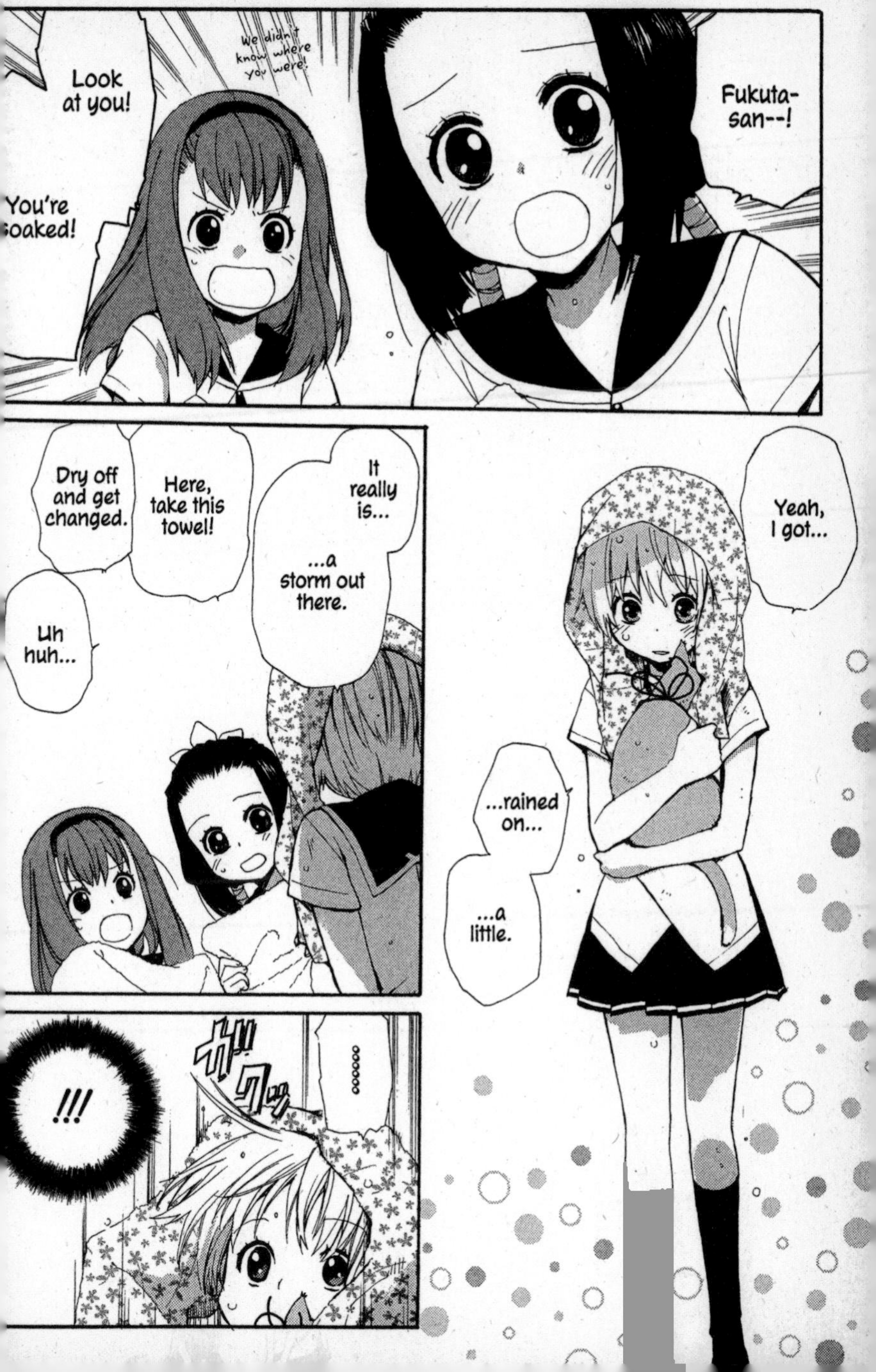
Fukuta-san--!
We didn't know where you were!
Look at you!
You're soaked!
Yeah, I got...
...rained on...
...a little.
It really is...
...a storm out there.
Here, take this towel!
Dry off and get changed.
Uh huh...
!!!

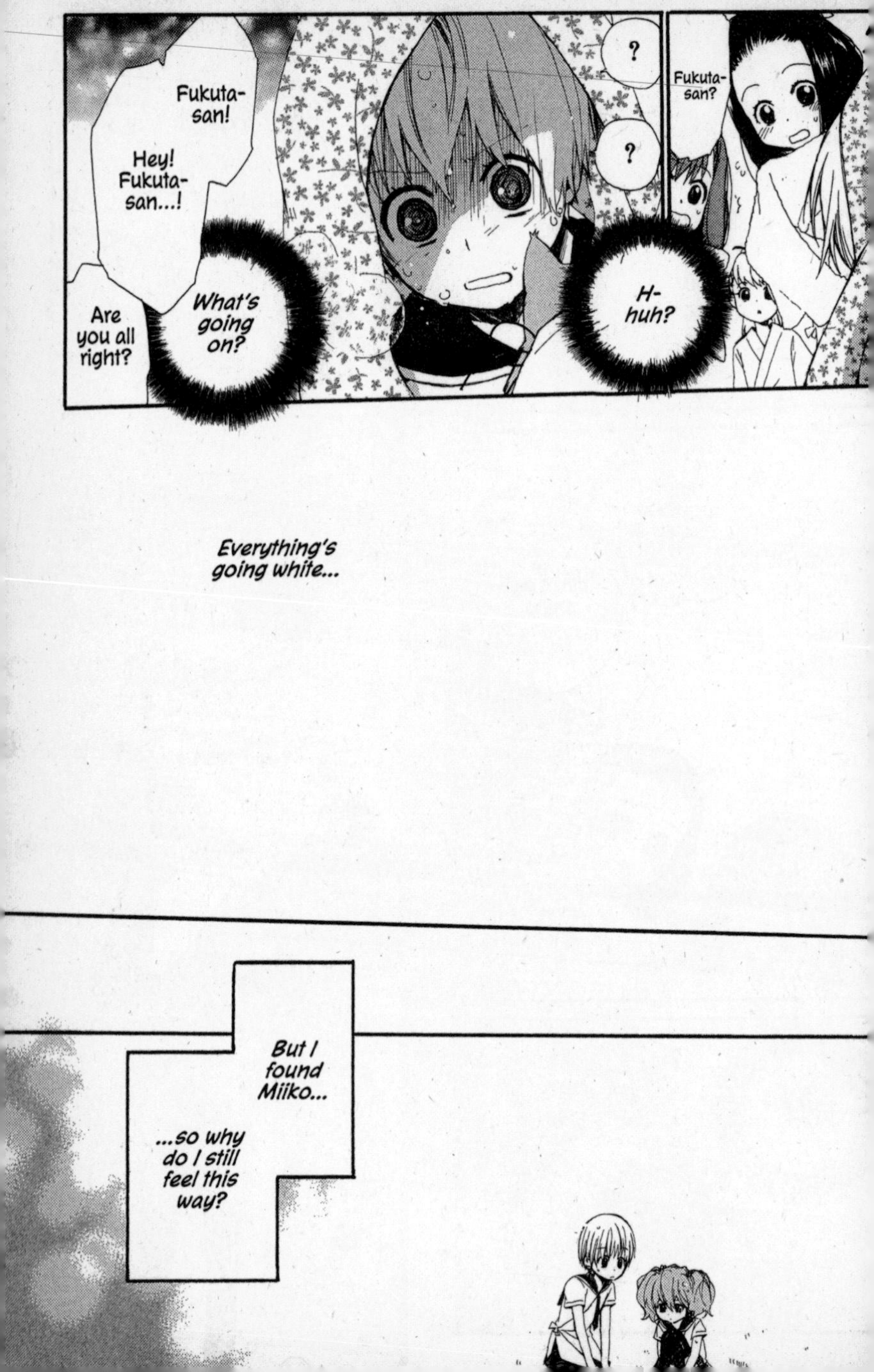
Fukuta-san?
?
?
H-huh?
Fukuta-san! Hey! Fukuta-san...!
What's going on?
Are you all right?
Everything's going white...
But I found Miiko...
...so why do I still feel this way?

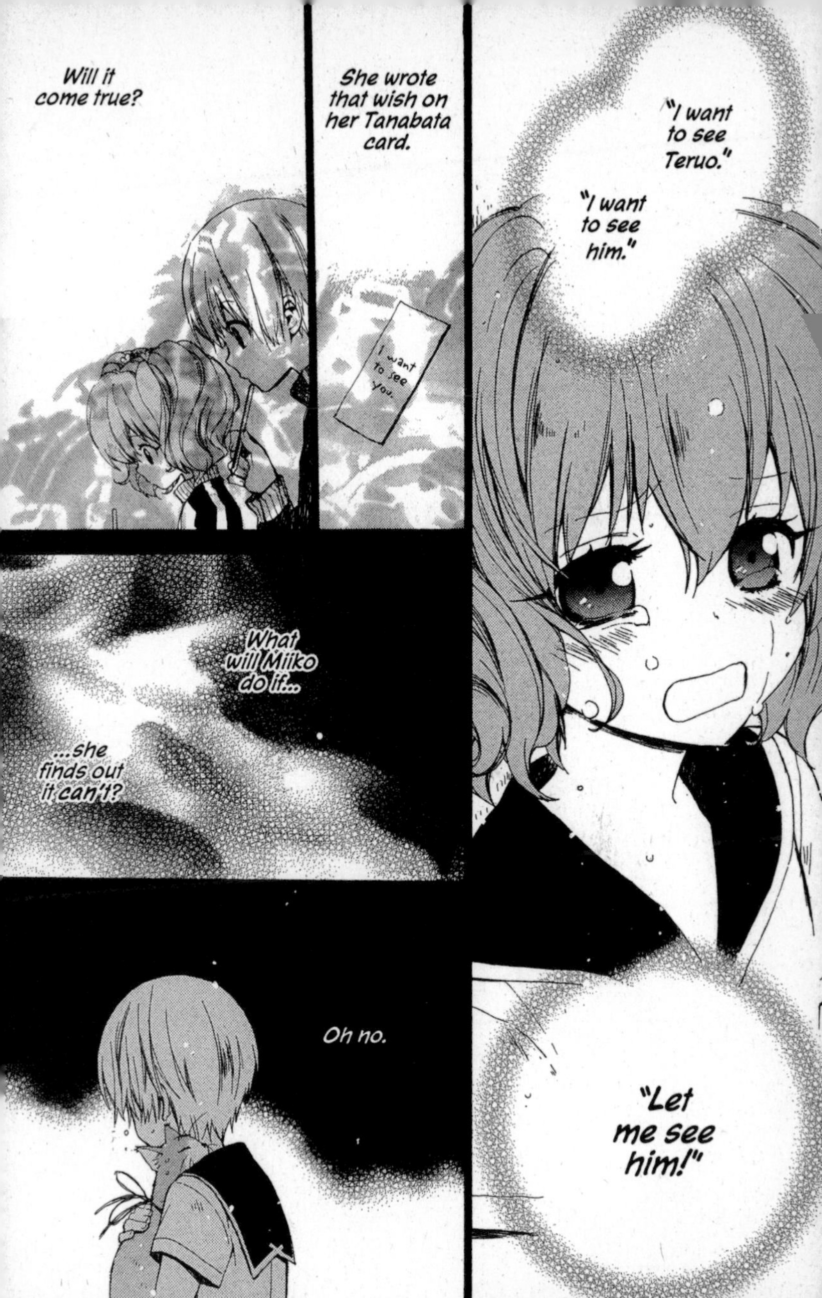
"I want to see Teruo."
"I want to see him."
"Let me see him!"
She wrote that wish on her Tanabata card.
I want to see you.
Will it come true?
What will Miiko do if...
...she finds out it can't?
Oh no.

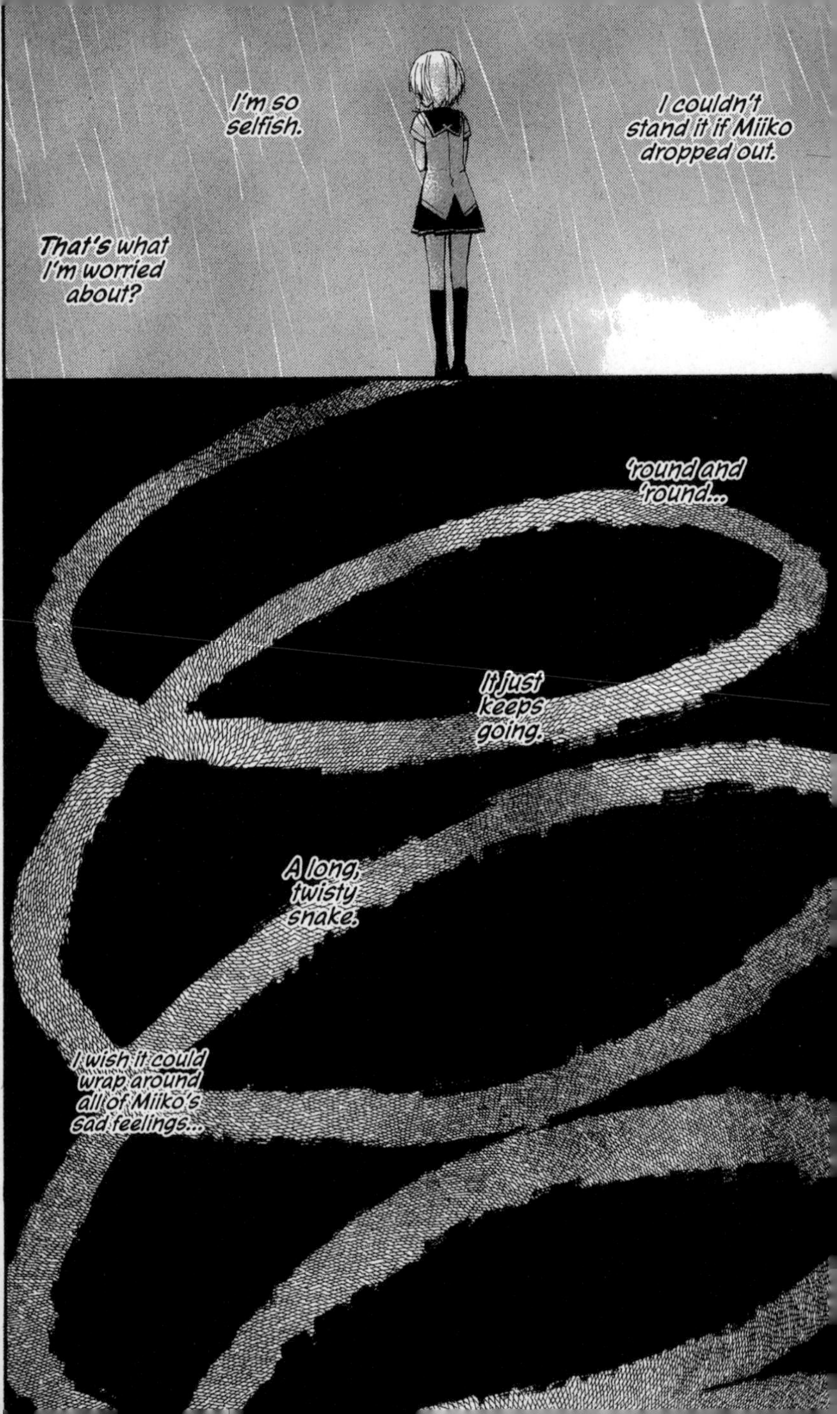
I couldn't stand it if Miiko dropped out.
I'm so selfish.
That's what I'm worried about?
'round and 'round...
It just keeps going.
A long, twisty snake.
I wish it could wrap around all of Miiko's sad feelings...

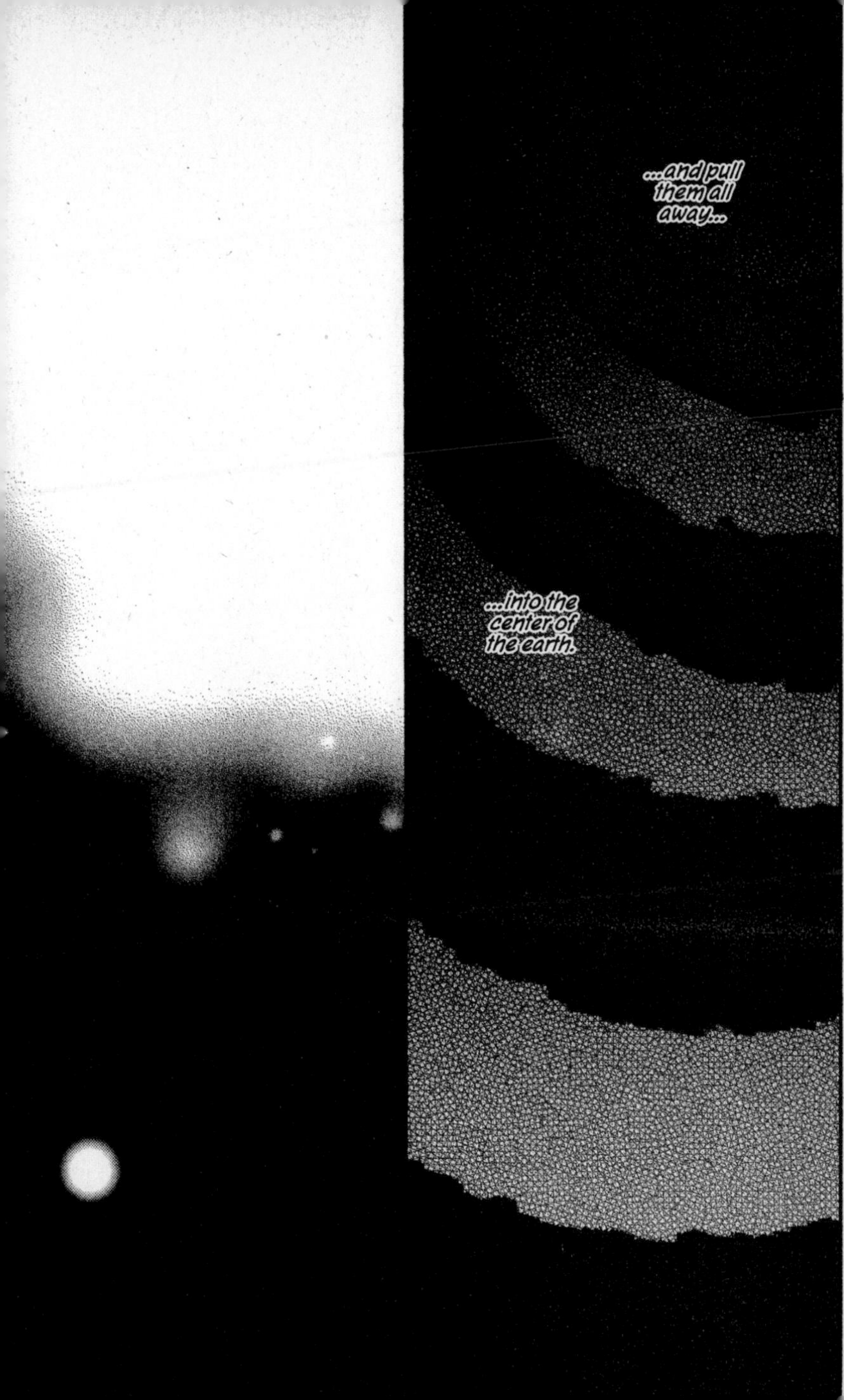
...and pull them all away...
...into the center of the earth.

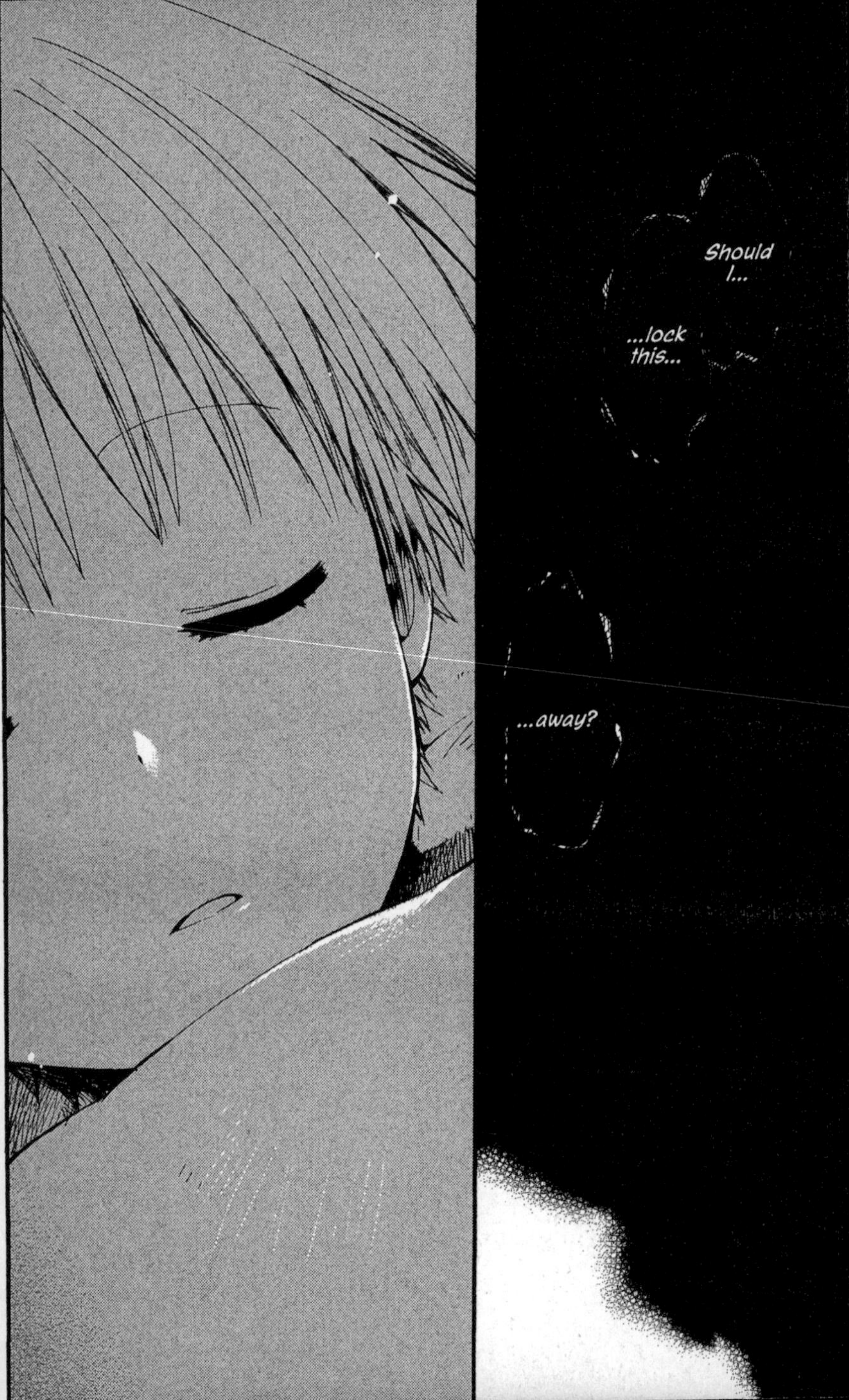
Should I...
...lock this...
...away?

Report.27 Sasuke

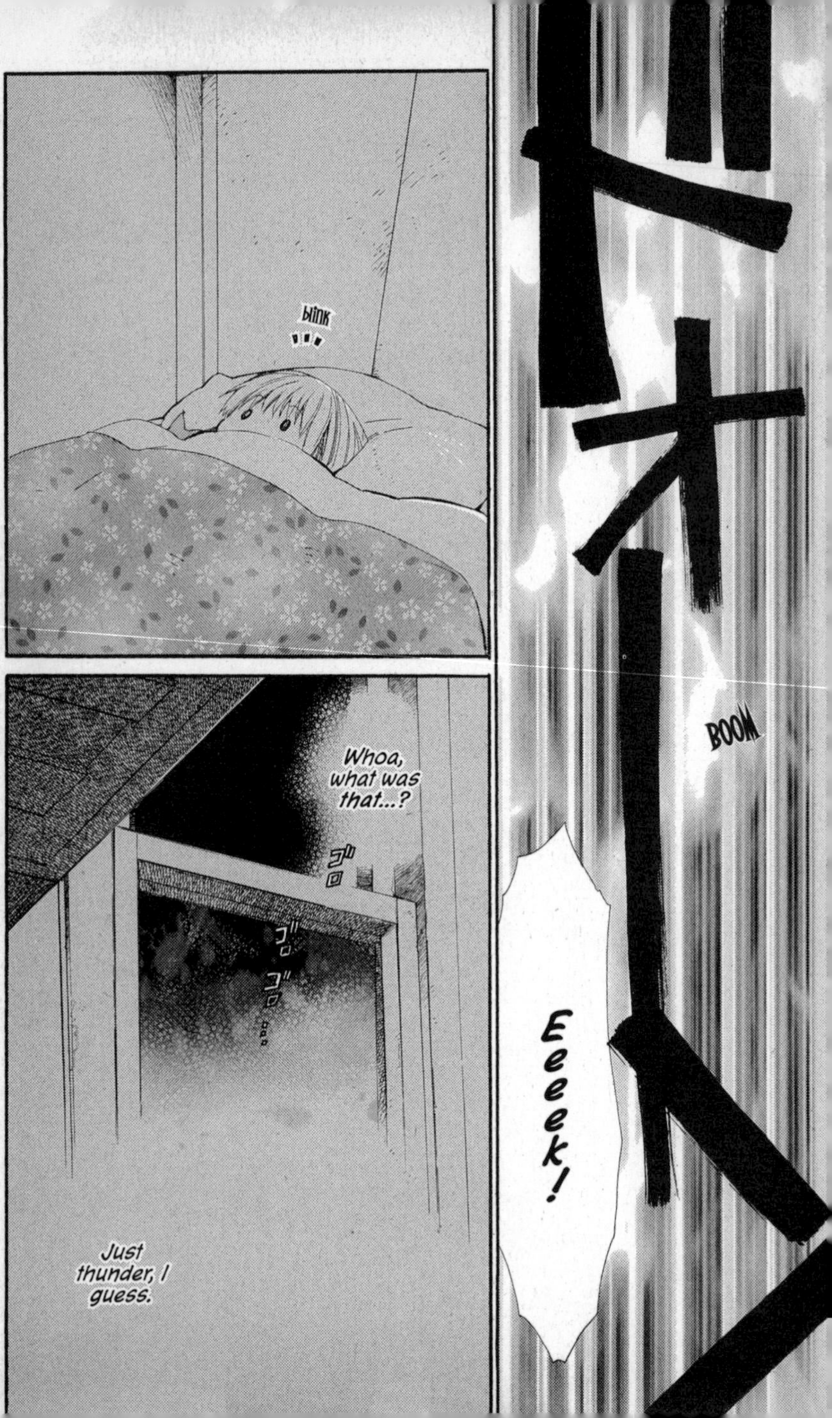
ドオーン
BOOM
Eeeek!
blink
Whoa, what was that...?
ゴロ
ゴロ ゴロ...
Just thunder, I guess.

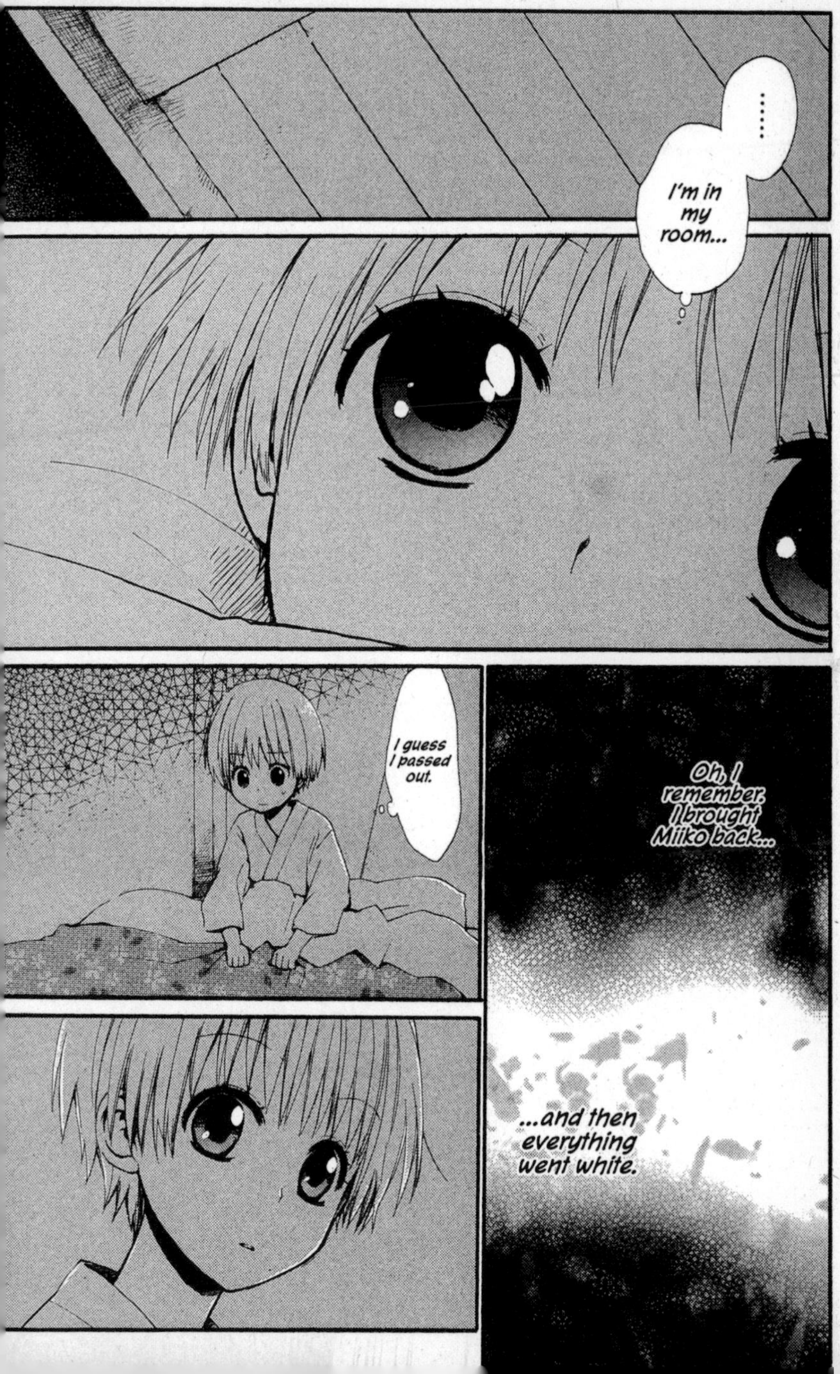
......
I'm in my room...
Oh, I remember. I brought Miiko back...
...and then everything went white.
I guess I passed out.

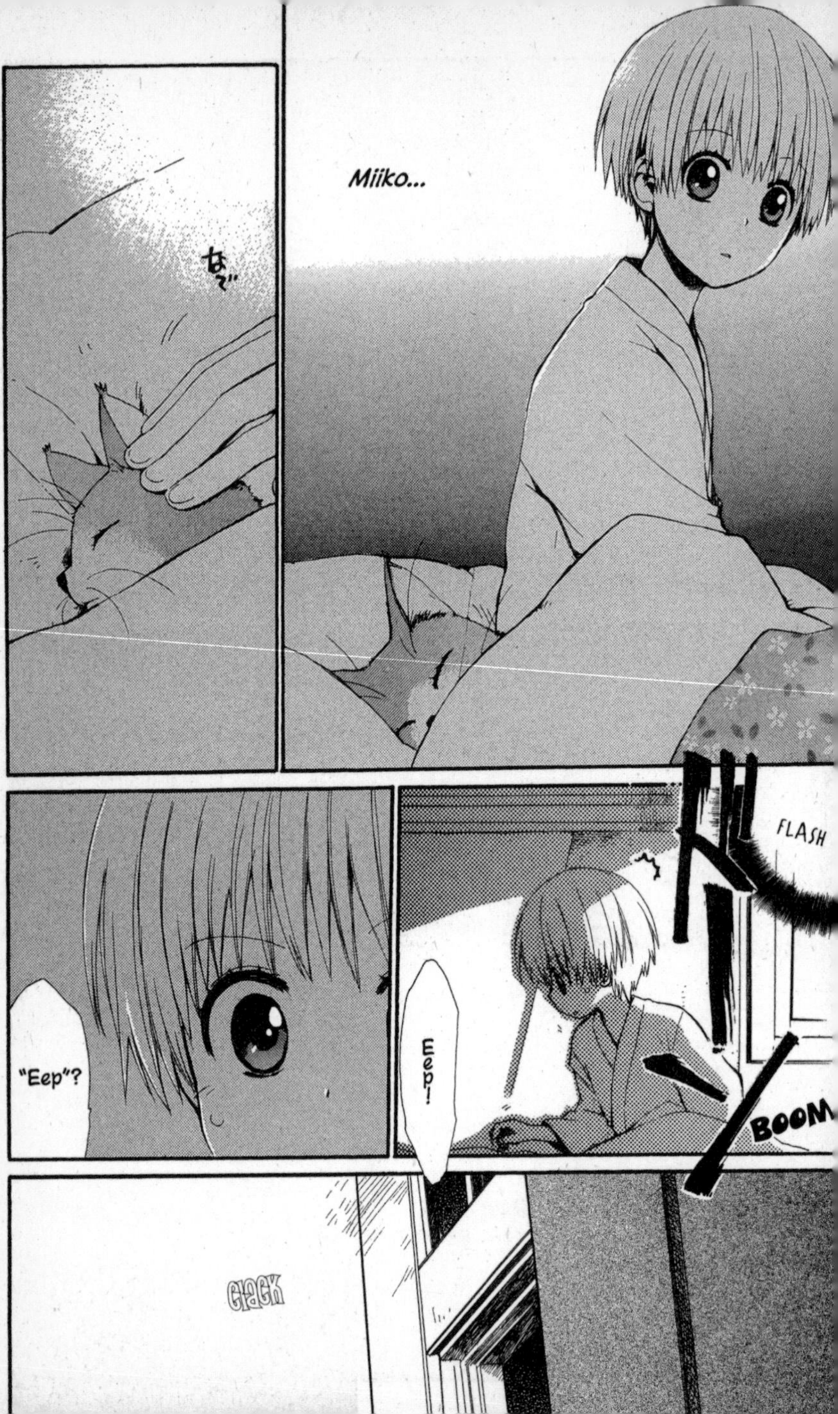
Miiko...
なで
FLASH
Eep!
BOOM
"Eep"?
CLACK

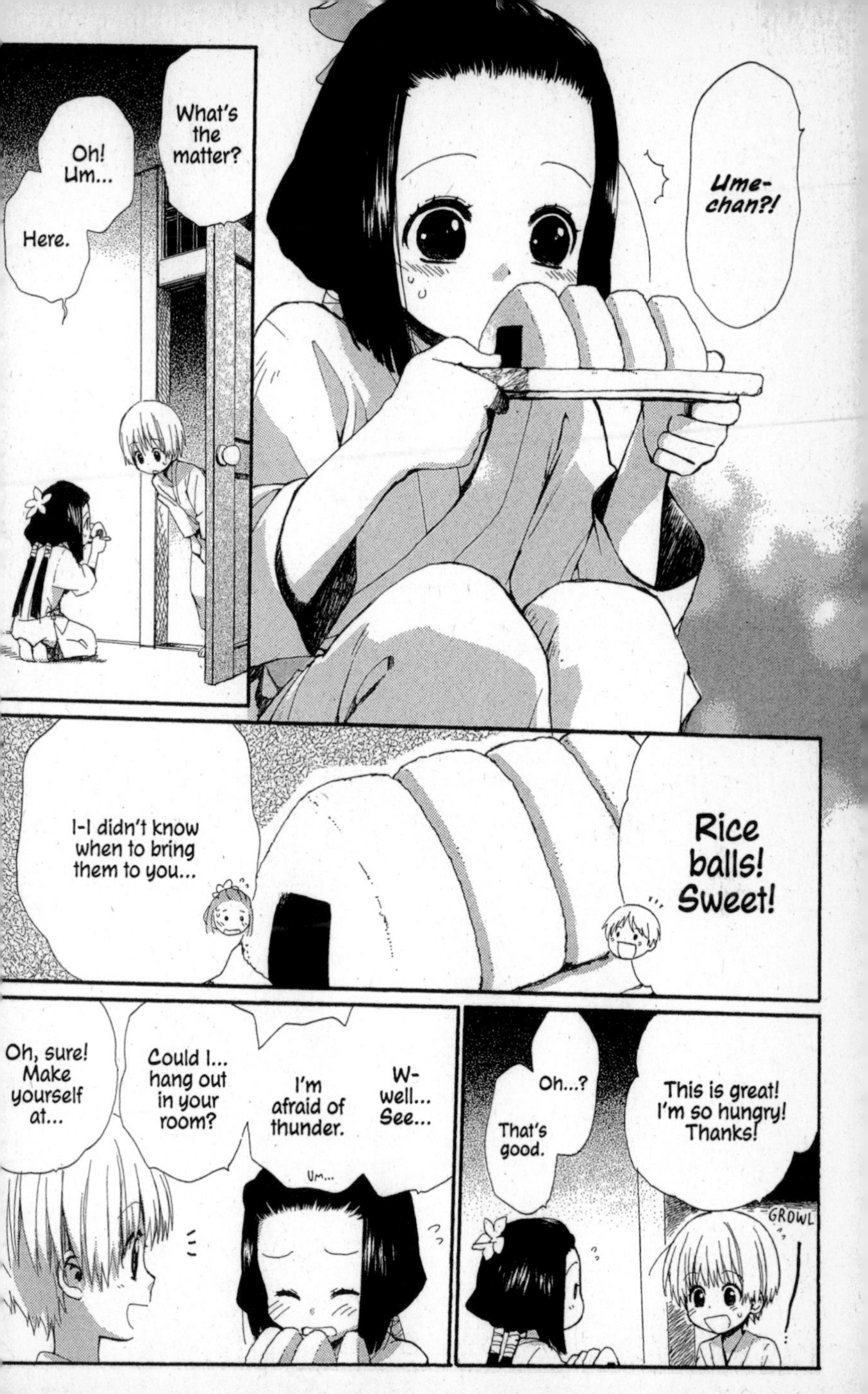

Ume-chan?!
What's the matter?
Oh! Um...
Here.
Rice balls! Sweet!
I-I didn't know when to bring them to you...
GROWL
This is great! I'm so hungry! Thanks!
Oh...?
That's good.
W-well... See...
I'm afraid of thunder.
Um...
Could I... hang out in your room?
Oh, sure! Make yourself at...

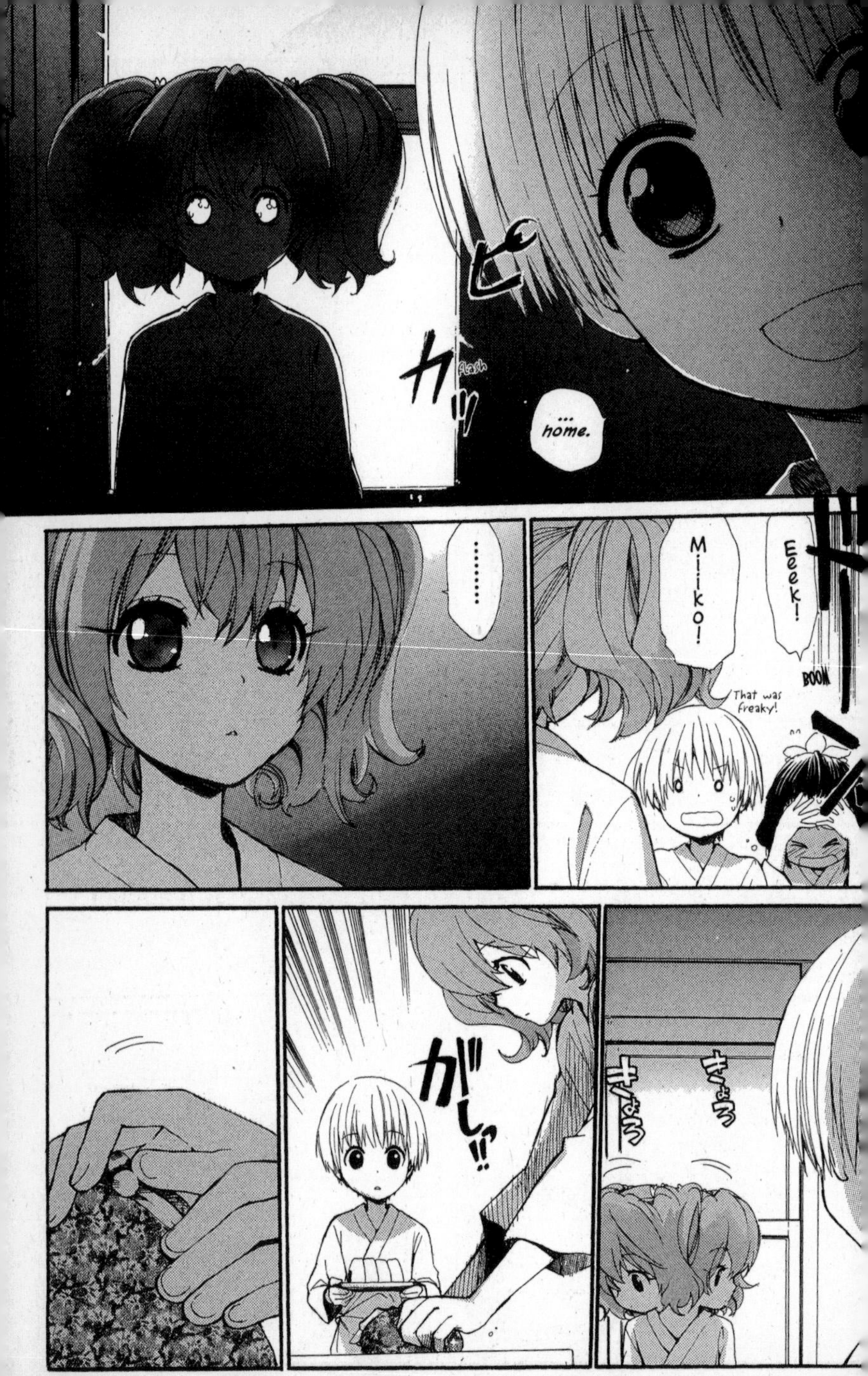
Flash
...home.
Eeeek!
Miiko!
BOOM
That was freaky!
......

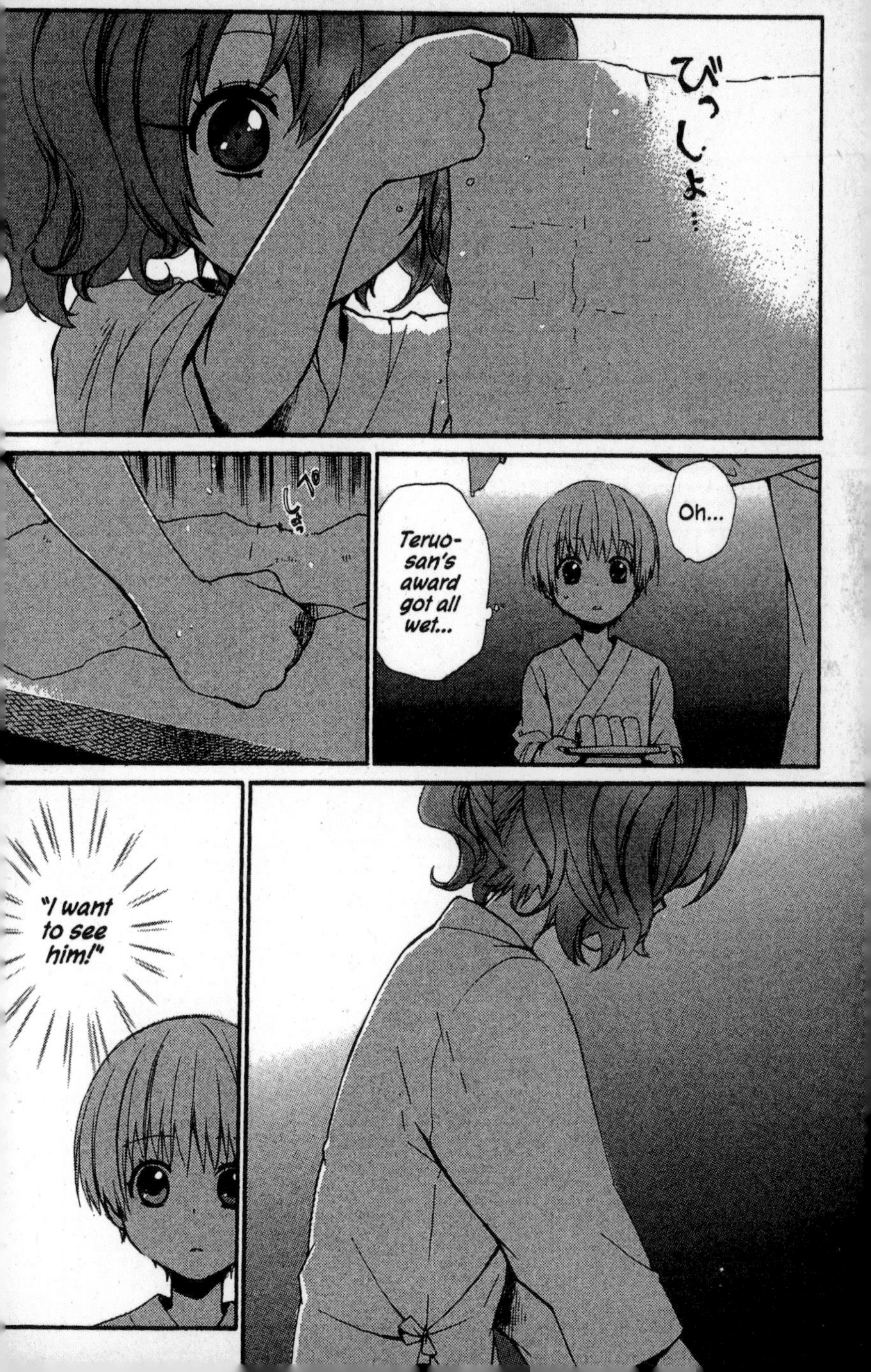
びっしょ…
Oh...
Teruo-san's award got all wet...
ぺしょ
"I want to see him!"

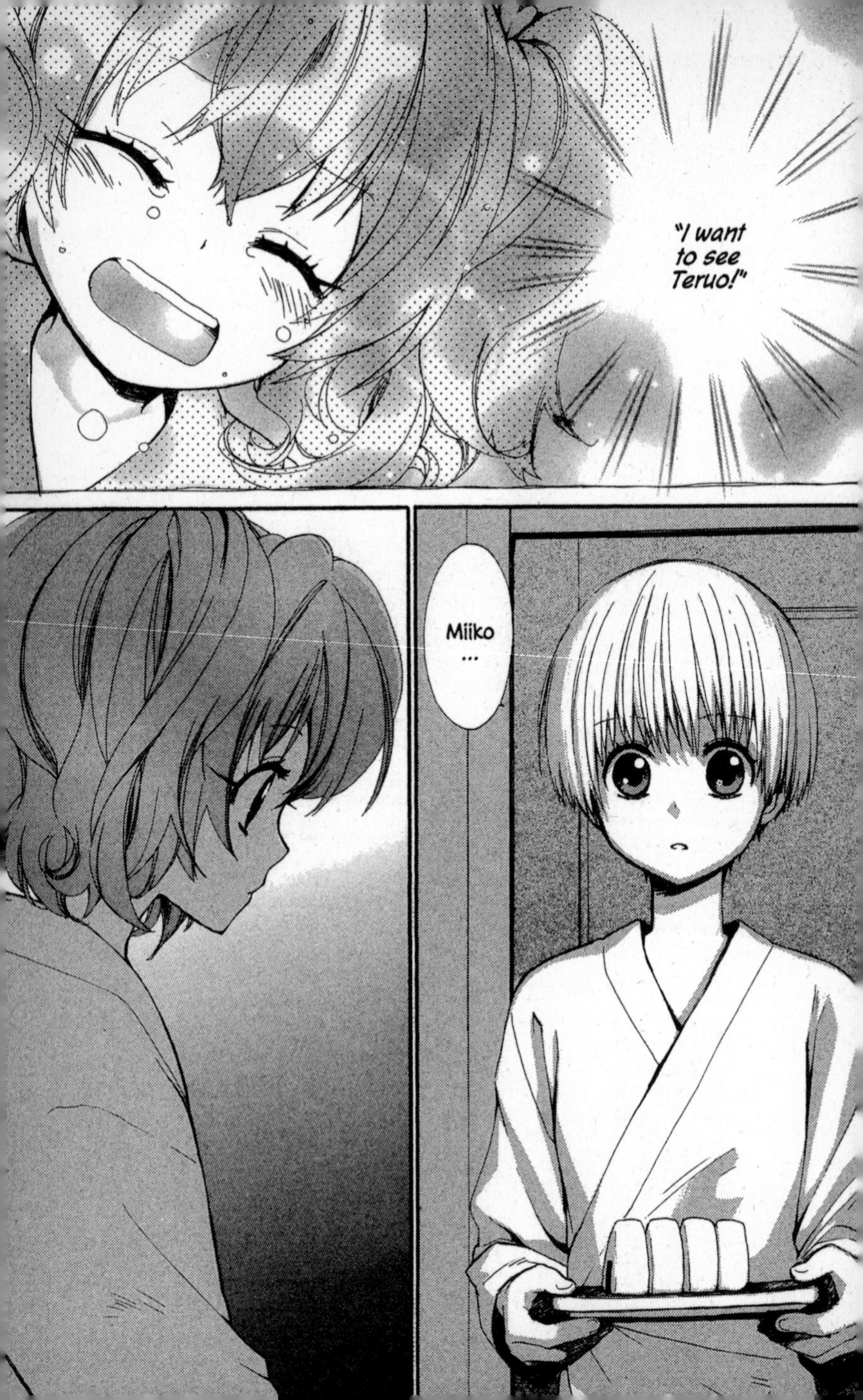
"I want to see Teruo!"
Miiko ...

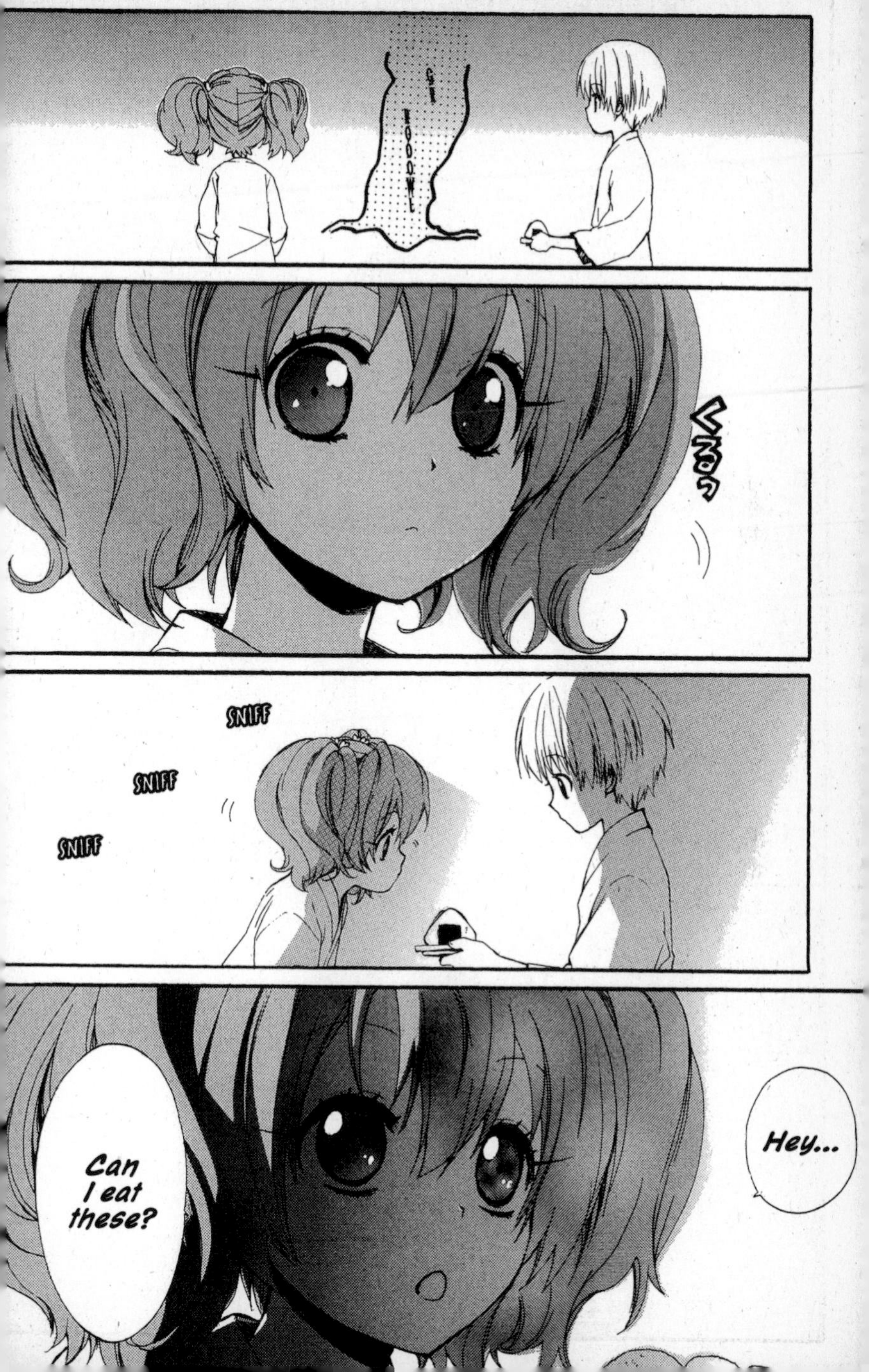
GROOOWL
くるっ
SNIFF
SNIFF
SNIFF
Hey...
Can I eat these?

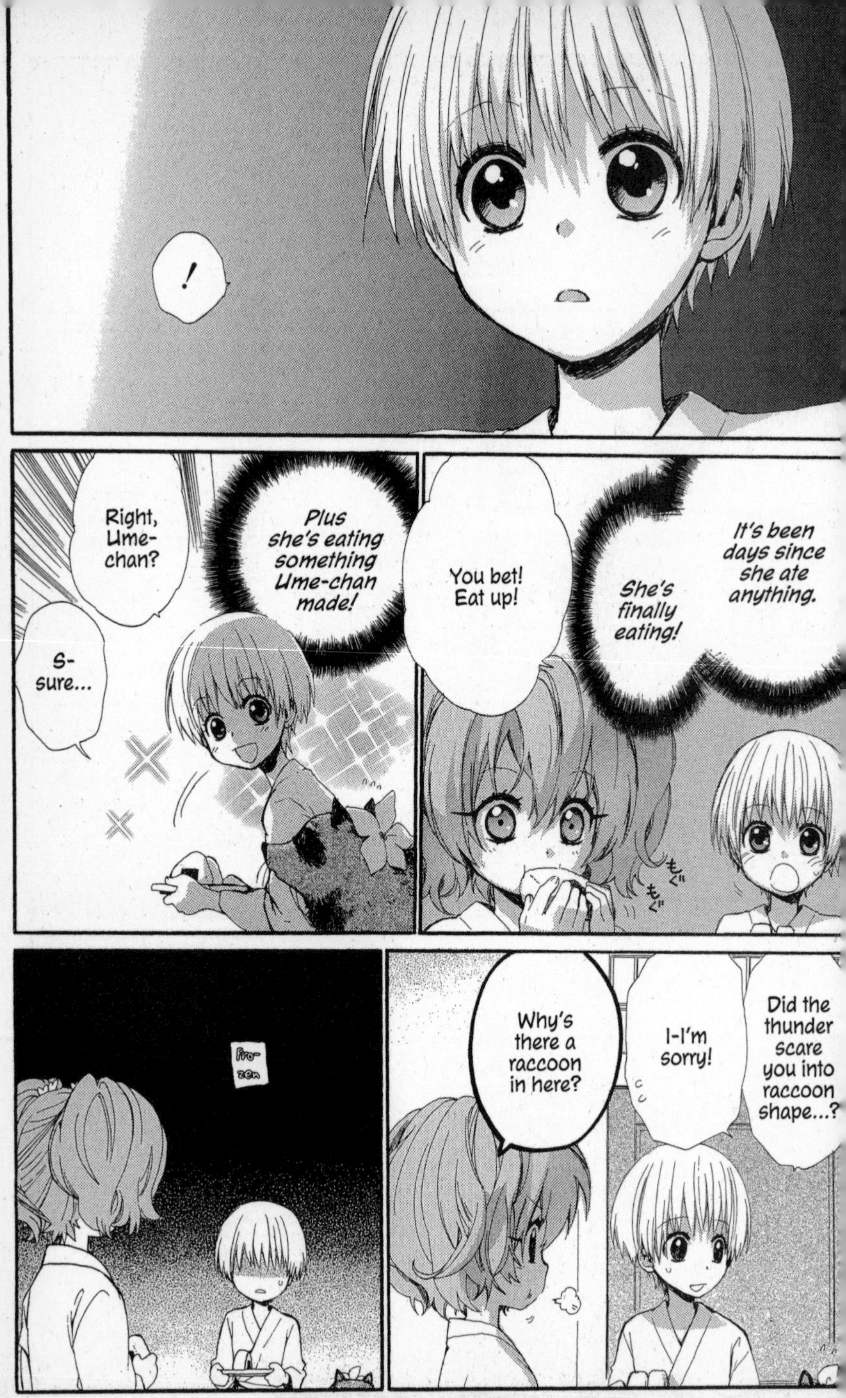
!
It's been days since she ate anything.
She's finally eating!
You bet! Eat up!
もぐ もぐ
Plus she's eating something Ume-chan made!
Right, Ume-chan?
S-sure...
Did the thunder scare you into raccoon shape...?
I-I'm sorry!
Why's there a raccoon in here?
Fro-zen

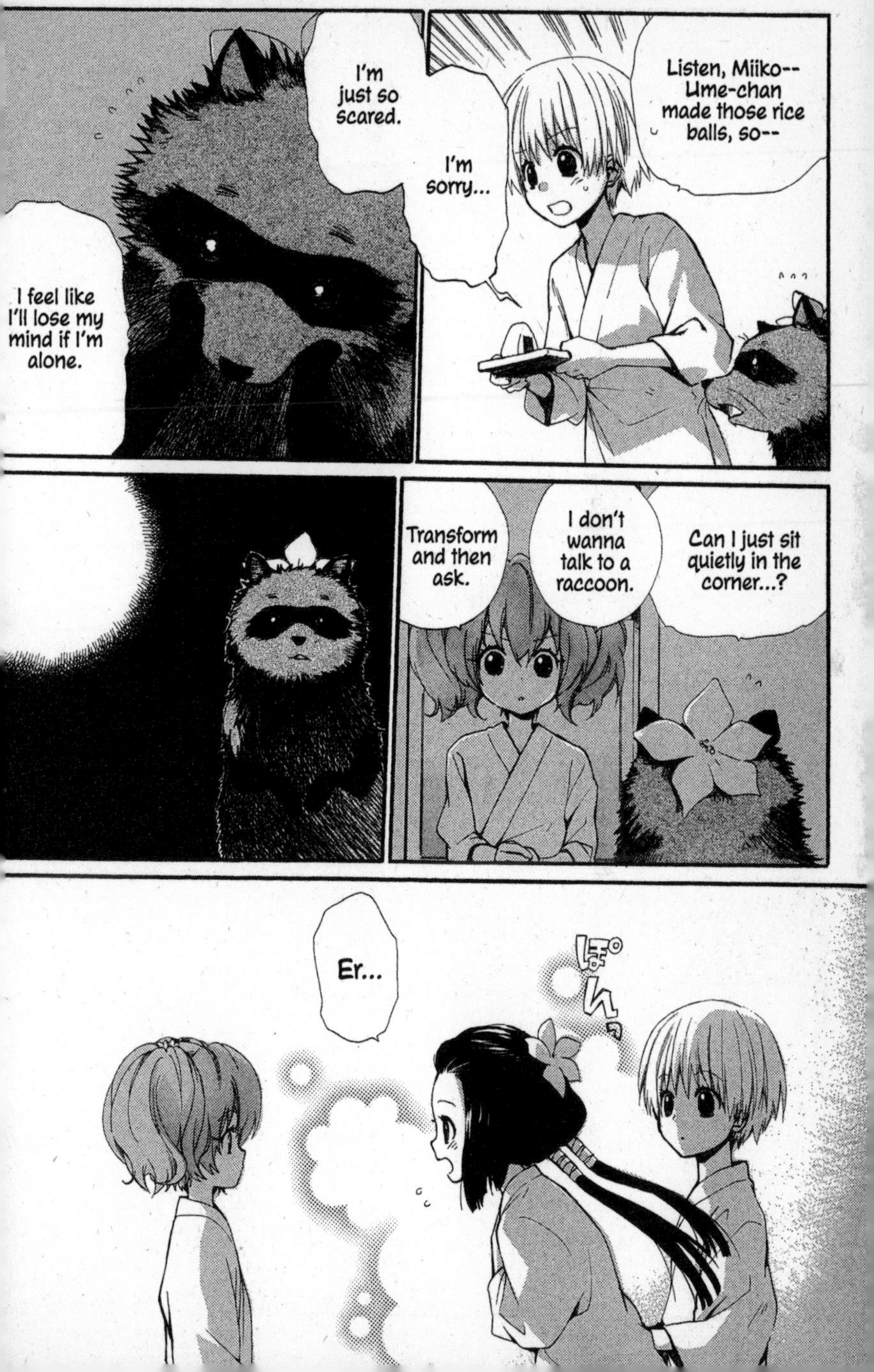
Listen, Miiko-- Ume-chan made those rice balls, so--
I'm sorry...
I'm just so scared.
I feel like I'll lose my mind if I'm alone.
Can I just sit quietly in the corner...?
I don't wanna talk to a raccoon.
Transform and then ask.
ぽんっ
Er...

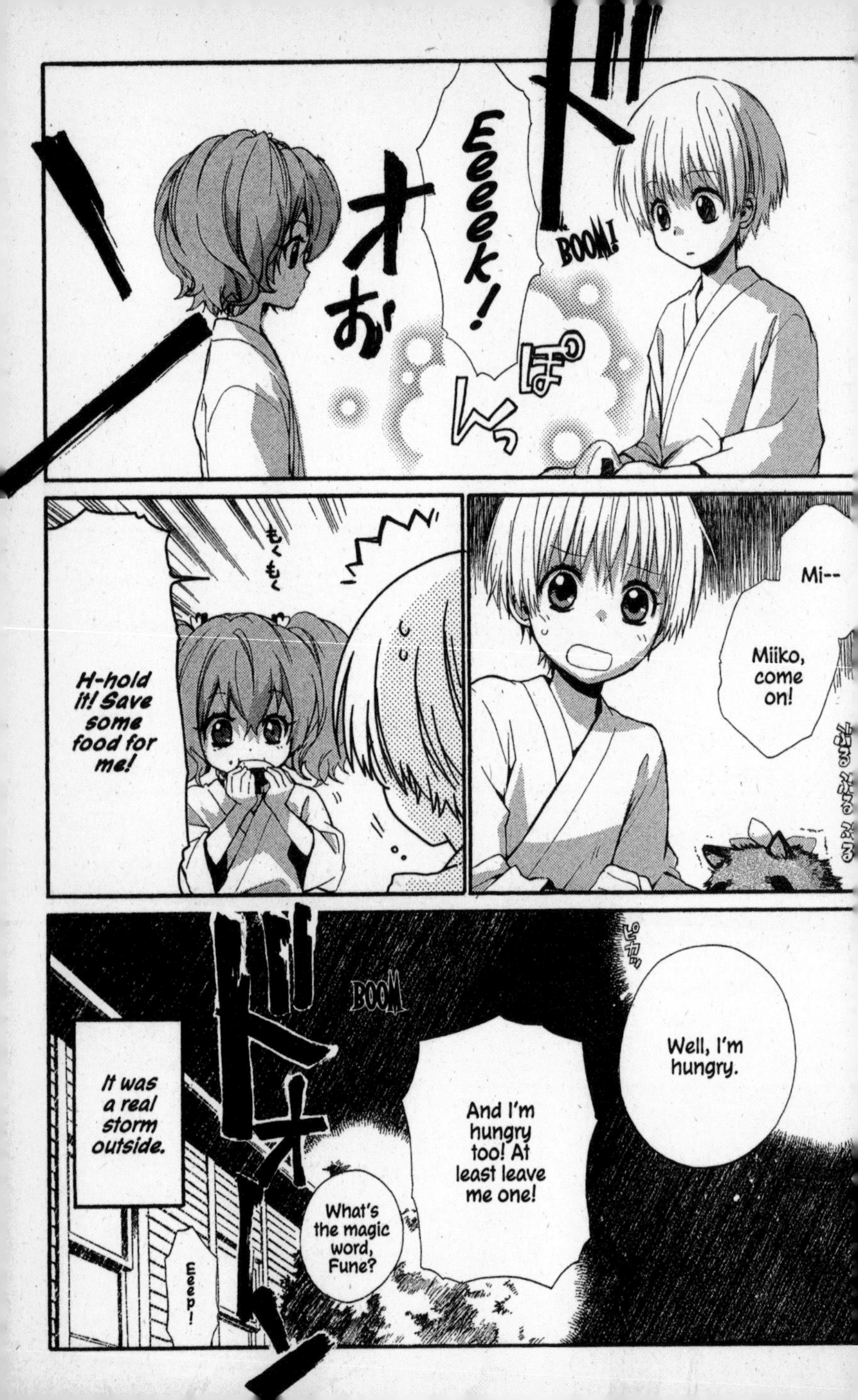
Eeeek!
BOOM!
ぽんっ
Mi--
Miiko, come on!
もくもく
H-hold it! Save some food for me!
Well, I'm hungry.
And I'm hungry too! At least leave me one!
BOOM
What's the magic word, Fune?
It was a real storm outside.
Eeep!

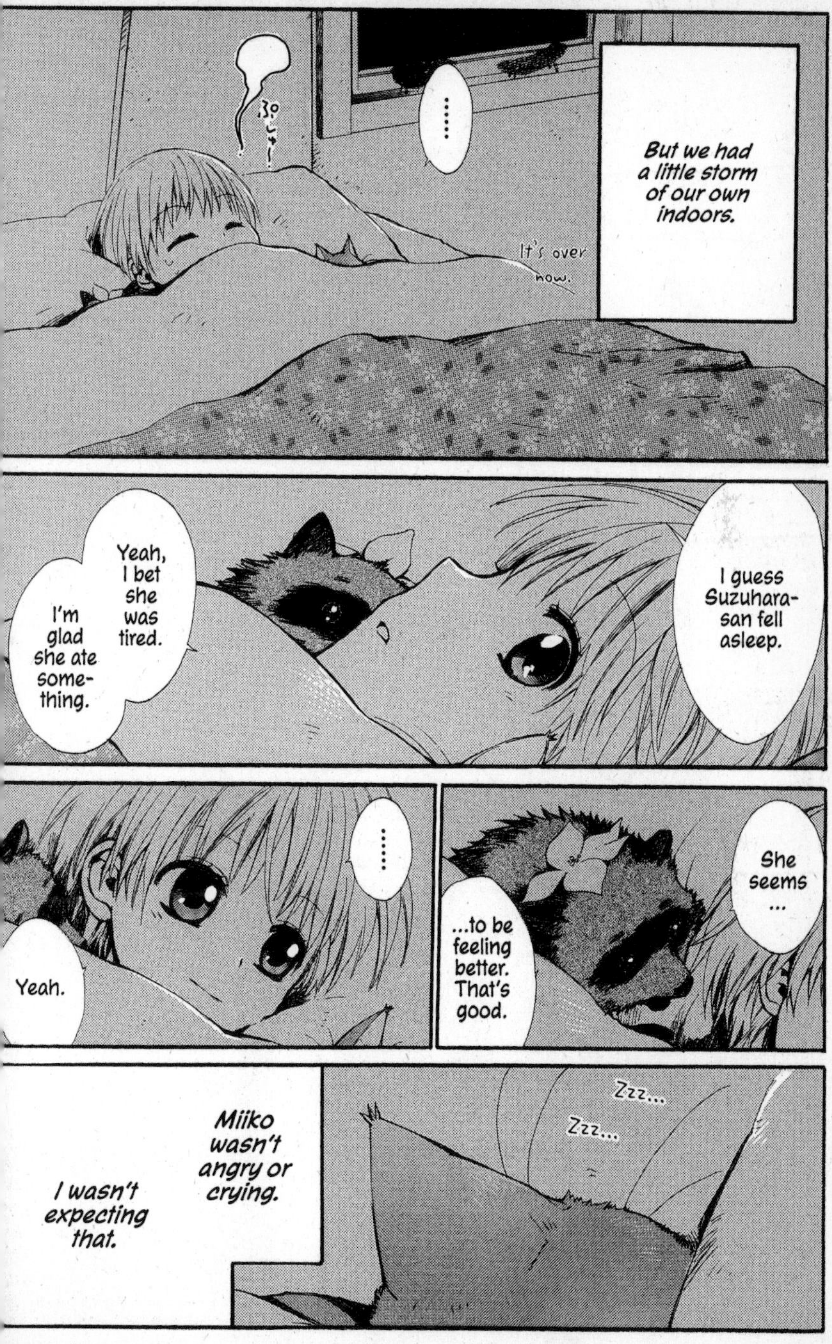
But we had a little storm of our own indoors.
……
ぷしゃー!
It's over now.
I guess Suzuhara-san fell asleep.
Yeah, I bet she was tired.
I'm glad she ate something.
She seems ...
...to be feeling better. That's good.
……
Yeah.
Zzz...
Zzz...
Miiko wasn't angry or crying.
I wasn't expecting that.

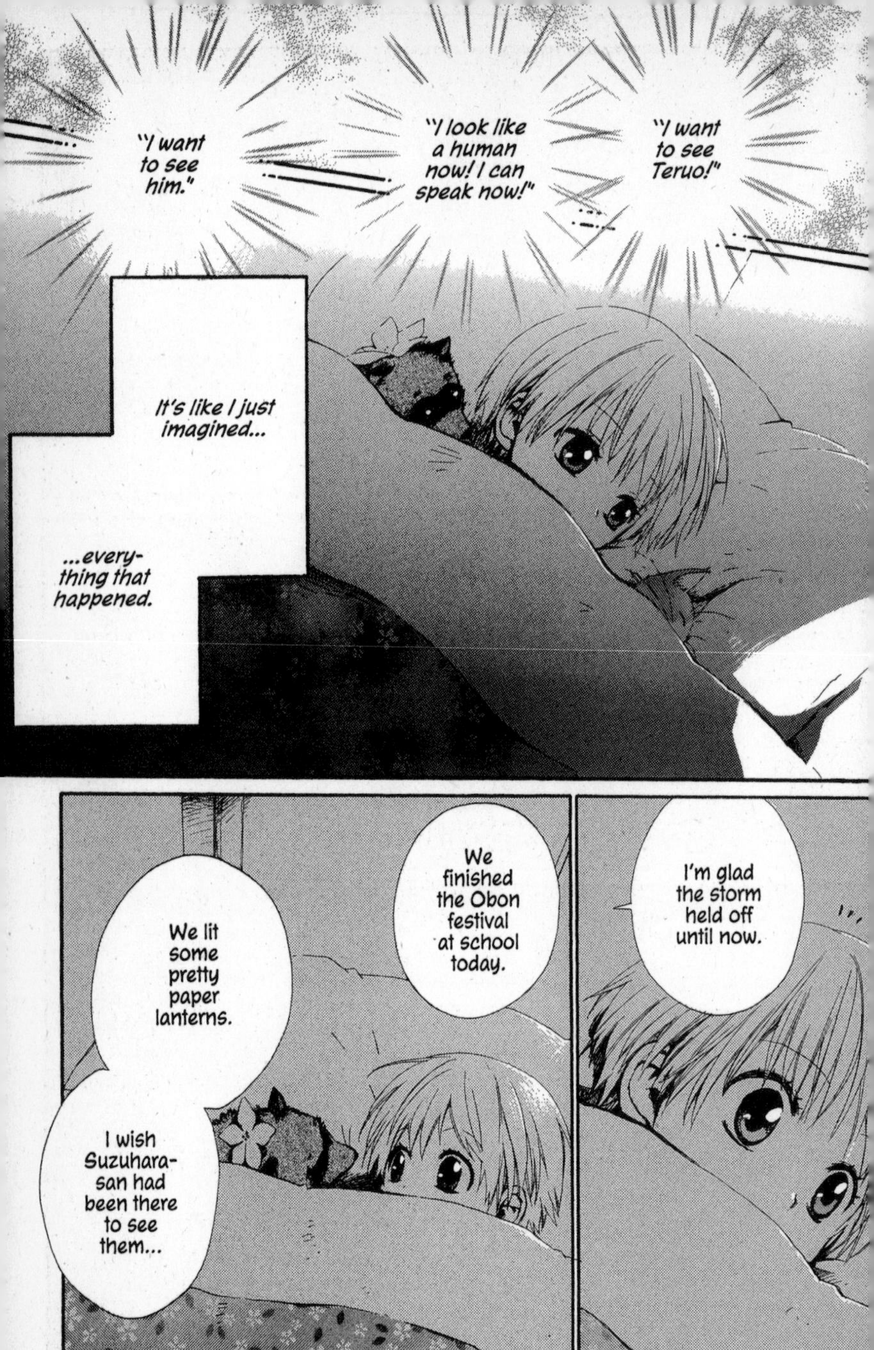
"I want to see Teruo!"
"I look like a human now! I can speak now!"
"I want to see him."
It's like I just imagined...
...every-thing that happened.
I'm glad the storm held off until now.
We finished the Obon festival at school today.
We lit some pretty paper lanterns.
I wish Suzuhara-san had been there to see them...

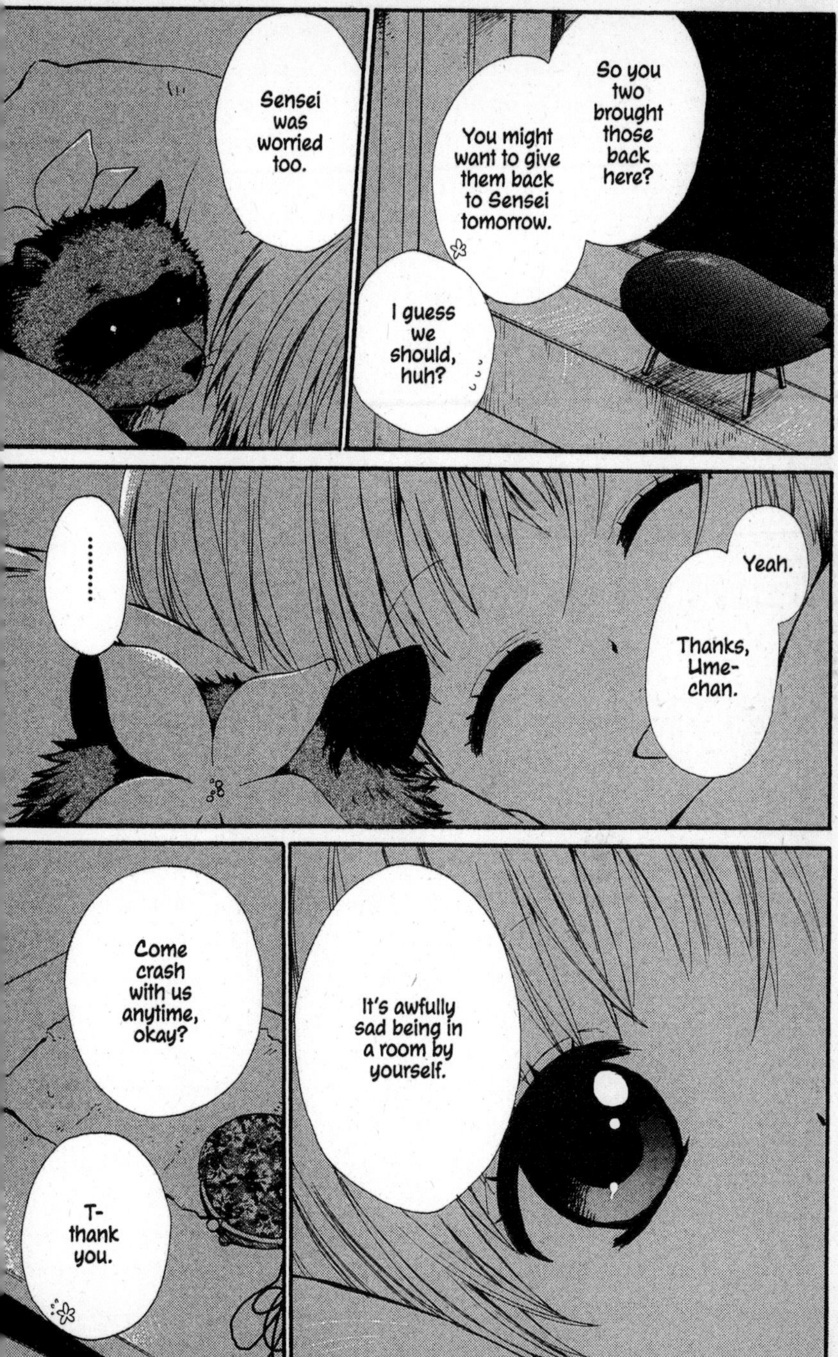
So you two brought those back here?
You might want to give them back to Sensei tomorrow.
I guess we should, huh?
Sensei was worried too.
Yeah.
Thanks, Ume-chan.
....
It's awfully sad being in a room by yourself.
Come crash with us anytime, okay?
T-thank you.

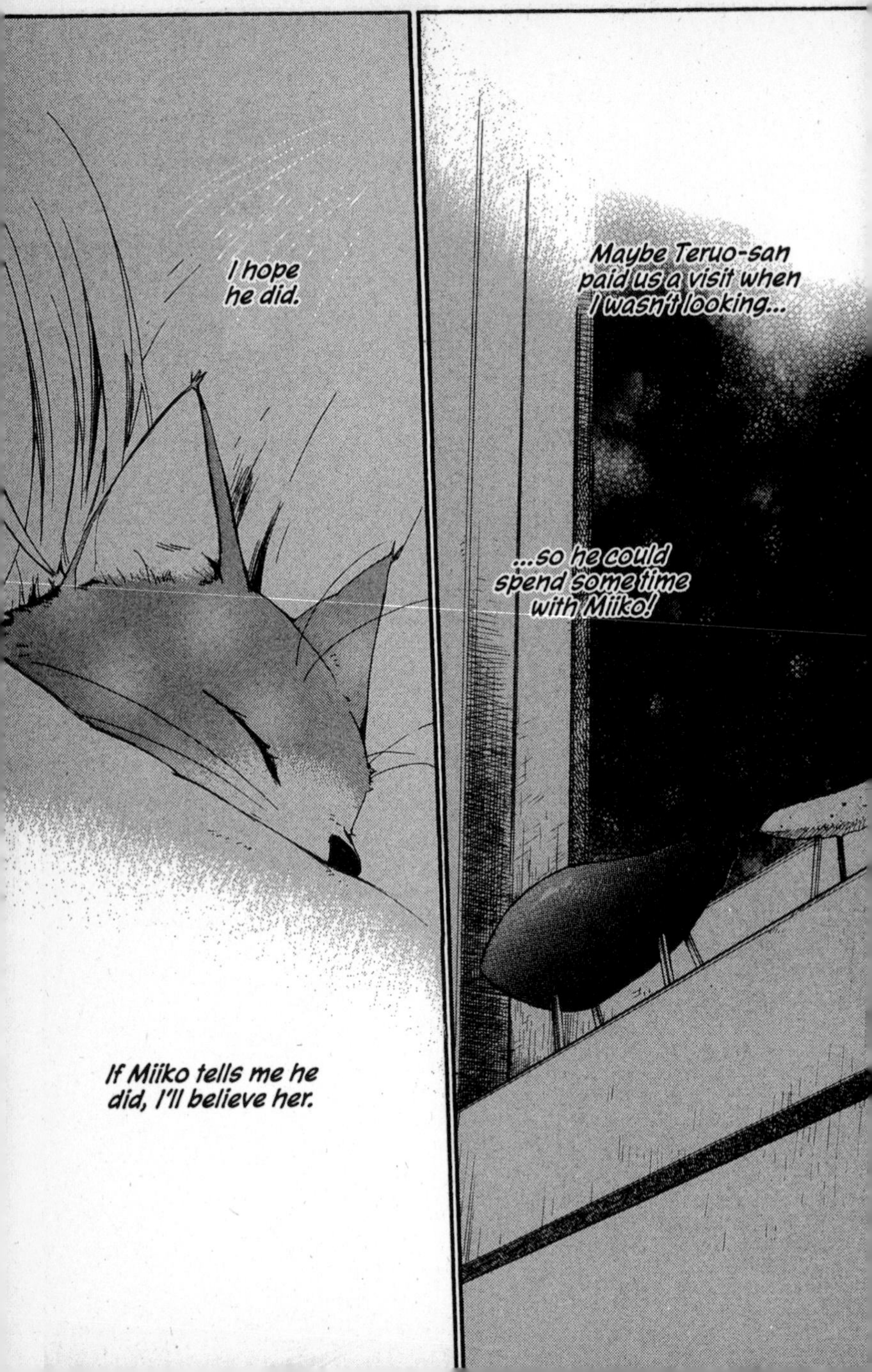
Maybe Teruo-san paid us a visit when I wasn't looking...
...so he could spend some time with Miiko!
I hope he did.
If Miiko tells me he did, I'll believe her.

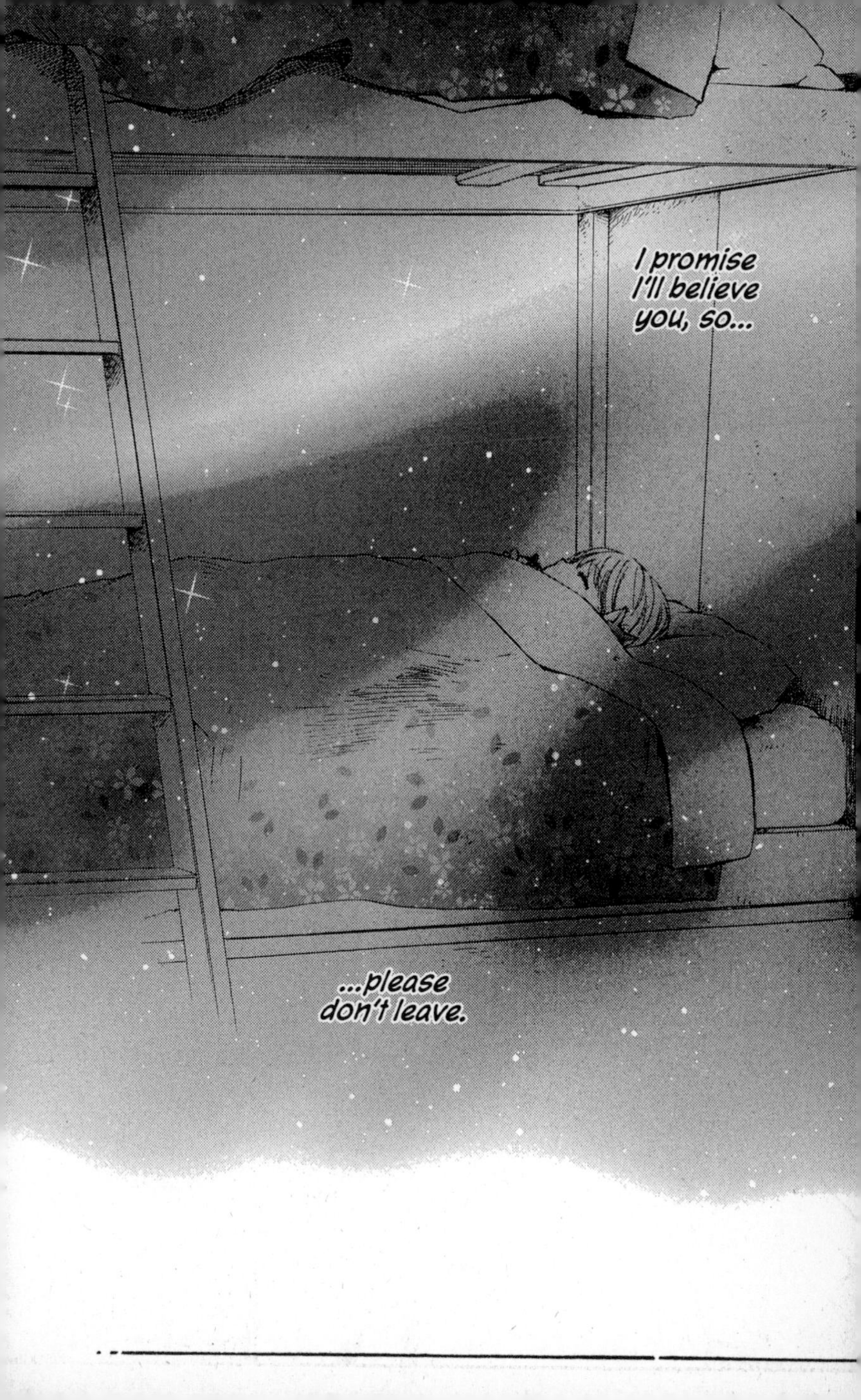
I promise I'll believe you, so...
...please don't leave.

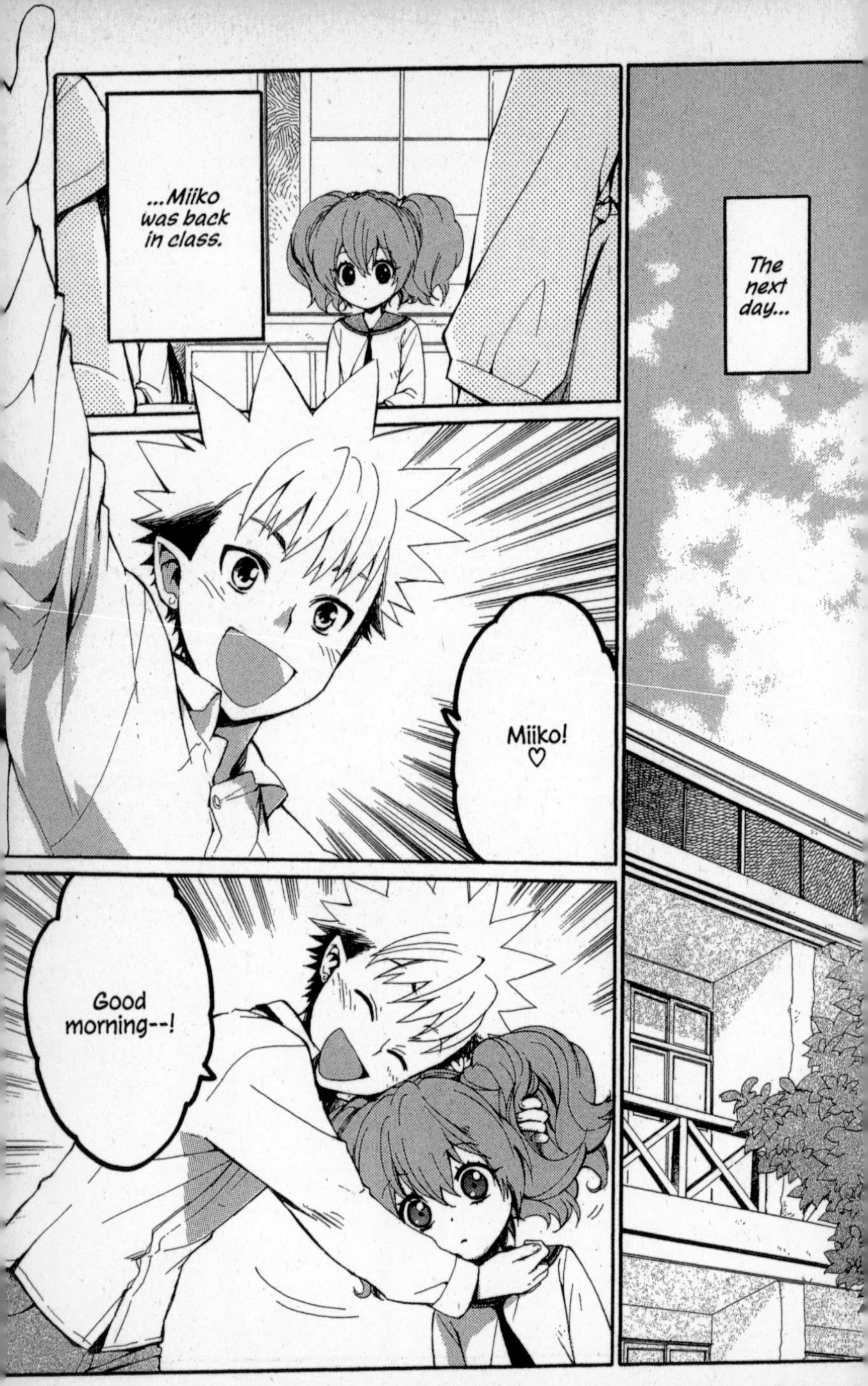
The next day...
...Miiko was back in class.
Miiko! ♡
Good morning--!

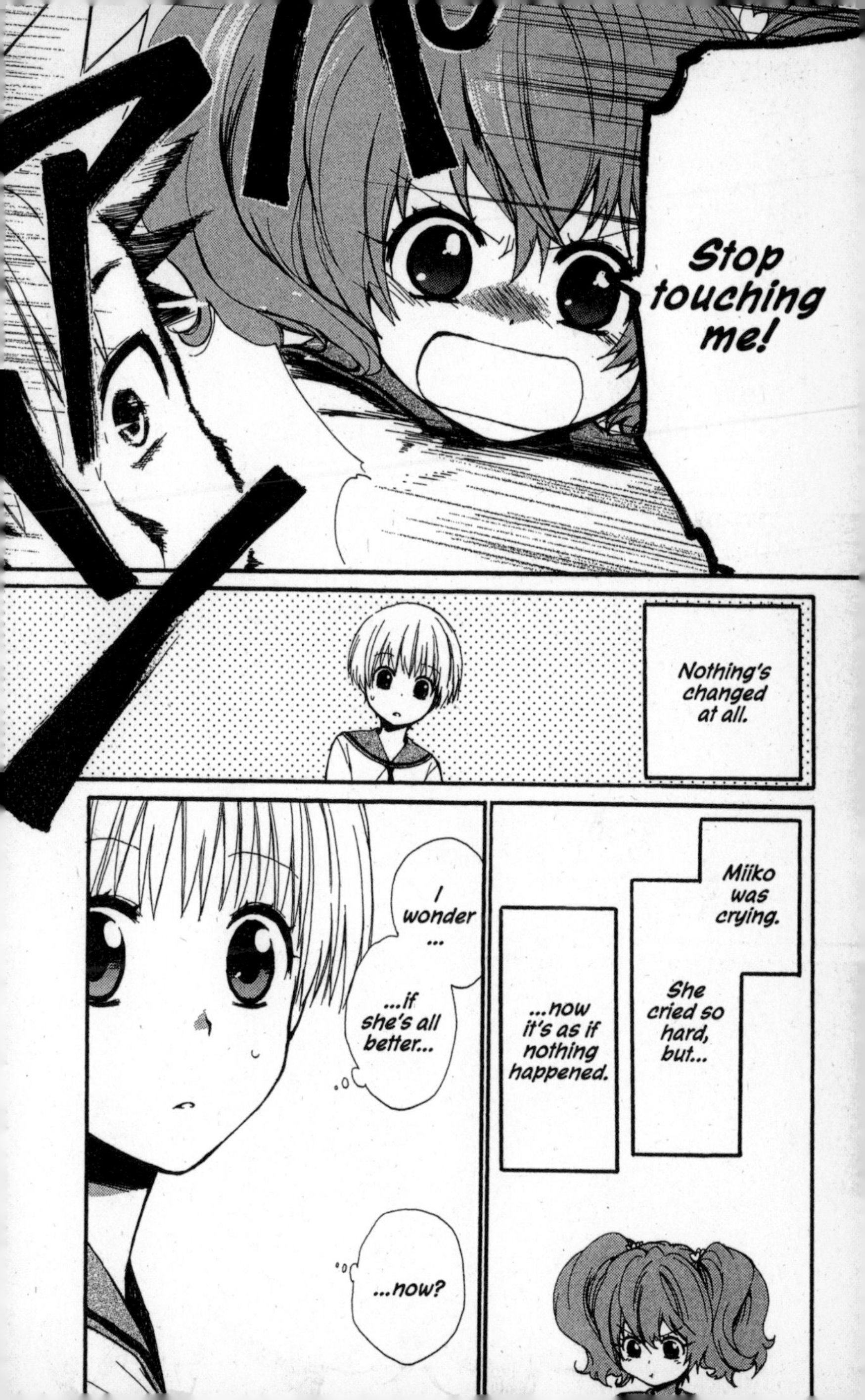
Stop touching me!
Nothing's changed at all.
Miiko was crying.
She cried so hard, but...
...now it's as if nothing happened.
I wonder...
...if she's all better...
...now?

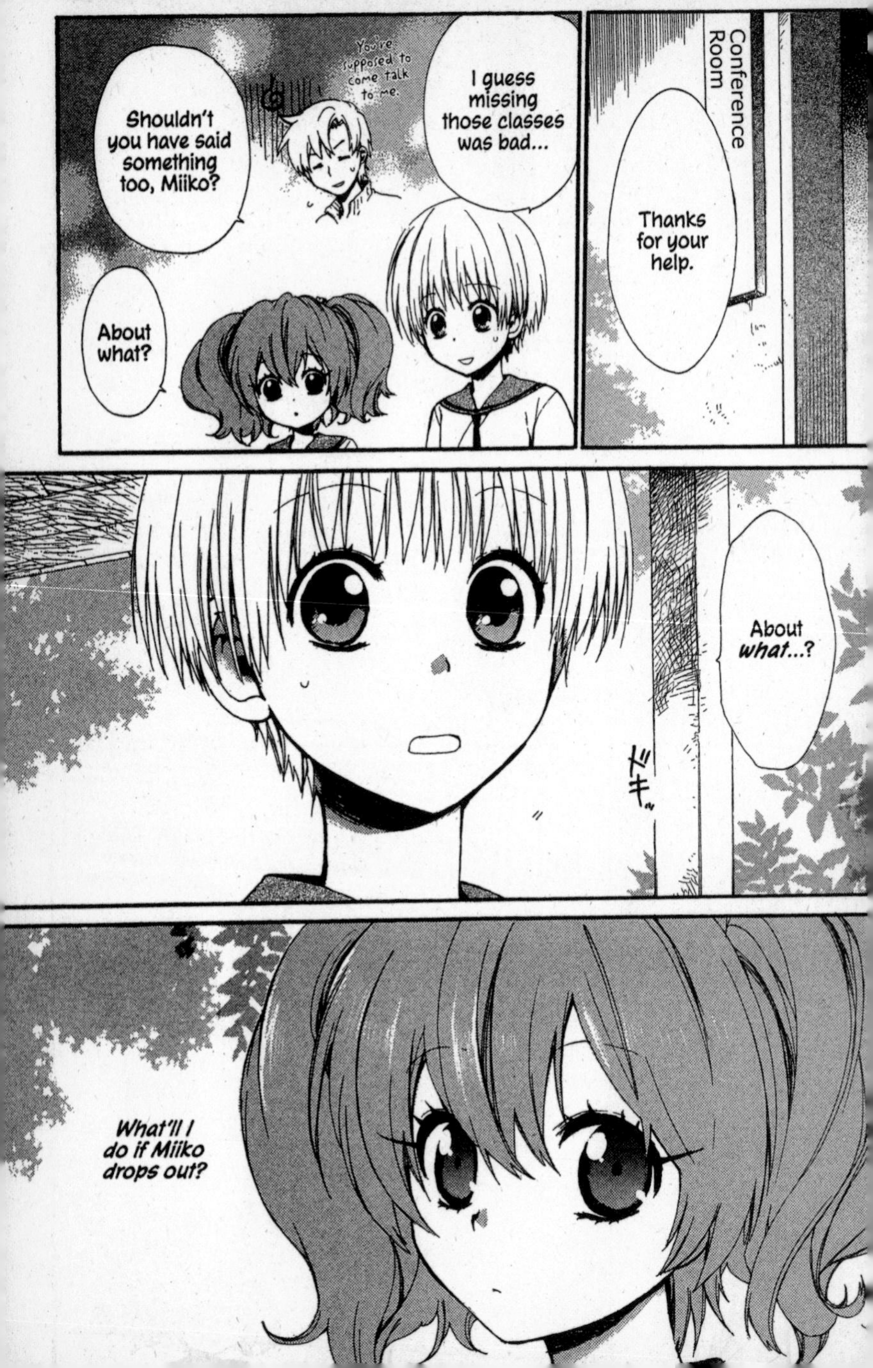
Conference Room
Thanks for your help.
I guess missing those classes was bad...
You're supposed to come talk to me.
Shouldn't you have said something too, Miiko?
About what?
About *what*...?
What'll I do if Miiko drops out?

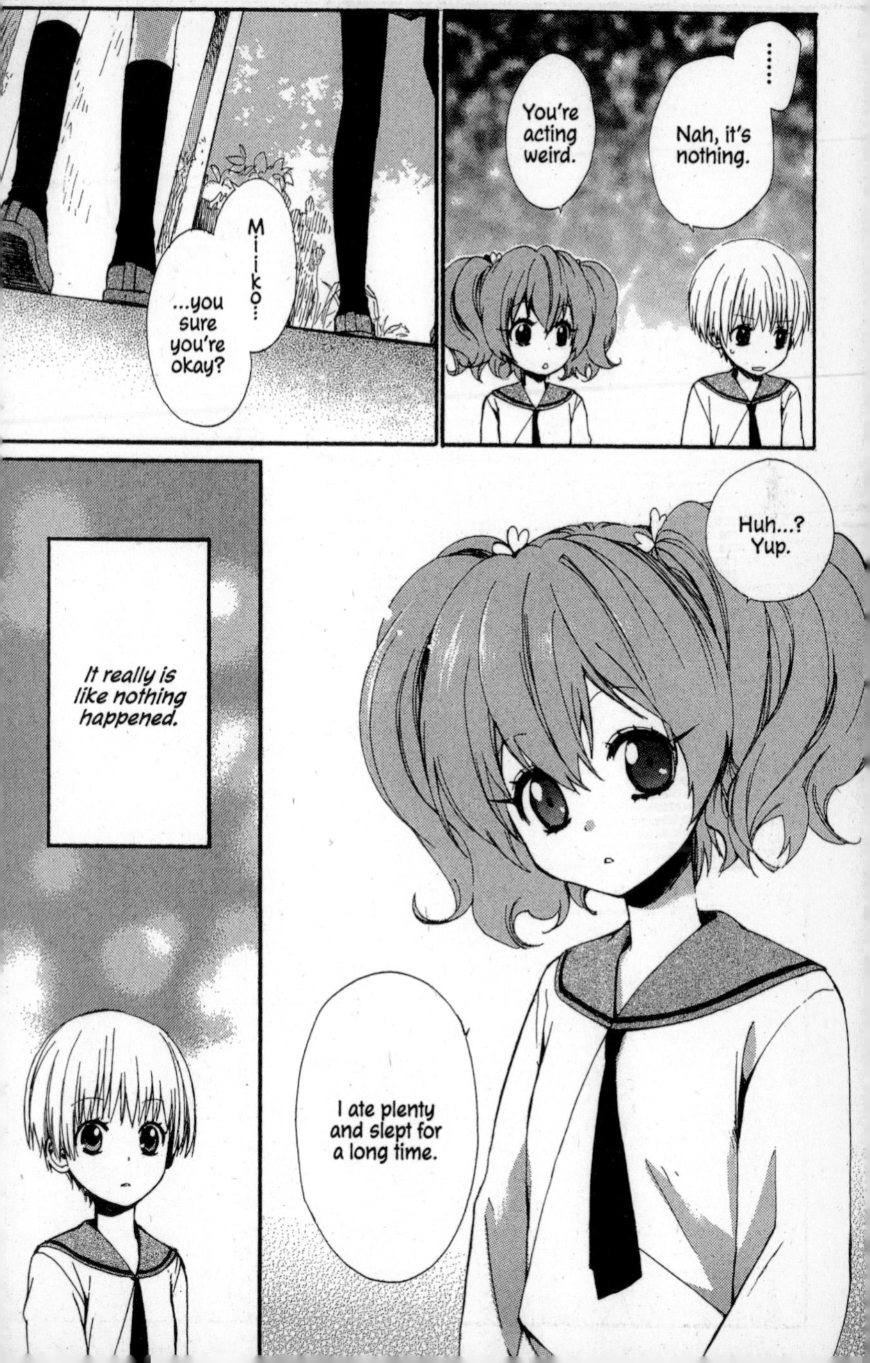
......
Nah, it's nothing.
You're acting weird.
Miiko...
...you sure you're okay?
Huh...? Yup.
I ate plenty and slept for a long time.
It really is like nothing happened.

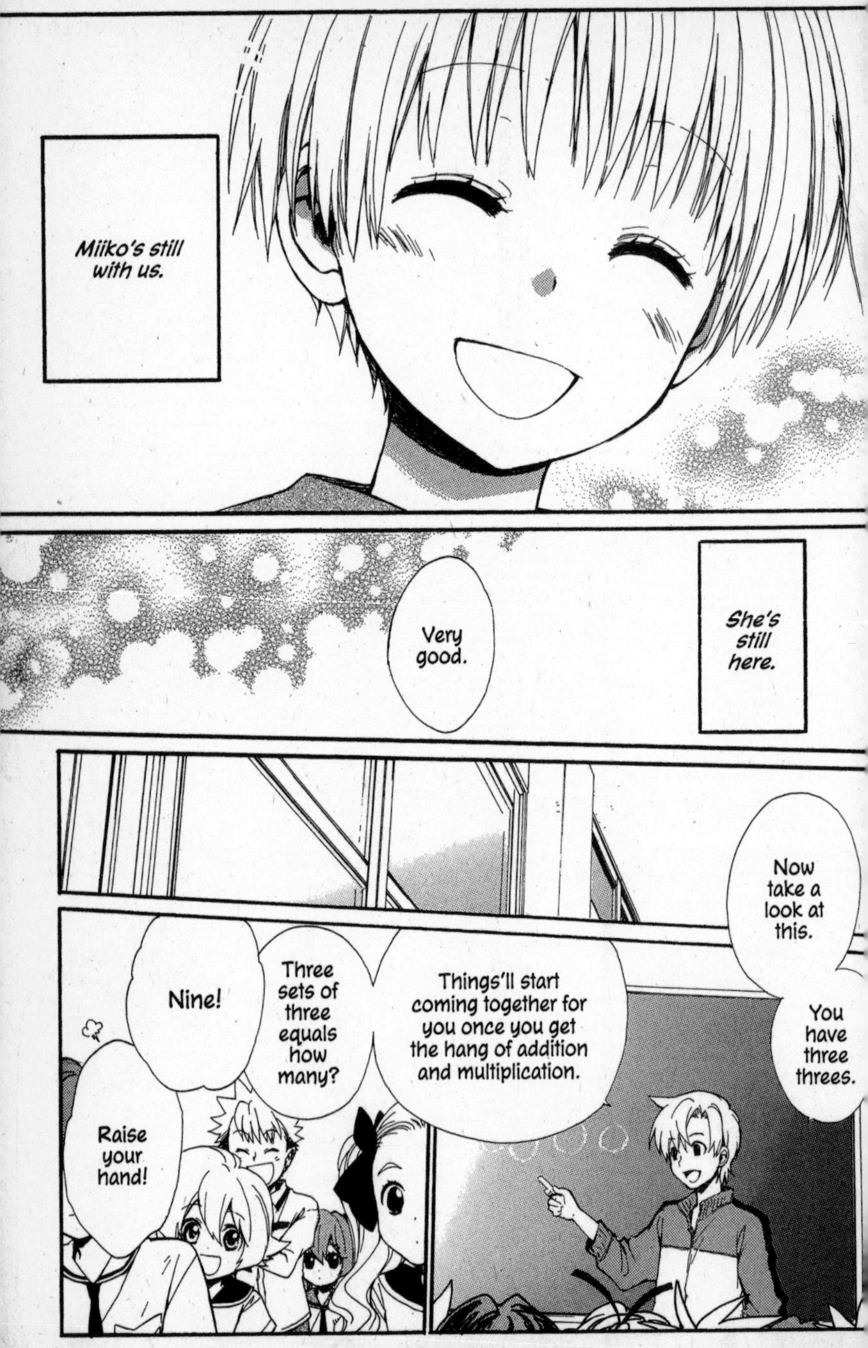
Miiko's still with us.
She's still here.
Very good.
Now take a look at this.
You have three threes.
Things'll start coming together for you once you get the hang of addition and multiplication.
Three sets of three equals how many?
Nine!
Raise your hand!

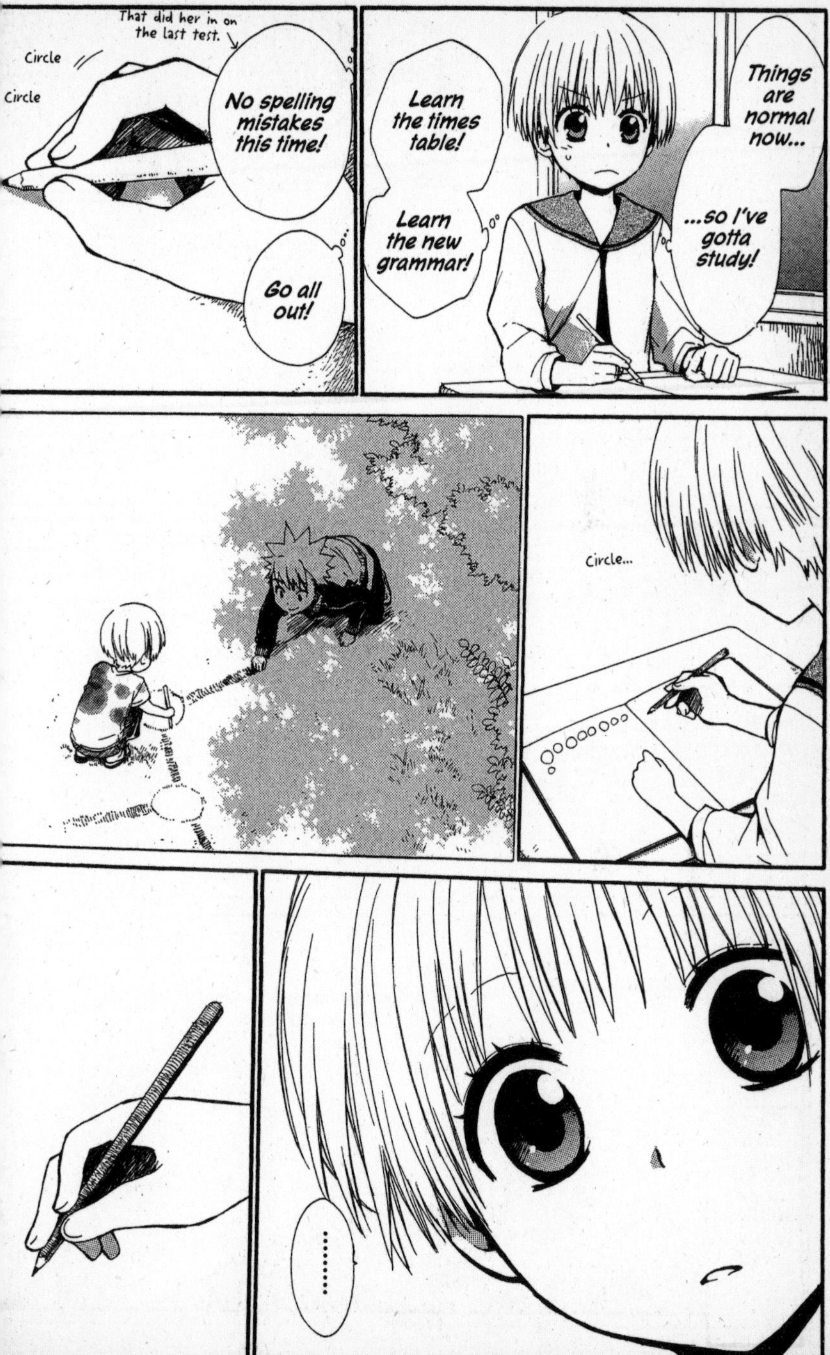
Things are normal now...
...so I've gotta study!
Learn the times table!
Learn the new grammar!
That did her in on the last test.
No spelling mistakes this time!
Go all out!
Circle
Circle
Circle...
....

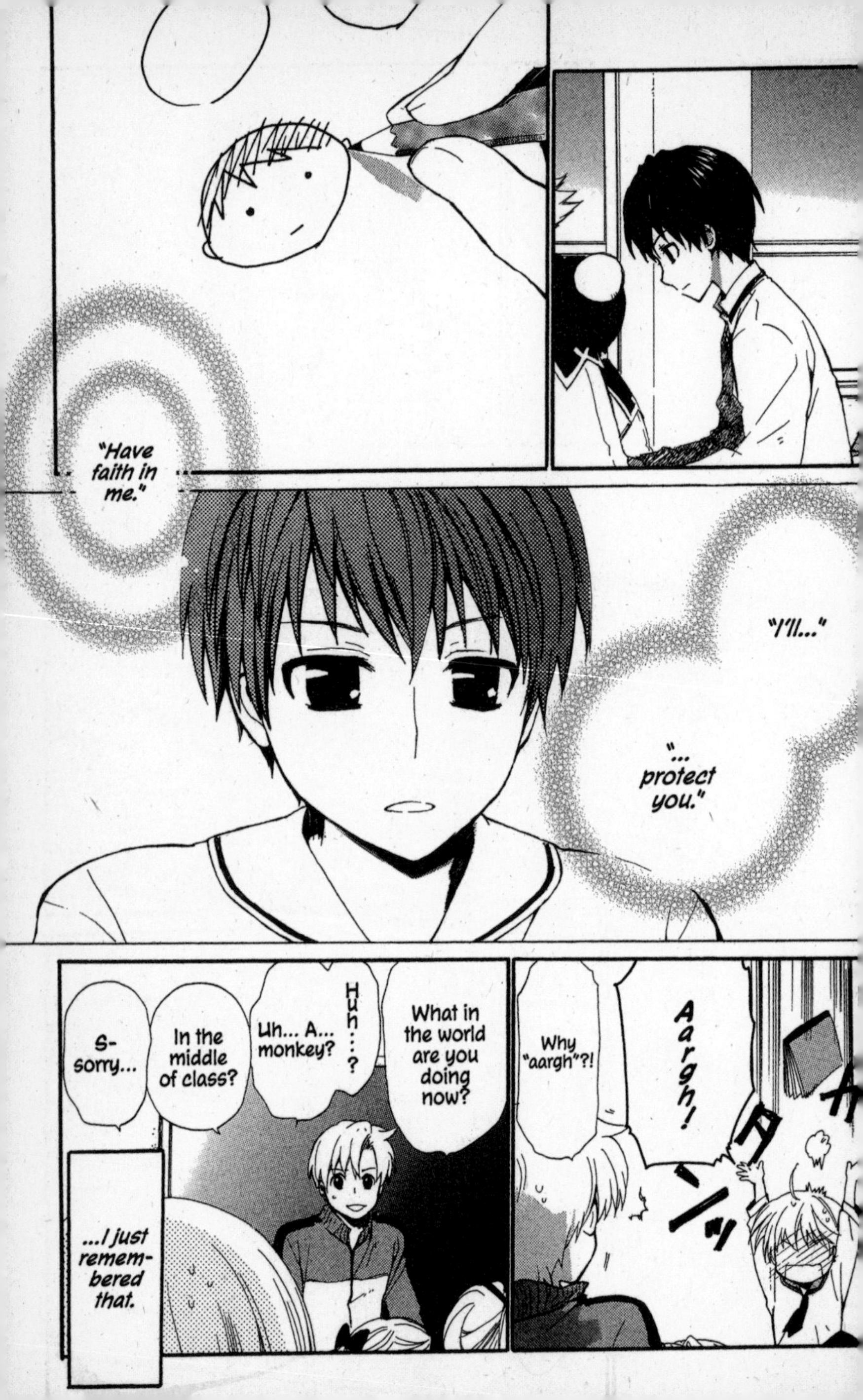
"Have faith in me."
"I'll..."
"...protect you."
Aargh!
Why "aargh"?!
What in the world are you doing now?
Huh...?
Uh... A... monkey?
In the middle of class?
S-sorry...
...I just remembered that.

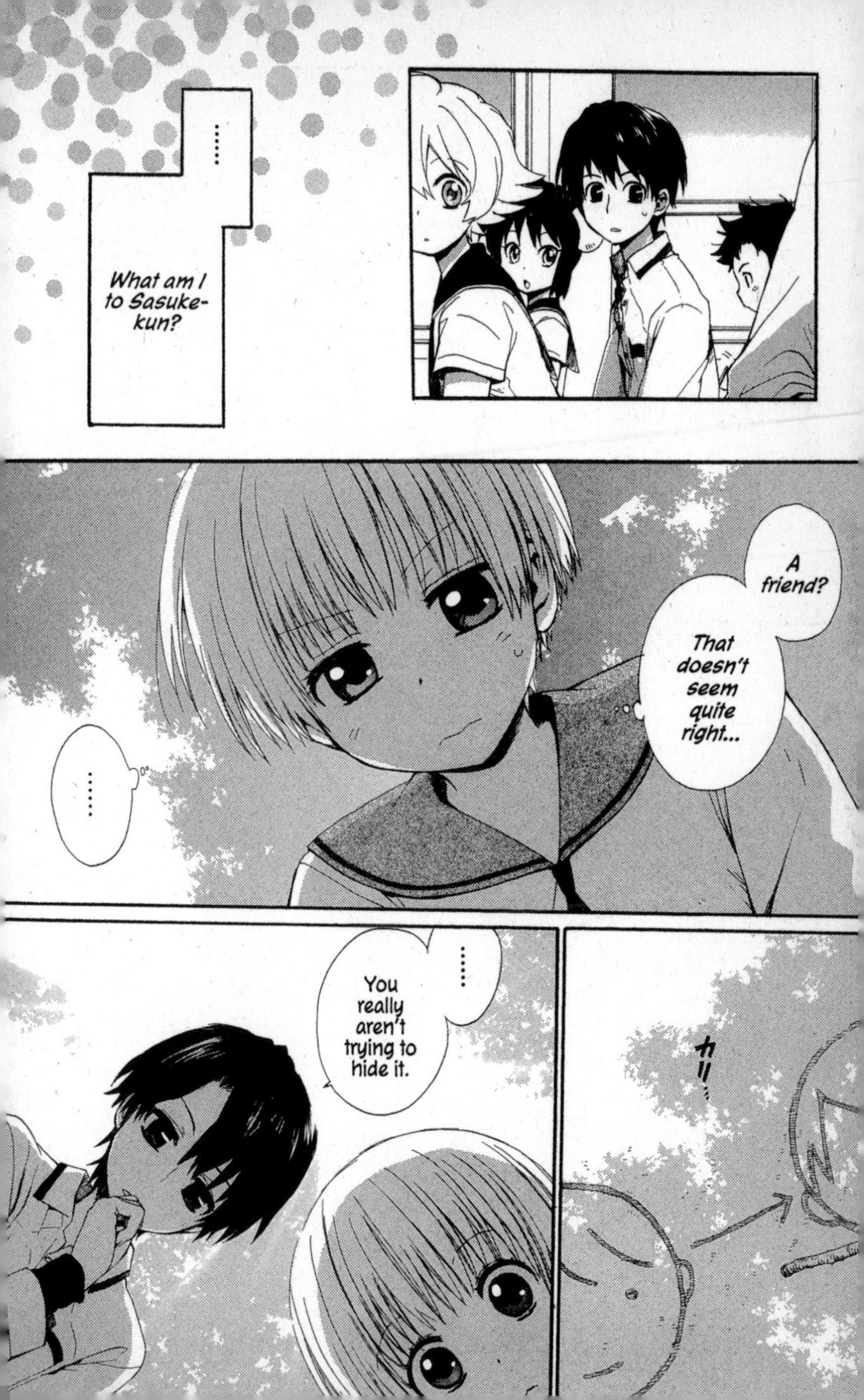
......
What am I to Sasuke-kun?
A friend? That doesn't seem quite right...
......
カリ…
...... You really aren't trying to hide it.

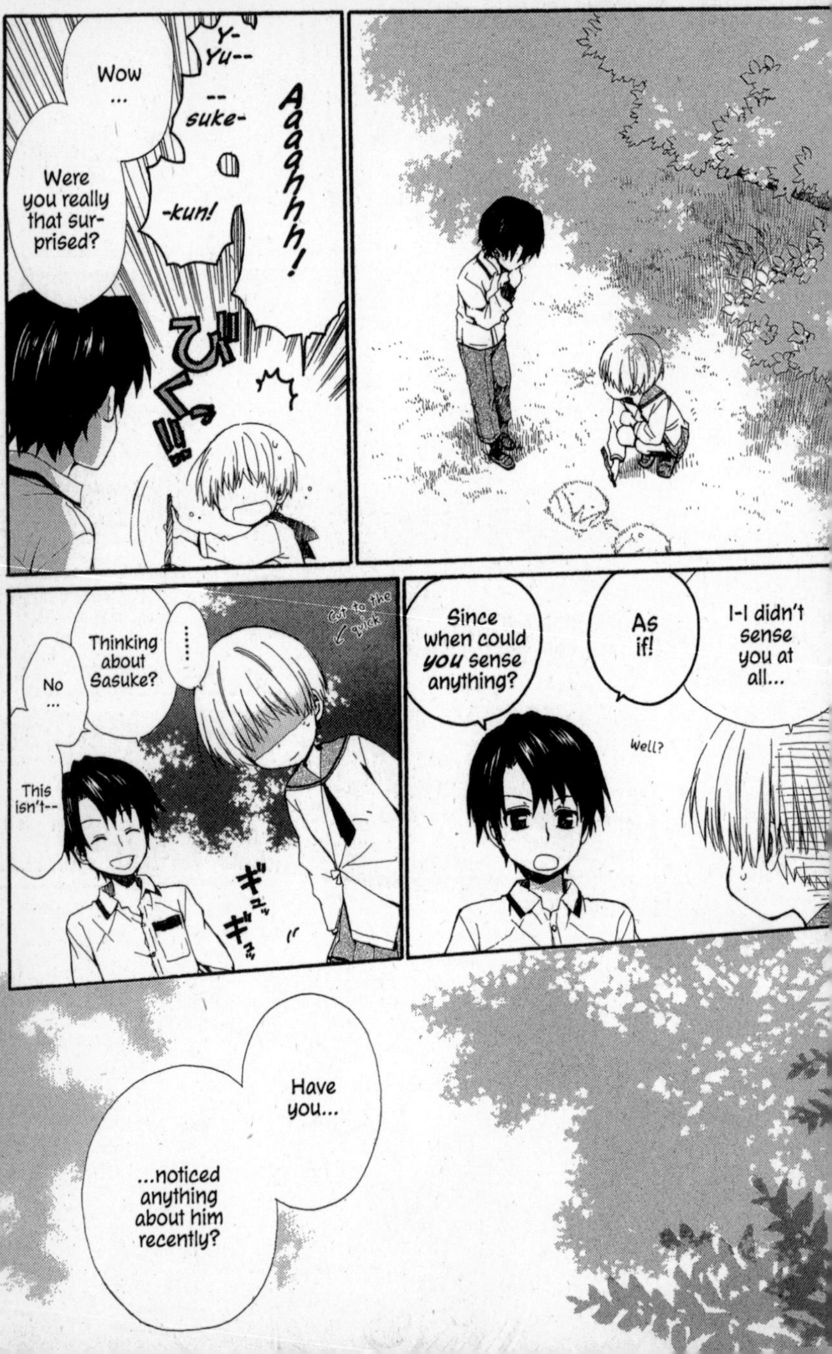
Aaaahhh!
Y-
Yu--
--suke-
-kun!
Wow ...
Were you really that surprised?
I-I didn't sense you at all...
As if!
Since when could *you* sense anything?
Well?
Cut to the quick
......
Thinking about Sasuke?
No ...
This isn't--
Have you...
...noticed anything about him recently?

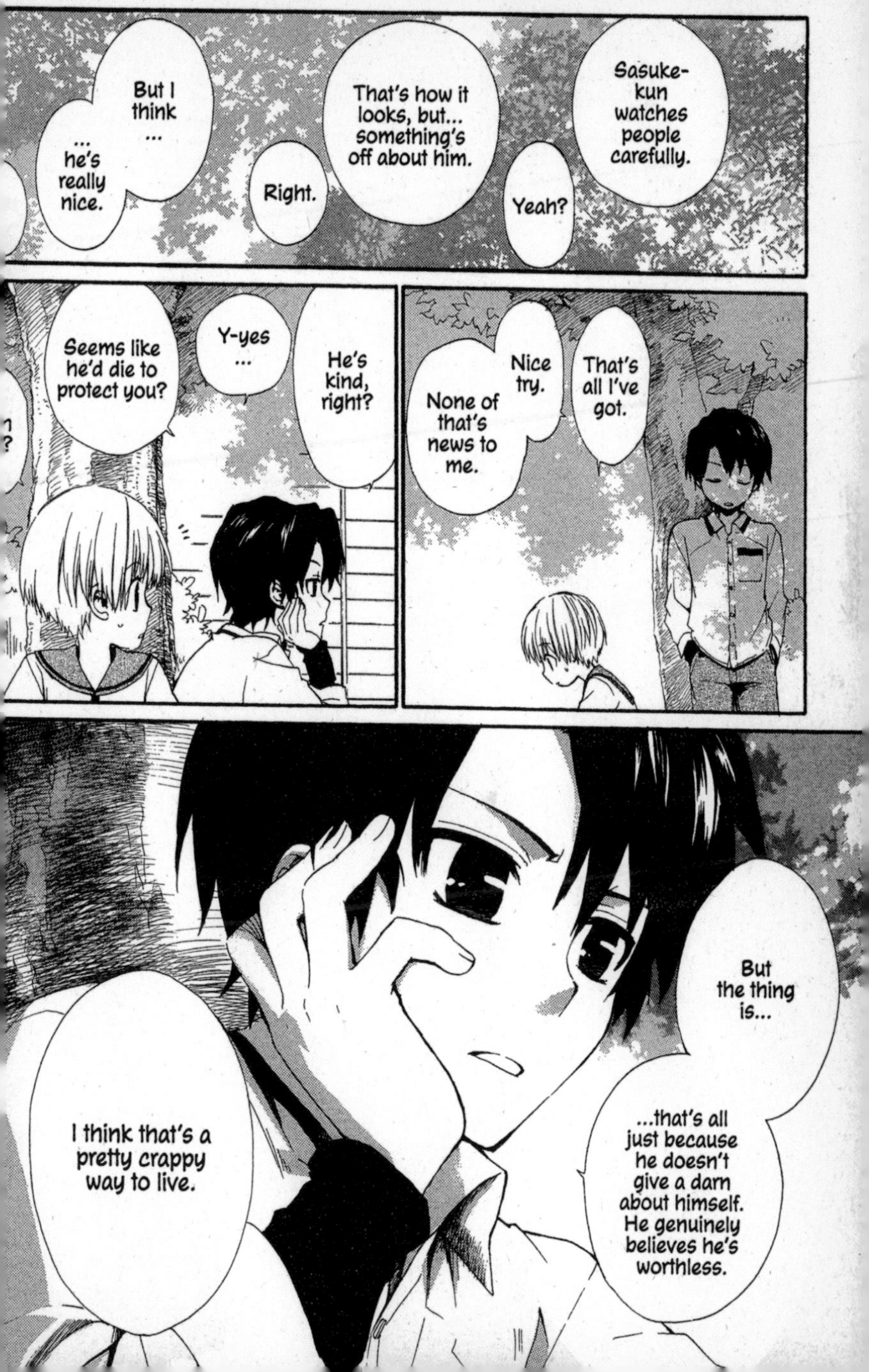
Sasuke-kun watches people carefully.
Yeah?
That's how it looks, but... something's off about him.
Right.
But I think ...
... he's really nice.
That's all I've got.
Nice try.
None of that's news to me.
He's kind, right?
Y-yes ...
Seems like he'd die to protect you?
But the thing is...
...that's all just because he doesn't give a darn about himself. He genuinely believes he's worthless.
I think that's a pretty crappy way to live.

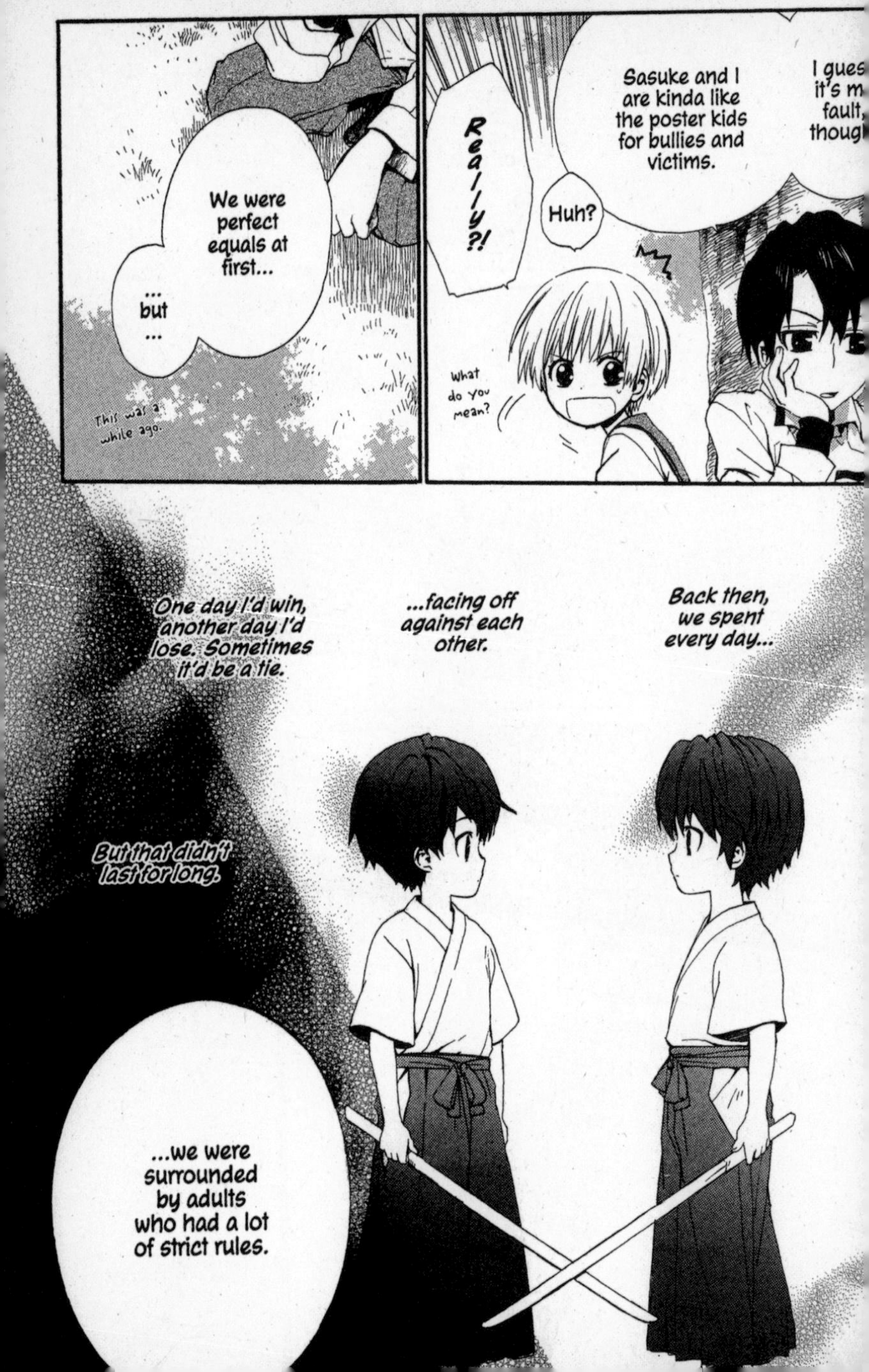
Sasuke and I are kinda like the poster kids for bullies and victims.
I gues it's m fault, thoug
Huh?
Really?!
What do you mean?
We were perfect equals at first...
...but...
This was a while ago.
Back then, we spent every day...
...facing off against each other.
One day I'd win, another day I'd lose. Sometimes it'd be a tie.
But that didn't last for long.
...we were surrounded by adults who had a lot of strict rules.

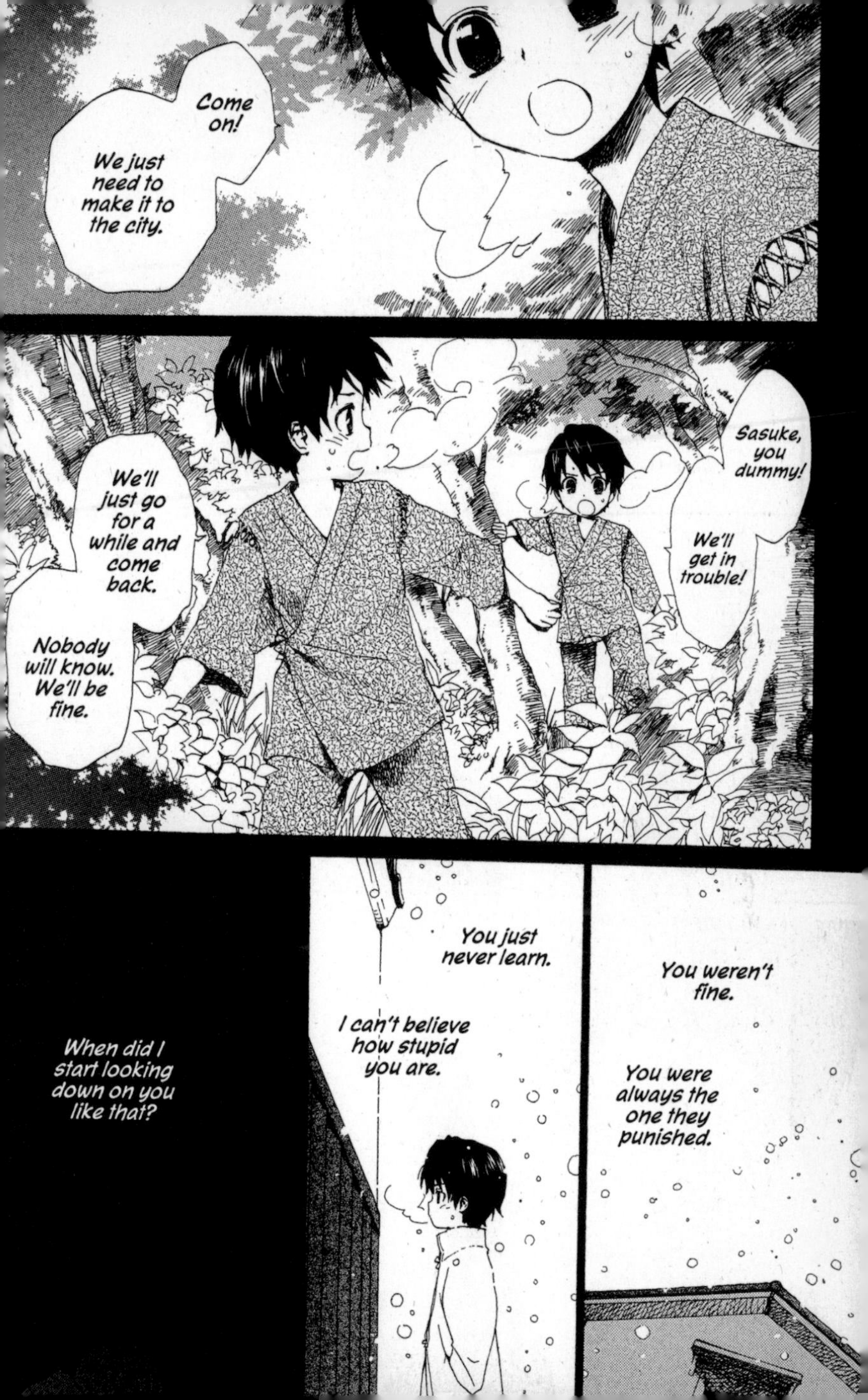
Come on!
We just need to make it to the city.
Sasuke, you dummy!
We'll get in trouble!
We'll just go for a while and come back.
Nobody will know. We'll be fine.
You weren't fine.
You were always the one they punished.
You just never learn.
I can't believe how stupid you are.
When did I start looking down on you like that?

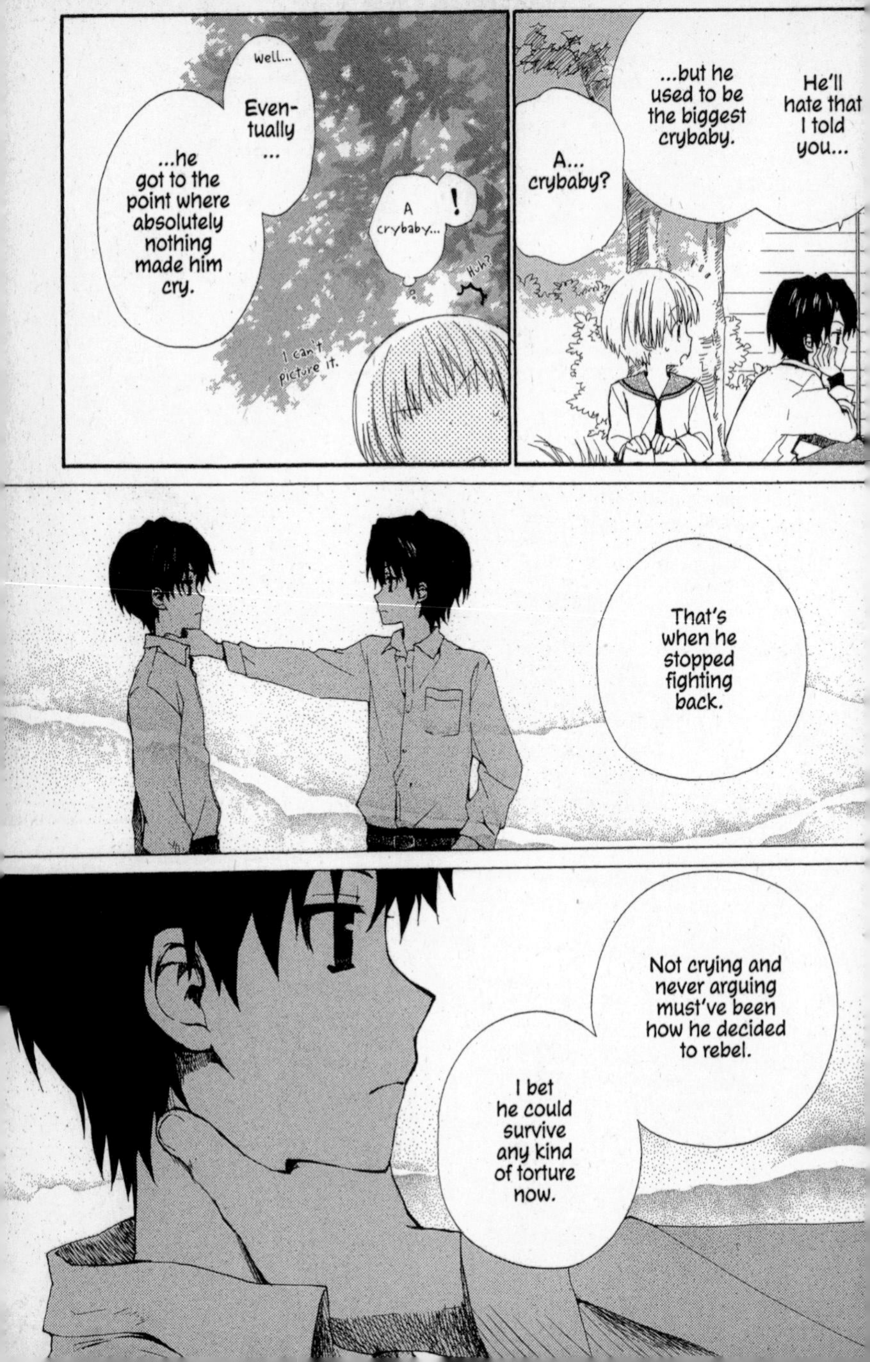
He'll hate that I told you...
...but he used to be the biggest crybaby.
A... crybaby?
A crybaby...
!
Huh?
Well...
Eventually...
...he got to the point where absolutely nothing made him cry.
I can't picture it.
That's when he stopped fighting back.
Not crying and never arguing must've been how he decided to rebel.
I bet he could survive any kind of torture now.

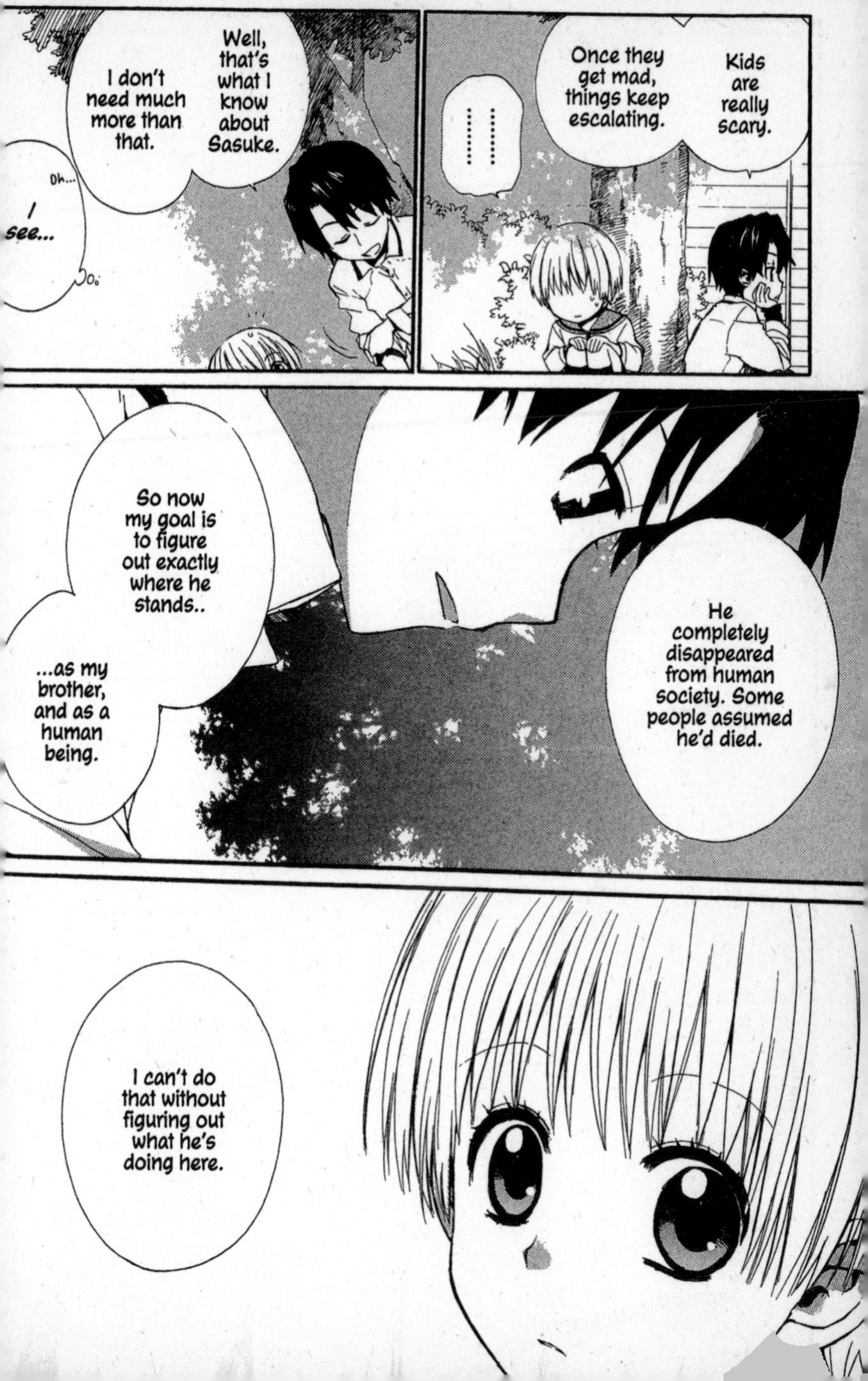
Kids are really scary.
Once they get mad, things keep escalating.
......
Well, that's what I know about Sasuke.
I don't need much more than that.
Oh... I see...
He completely disappeared from human society. Some people assumed he'd died.
So now my goal is to figure out exactly where he stands..
...as my brother, and as a human being.
I can't do that without figuring out what he's doing here.

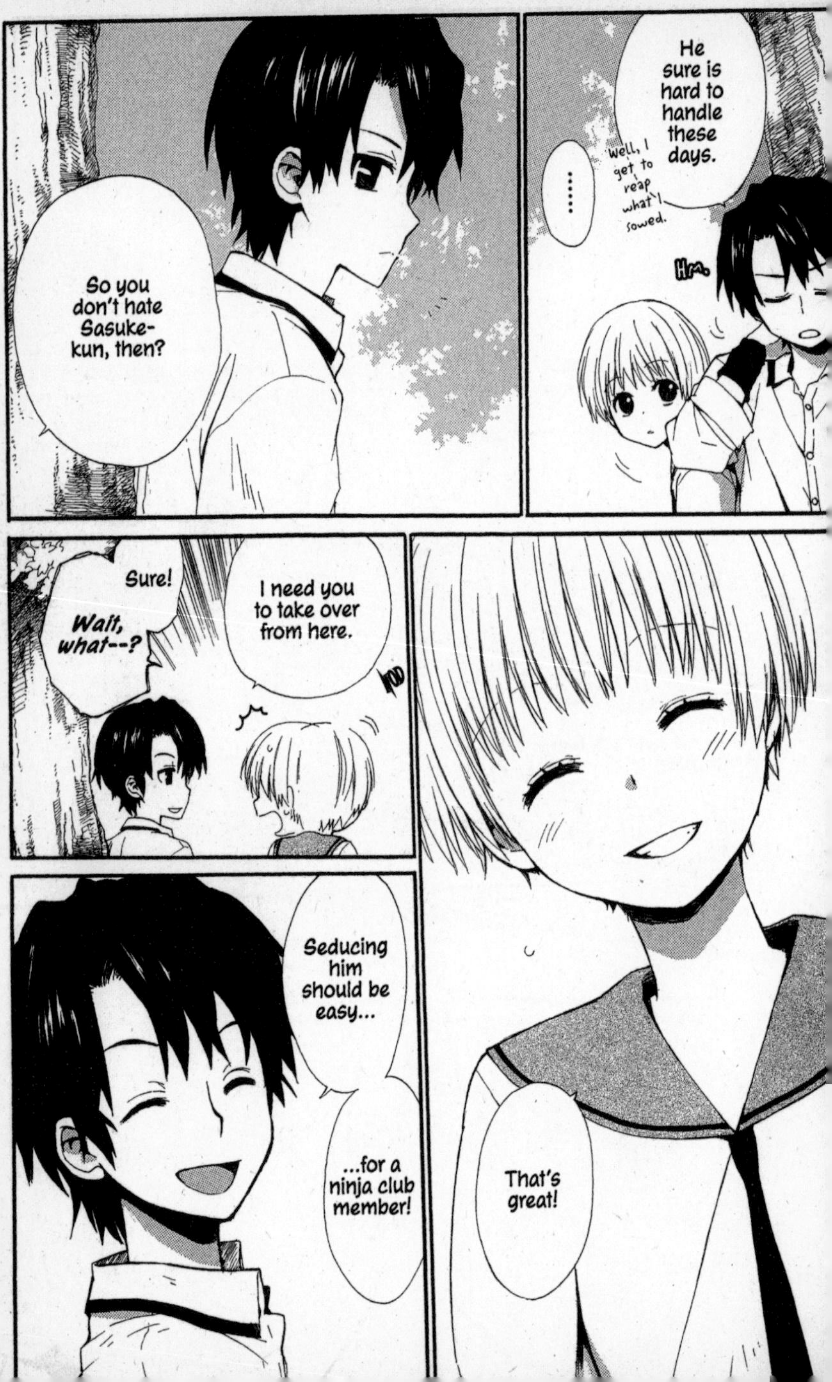
He sure is hard to handle these days.
well, I get to reap what I sowed.
......
Hm.
So you don't hate Sasuke-kun, then?
That's great!
I need you to take over from here.
NOD
Sure!
Wait, what--?
Seducing him should be easy...
...for a ninja club member!

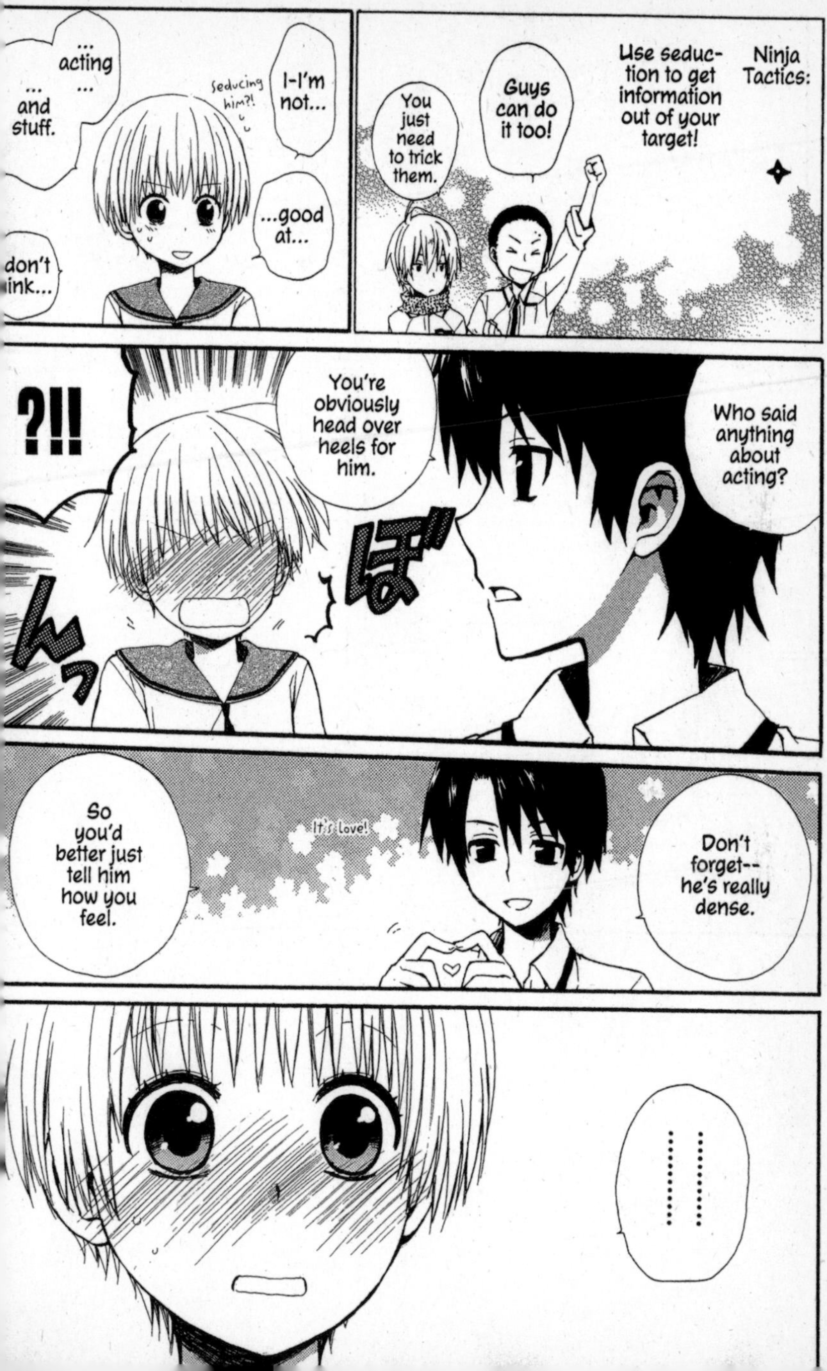
Ninja Tactics:
Use seduction to get information out of your target!
Guys can do it too!
You just need to trick them.
I-I'm not...
Seducing him?!
...good at...
... acting ...
... and stuff.
don't ink...
Who said anything about acting?
You're obviously head over heels for him.
?!!
ぼ
ん
Don't forget-- he's really dense.
It's love!
So you'd better just tell him how you feel.
......

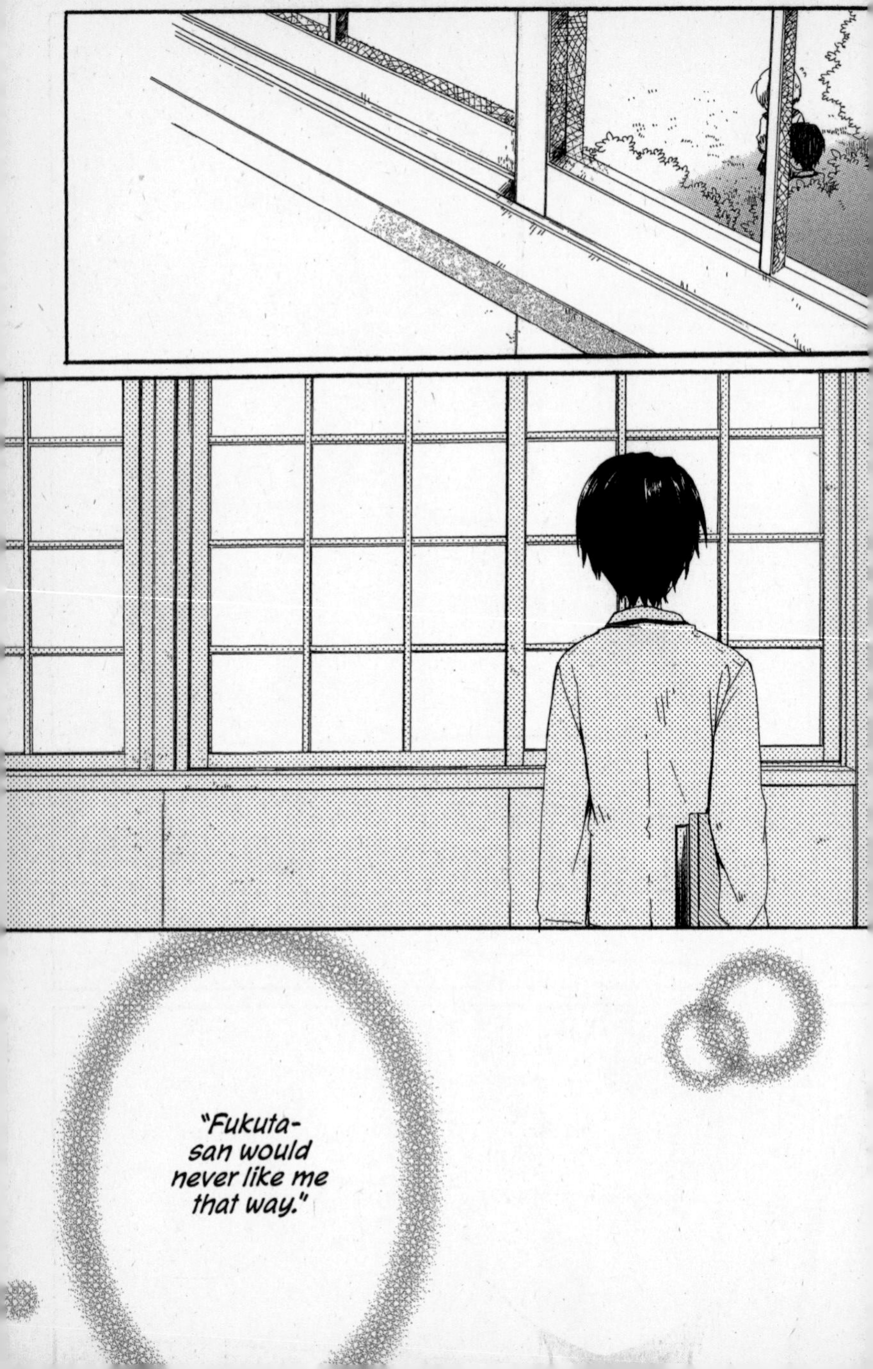
"Fukuta-san would never like me that way."

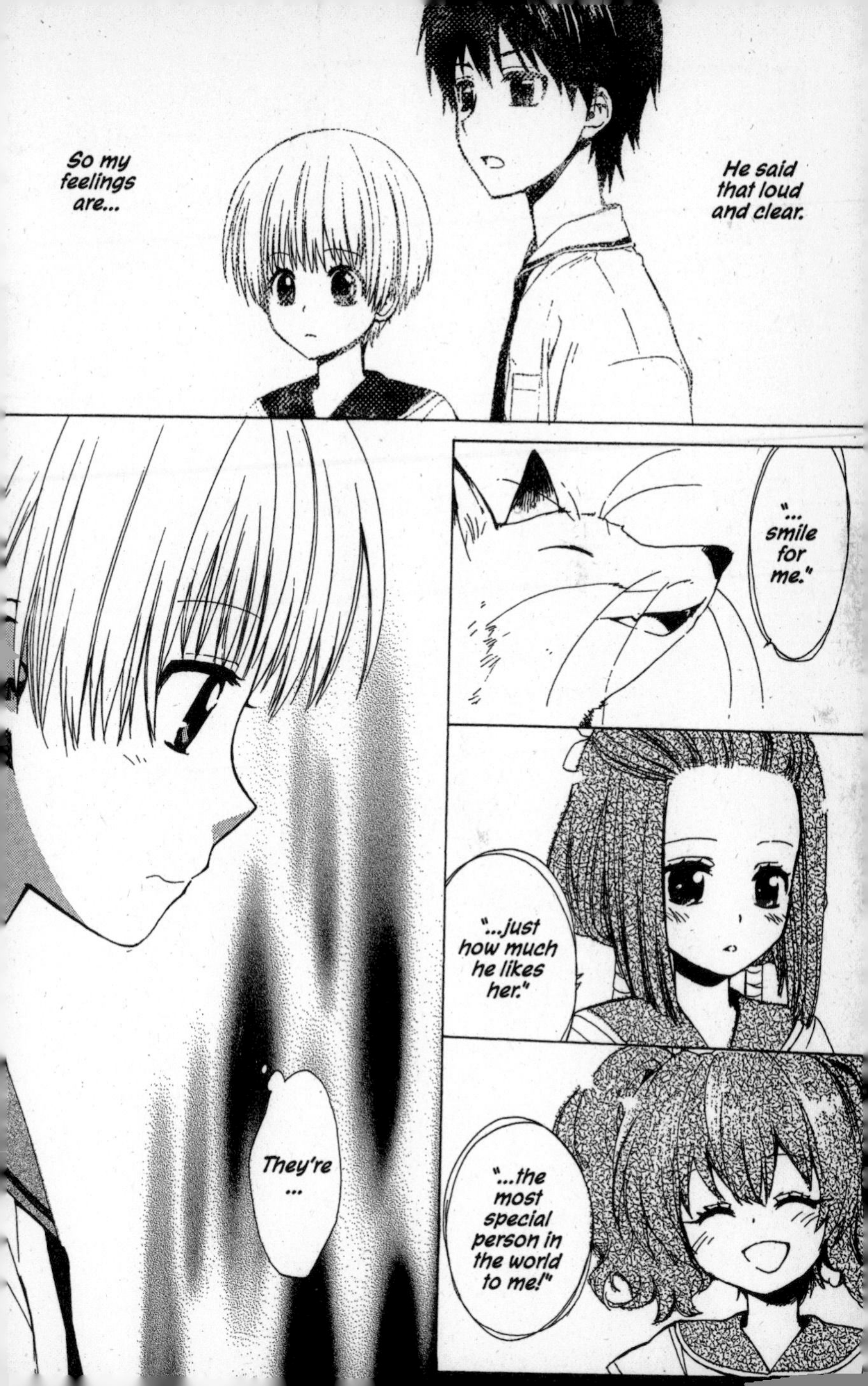
He said that loud and clear.
So my feelings are...
"...smile for me."
"...just how much he likes her."
"...the most special person in the world to me!"
They're ...

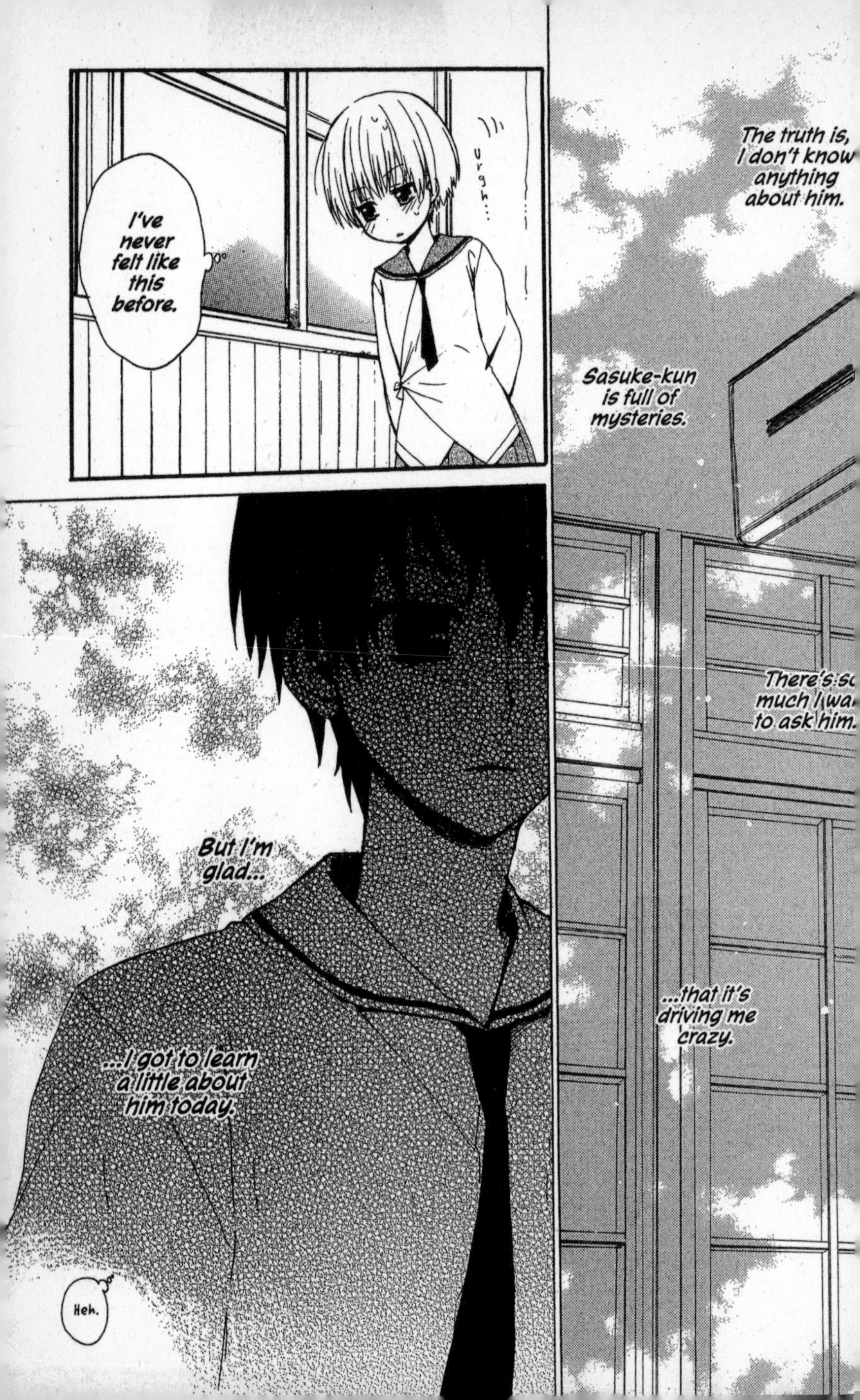
The truth is, I don't know anything about him.
Sasuke-kun is full of mysteries.
There's s much I wa to ask him.
...that it's driving me crazy.
Urgh...
I've never felt like this before.
But I'm glad...
...I got to learn a little about him today.
Heh.

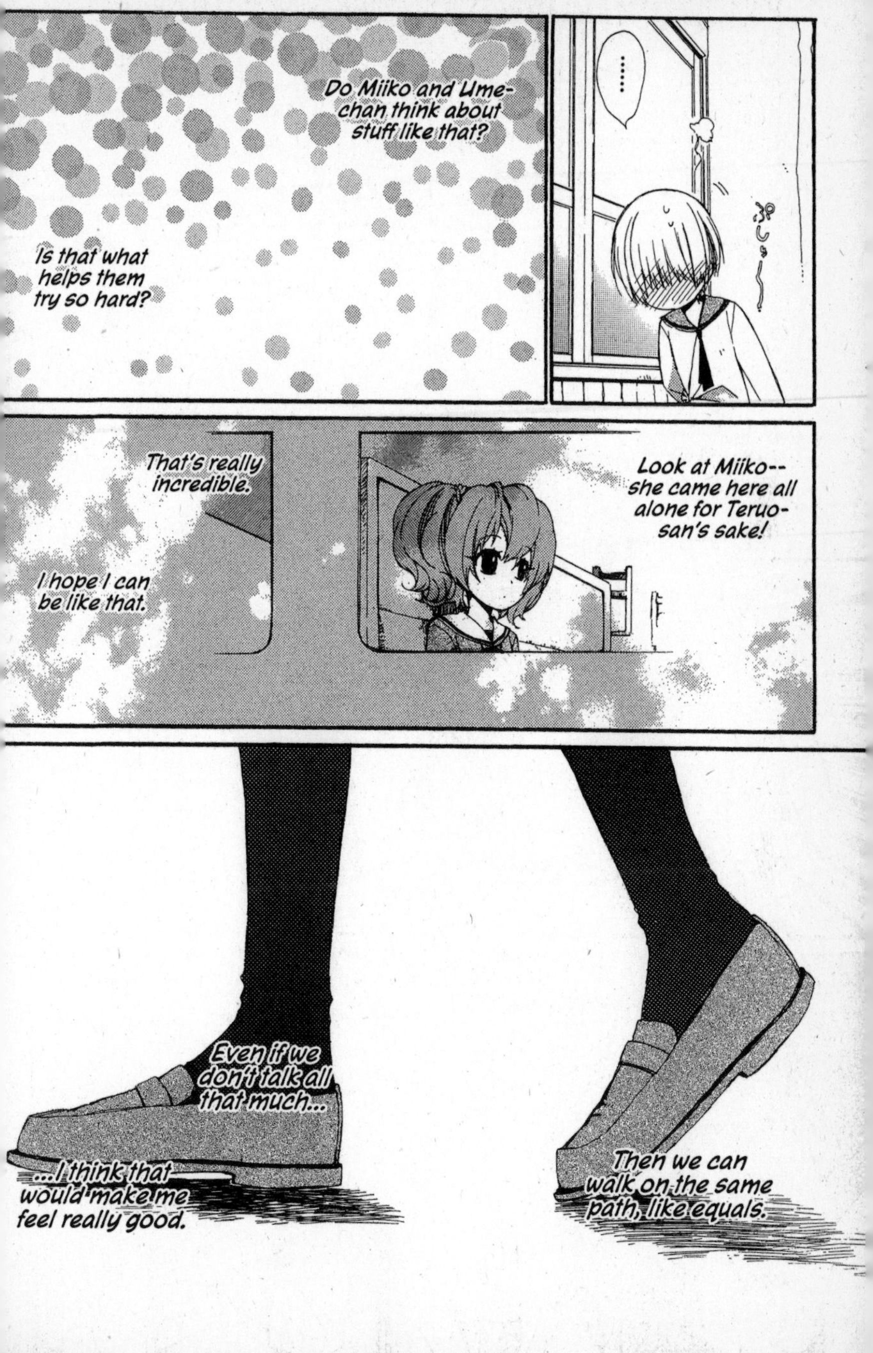
......
ぷしゅ～
Do Miiko and Ume-chan think about stuff like that?
Is that what helps them try so hard?
Look at Miiko--she came here all alone for Teruo-san's sake!
That's really incredible.
I hope I can be like that.
Even if we don't talk all that much...
Then we can walk on the same path, like equals.
...I think that would make me feel really good.

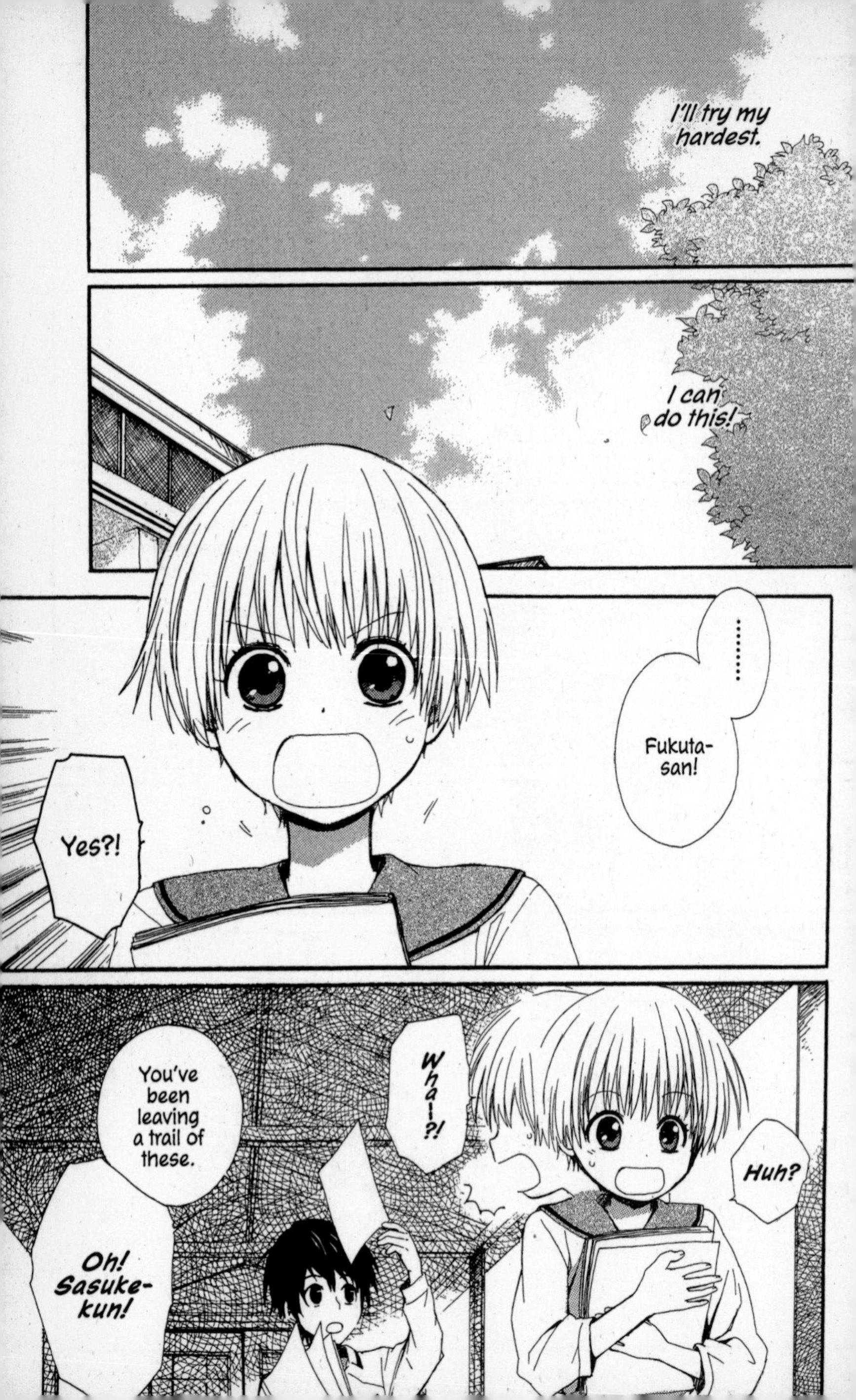
I'll try my hardest.
I can do this!
......
Fukuta-san!
Yes?!
Huh?
Wha-?!
You've been leaving a trail of these.
Oh! Sasuke-kun!

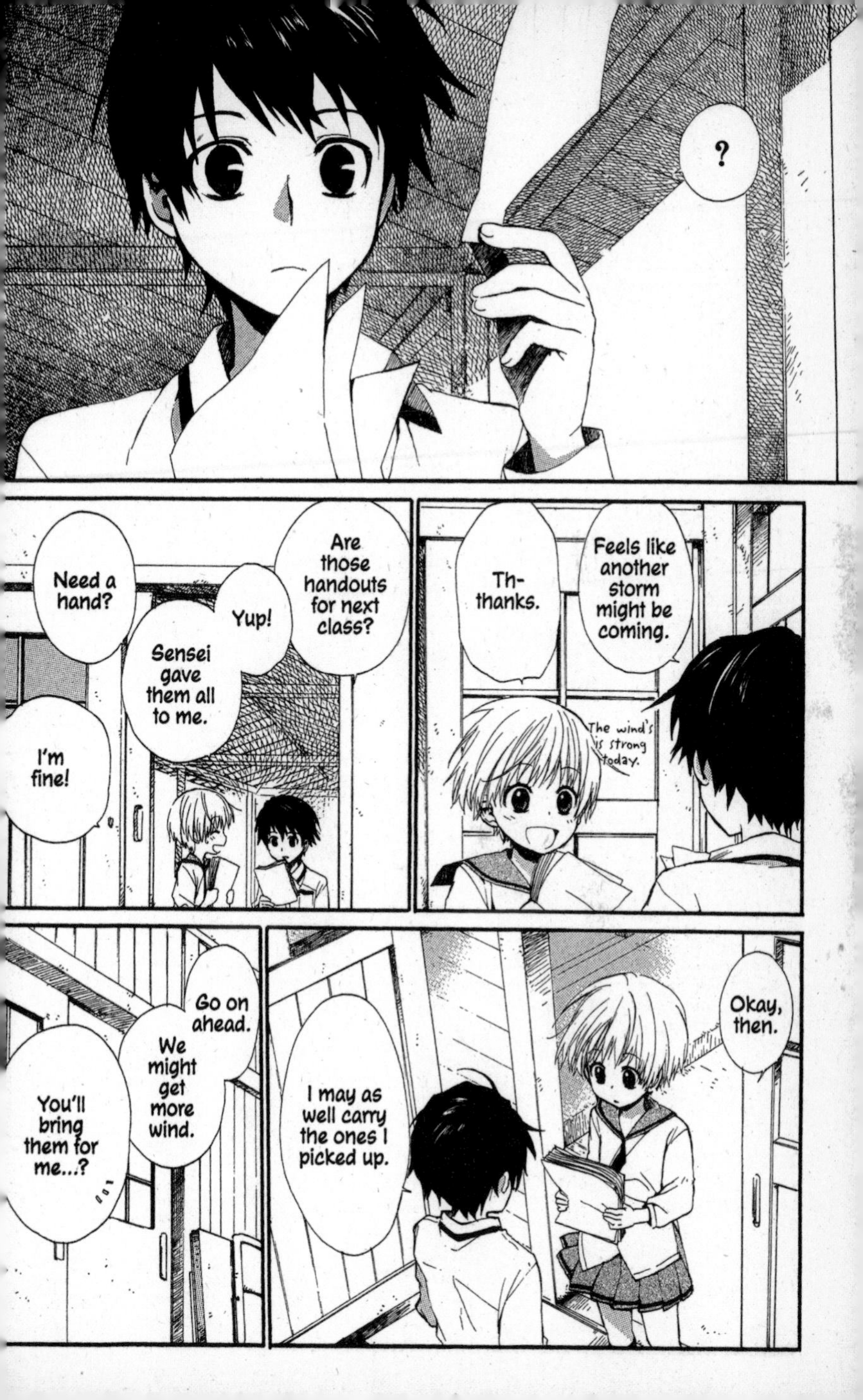
?
Feels like another storm might be coming.
Th- thanks.
The wind's is strong today.
Are those handouts for next class?
Yup!
Need a hand?
Sensei gave them all to me.
I'm fine!
Okay, then.
I may as well carry the ones I picked up.
Go on ahead.
We might get more wind.
You'll bring them for me...?

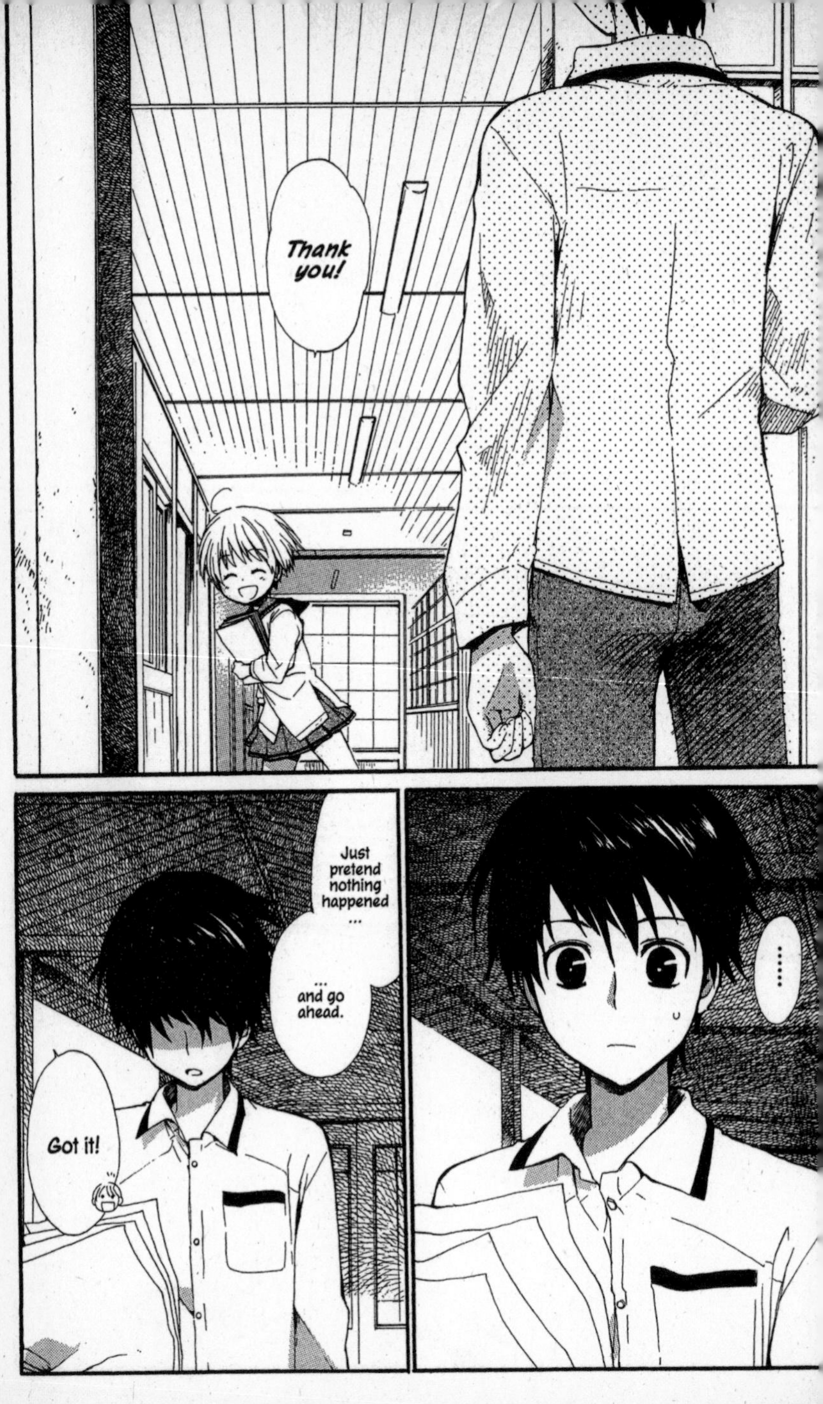
Thank you!
......
Just pretend nothing happened ...
... and go ahead.
Got it!

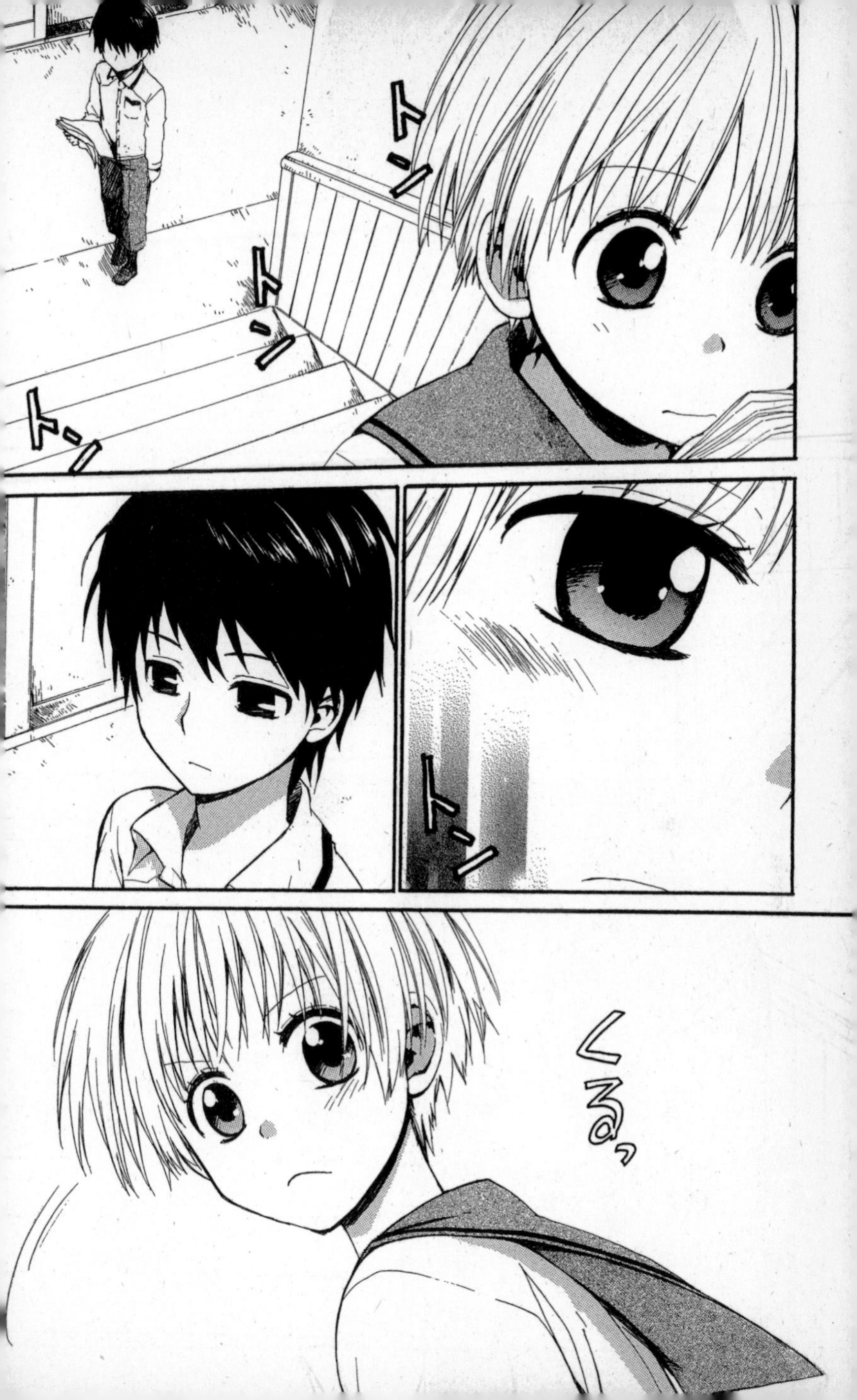
トーン
トーン
トーン
トーン
くるっ

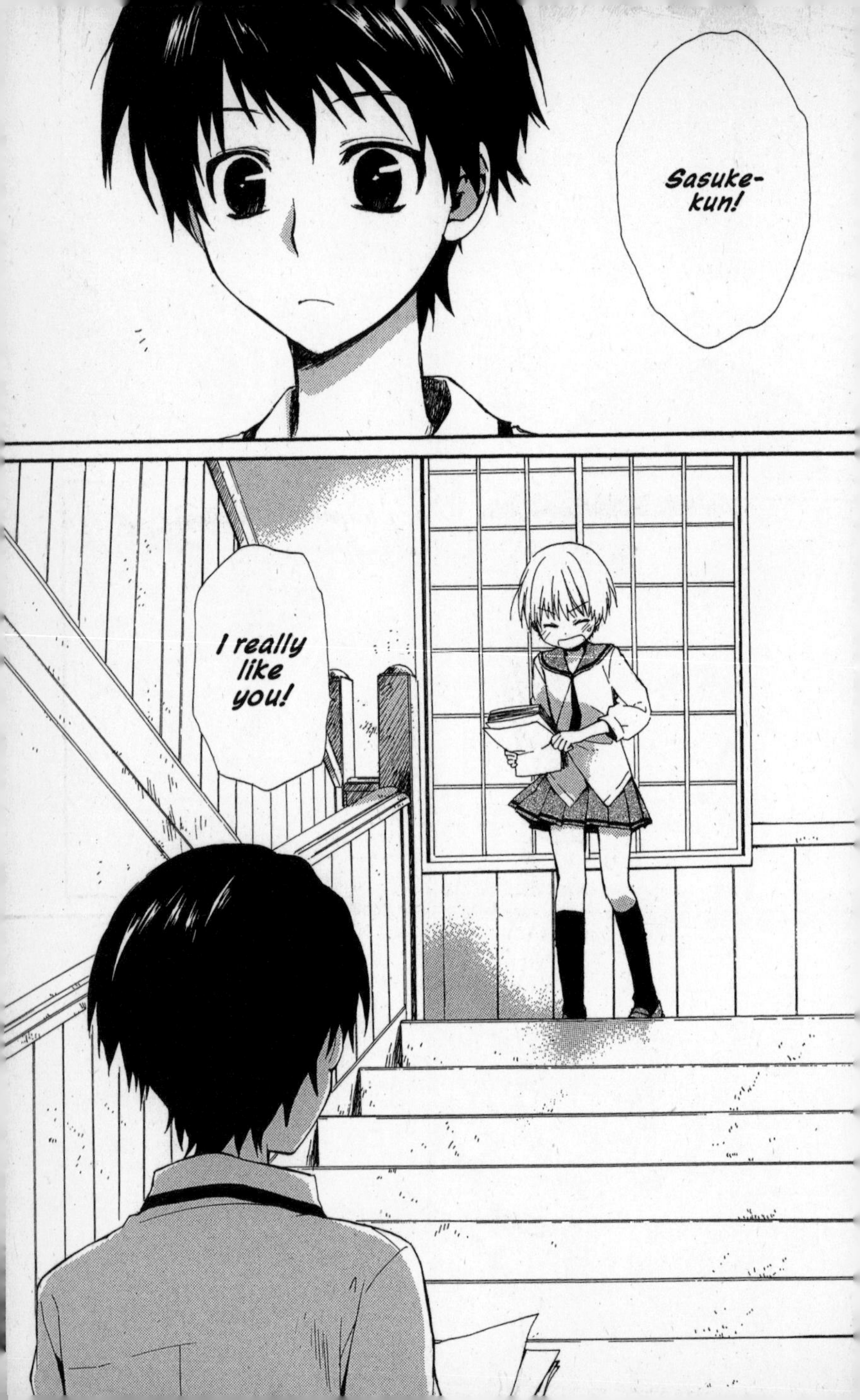
Sasuke-kun!
I really like you!

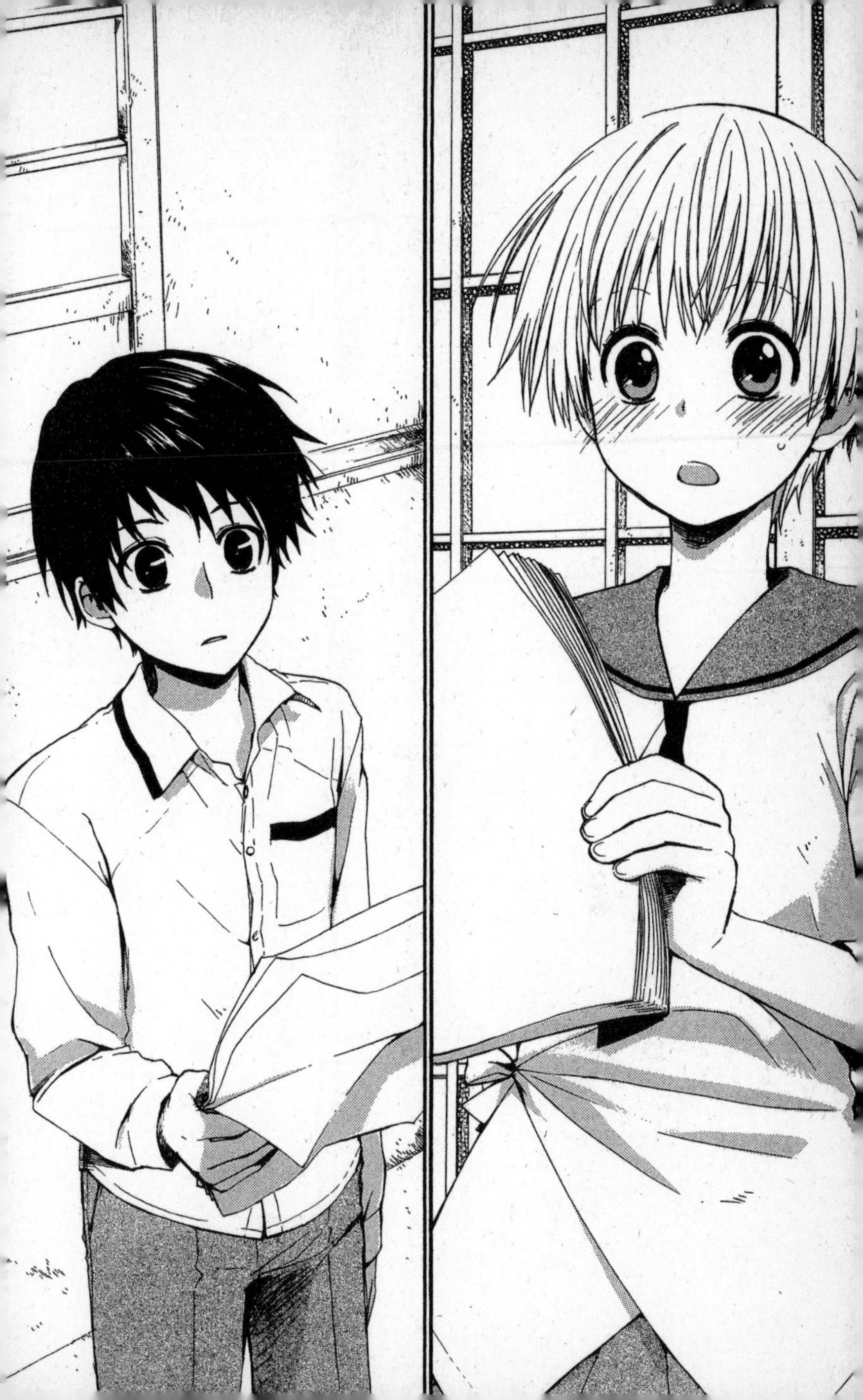

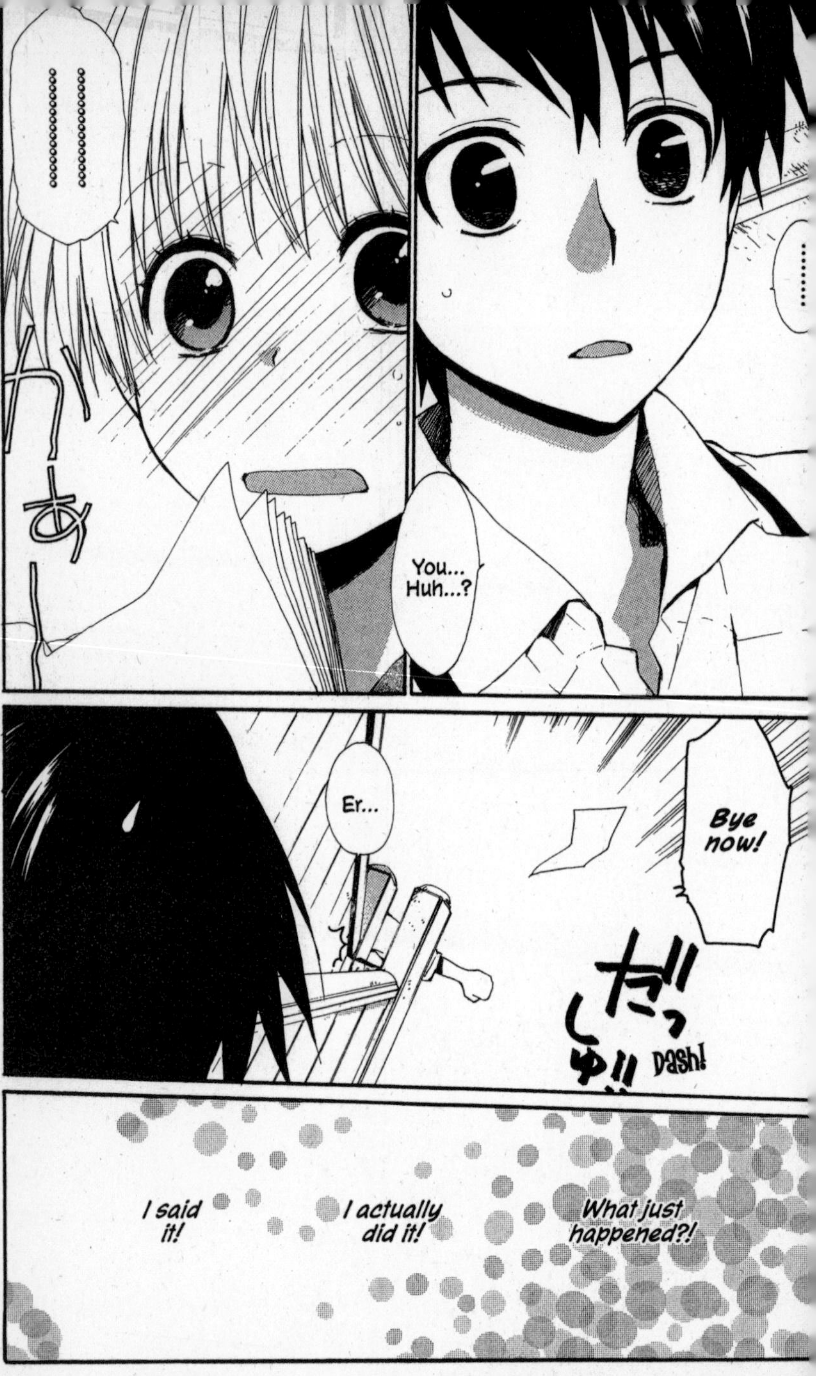

You...
Huh...?
......
Bye now!
だっしゅ!!
DASH!
Er...
What just happened?!
I actually did it!
I said it!

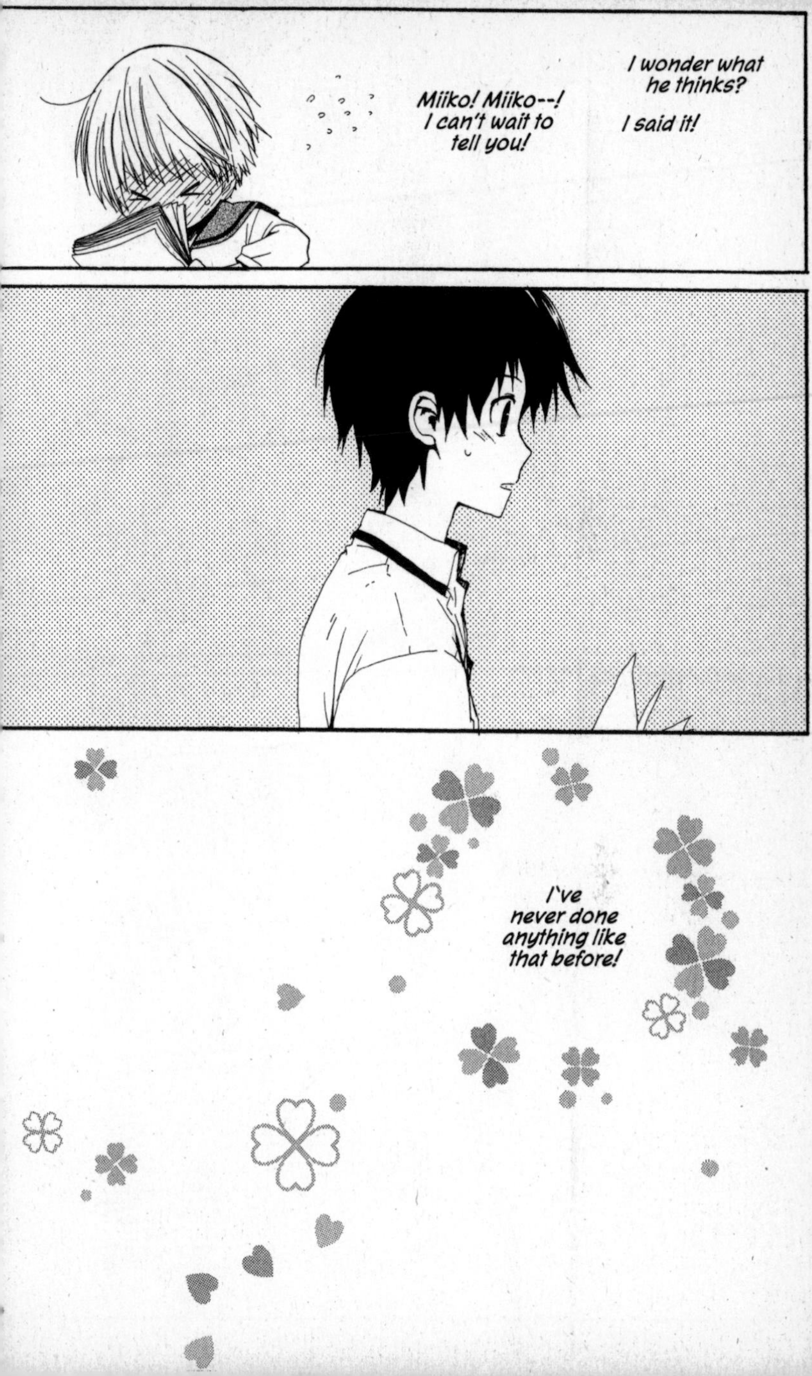
I wonder what he thinks?
I said it!
Miiko! Miiko--! I can't wait to tell you!
I've never done anything like that before!

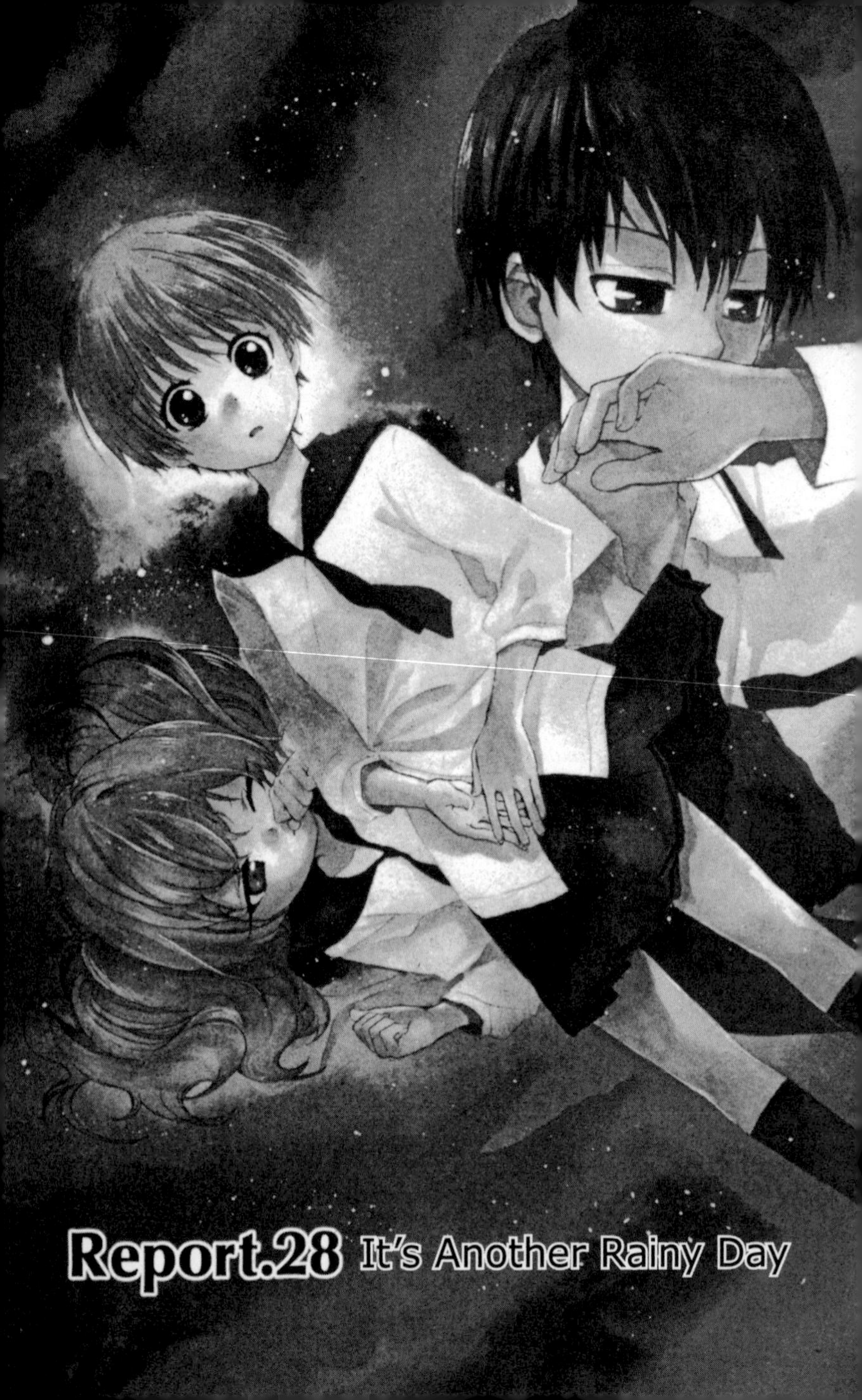
Report.28 It's Another Rainy Day

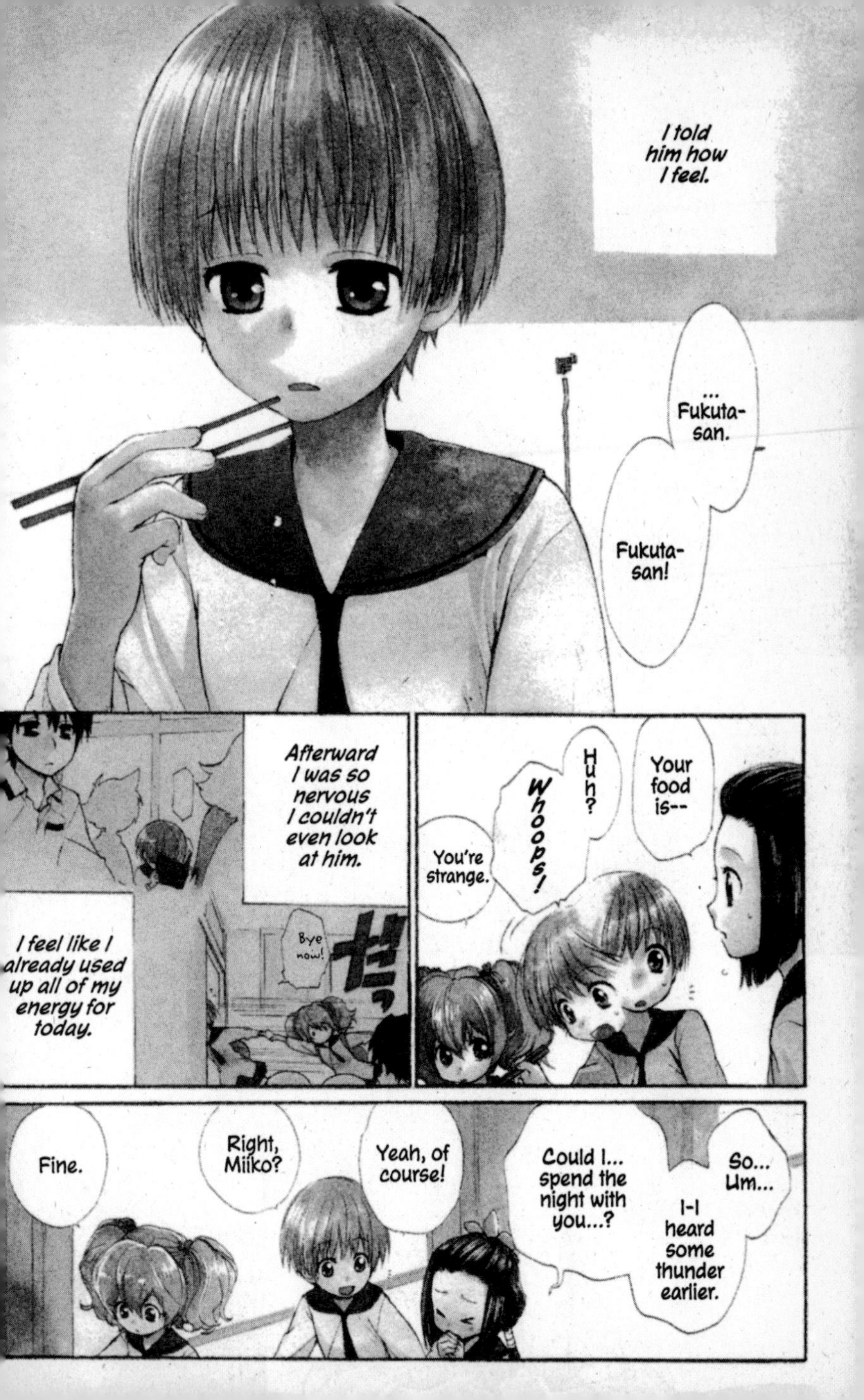
I told him how I feel.
... Fukuta-san.
Fukuta-san!
Your food is--
Huh?
Whoops!
You're strange.
Afterward I was so nervous I couldn't even look at him.
Bye now!
I feel like I already used up all of my energy for today.
So... Um...
I-I heard some thunder earlier.
Could I... spend the night with you...?
Yeah, of course!
Right, Miiko?
Fine.

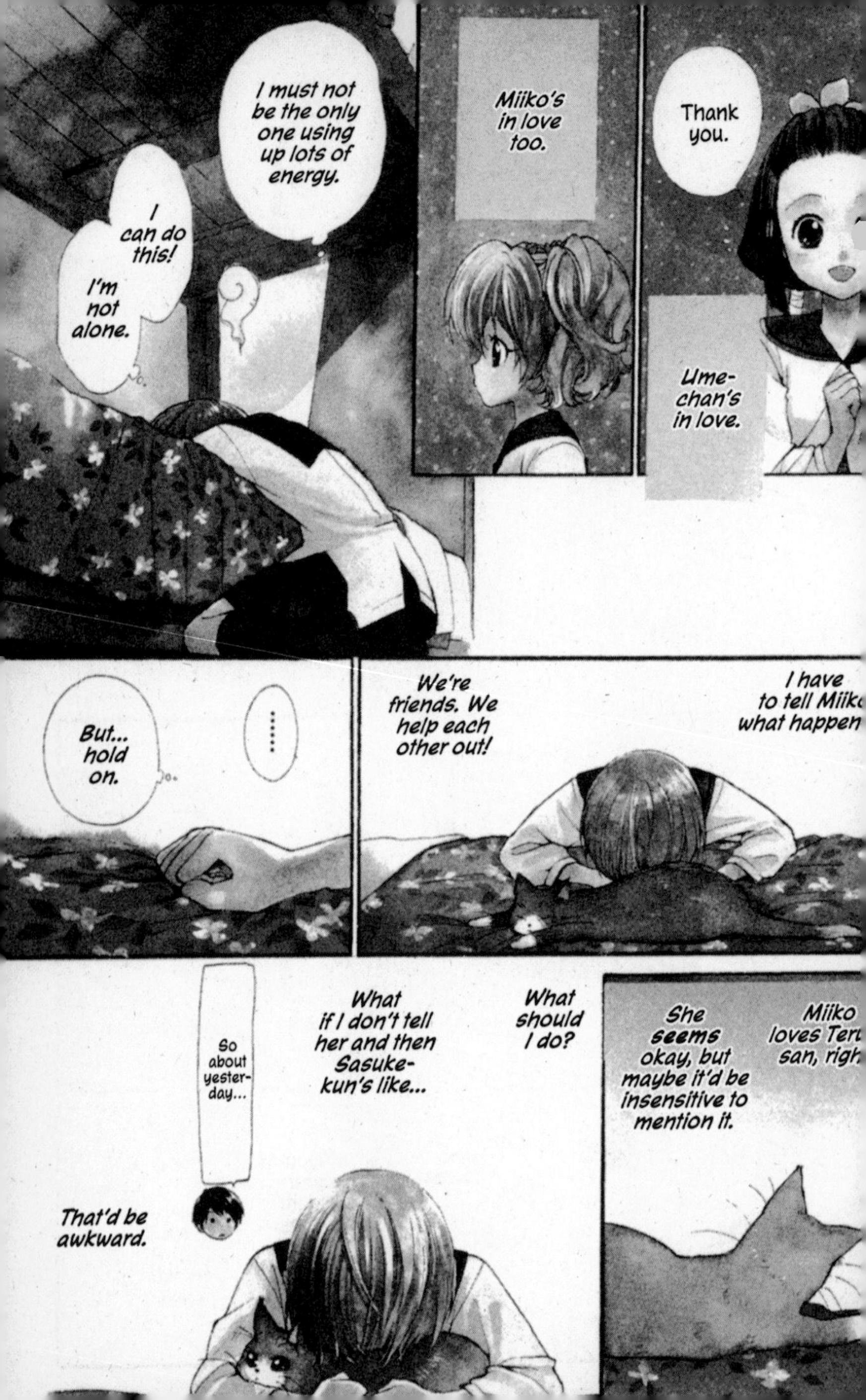
Thank you.
Ume-chan's in love.
Miiko's in love too.
I must not be the only one using up lots of energy.
I can do this!
I'm not alone.
I have to tell Miik
what happen
We're friends. We help each other out!
......
But... hold on.
Miiko loves Ter
san, righ
She seems okay, but maybe it'd be insensitive to mention it.
What should I do?
What if I don't tell her and then Sasuke-kun's like...
So about yester-day...
That'd be awkward.

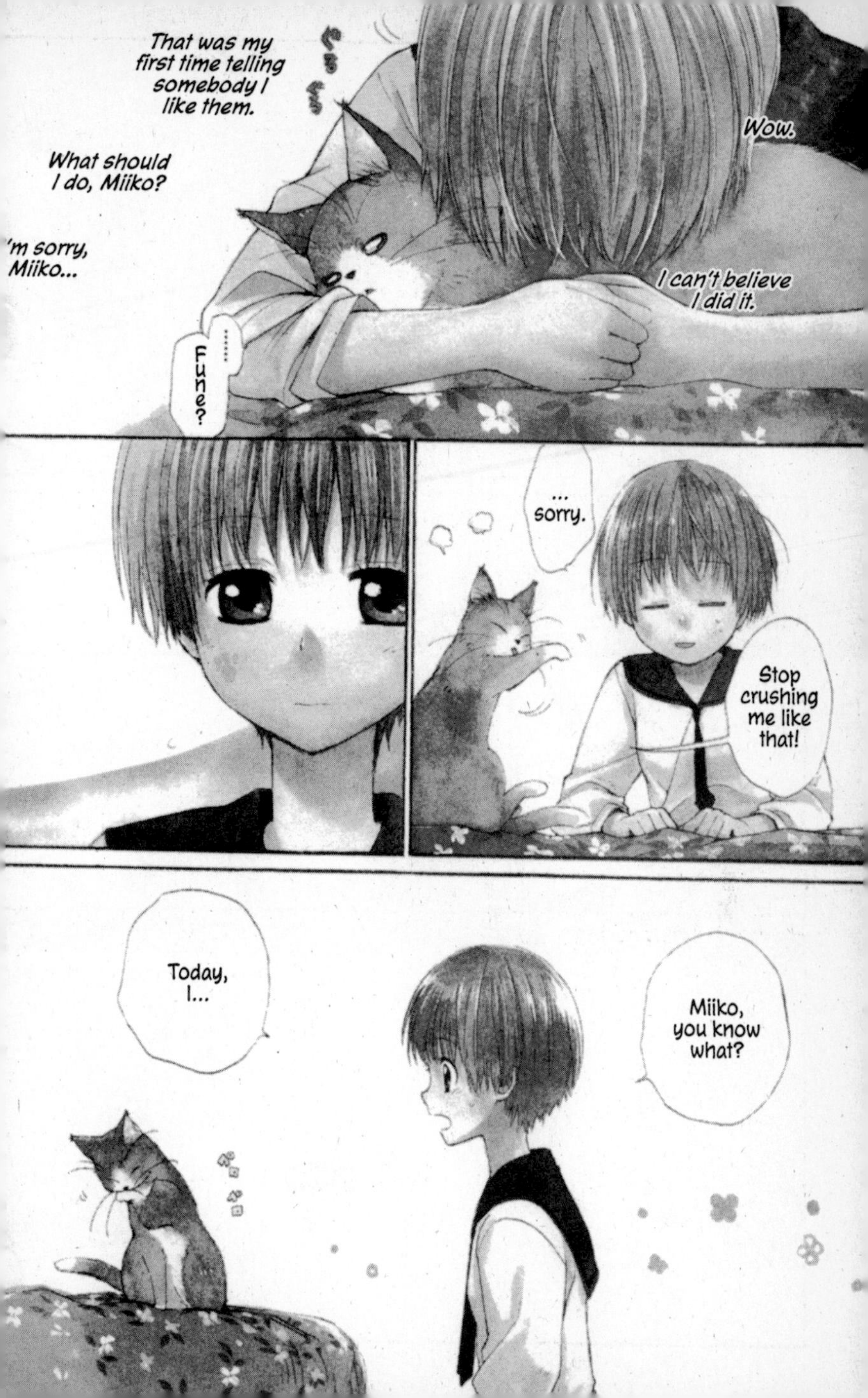
Wow.
I can't believe I did it.
That was my first time telling somebody I like them.
What should I do, Miiko?
'm sorry, Miiko...
......Fune?
... sorry.
Stop crushing me like that!
Miiko, you know what?
Today, I...

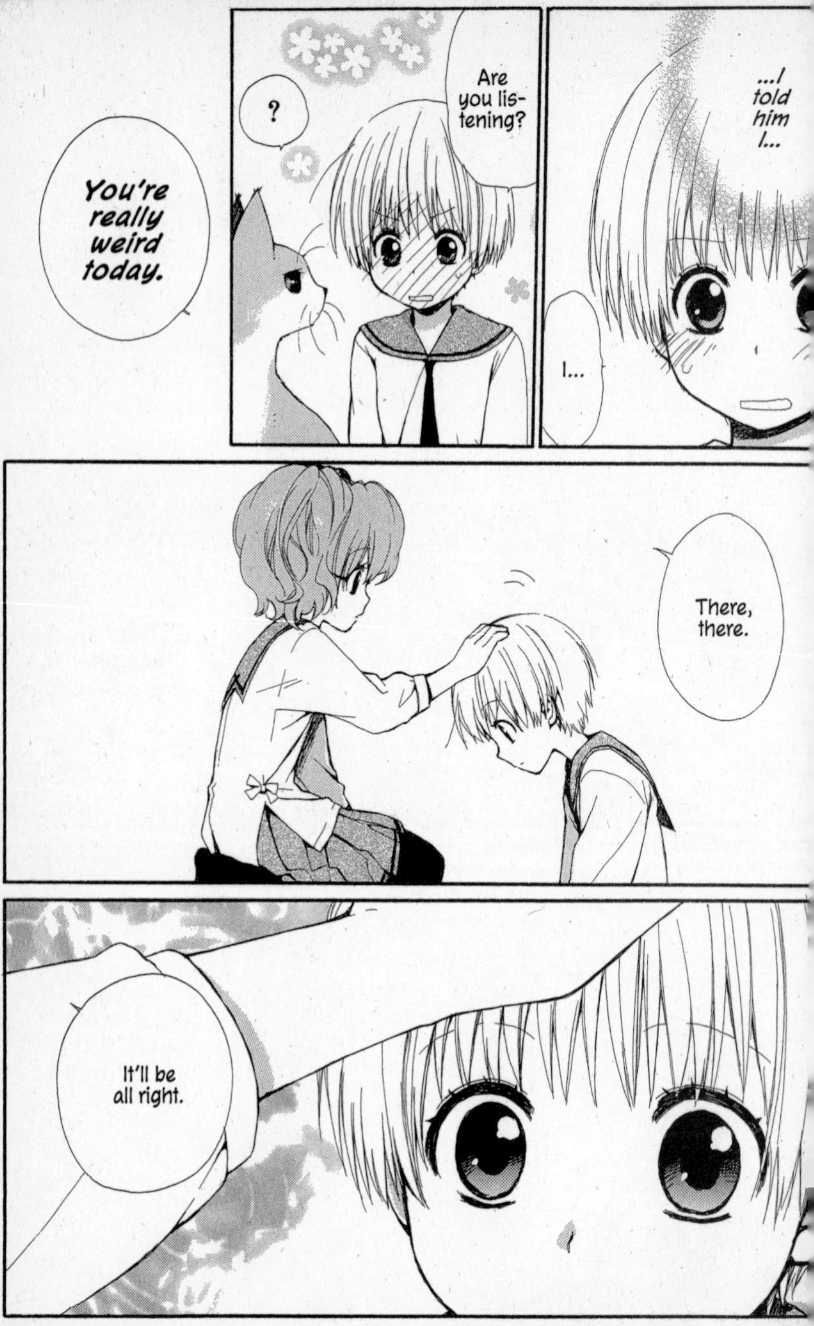
...I told him I...
I...
Are you lis-tening?
?
You're really weird today.
There, there.
It'll be all right.

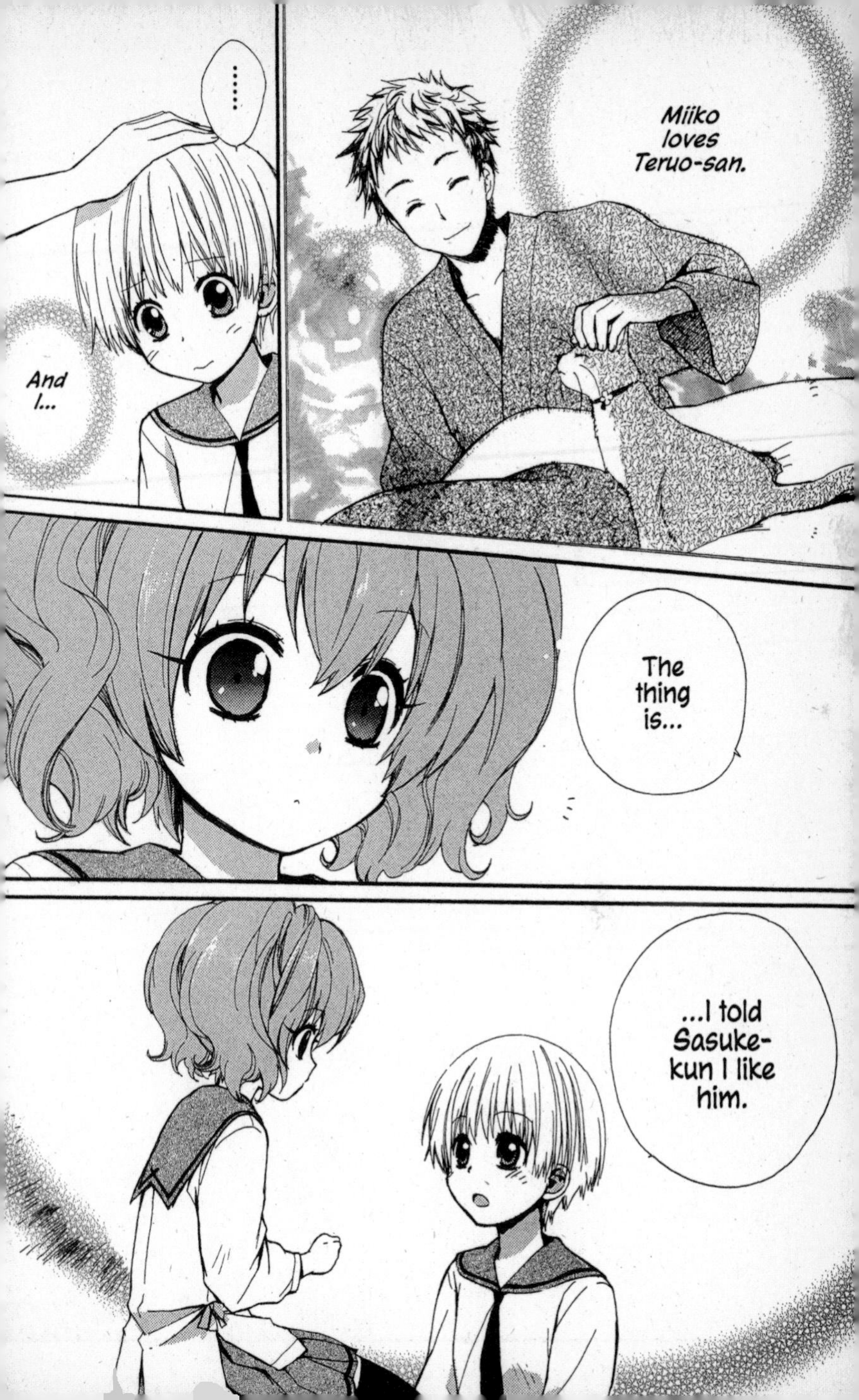
Miiko loves Teruo-san.
......
And I...
The thing is...
...I told Sasuke-kun I like him.

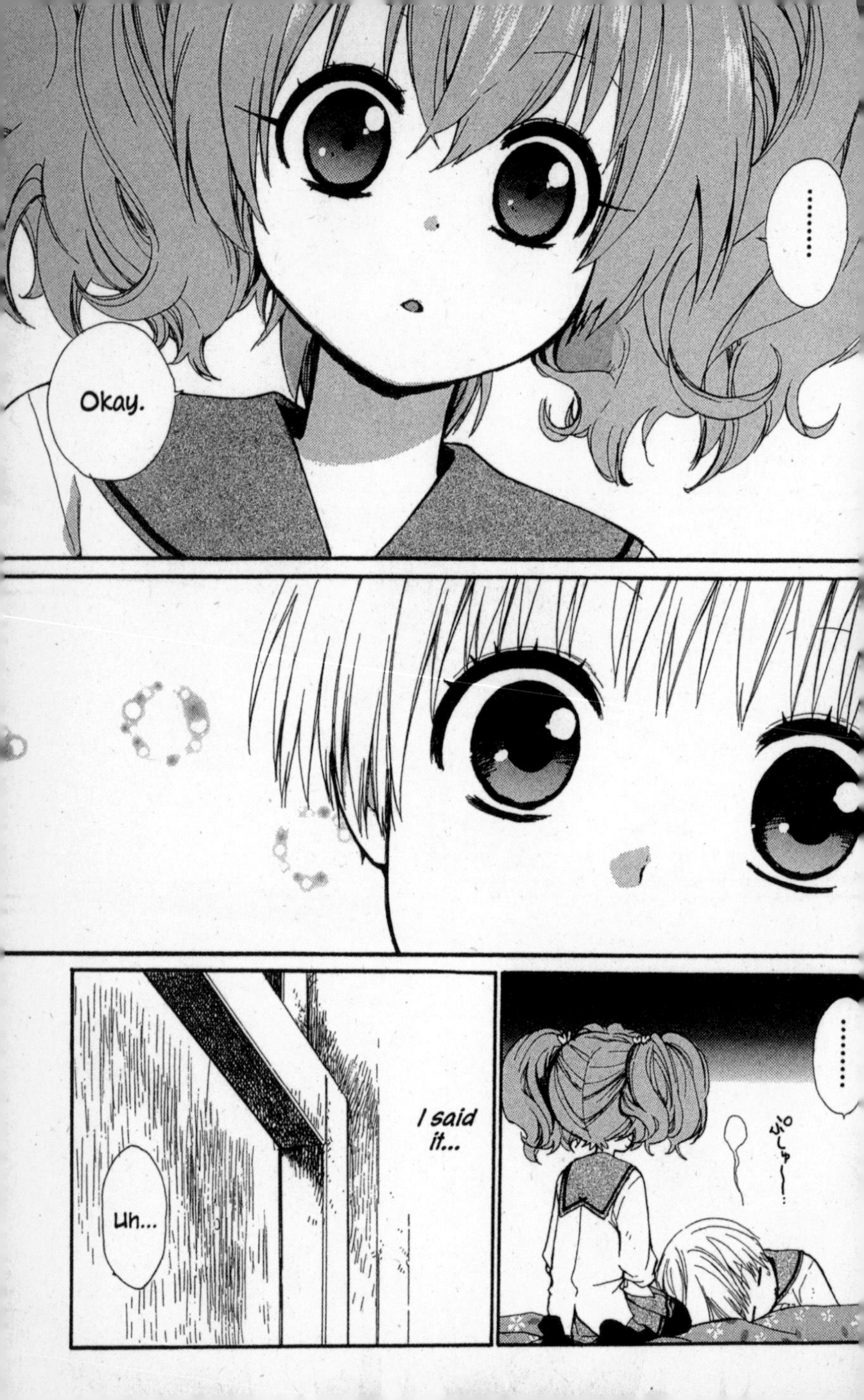
......
Okay.
......
ぷしゅ〜〜…
I said it...
Uh...

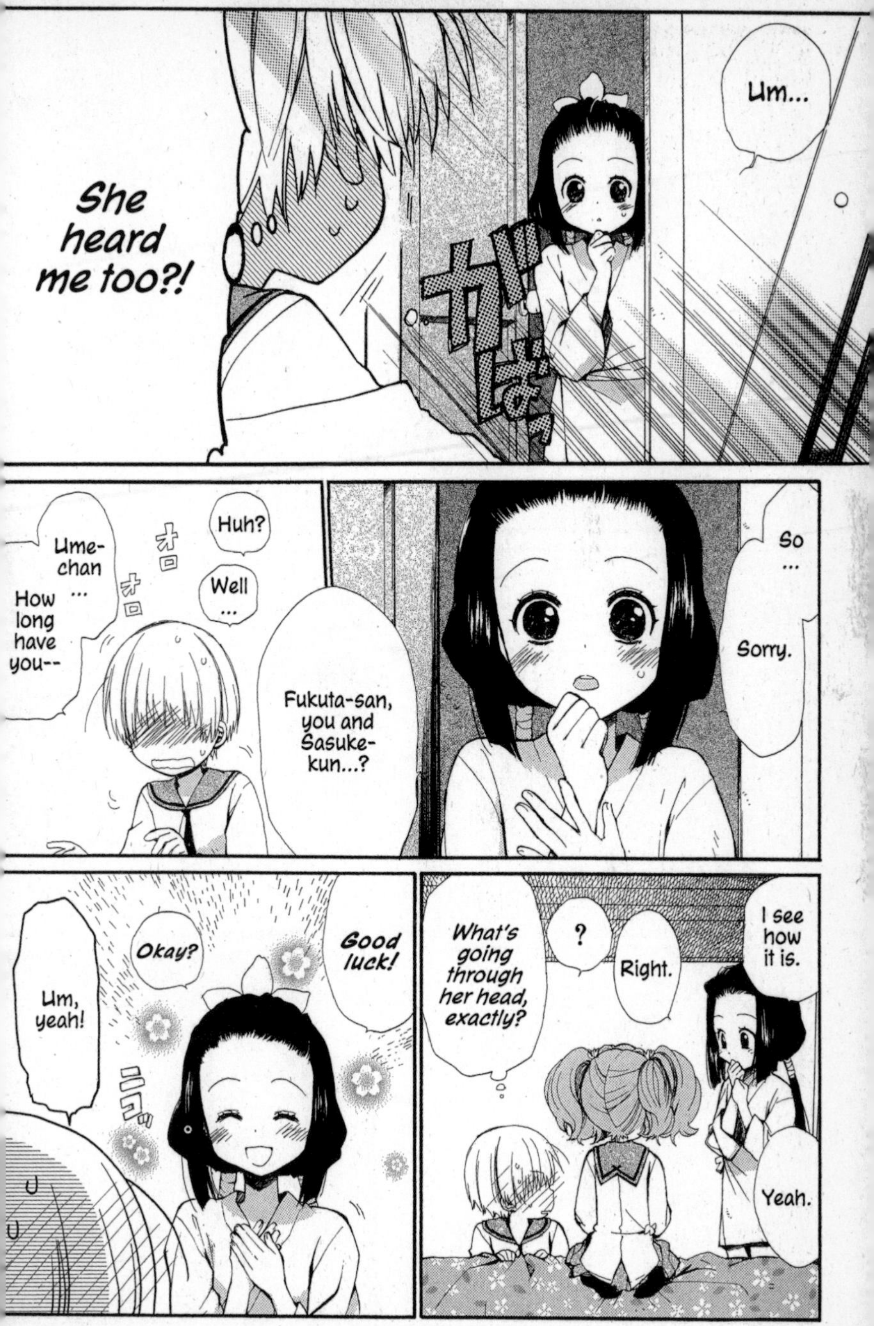
Um...
ガばっ
She heard me too?!
So ... Sorry.
Fukuta-san, you and Sasuke-kun...?
Huh?
Well ...
オロ オロ
Ume-chan ... How long have you--
I see how it is.
Right.
?
What's going through her head, exactly?
Yeah.
Good luck!
Okay?
ニコッ
Um, yeah!

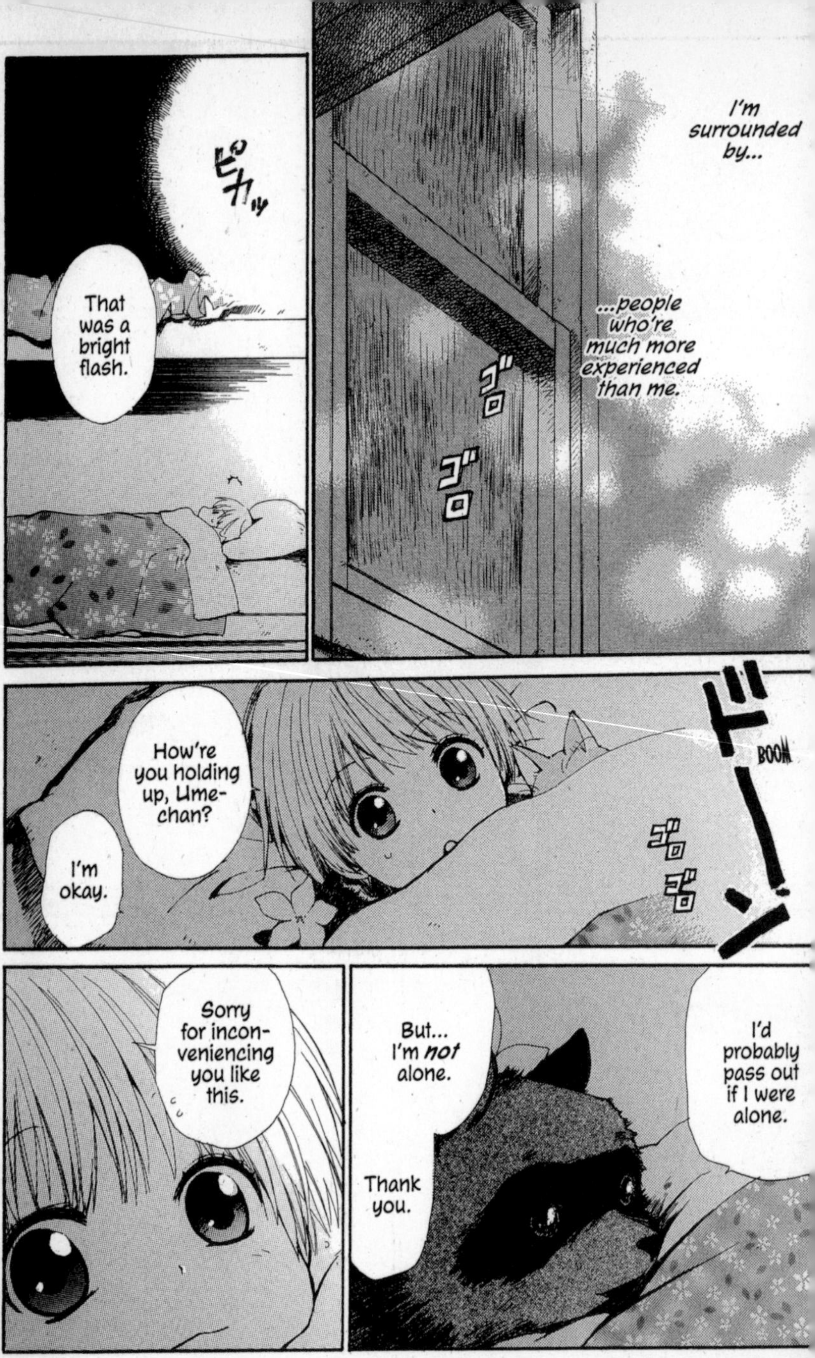
I'm surrounded by...
...people who're much more experienced than me.
ゴロ
ゴロ
ピカッ
That was a bright flash.
ドーン
BOOM
ゴロ
ゴロ
How're you holding up, Ume-chan?
I'm okay.
I'd probably pass out if I were alone.
But... I'm *not* alone.
Thank you.
Sorry for inconveniencing you like this.

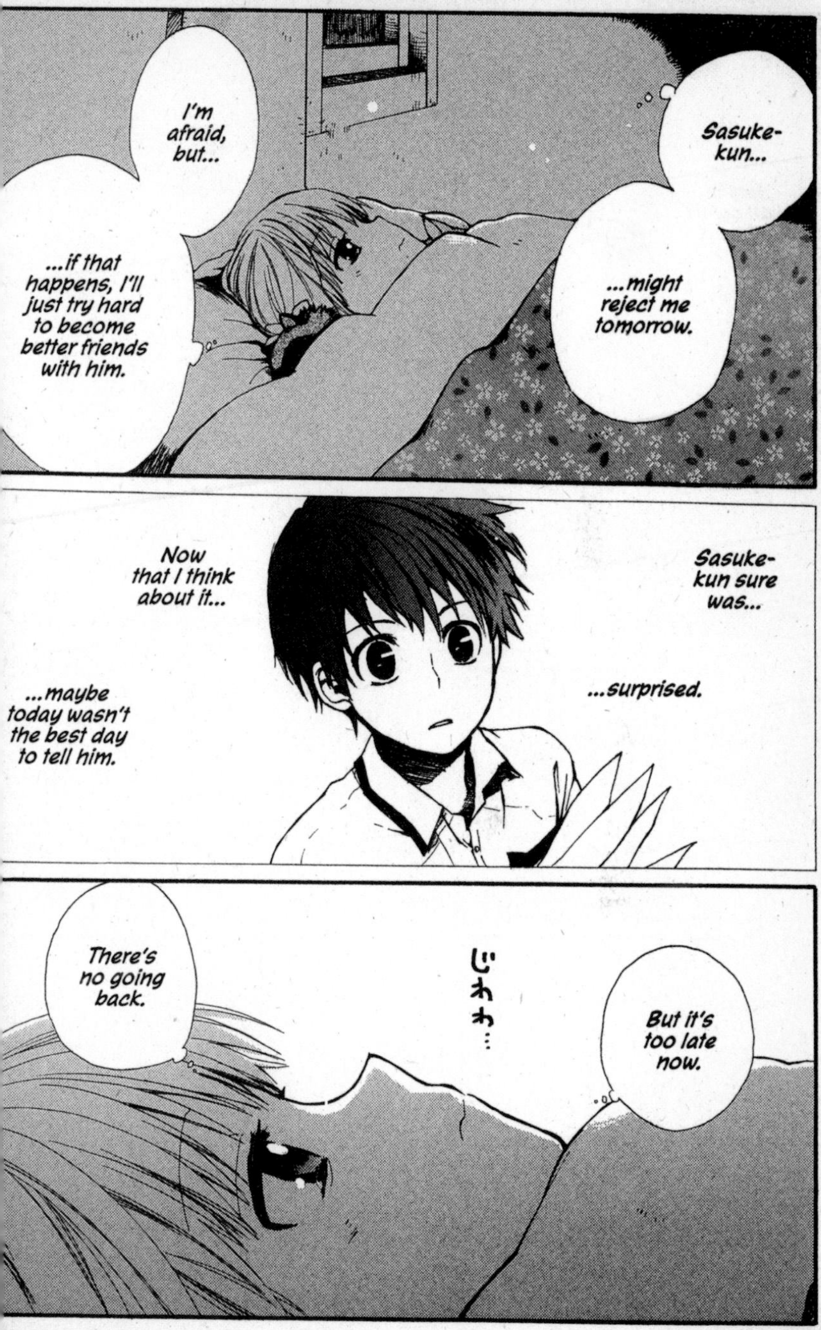
Sasuke-kun...
...might reject me tomorrow.
I'm afraid, but...
...if that happens, I'll just try hard to become better friends with him.
Sasuke-kun sure was...
...surprised.
Now that I think about it...
...maybe today wasn't the best day to tell him.
But it's too late now.
じわわ…
There's no going back.

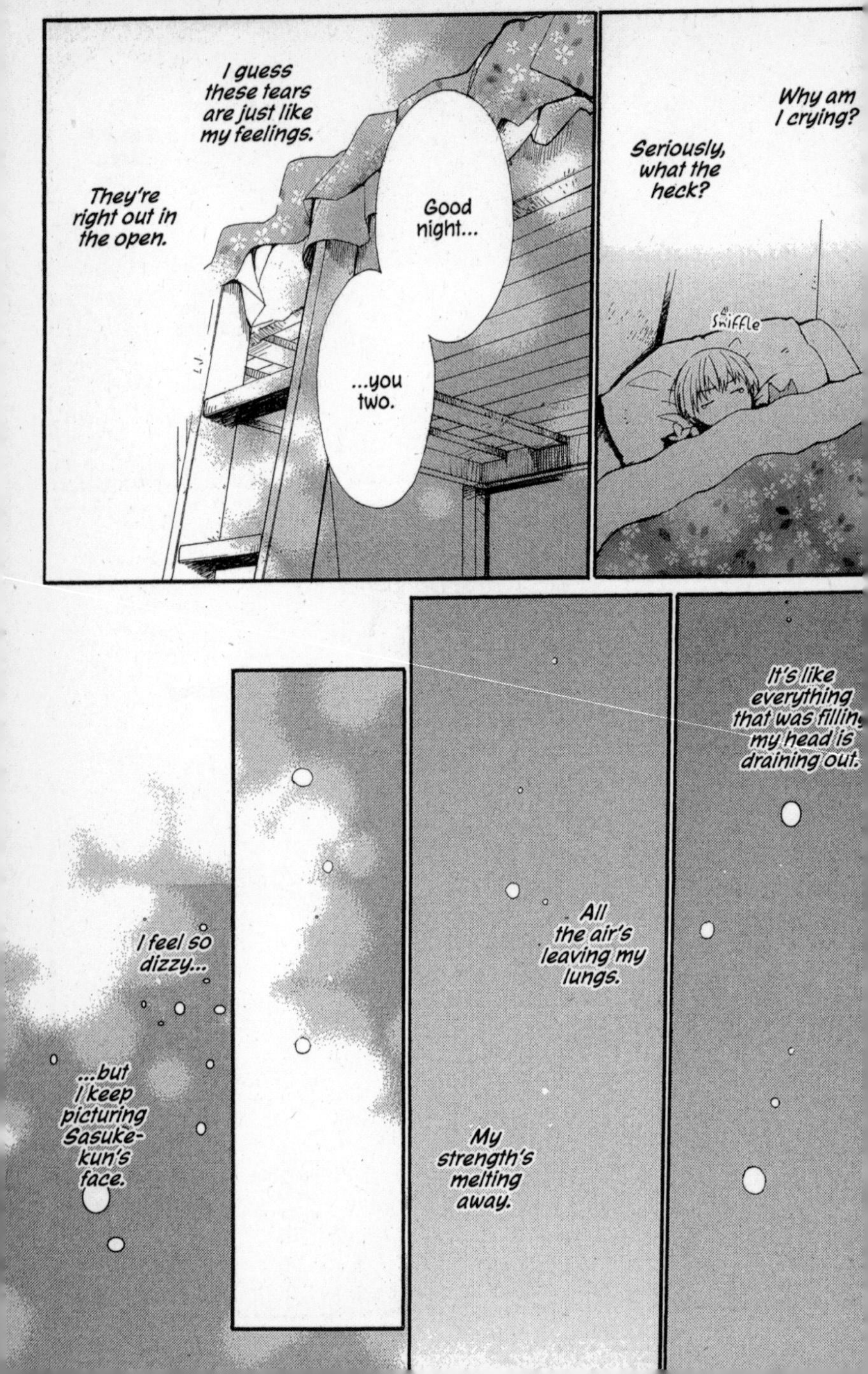
Why am I crying?
Seriously, what the heck?
Sniffle
Good night...
...you two.
I guess these tears are just like my feelings.
They're right out in the open.
It's like everything that was fillin my head is draining out.
All the air's leaving my lungs.
My strength's melting away.
I feel so dizzy...
...but I keep picturing Sasuke-kun's face.

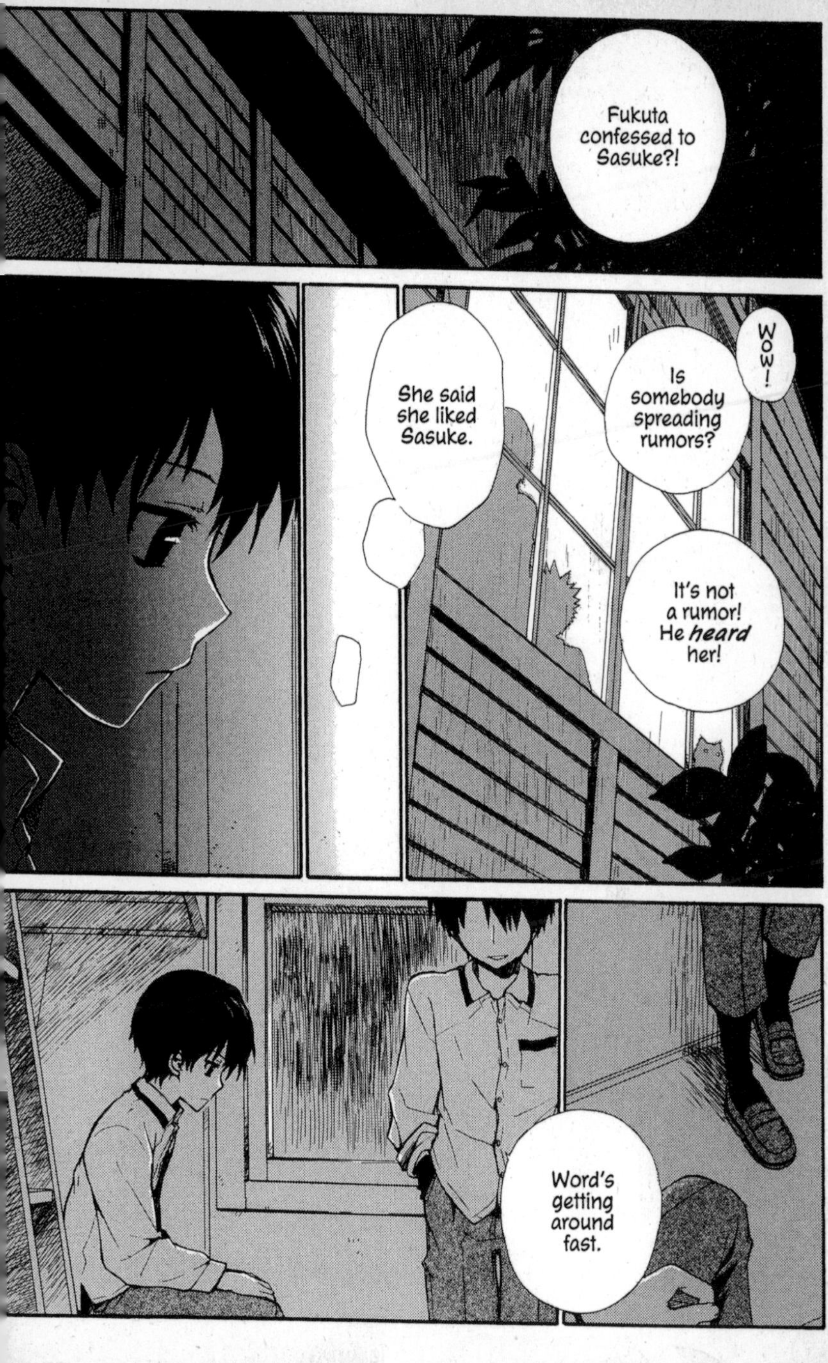
Fukuta confessed to Sasuke?!
Wow!
Is somebody spreading rumors?
She said she liked Sasuke.
It's not a rumor! He *heard* her!
Word's getting around fast.

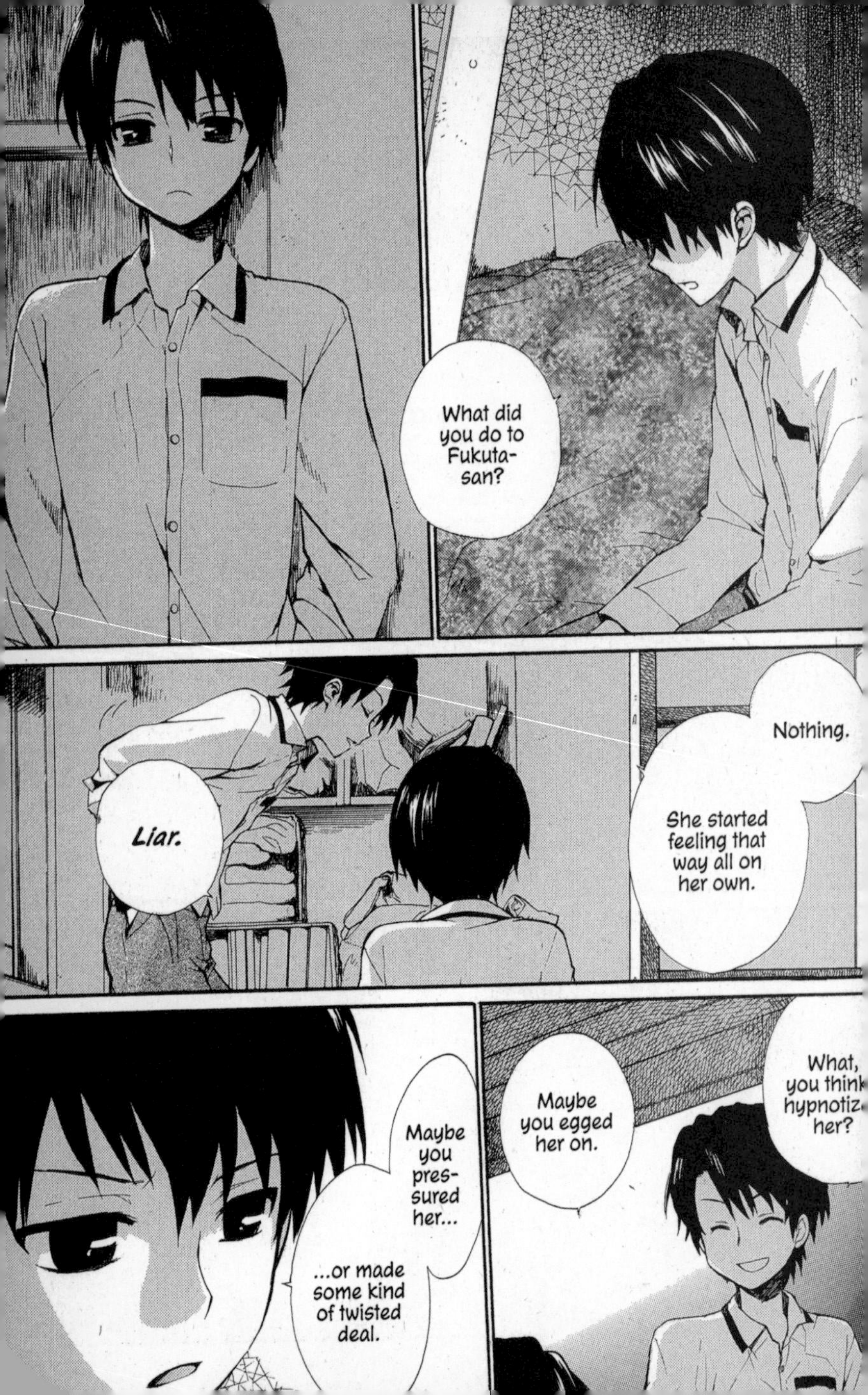

What did you do to Fukuta-san?
Nothing.
She started feeling that way all on her own.
Liar.
What, you think hypnotiz her?
Maybe you egged her on.
Maybe you pres-sured her...
...or made some kind of twisted deal.

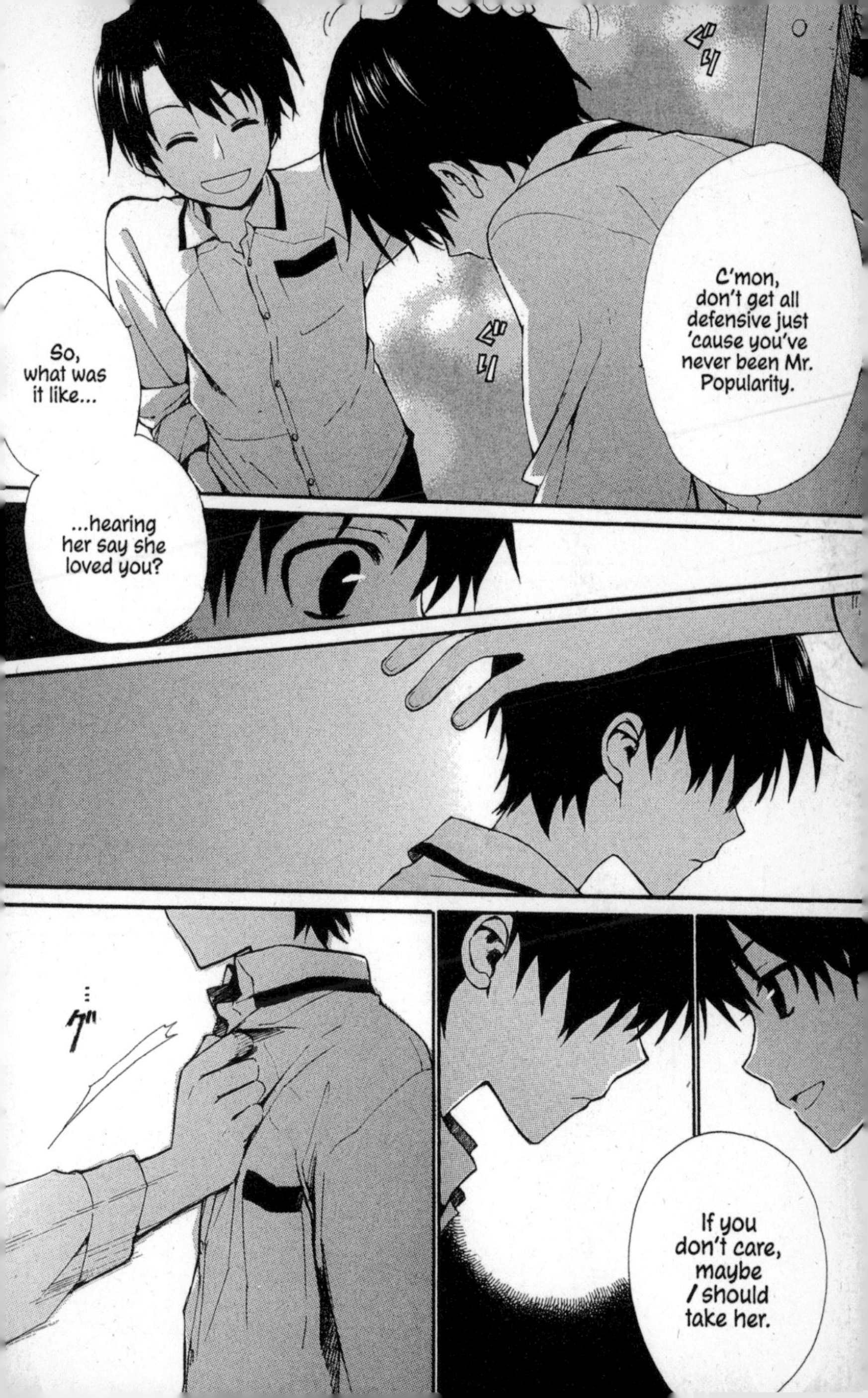
ぐい
ぐい
C'mon, don't get all defensive just 'cause you've never been Mr. Popularity.
So, what was it like...
...hearing her say she loved you?
If you don't care, maybe *I* should take her.

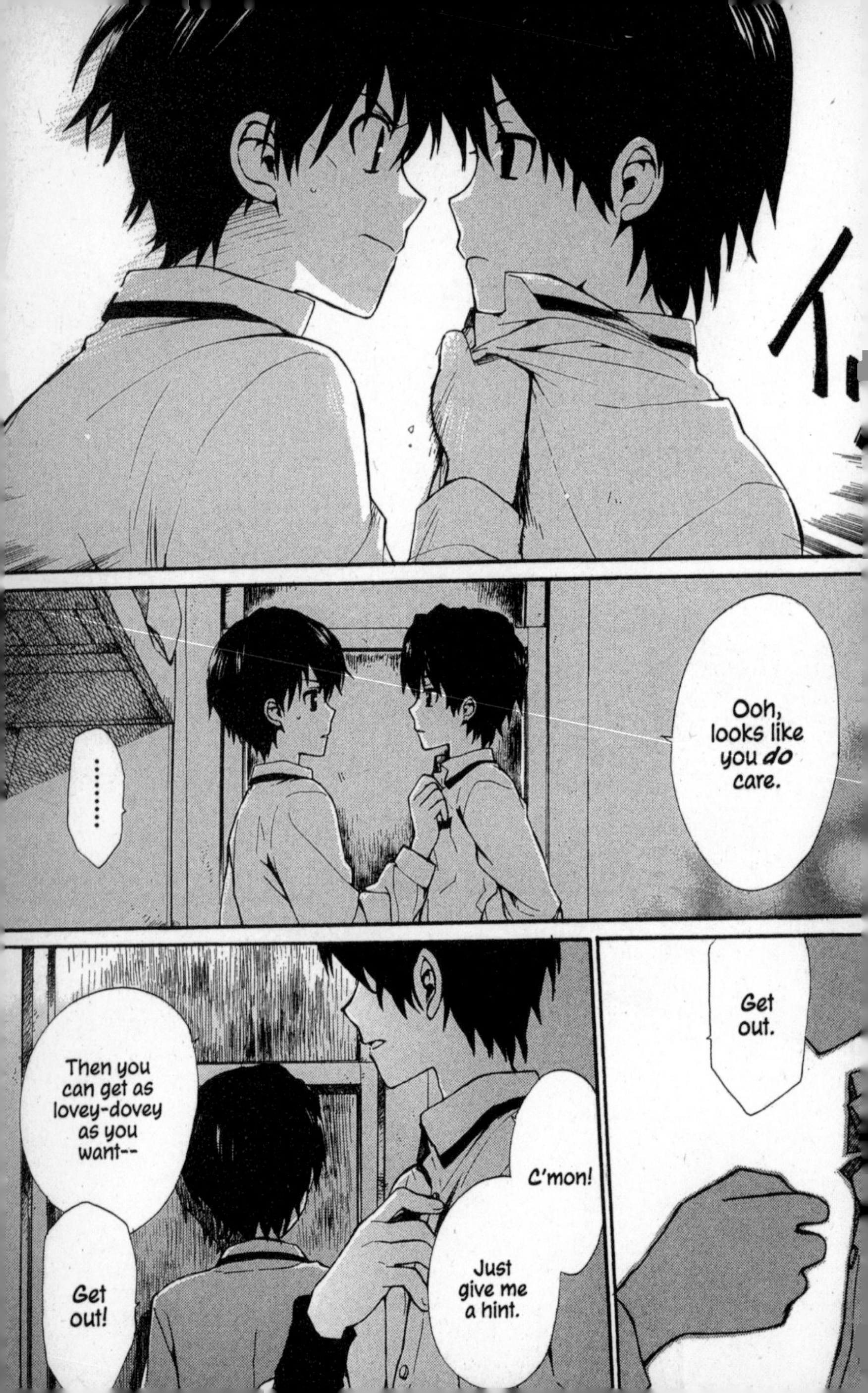
Ooh, looks like you *do* care.
....
Get out.
C'mon!
Just give me a hint.
Then you can get as lovey-dovey as you want--
Get out!

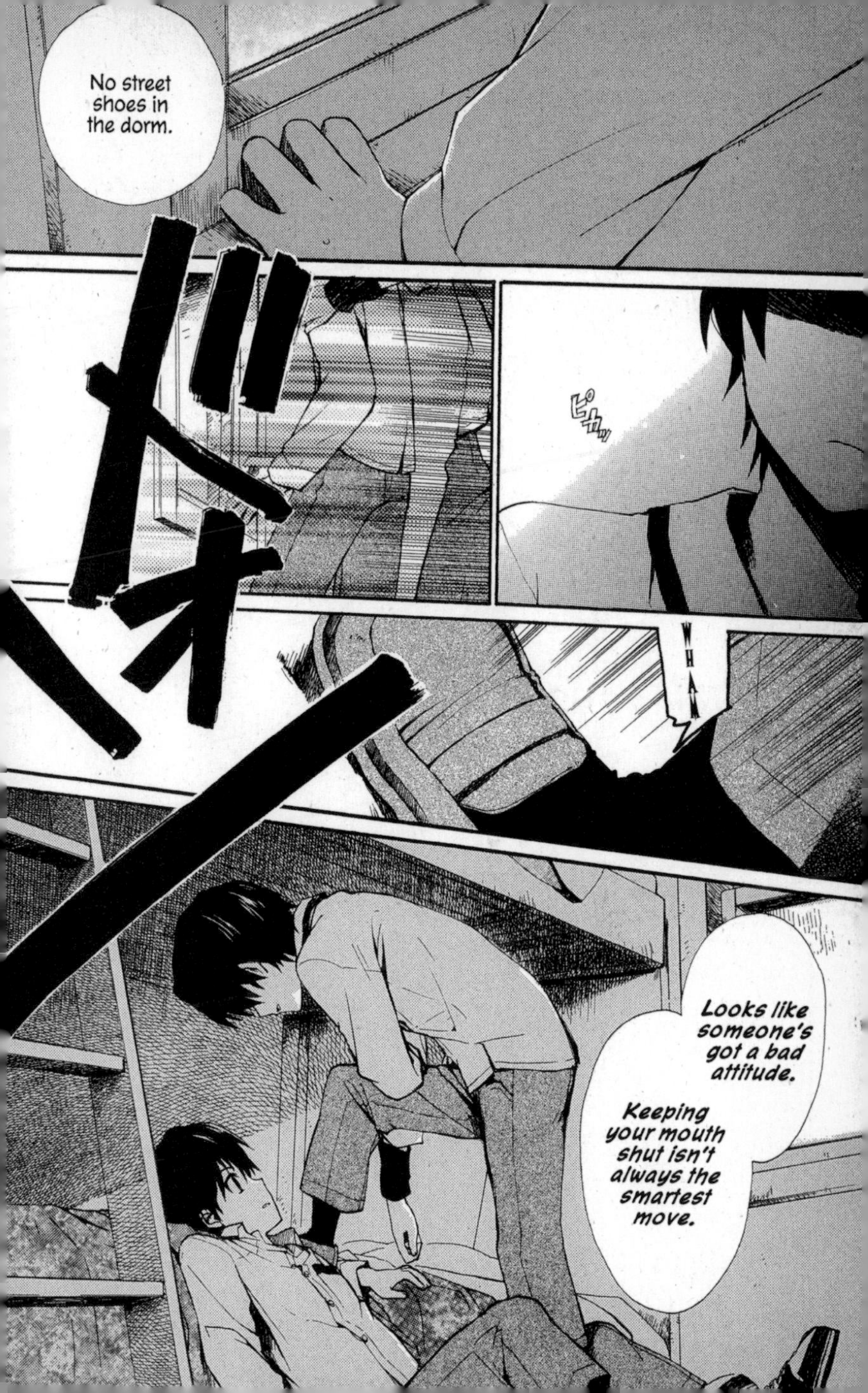
No street shoes in the dorm.
ピカッ
WHAM
Looks like someone's got a bad attitude.
Keeping your mouth shut isn't always the smartest move.

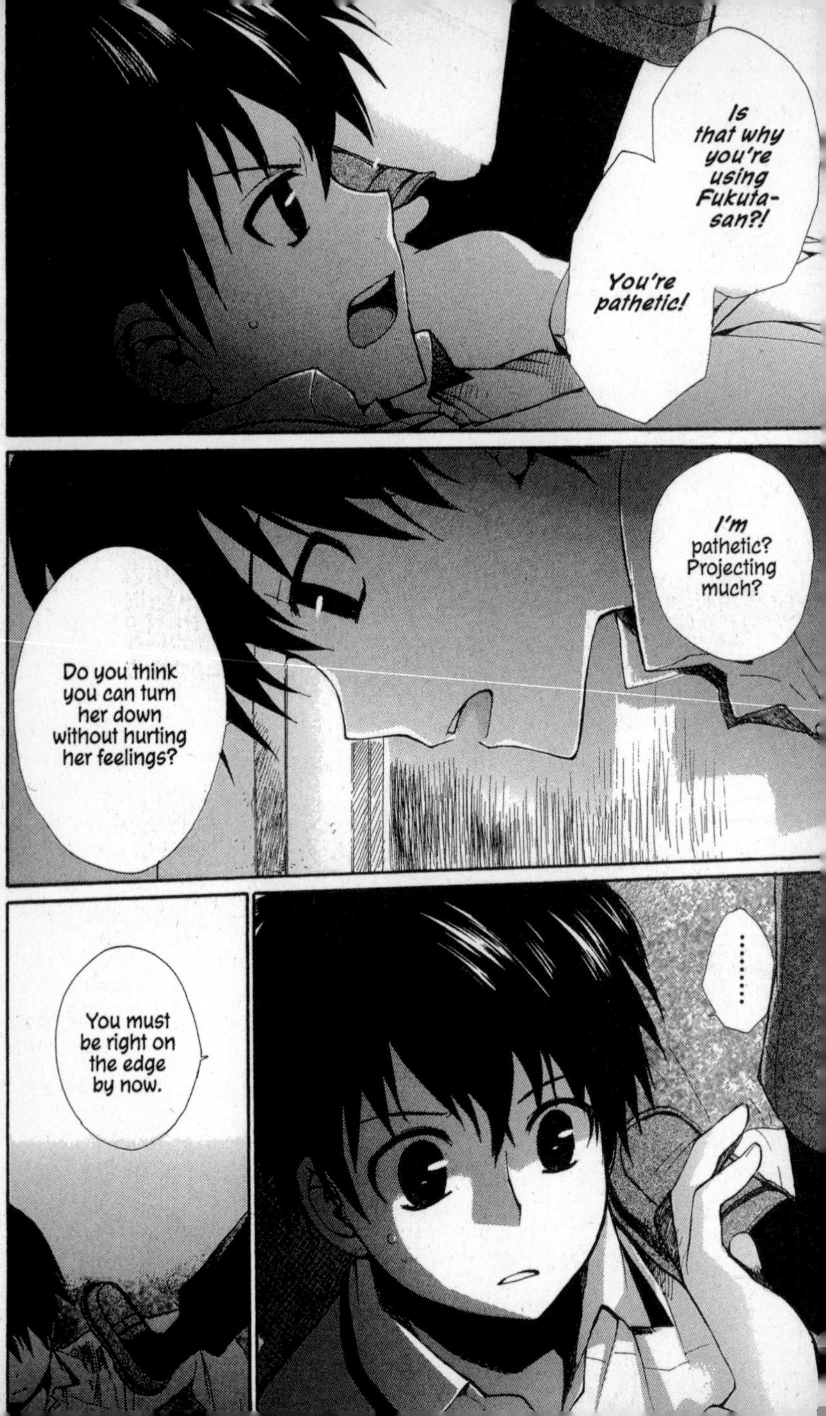
Is that why you're using Fukuta-san?!
You're pathetic!
I'm pathetic? Projecting much?
Do you think you can turn her down without hurting her feelings?
....
You must be right on the edge by now.

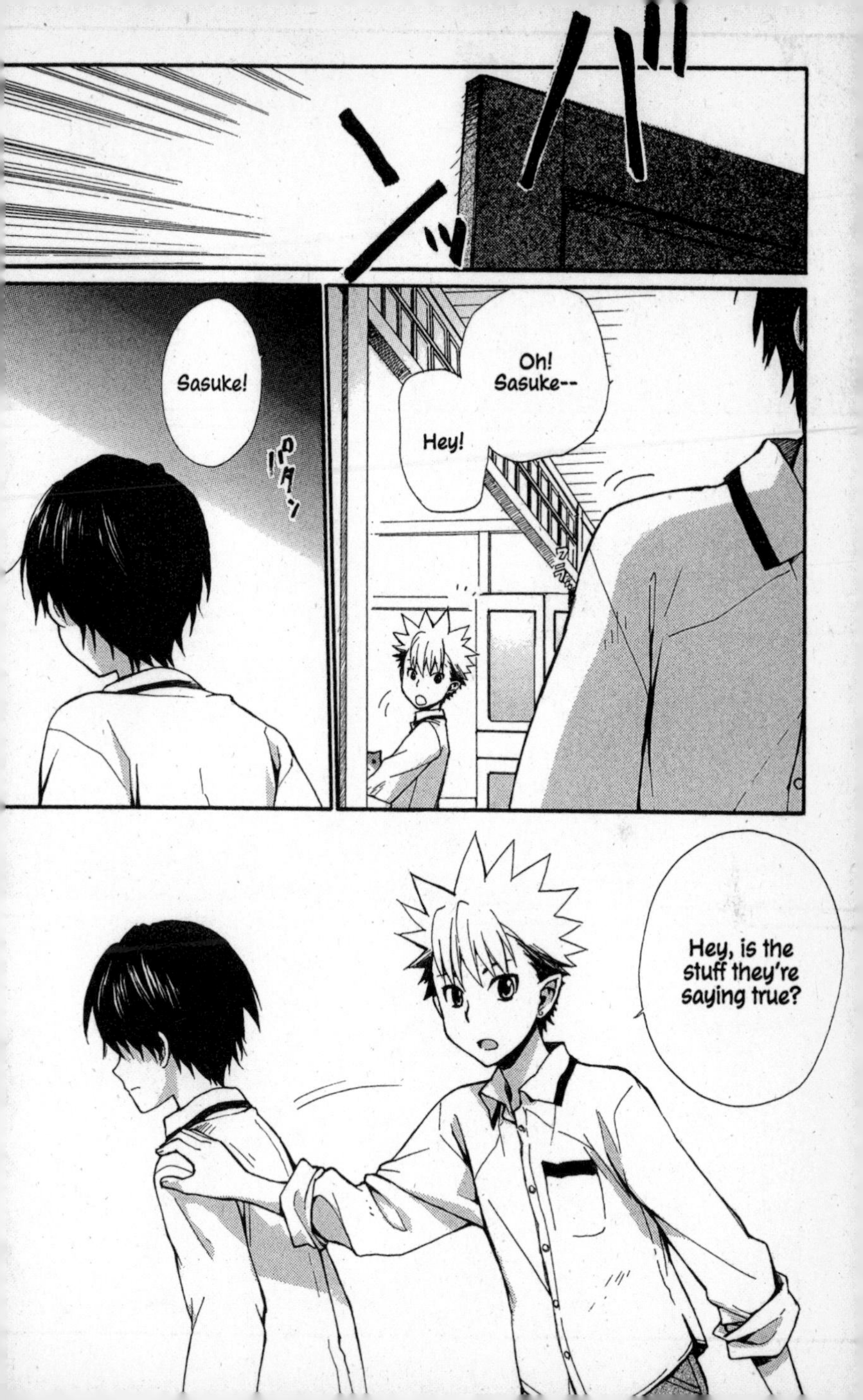
Oh! Sasuke--
Hey!
Sasuke!
Hey, is the stuff they're saying true?

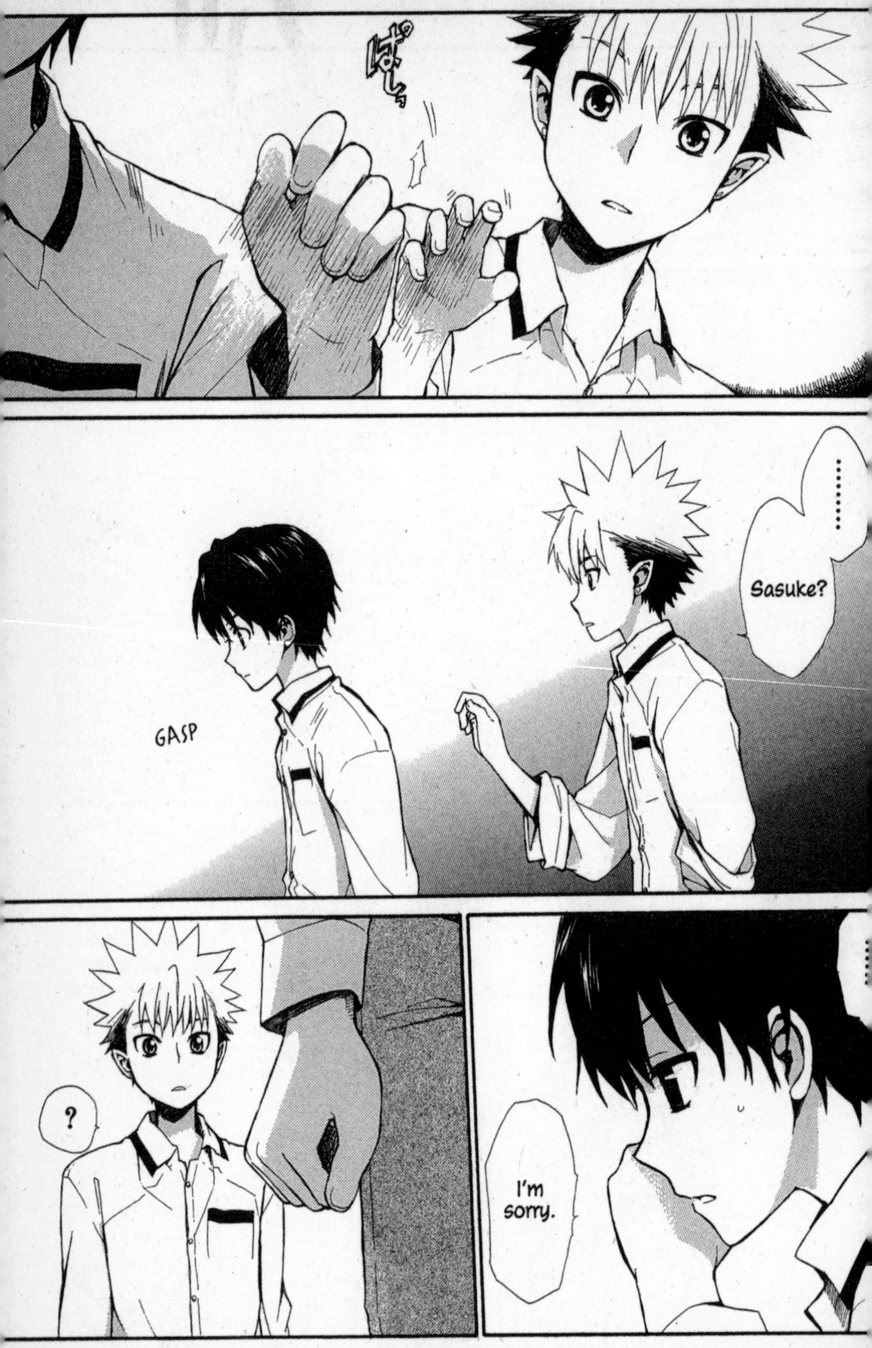
ぱしっ
......
Sasuke?
GASP
I'm sorry.
?

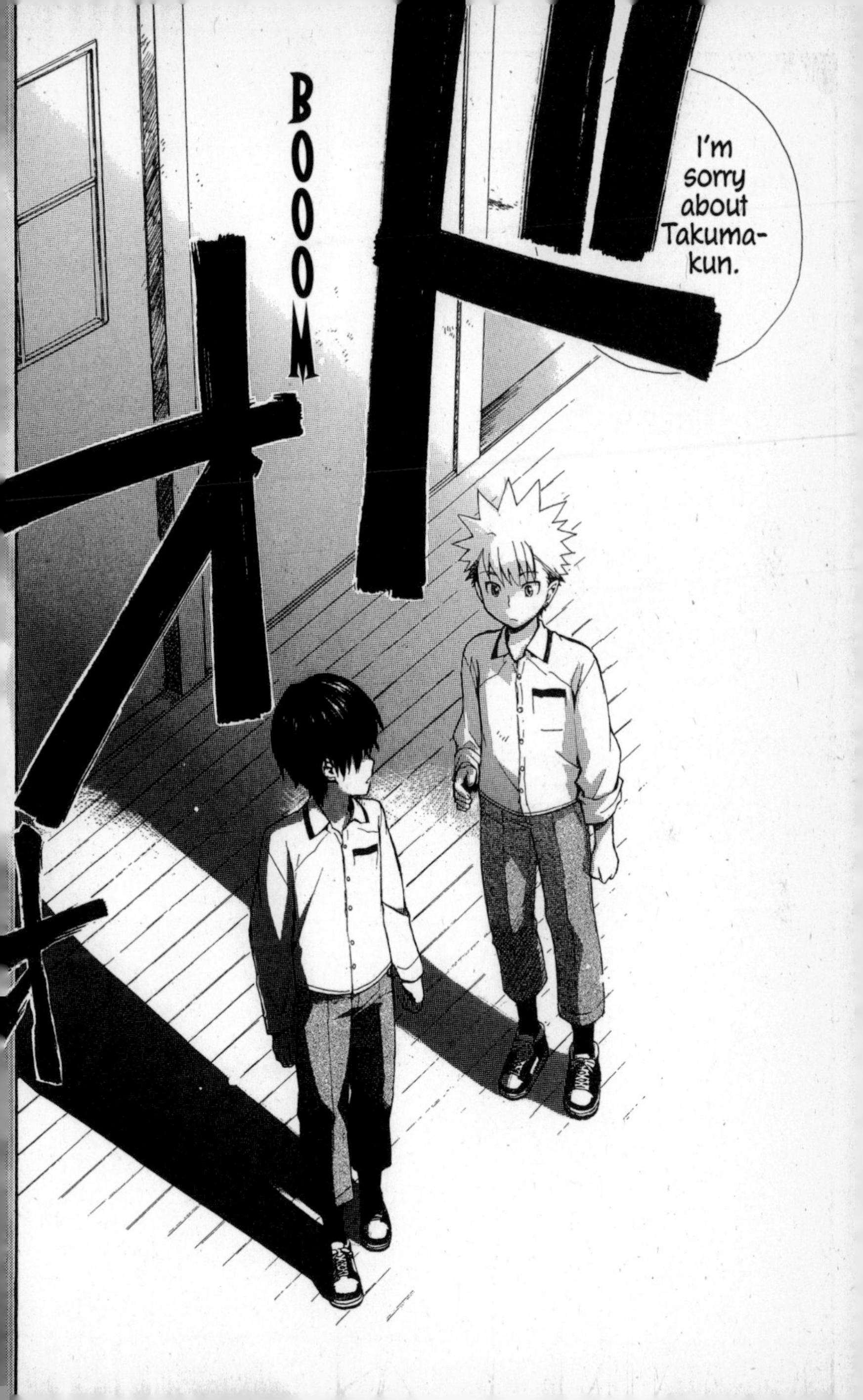
I'm sorry about Takuma-kun.
BOOOM

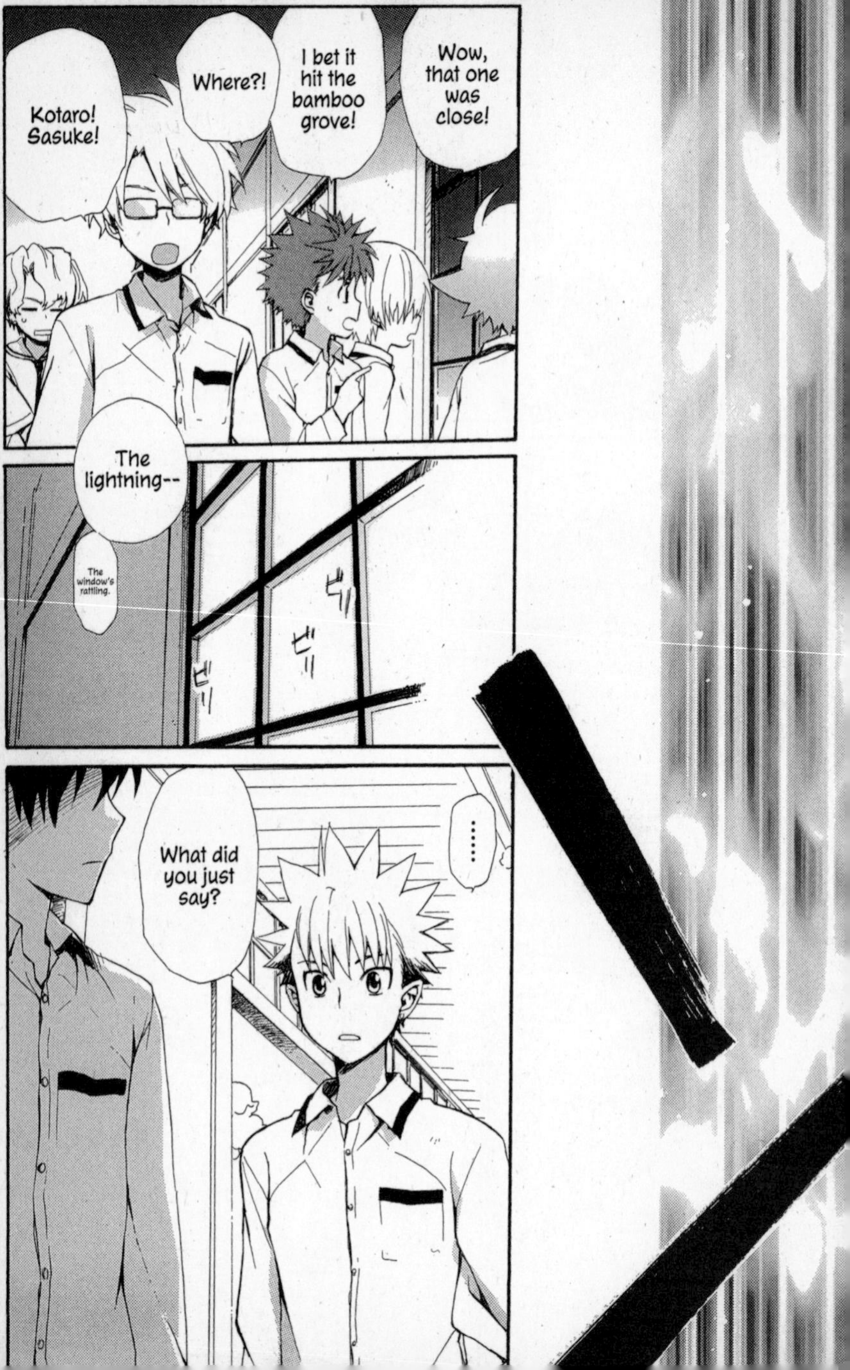
Wow, that one was close!
I bet it hit the bamboo grove!
Where?!
Kotaro! Sasuke!
The lightning--
The window's rattling.
ビリ
ビリ
ビリ
......
What did you just say?

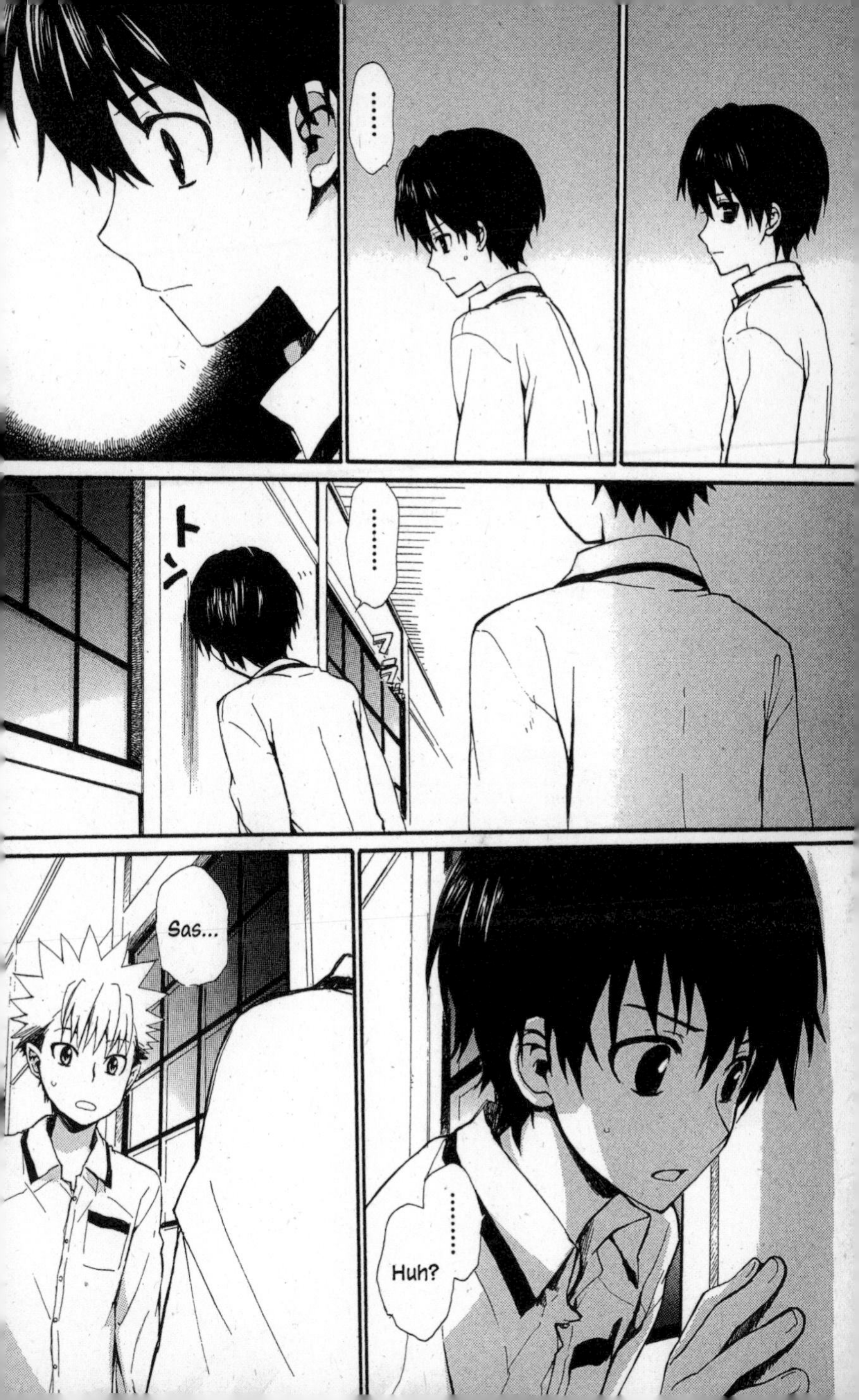
......
......
トン
......
Huh?
Sas...

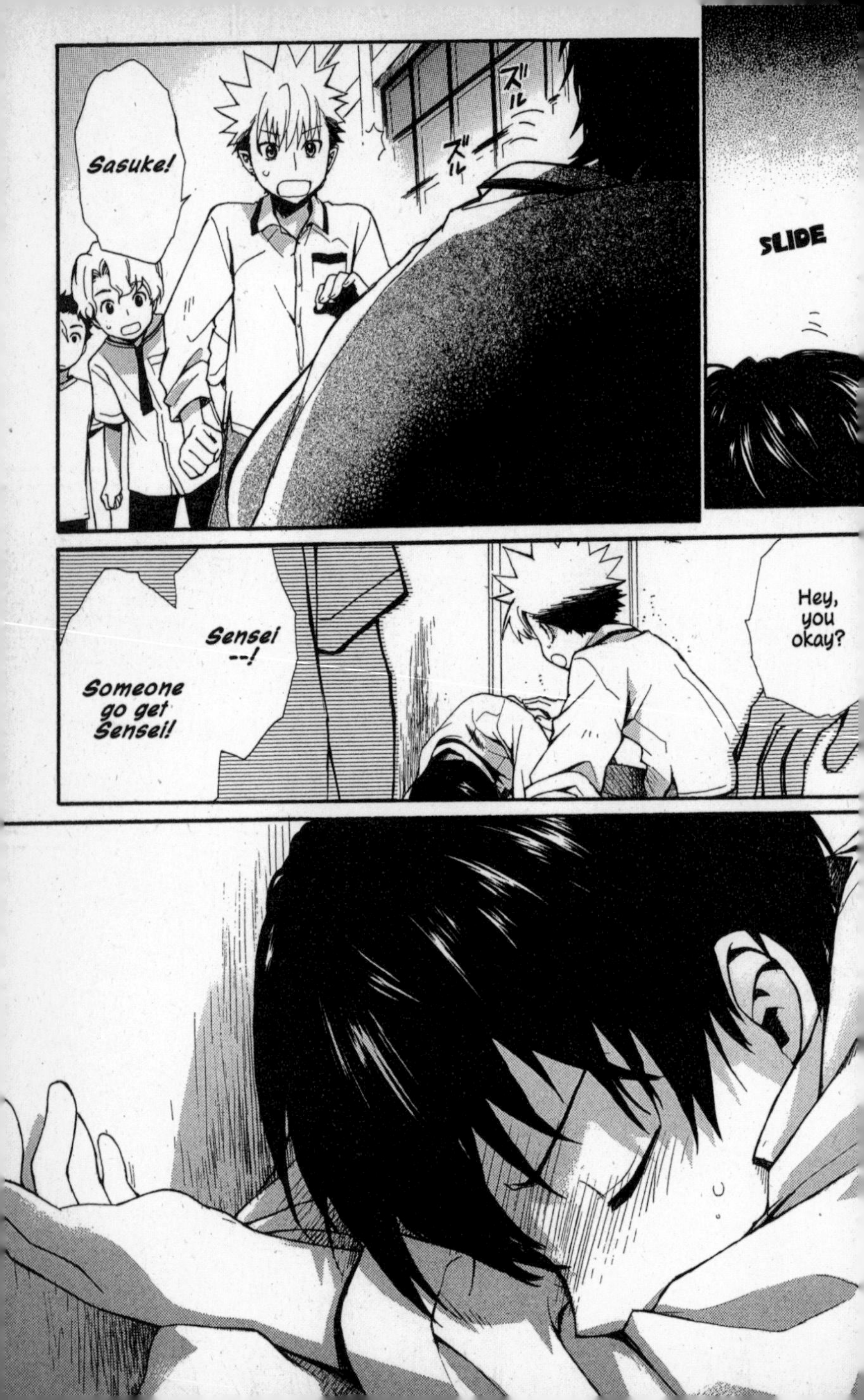
SLIDE
ズル
ズル
Sasuke!
Hey, you okay?
Sensei --!
Someone go get Sensei!

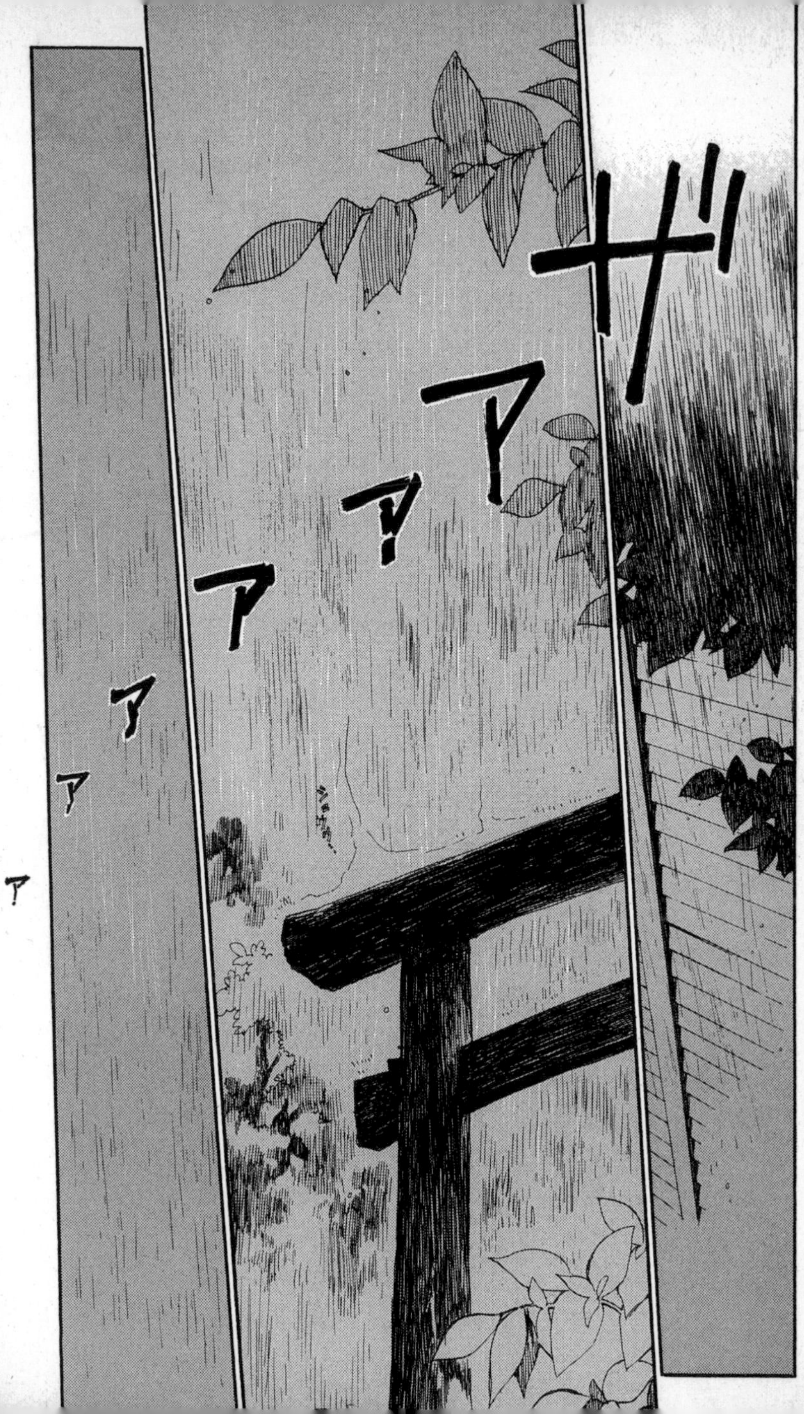
ザァァァァァァ

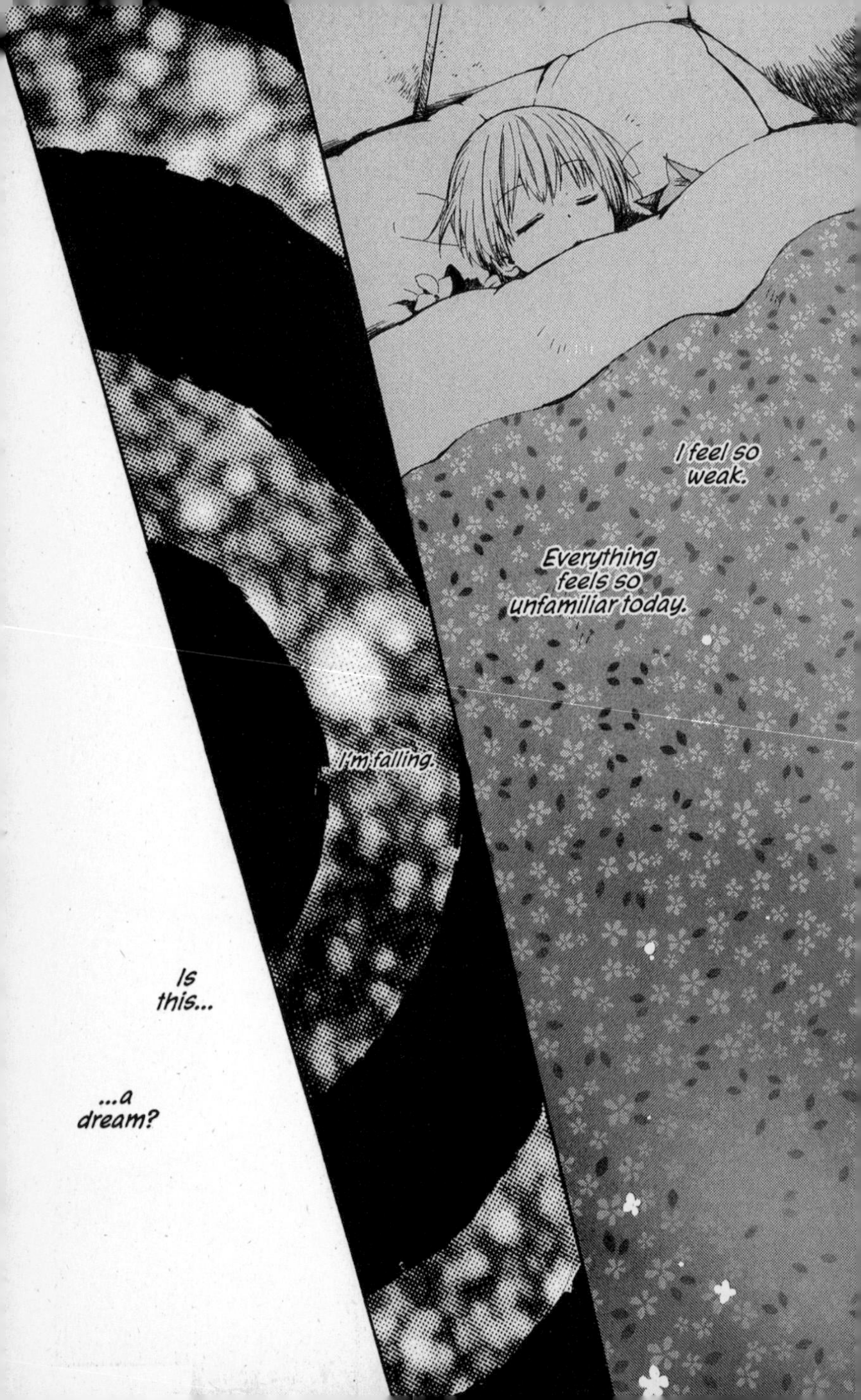
I feel so weak.
Everything feels so unfamiliar today.
I'm falling.
Is this...
...a dream?

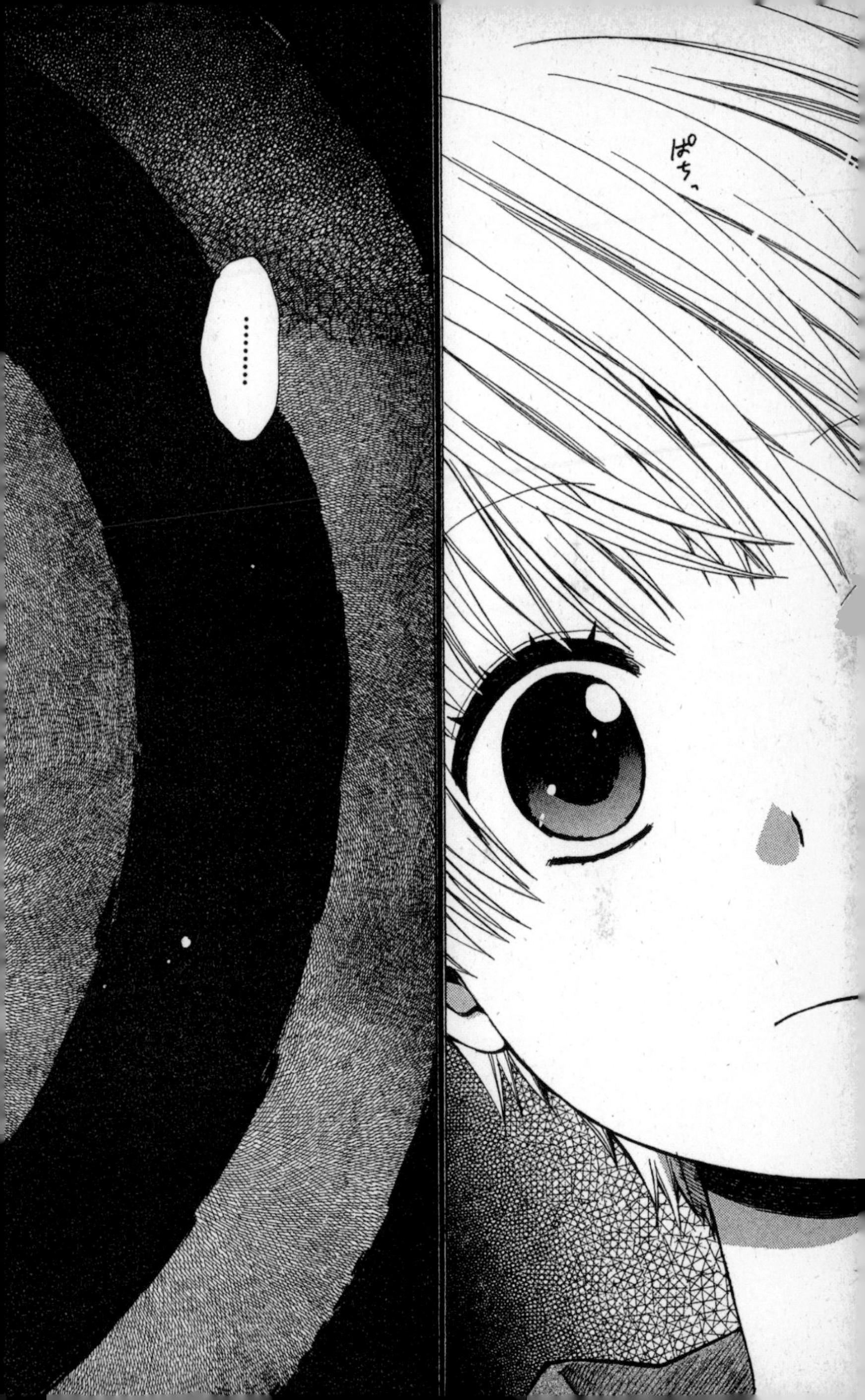
ぱち、
……

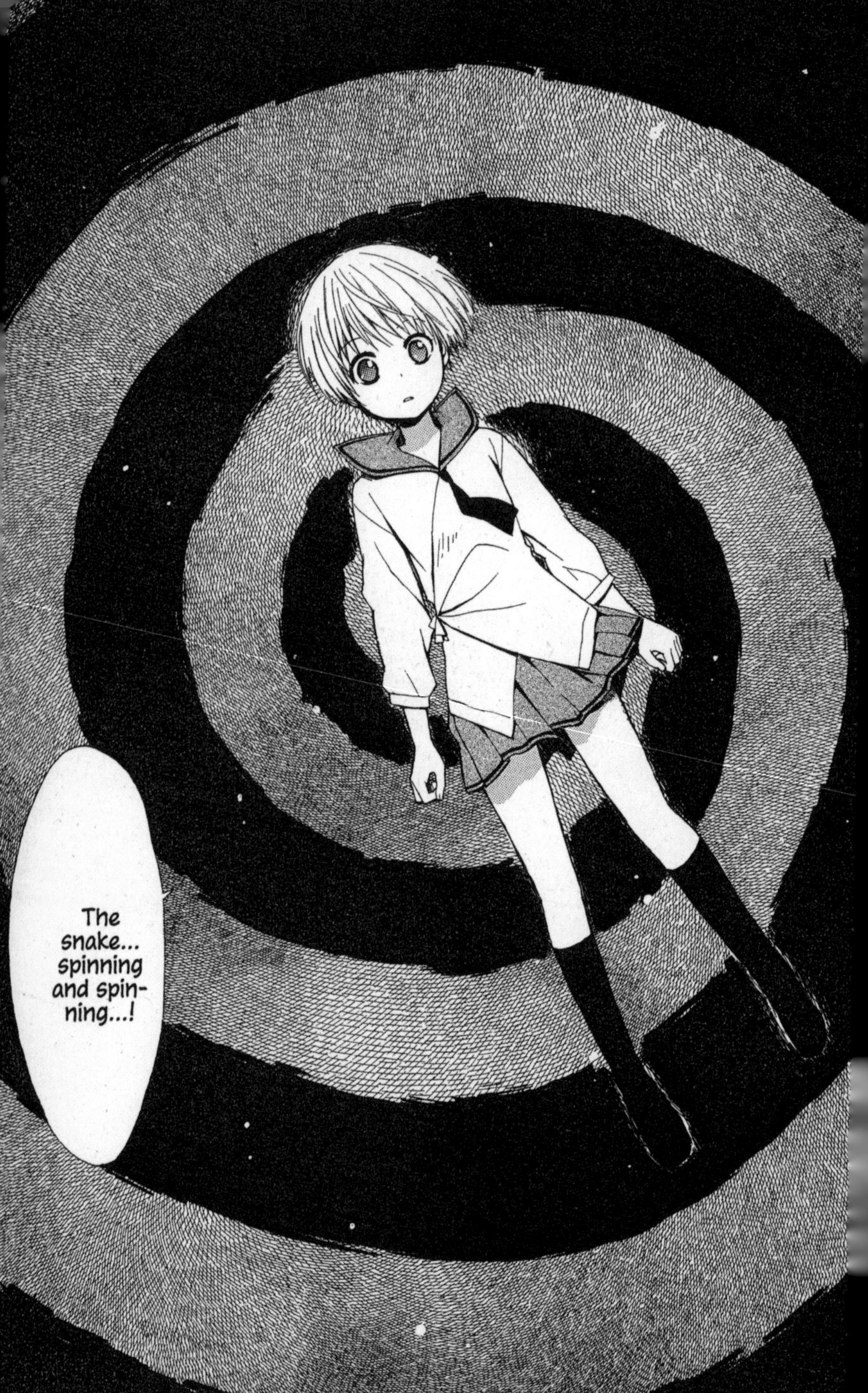
The snake... spinning and spin-ning...!

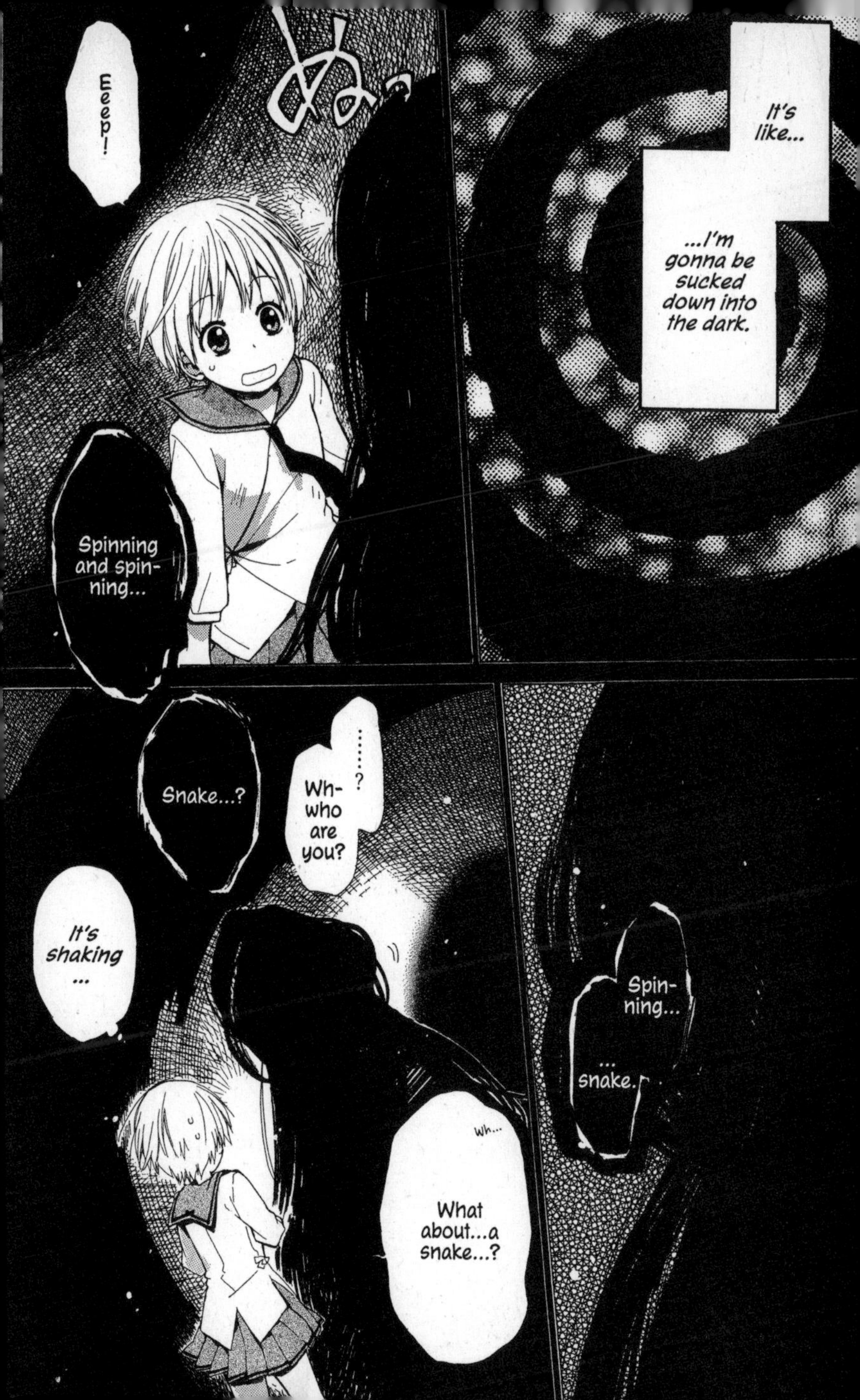
It's like...
...I'm gonna be sucked down into the dark.
Eeep!
Spinning and spinning...
Spinning...
...snake.
......?
Wh-who are you?
Snake...?
It's shaking...
Wh...
What about...a snake...?

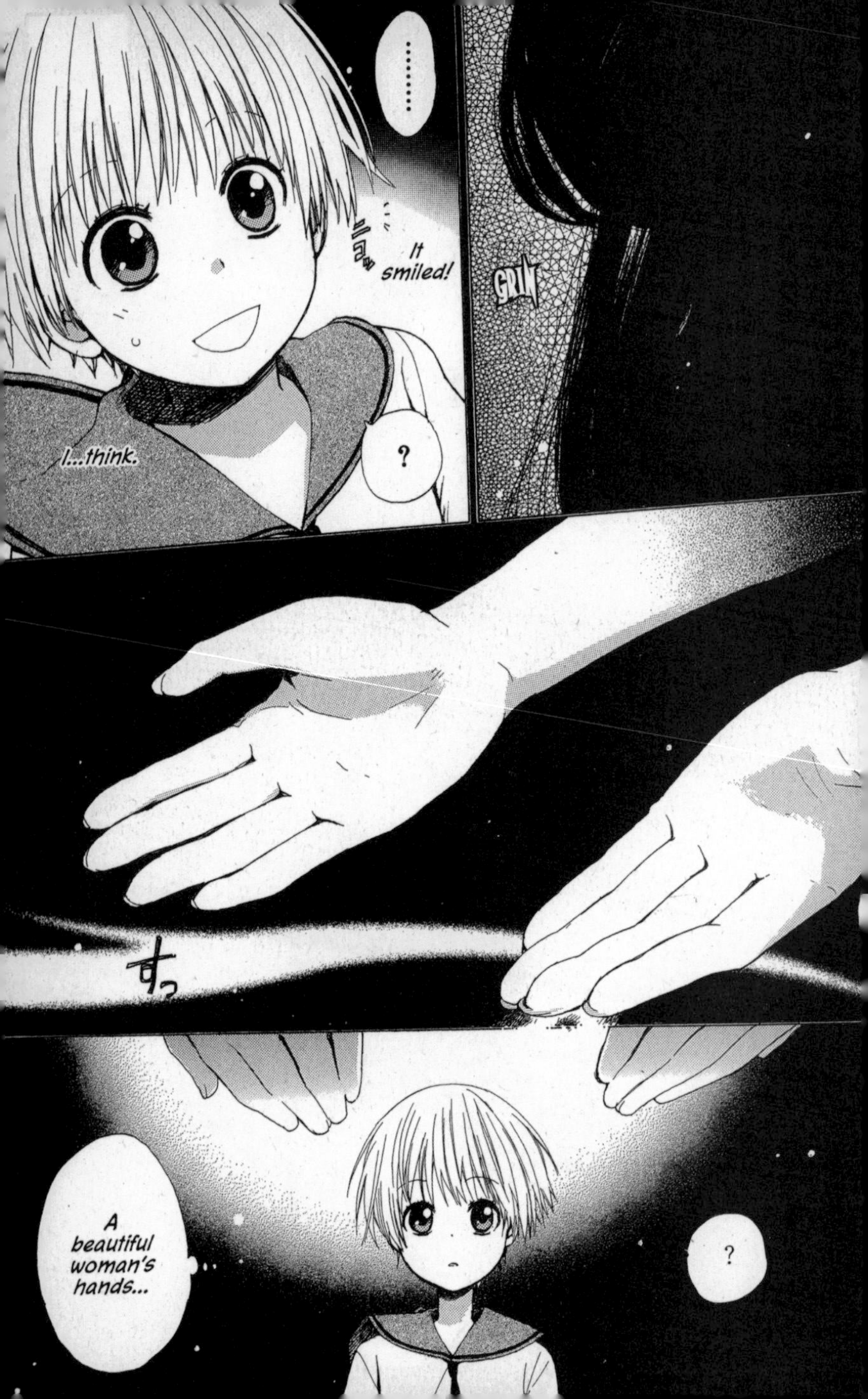
GRIN
......
It smiled!
?
I...think.
すっ
?
A beautiful woman's hands...

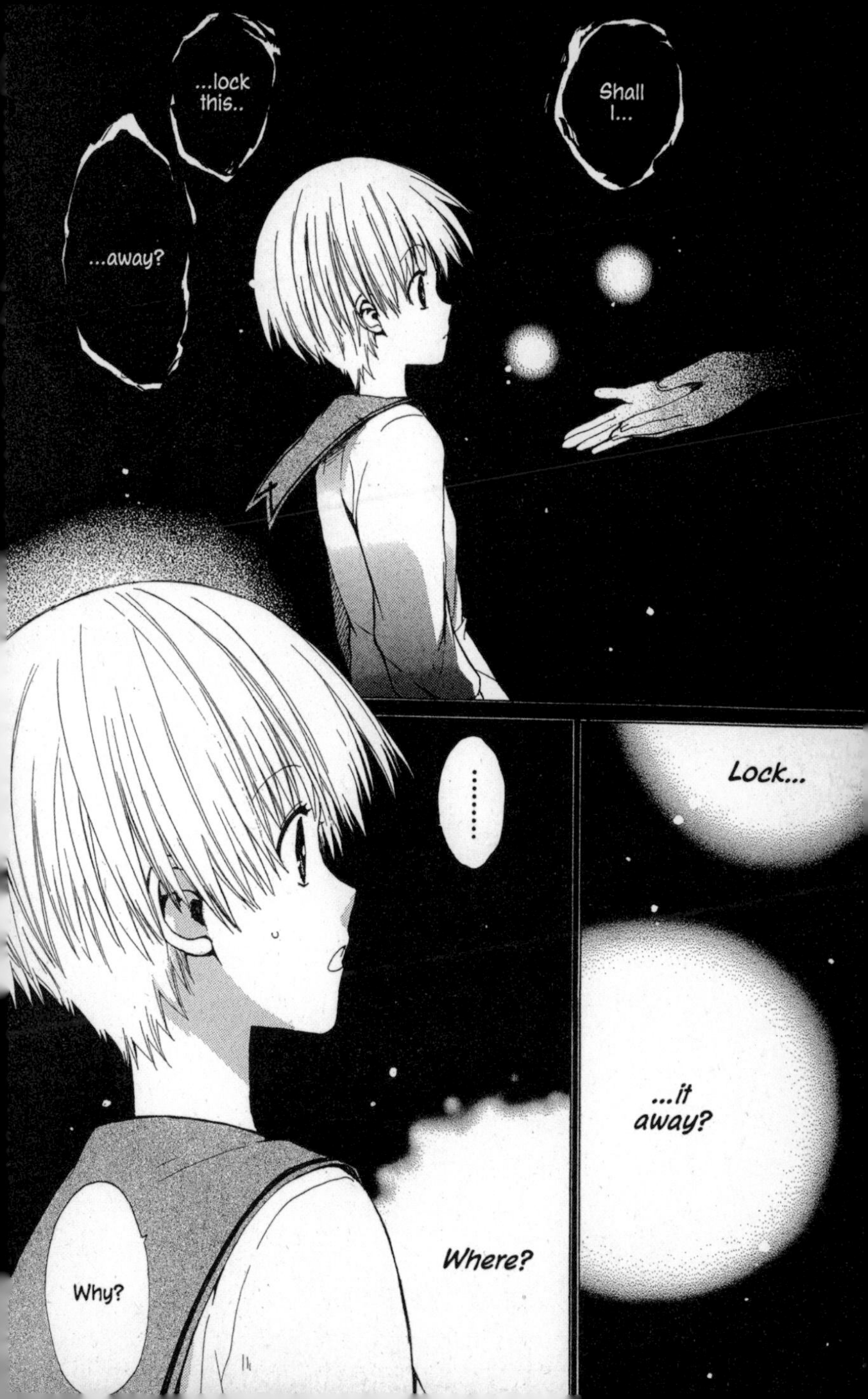
Shall I...
...lock this..
...away?
Lock...
...it away?
....
Where?
Why?

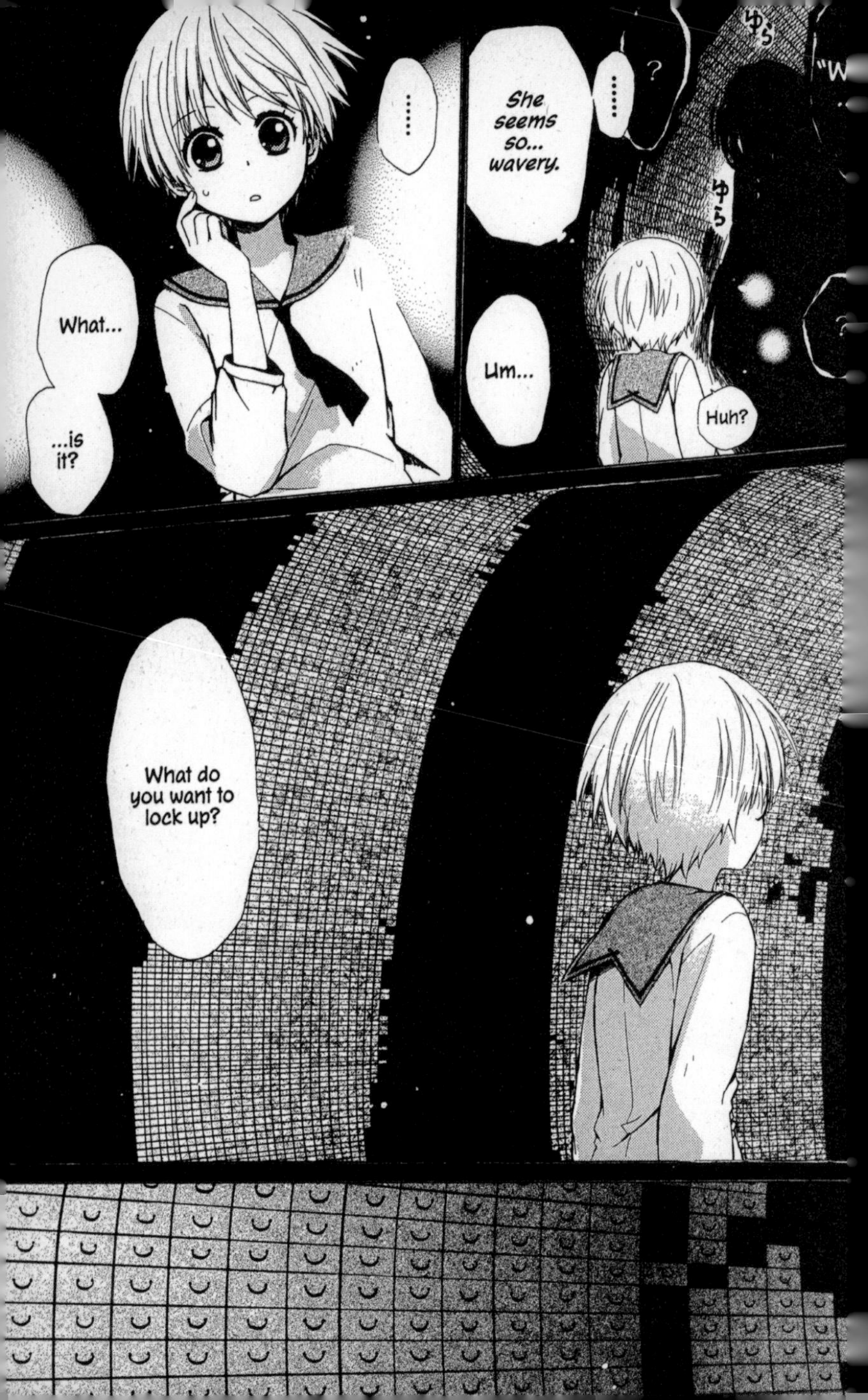

ゆら
?
ゆら
Huh?
......
She seems so... wavery.
Um...
......
What...
...is it?
What do you want to lock up?

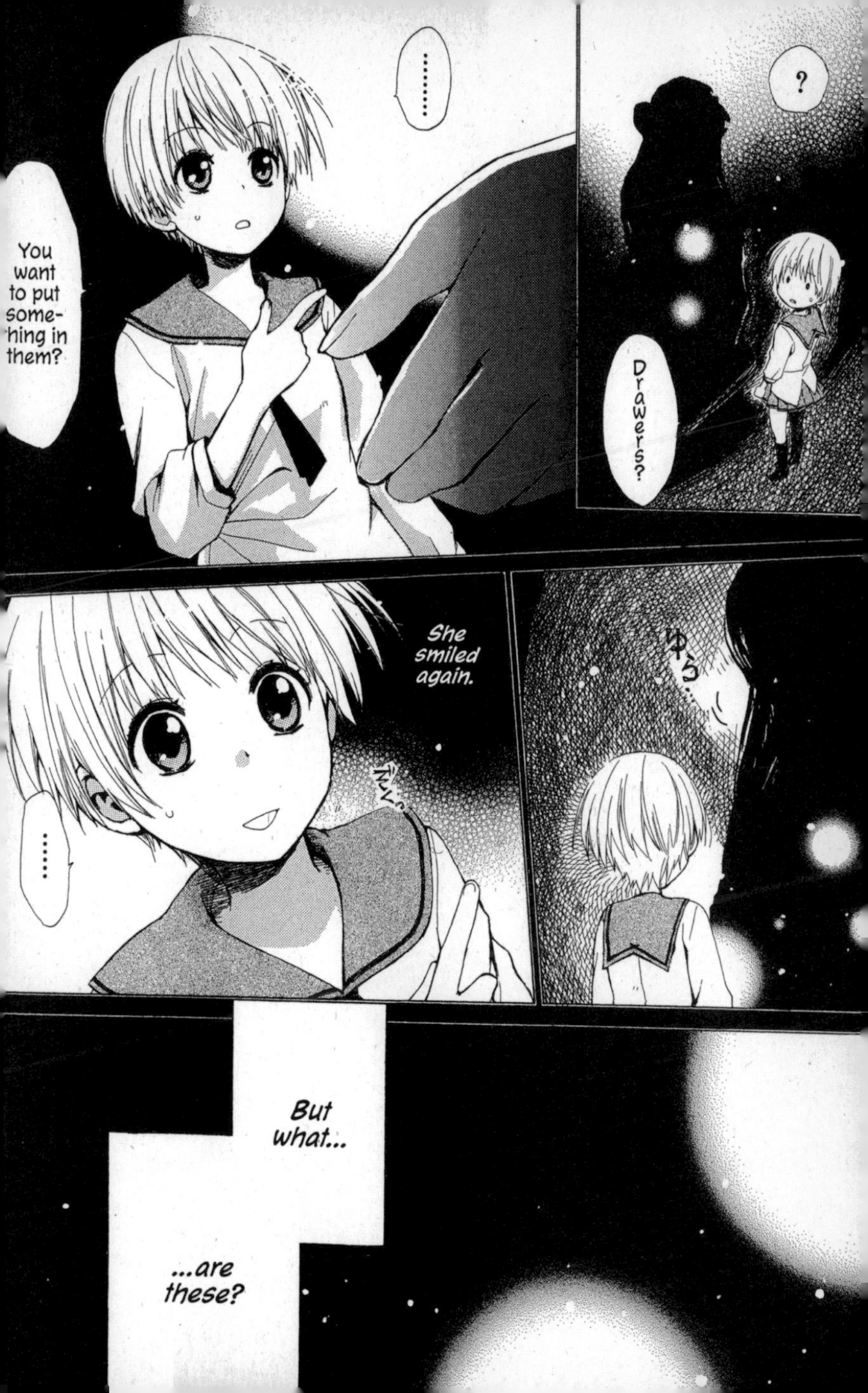
?
Drawers?
......
You want to put some-hing in them?
She smiled again.
......
But what...
...are these?

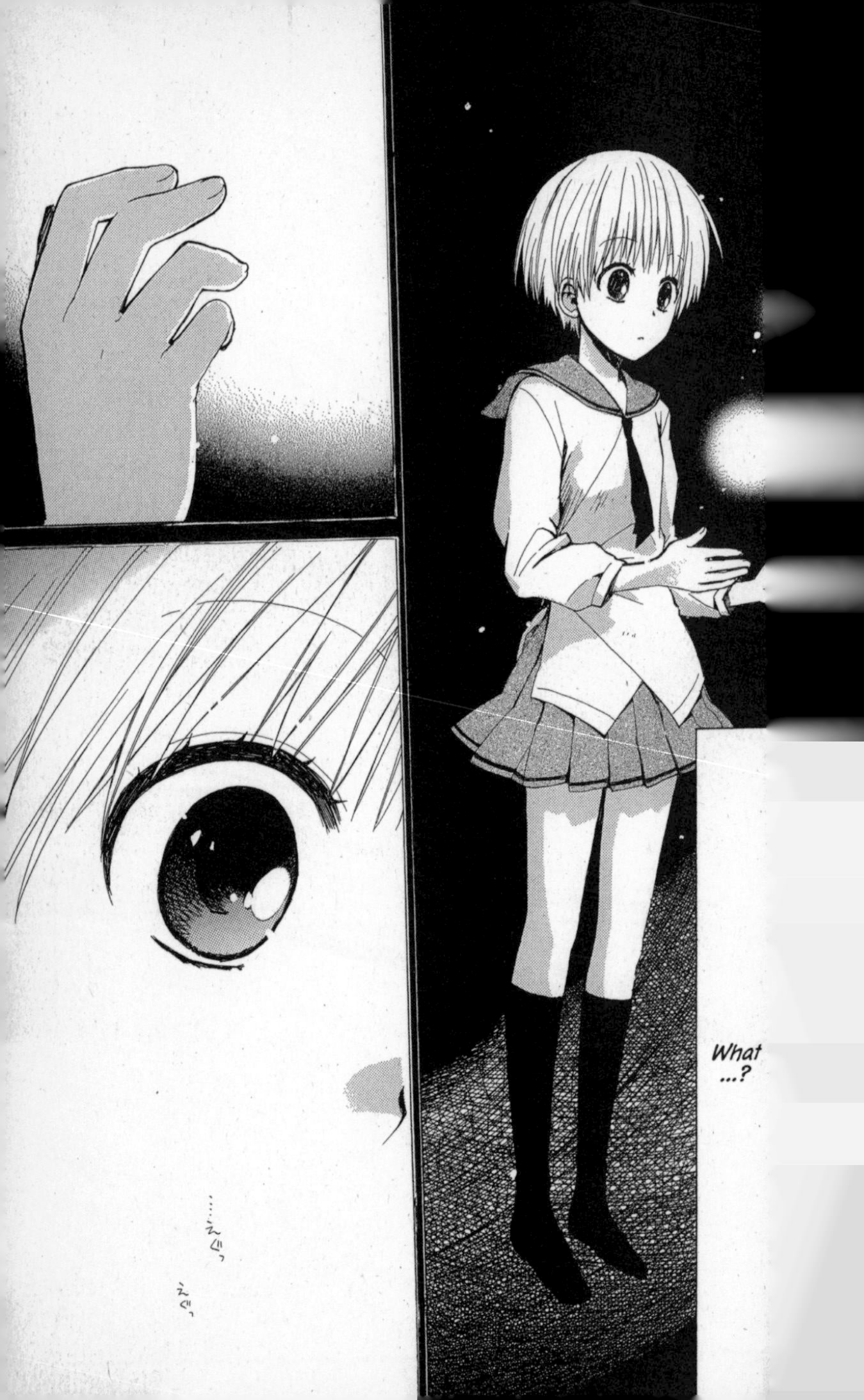
What
...?
…えぐっ
えぐっ

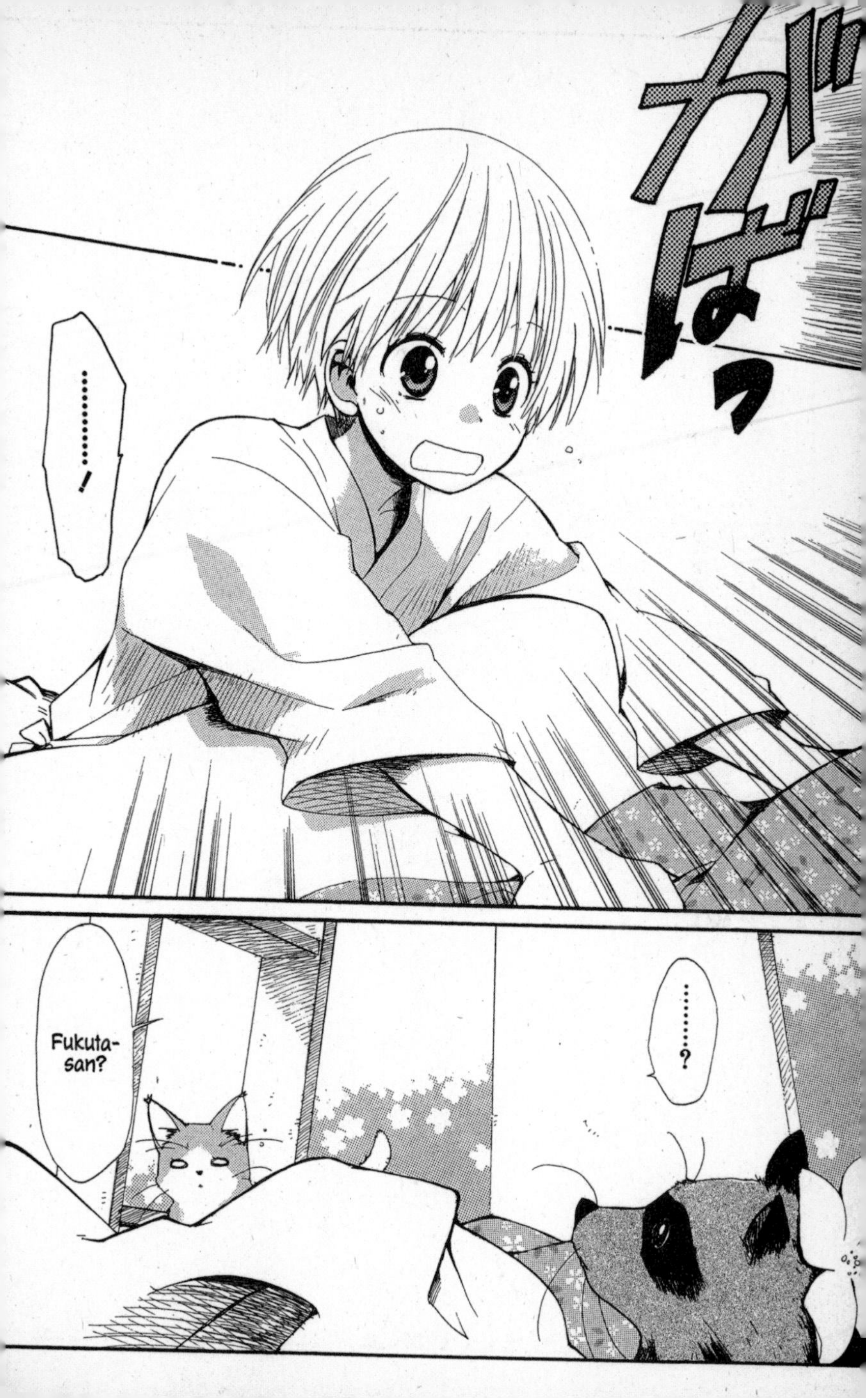
がばっ
.........!
.........?
Fukuta-san?

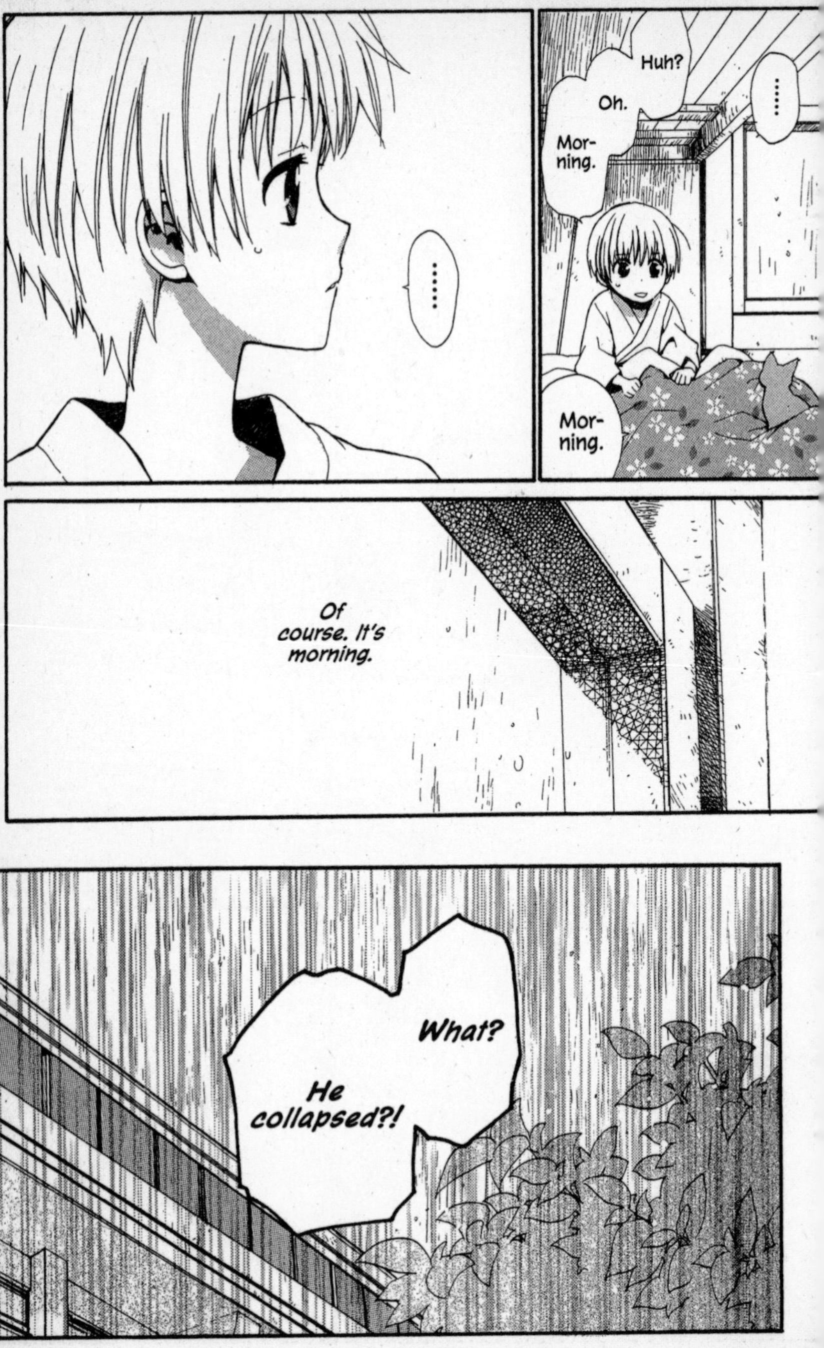

……
Huh?
Oh.
Mor-ning.
Mor-ning.
……
Of course. It's morning.
What?
He collapsed?!

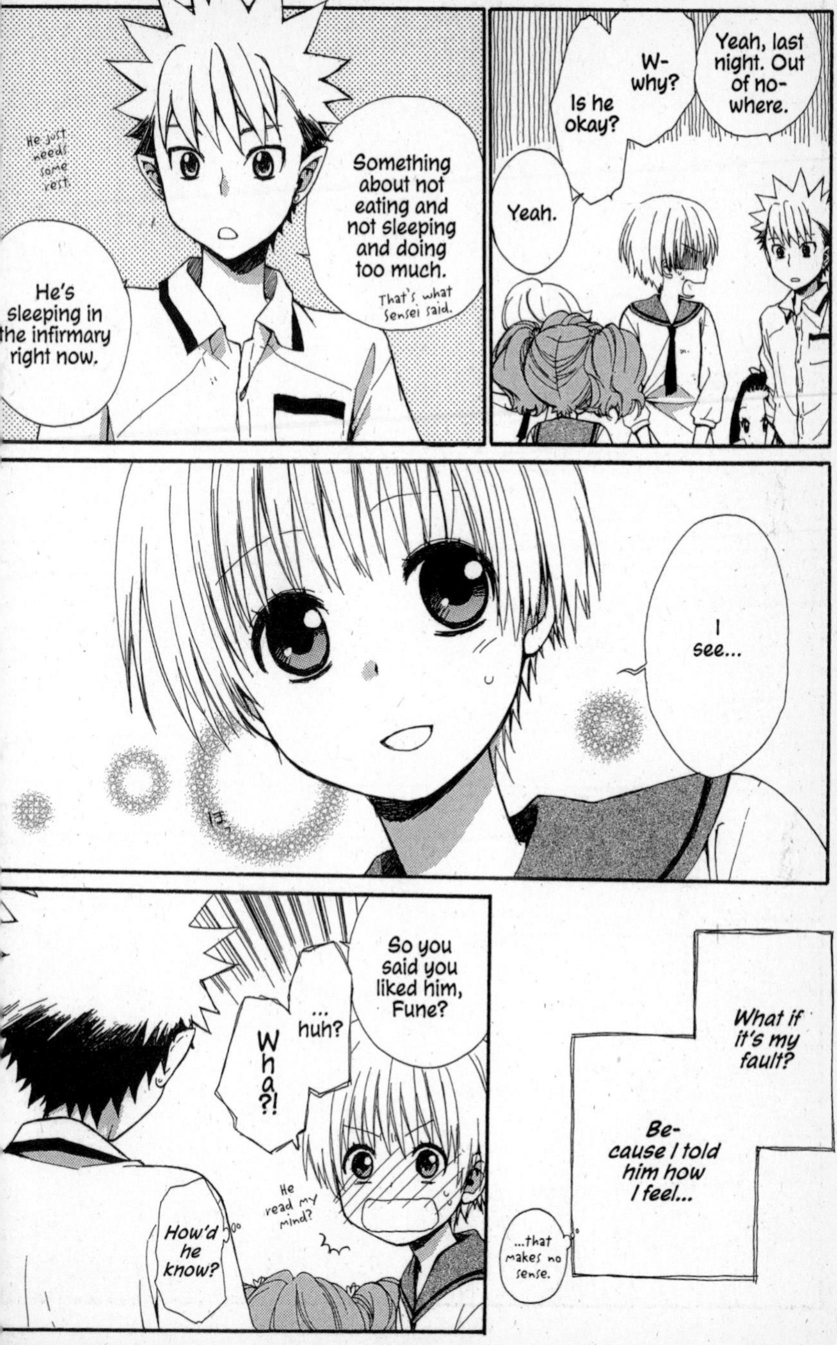
Yeah, last night. Out of no-where.
W-why?
Is he okay?
Yeah.
Something about not eating and not sleeping and doing too much.
That's what Sensei said.
He's sleeping in the infirmary right now.
He just needs some rest.
I see...
What if it's my fault?
Be-cause I told him how I feel...
...that makes no sense.
So you said you liked him, Fune?
...huh?
Wha?!
He read my mind?
How'd he know?

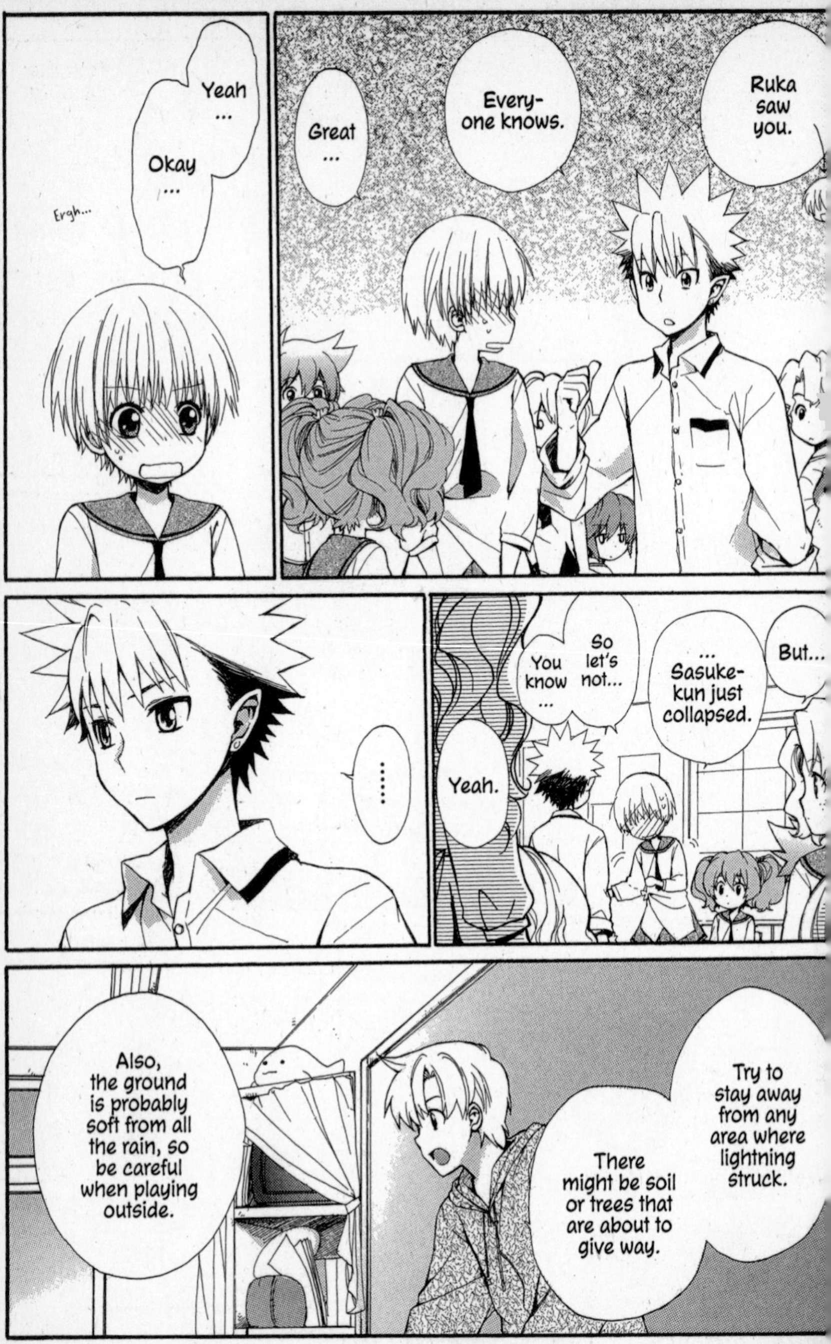
Ruka saw you.
Every-one knows.
Great ...
Yeah ... Okay ...
Ergh...
But...
... Sasuke-kun just collapsed.
So let's not...
You know ...
Yeah.
......
Try to stay away from any area where lightning struck.
There might be soil or trees that are about to give way.
Also, the ground is probably soft from all the rain, so be careful when playing outside.

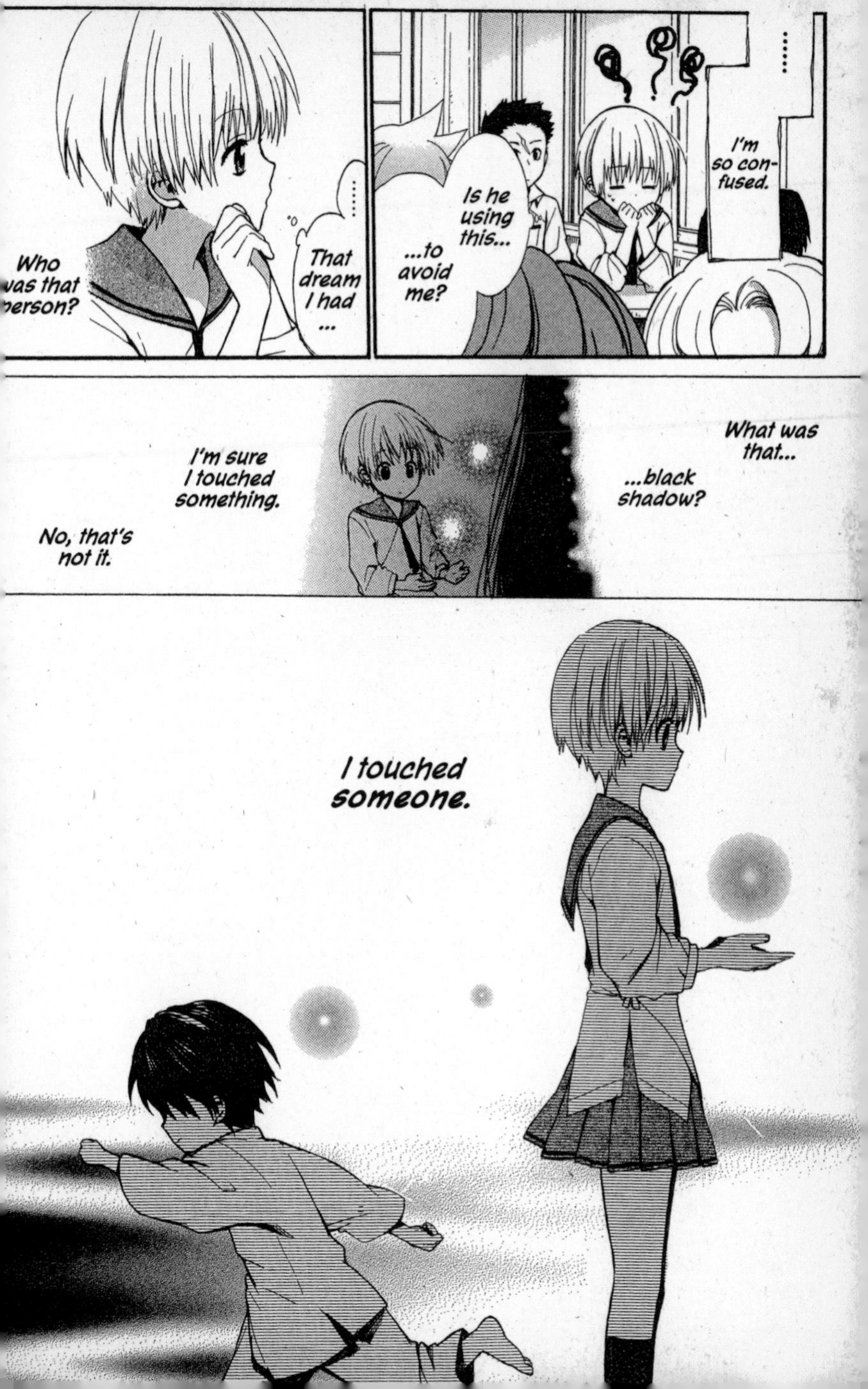
......
I'm so con-fused.
Is he using this...
...to avoid me?
......
That dream I had ...
Who vas that erson?
What was that...
...black shadow?
I'm sure I touched something.
No, that's not it.
I touched someone.

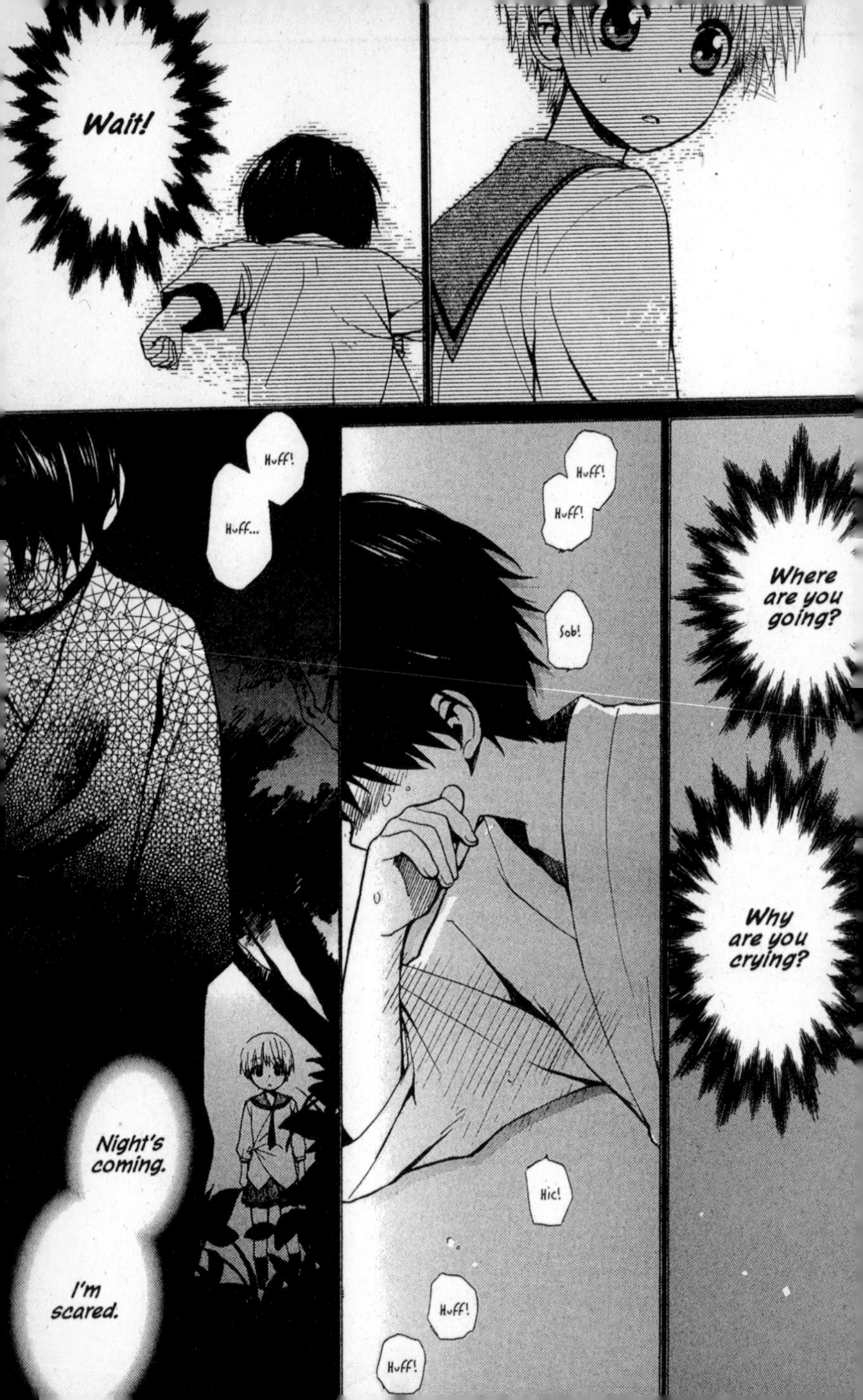
Wait!
Where are you going?
Why are you crying?
Huff!
Huff!
Sob!
Hic!
Huff!
Huff!
Huff!
Huff...
Night's coming.
I'm scared.

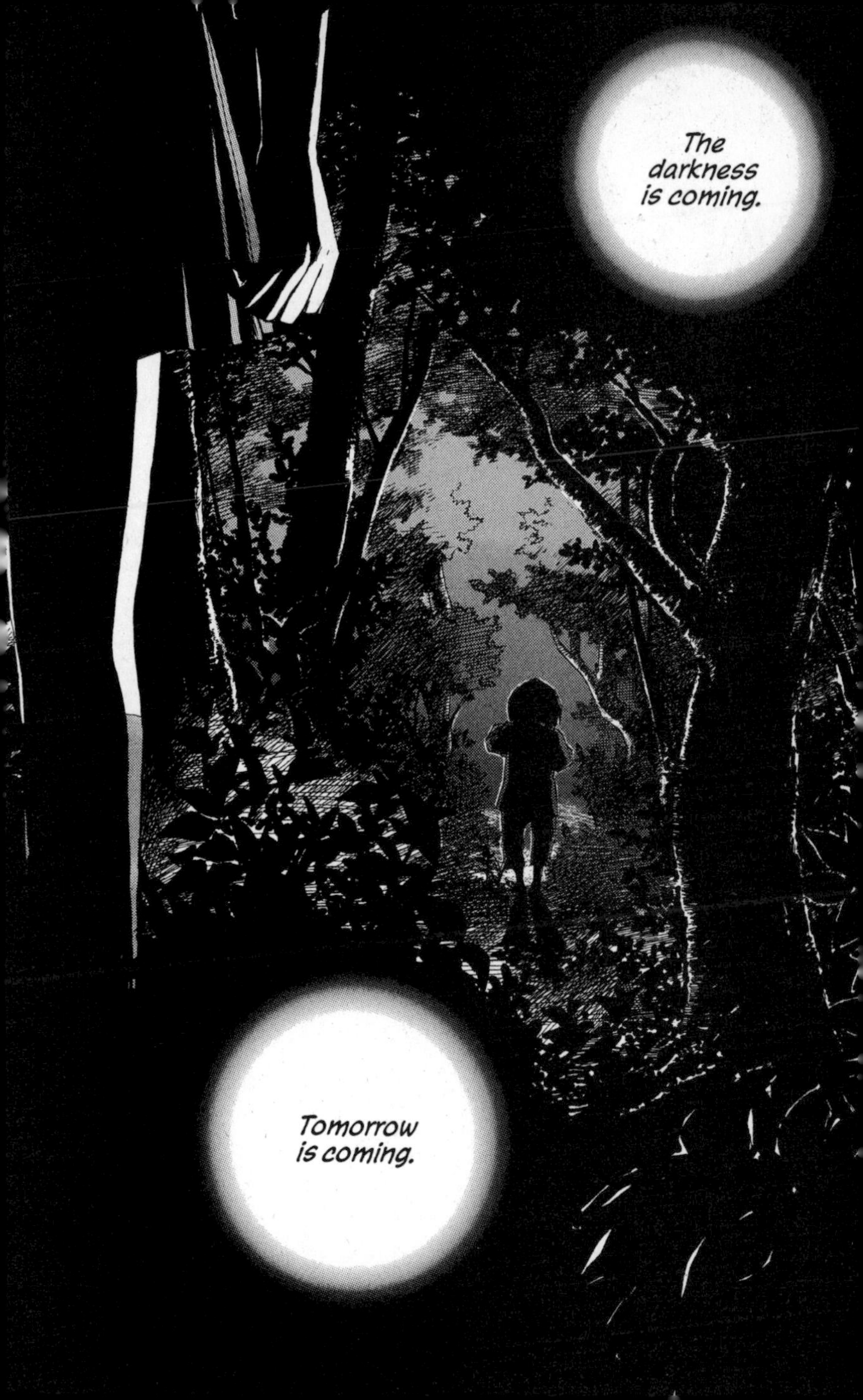
The darkness is coming.
Tomorrow is coming.

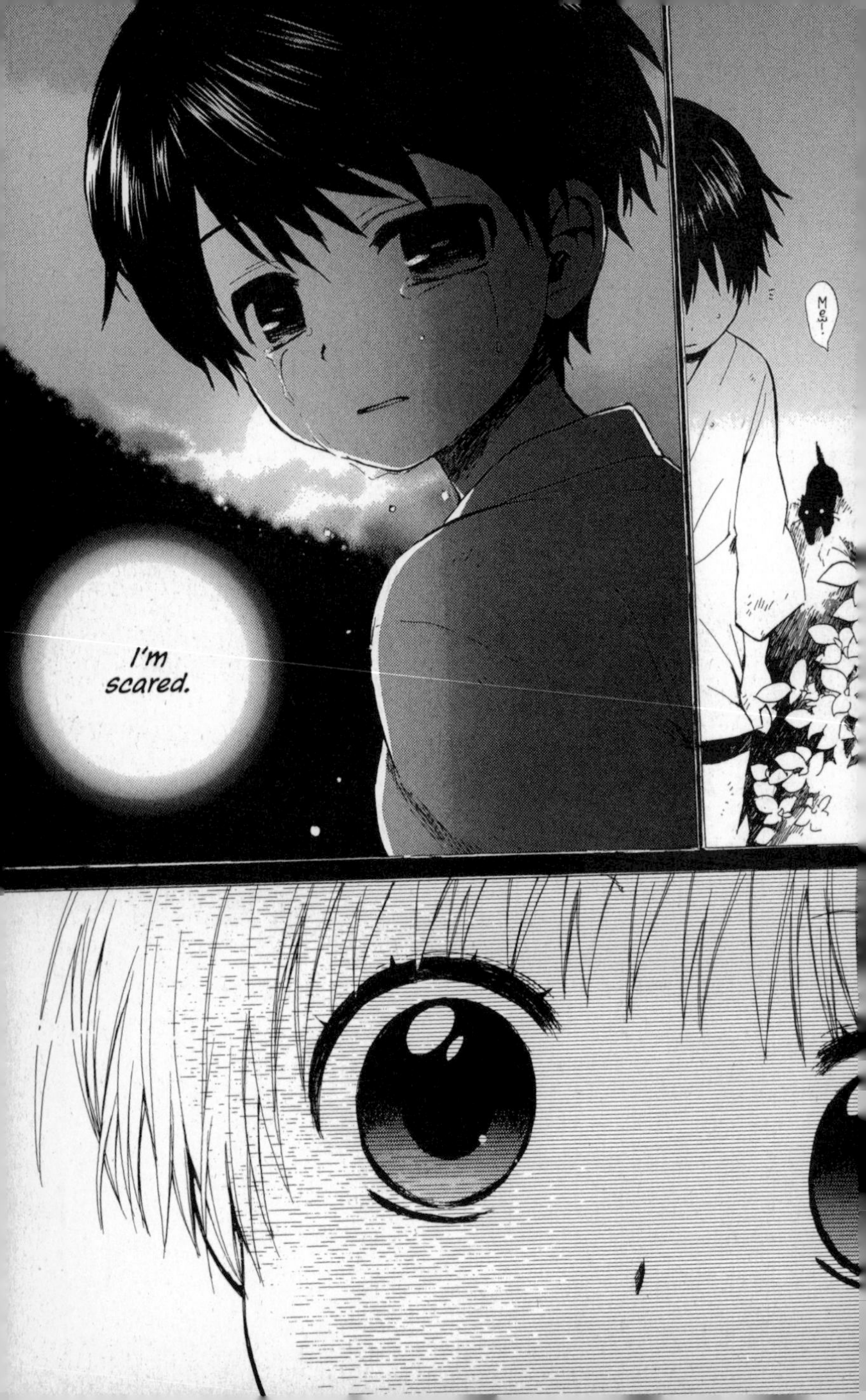
Mew!
I'm scared.

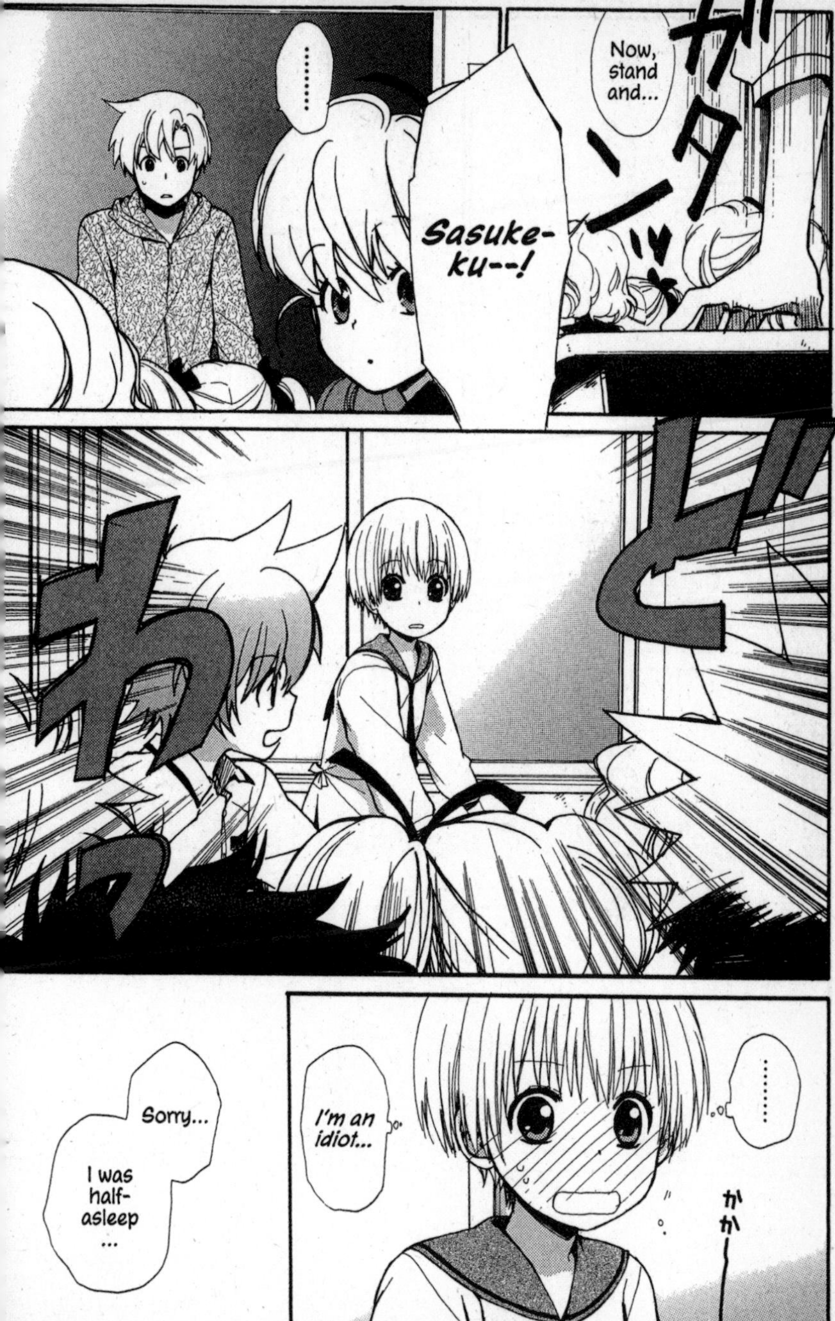
ガタンッ
Now, stand and...
Sasuke-ku--!
......
どど
わわ
......
かかー
I'm an idiot...
Sorry...
I was half-asleep ...

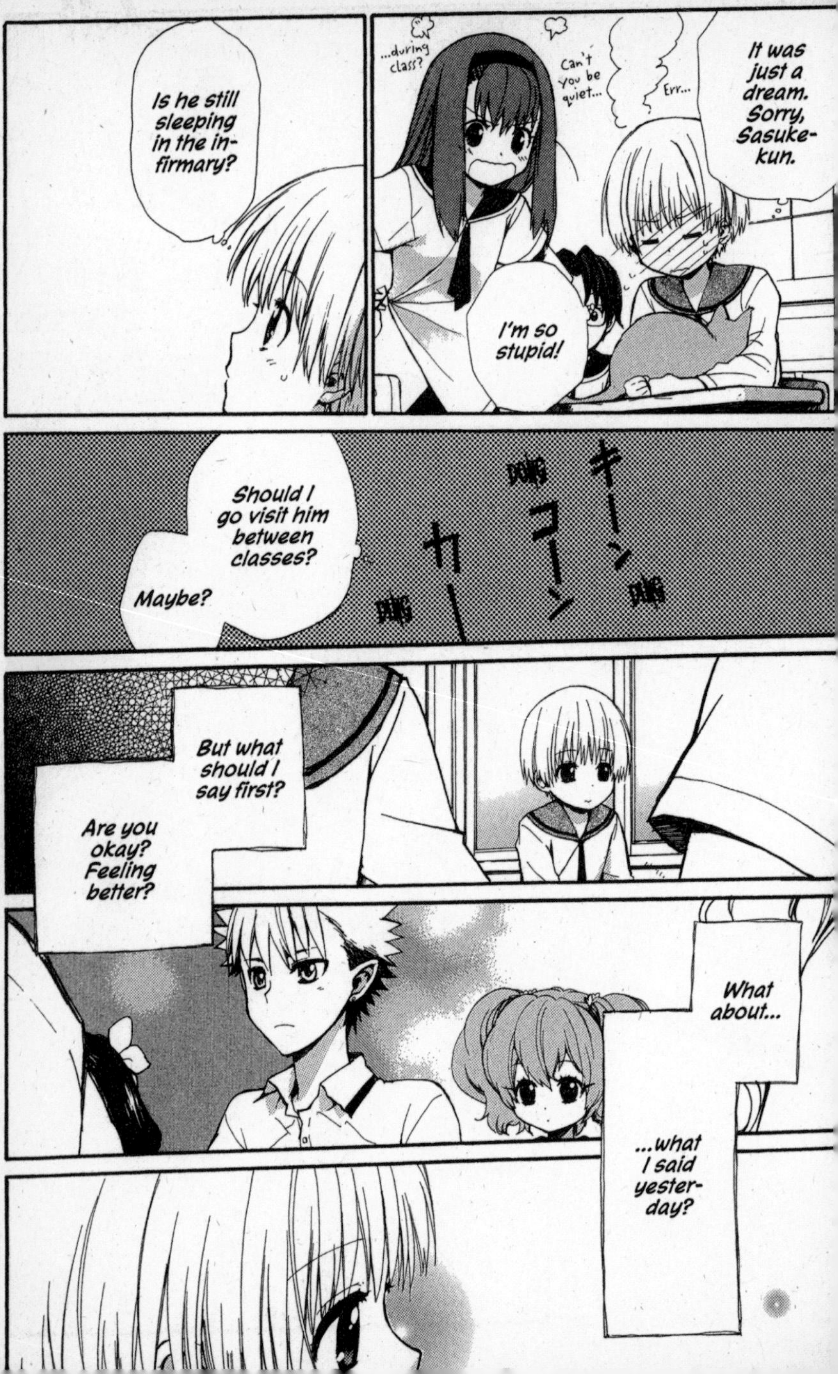
It was just a dream. Sorry, Sasuke-kun.
Err...
Can't you be quiet...
...during class?
I'm so stupid!
Is he still sleeping in the infirmary?
キーン
DING
コーン
DING
カーン
DING
Should I go visit him between classes?
Maybe?
But what should I say first?
Are you okay? Feeling better?
What about...
...what I said yesterday?

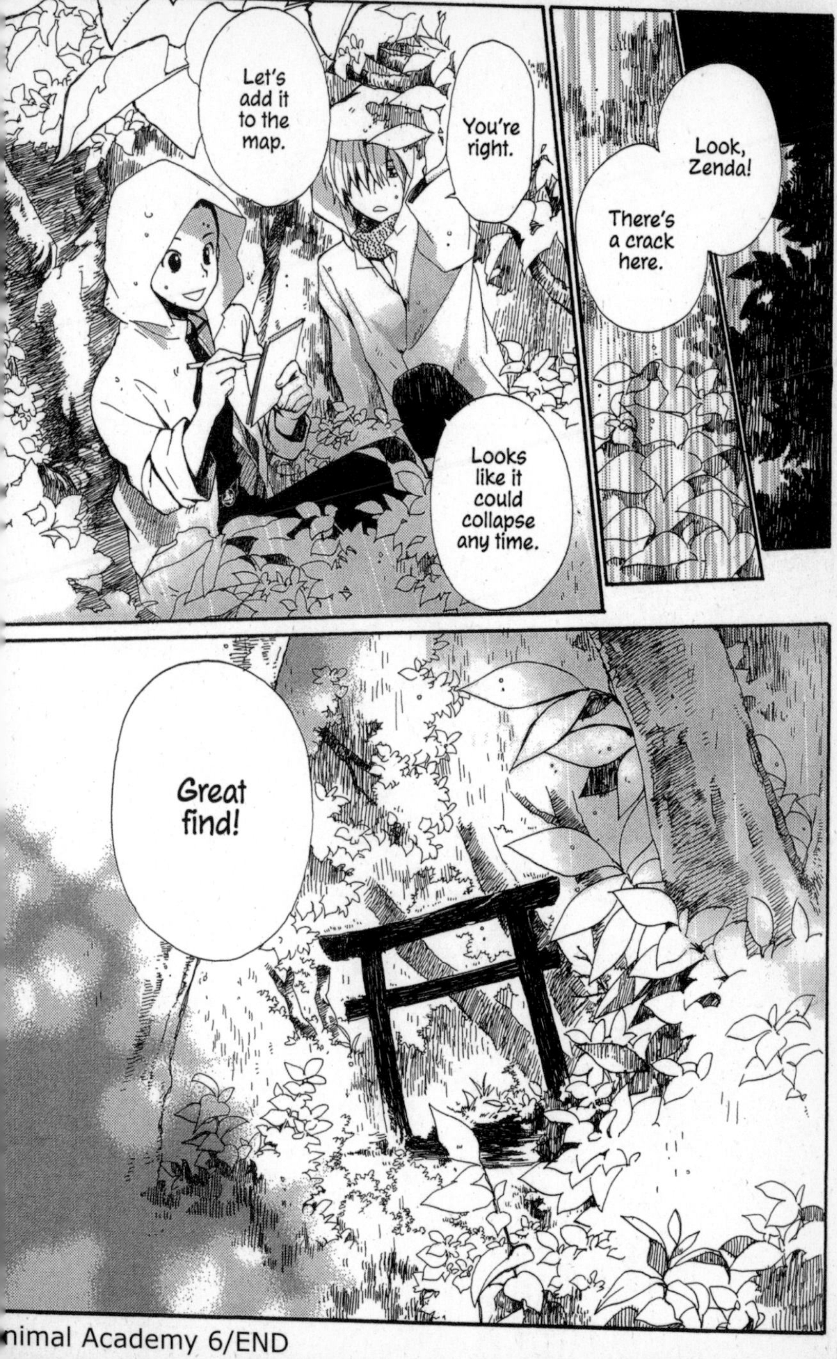
Look, Zenda!
There's a crack here.
You're right.
Let's add it to the map.
Looks like it could collapse any time.
Great find!

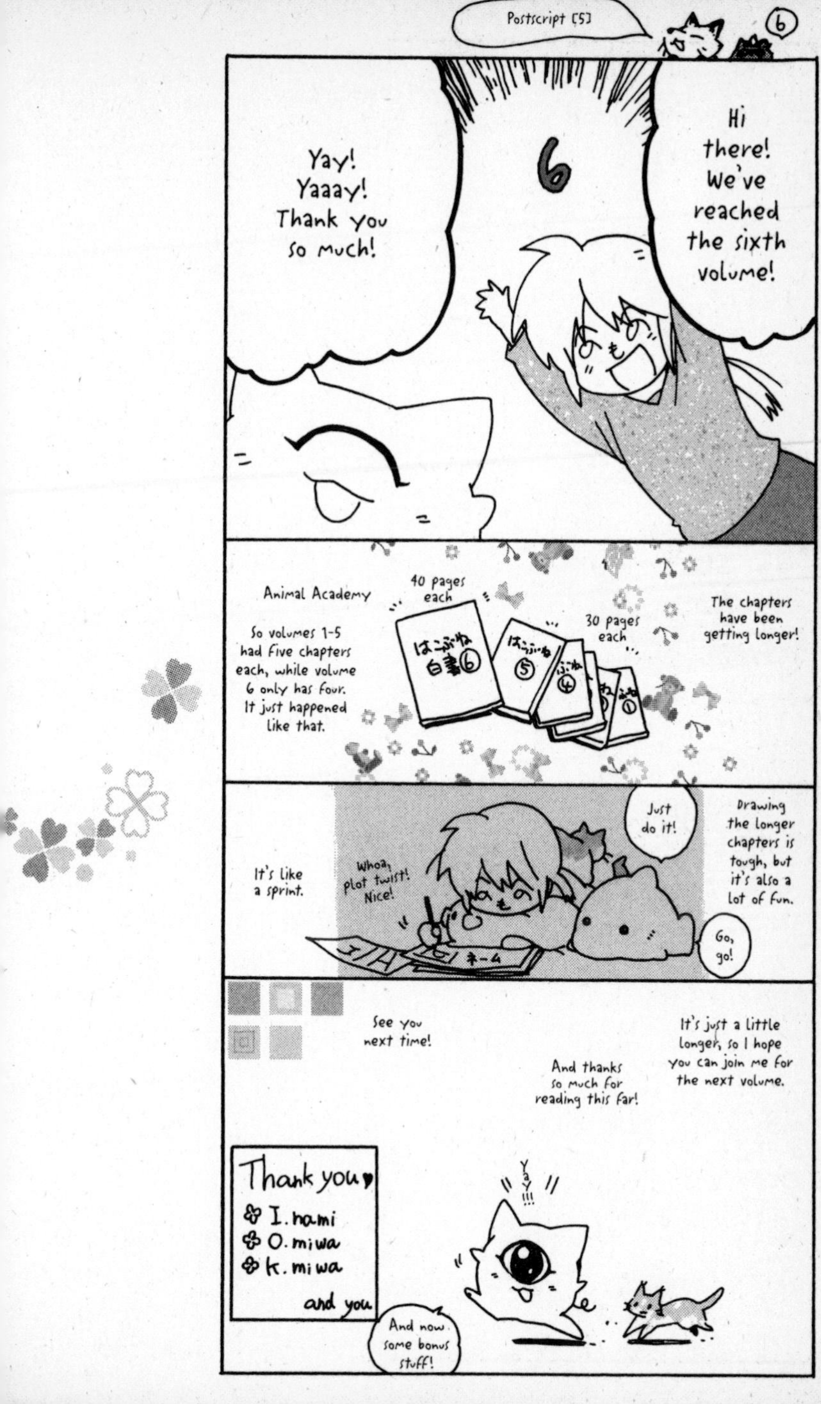
Postscript [5]
6
Hi there! We've reached the sixth volume!
6
Yay! Yaaay! Thank you so much!
The chapters have been getting longer!
30 pages each
40 pages each
はこぶね白書⑥
Animal Academy
So volumes 1-5 had five chapters each, while volume 6 only has four. It just happened like that.
Drawing the longer chapters is tough, but it's also a lot of fun.
Just do it!
Go, go!
Whoa, plot twist! Nice!
ネーム
It's like a sprint.
It's just a little longer, so I hope you can join me for the next volume.
And thanks so much for reading this far!
See you next time!
Thank you♥
I.nami
O.miwa
K.miwa
and you
Yay!!!
And now some bonus stuff!

A story I considered doing, #1: How Miiko came to the school

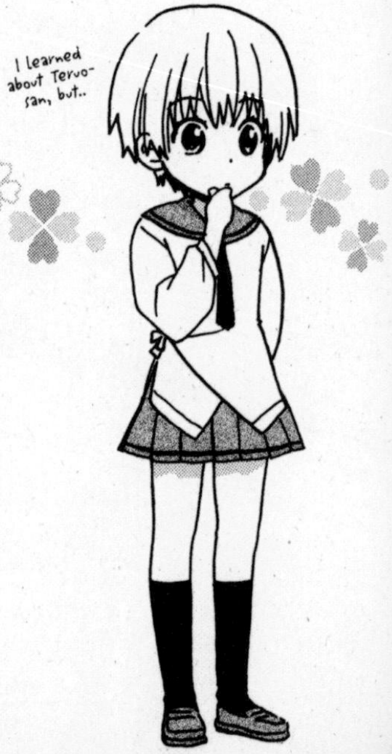
I learned about Teruo-san, but..

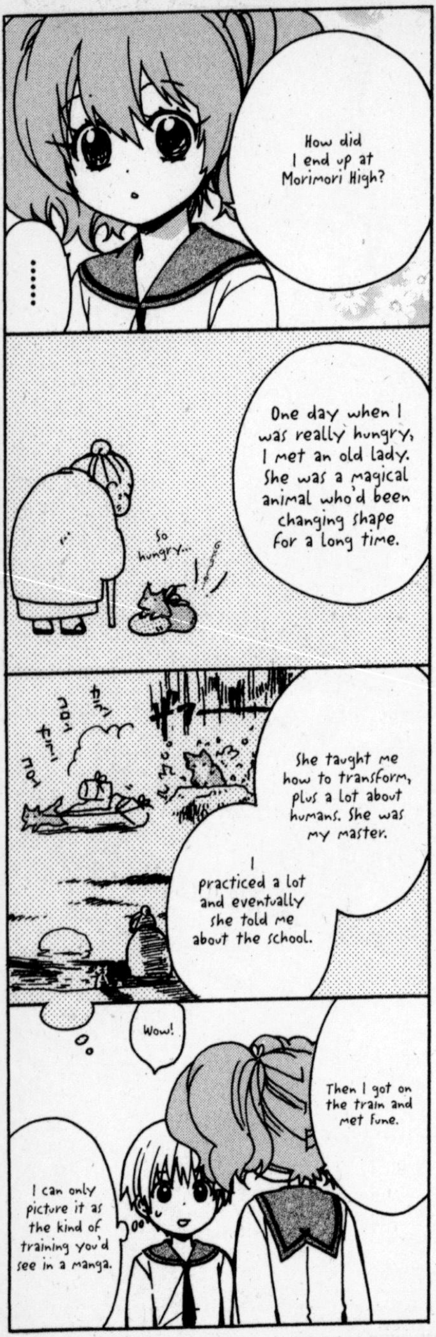
How did I end up at Morimori High?
......
One day when I was really hungry, I met an old lady. She was a magical animal who'd been changing shape for a long time.
So hungry..
She taught me how to transform, plus a lot about humans. She was my master.
I practiced a lot and eventually she told me about the school.
Then I got on the train and met Fune.
Wow!
I can only picture it as the kind of training you'd see in a manga.

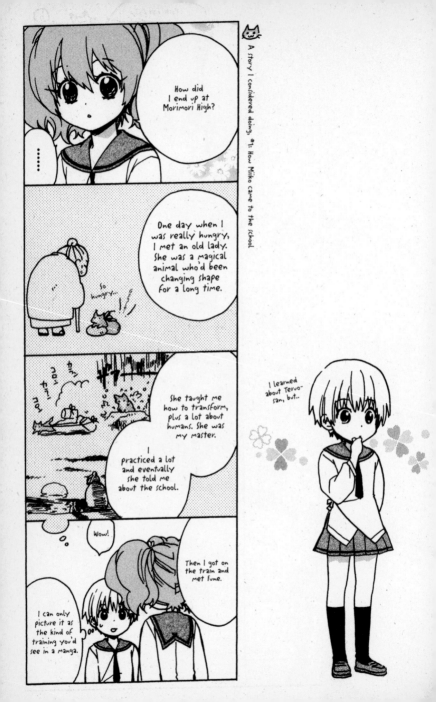

A story I considered doing, #2: The Sagami Brothers' Birthday

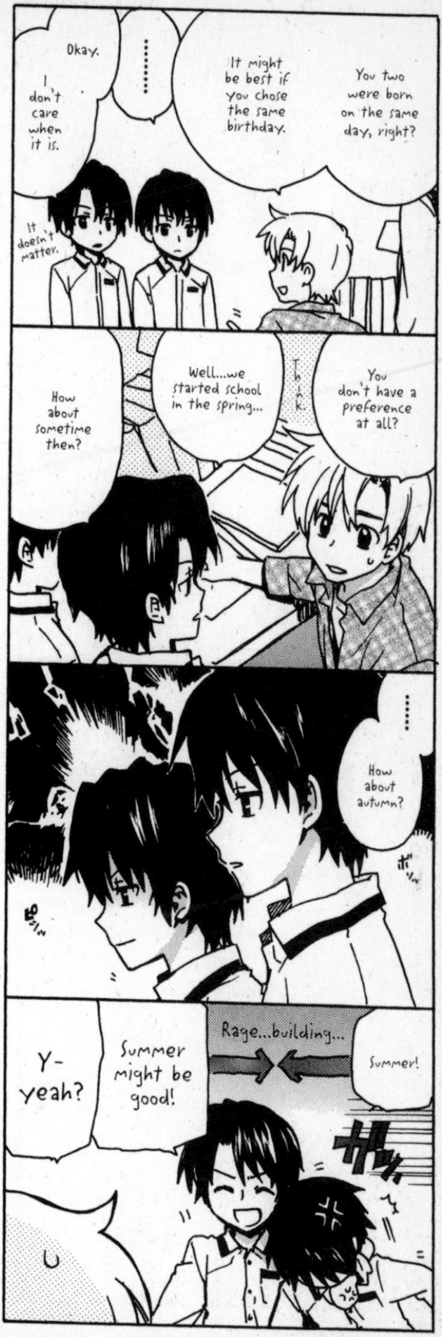

You two were born on the same day, right?
It might be best if you chose the same birthday.
......
Okay.
I don't care when it is.
It doesn't matter.
You don't have a preference at all?
Think
Well...we started school in the spring...
How about sometime then?
......
How about autumn?
Summer!
Rage...building...
Summer might be good!
Y-yeah?

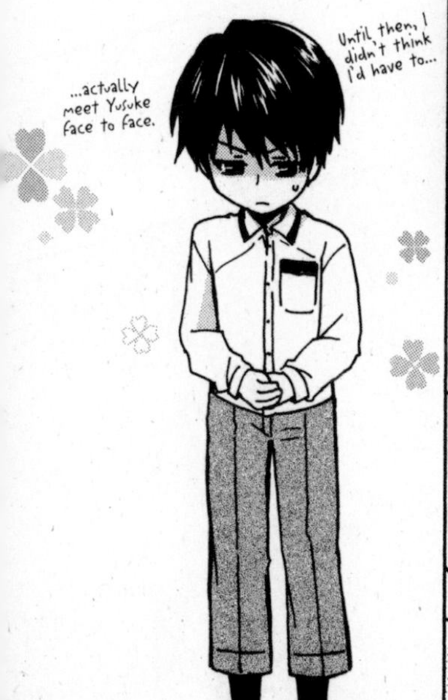

Until then, I didn't think I'd have to...
...actually meet Yusuke face to face.

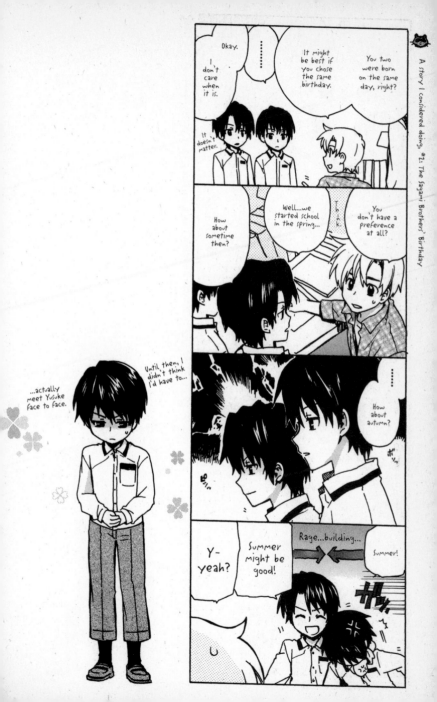

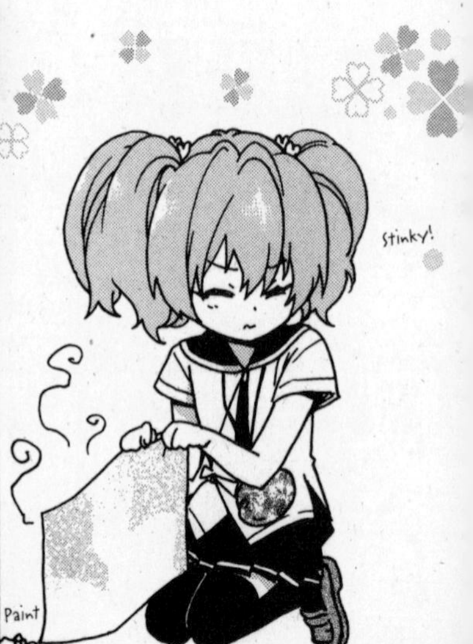
Stinky!
Paint

A story I considered doing, #3: Art club member Silvino, jealous of Miiko's talents

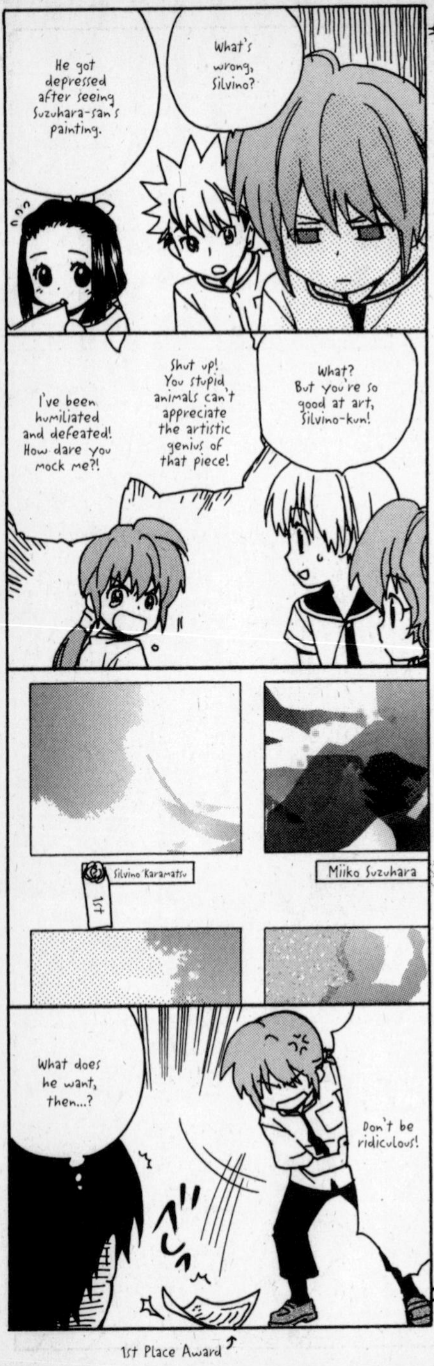
What's wrong, Silvino?
He got depressed after seeing Suzuhara-san's painting.
What? But you're so good at art, Silvino-kun!
Shut up! You stupid animals can't appreciate the artistic genius of that piece!
I've been humiliated and defeated! How dare you mock me?!
Miiko Suzuhara
Silvino Karamatsu
1st
Don't be ridiculous!
What does he want, then...?
1st Place Award

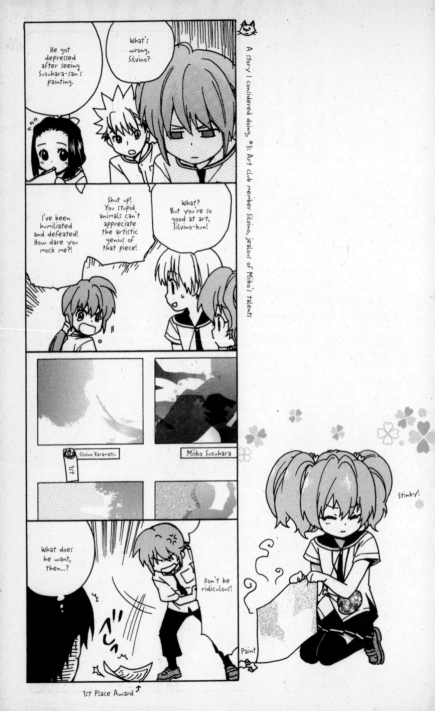

HAKOBUN HOKUSHO.6

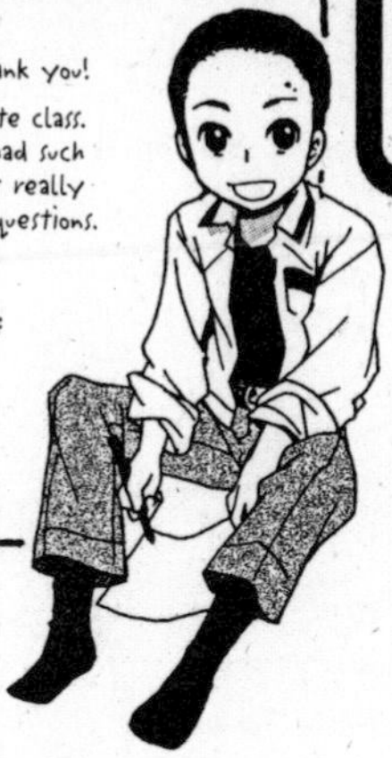

Just before I sat down to write this, I received some fan mail. Thank you!

A lot of you wrote and asked questions about the first-year white class. I was surprised to see that so many of you were interested and had such specific questions. But hey, that's what this page is for! This isn't really important information, but I've tried hard to answer some of your questions.

I have to admit that I came up with a lot of this just now, but I had fun. Hope you like it!

st Year, White Class

heir classroom is located between the red class and blue class.

Name →
(Species/Birthday)→

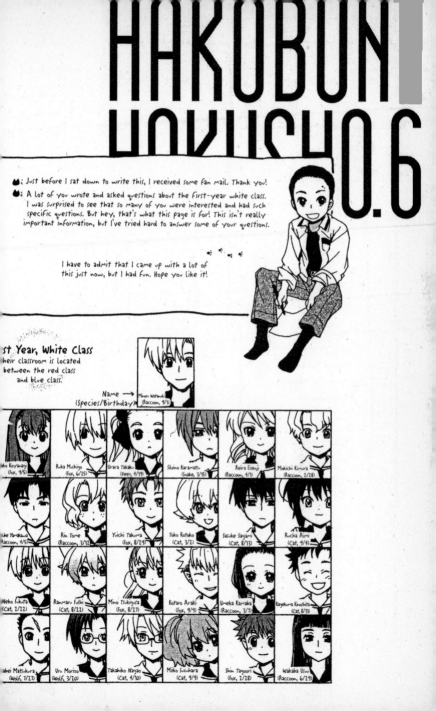

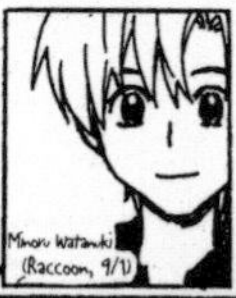
Minoru Watanuki
(Raccoon, 9/1)

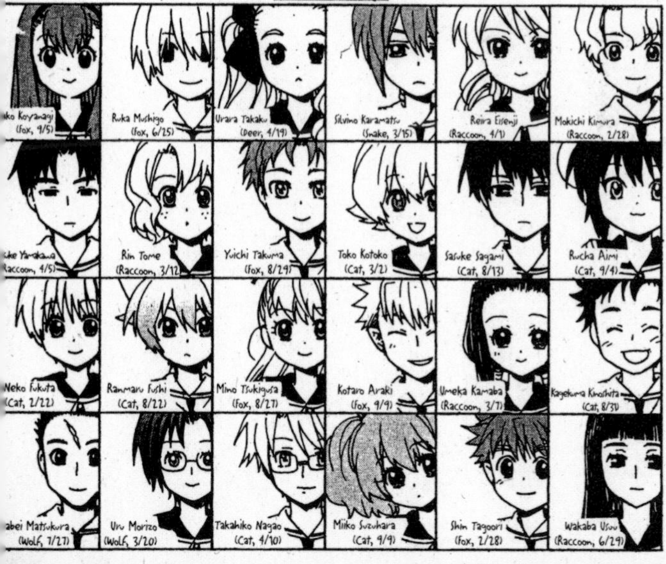
ko Koyanagi (Fox, 9/5)
Ruka Mushigo (Fox, 6/25)
Urara Takaku (Deer, 4/19)
Silvino Karamatsu (Snake, 3/15)
Reira Eisenji (Raccoon, 4/1)
Mokichi Kimura (Raccoon, 2/28)
uke Yarakawa (accoon, 4/5)
Rin Tome (Raccoon, 3/12)
Yuichi Takuma (Fox, 8/29)
Toko Kotoko (Cat, 3/2)
Sasuke Sagami (Cat, 8/13)
Rucha Aimi (Cat, 9/4)
Neko Fukuta (Cat, 2/22)
Ranmaru Fushi (Cat, 8/22)
Mino Tsukigusa (Fox, 8/27)
Kotaro Araki (Fox, 9/9)
Umeka Kamaba (Raccoon, 3/7)
Kagekura Kinoshita (Cat, 8/31)
abei Matsukura (Wolf, 7/27)
Uru Morizo (Wolf, 3/20)
Takahiko Nagao (Cat, 4/10)
Miiko Suzuhara (Cat, 9/9)
Shin Tagoori (Fox, 2/28)
Wakaba Usuu (Raccoon, 6/29)

Q. Can you list the characters by height?

Q.. Who's the smartest?

Tallest

Manjiro Uesugi ← Bonus
Zenda Miyoshi
Harabei Matsukura
Chosuke Yamakawa
Kotaro Araki
Takahiko Nagao
Sasuke Sagami
Yusuke Sagami
Wakaba Usuu
Uru Morizo
Mokichi Kimura
Ruka Mushigo
Shin Tagoori
Yuichi Takuma
Mino Tsukigusa
Neko Fukuta
Ranmaru Fushi
Reira Eisenji
Umako Koyanagi
Kagekuma Kinoshita
Toko Kotoko
Silvino Karamatsu
Umeka Kamaba
Rucha Aimi
Rin Tome
Urara Takaku
Miiko Suzuhara

Shortest

...something like that?

Intelligent

Miiko Suzuhara
Chosuke Yamakawa
Wakaba Usuu
Rucha Aimi
Sasuke Sagami
Takahiko Nagao
Urara Takaku
Reira Eisenji
Umako Koyanagi
Ranmaru Fushi
Kagekuma Kinoshita
Zenda Miyoshi
Umeka Kamaba
Shin Tagoori

Careless ──── Mokichi Kimura ──── **Overcompensating**

Rin Tome
Ruka Mushigo
Minoru Watanuki
Mino Tsukigusa
Uru Morizo
Harabei Matsukura
Yuichi Takuma
Neko Fukuta
Yusuke Sagami
Kotaro Araki
Manjiro Uesugi
Toko Kotoko
Silvino Karamatsu

Sensitive

It breaks down something like that, but of course there are lots of factors that affect their grades.

And so....

Thanks to everyone who sent me letters. I love reading them (and hearing them and seeing them)! Thank you for all the comments and fanart you've sent.

To everyone who's asked things like, "Who does that character in the corner like?" I'll leave that to your imagination. I'm happy to know that you're out there thinking about this stuff. It's more fun for me that way.

That's it for now.

Bye!

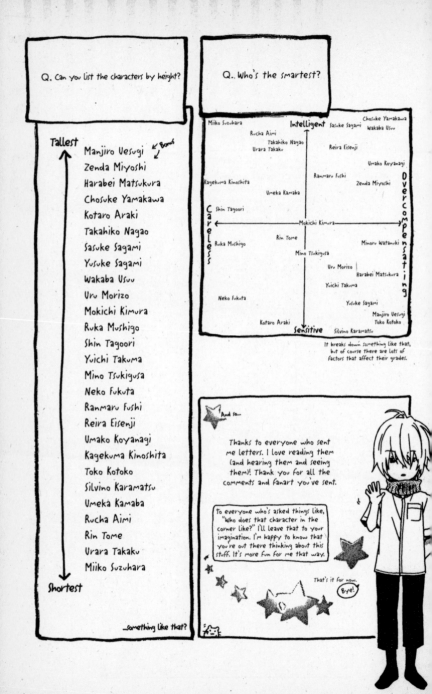

In the next volume of...

Animal Academy
HAKOBUNE HAKUSHO
はこぶね白書

Neko summoned all of her courage to tell Sasuke that she likes him only to have him collapse! What secrets are Sasuke and Yusuke still hiding? And how are they connected to Neko's very presence at the school? Will Neko ever be able to unravel the mystery of the headmaster, and help her friends overcome their sad pasts?

THE SMALLEST HERO!?
RATMAN
ラットマン

Not your typical good versus evil story

Even with a successful caper under his belt, Shuto Katsuragi is still not very comfortable his role as the dark anti-hero "Ratman" for the evil secret organization "Jackal." Deciding to advantage of Ratman's abilities, he tries his H at some vigilante heroism on his off time fro the organization. The first attempt goes well, he even shows up in the papers as a "myste ous, unnamed hero." The second attempt d not go nearly as well, as he is mistaken for th criminal instead of the guy trying to stop the crime. The misunderstandings continue whe he tries to break up a fight between membe a hero sentai team. He has to knock them o do it, and a late-coming Ankaiser pounces o the excuse to pick a fight of his own!

the smallest hero?!
Story and Art by INUI Sekihiko
2

ACTION

OT OLDER TEEN AGE 16+

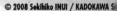

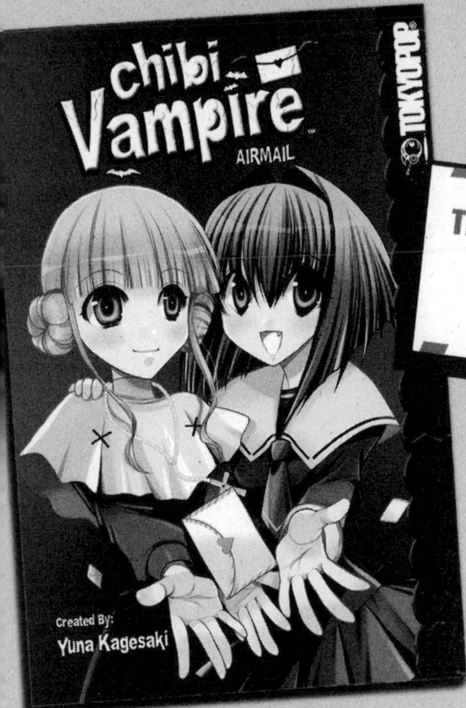
chibi Vampire
AIRMAIL
TOKYOPOP
Created By:
Yuna Kagesaki

The wait is over, Karin Fans, Chibi Vampire: Airmail is here!

A collection of manga stories that follows the continuing adventures of our favorite vampire, Karin! In these short stories, you'll find out what happened to our favorite characters and even get a glimpse of some European vampires that were never seen in the main series! Also included are some manga strips detailing creator Yuna Kagesaki's trip to Seattle's Sakura-Con!

COMEDY OT OLDER TEEN AGE 16+

BE SURE TO VISIT WWW.TOKYOPOP.COM/SHOP FOR EVERYTHING YOU COULD EVER WANT!

DISCOVER STARCRAFT GHOST ACADEMY

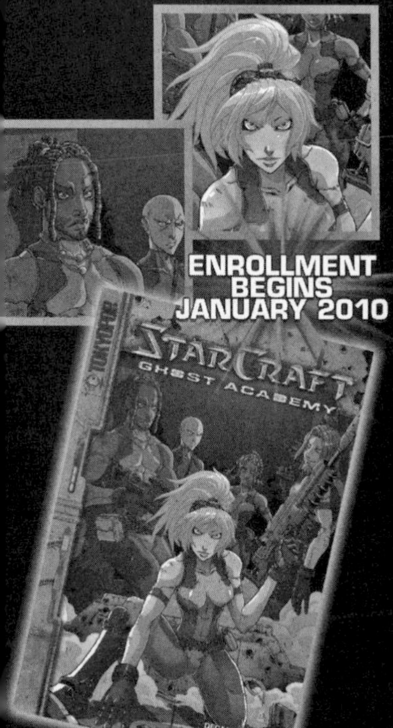
ENROLLMENT
BEGINS
JANUARY 2010
TOKYOPOP
STARCRAFT
GHOST ACADEMY
DECANDIDO
FURUKAWA
1

Ghosts – the terrans' powerful assassins, capable of reading minds and calling down nuclear strikes... These ultimate weapons of Emporer Mengsk's arsenal are crafted at a sinister instiution – the Ghost Academy.

In this never-before-seen chapter in ghost prodigy Nova's life, the doors of the Ghost Academy are flung wide open! Join Nova as she navigates the challenges of brutal training, both physical and psychological, along with fellow cadets whose unusual telepathic and telekinetic powers are being twisted to serve the Dominion. But the cadets have no choice other than to endure and overcome, because at this school, failure is not an option.

THE MANGA REVOLUTION · LEADING · THE MANGA REVOLUTION · LEADING
漫画革命

SCI-FI

T TEEN AGE 13+

LICENSED BLIZZARD ENTERTAINMENT PRODUCT

FOR MORE INFORMATION VISIT: WWW.TOKYOPOP.COM/STARCRAFT

STOP!

This is the back of the book.
You wouldn't want to spoil a great ending!

This book is printed "manga-style," in the authentic Japanese right-to-left format. Since none of the artwork has been flipped or altered, readers get to experience the story just as the creator intended. You've been asking for it, so TOKYOPOP® delivered: authentic, hot-off-the-press, and far more fun!

1
2
3
4
5
6
7
8
9
10

DIRECTIONS

If this is your first time reading manga-style, here's a quick guide to help you understand how it works.

It's easy... just start in the top right panel and follow the numbers. Have fun, and look for more 100% authentic manga from TOKYOPOP®!

THE MANGA REVOLUTION • LEADING THE MANGA REVOLUTION • LEADING
漫画革命